I0759725

RECIPES FROM THE AMERICAN SOUTH

MICHAEL W.
TWITTY

RECIPES FROM THE AMERICAN SOUTH

INTRODUCTION

Recipes from The American South is a book that strives to give an introductory taste of the culinary sweep that Southern history and its many cultures represent. The South is not a monolith; no state or area can provide the breadth of the Southern story or fully set the Southern table.

PLACE, TIME, AND PEOPLE

The American South stretches from the Chesapeake Bay region to the Bluegrass country over to the Mississippi River Valley and over to the Ozarks, the Southern plains west to Texas Hill Country, and the Deep East southward toward the coast of the Gulf of Mexico. The United States Census Bureau also considers Delaware, Maryland, Missouri, West Virginia, and Oklahoma part of the South—which may infuriate those who define the South merely by the borders of the Confederacy (1861–1865). This definition and redefinition of Southern identity related to its Confederate past isn't sufficient for this volume. The largest culinary region in America doesn't stop at the Mason-Dixon line or the Ohio River or St. Louis, Missouri, which bills itself as the gateway to the American West. That narrow definition leaves out so many other essential populations, including Southern women, Native people, enslaved West and Central Africans, and non-European immigrants—a profound story of human migration in and out of the South that began thirteen thousand years ago.

Native Americans set the Southern table first. Even before the expansion of the cultivation of maize, beans, squash, sunflowers, Chenopodium, and maypop, there existed a virgin forest brimming with millions of freely available hickory nuts, persimmons, and wild grapes, along with a bevy of other foraged foods from maple sap to coontie root, also known as Florida arrowroot. This abundance of food provided the background for the rich culture of the Mound Builders and their descendants. So many foods of the adjacent Caribbean, Mesoamerica and beyond that are central to Southern cooking—tomatoes, sweet potatoes, peanuts, peppers, and more—came through the South and often through cultural mixing with West and Central Africans. The profusion of game and fish, the use of bear oil, plus grilling, smoking, and boiling different bits and pieces into a pot of stew, reverberates to this day in Southern food.

Most historical narratives introduce Europeans to the story at this point, but to understand the South, we turn to West Central Africans. Many of those indigenous foods had already made it east across the Atlantic by the time enslaved Africans were forced to American shores—with similar seasonal cooking advancements familiar to Native peoples. Africans loved grilled and smoked goods, and their daily meal was typically a stew served with starch. The new African palate—already enriched by yams, rice, okra, cowpeas, sorghum, melons, and spices—now married those staples with the crops they found in the South. Africans arrived empty-handed but not empty-headed. They were prepared to encounter the wild resources of the South, and many had centuries of experience with Islamic and Western European dishes.

The European colonization of the South ties all the pieces together. The Spanish and French feverishly moved to West Africa, the West Indies, and North America. They zealously worked to establish their distinct cooking traditions based on rouxs, sauces, paellas, and soups, eagerly taking in all the new Atlantic world had to offer, while imposing what they could from the Old World. British and Germanic customs came to dominate the South, along with traditions from their Protestant faith. Pies, wheat-based breads, cakes, puddings, smoked meats, and roasts, among other dishes hearty for the cold but sufficient for warm weather, became central parts of the Southern diet, while melding with flavors and ideas from the South's other foundational peoples.

Beyond Southern borders, an ongoing relationship with the colonial worlds to the south and west influenced Southern food like no other American culinary region. Migration by European colonists and the forced migration of enslaved Africans from the Caribbean into the American South connects the Southeastern United States with the broader African Atlantic world. In this nexus, different mixtures of Native, African, and European would forge parallel novel collisions, engagements, and innovations. This new cuisine would include hot sauce, barbecue, red beans and rice, dessert made with sweet potatoes and pumpkins, tropical fruit, cane syrup, and molasses (treacle).

To add to this multicultural gumbo, immigrant stories outside these cultures also played a part. Immigrants, both willing and coerced from East Asia and Latin America, have long been present in the South, starting in the Colonial period and becoming cemented from the late nineteenth into the mid-twentieth centuries. From the 1970s through the 1990s, the South became more Southeast Asian, Latino, Middle Eastern, and Korean. This period led to an influx of South Asian and African immigrant dishes with their culinary commentaries on Southern staples like rice, hot peppers, corn, okra, and leafy greens. These migrations laid their traditional foodways on the table with winks, nods, and borrowings from five hundred years of Southern traditions to draw on.

Southerners are different from other Americans. Southern food gives us clues as to why. Like Southern culture, Southern food is a product of fortunate collisions, cooperation, and sometimes chaos or confusion. Was "Sally Lunn" an English corruption of the French *soleil lune*? Is "barbecue" French, Taíno, or Hausa? Is the datil pepper Minorcan or Mandinka? Can a collard green fill an empanada, be stir-fried, go into a spring roll, or be stuffed for Jewish Sukkot? Is Brunswick stew Virginian, Carolinian, or Georgian? How do we make room for okra soup, gumbo, jambalaya, Hoppin' John, and red beans and rice?

Southerners have transmitted recipes and ideas about food in several varieties of Gaelic and dialects of Cherokee. Our Ancestors prayed over their food in Arabic, Hebrew, Latin, and Yoruba for centuries. For a long time, we have discussed the influence of Filipinos, Acadians, Germans from the Palatinate, Ulster Scots, Mexicans, and Melungeons. A large portion of Southern culture is the result of the British interacting with West and Central Africans because of chattel slavery and the interplay of class and gender between Black and white. In all cases—whether Lebanese, Greek, Italian, Chinese, Vietnamese, Cuban, Salvadoran, Ashkenazi Jewish, or Kurdish Muslim—the generations have produced a Southern people with a language, food preferences, and sense of self and place that point first to the American South, and not merely to America at large.

INGREDIENTS AND FLAVORS

If you ask someone what Southern ingredients are, they might list peaches for cobbler, apples for butter and fried pies, or mint for iced tea and juleps—all based on sense memory or nostalgia. Their mind might go to chicken and pork rather than beef, nutmeg in orange sweet potatoes, fried hickory-smoked bacon (streaky) or ham, or the texture and taste of quality cornmeal, used to dredge freshly caught trout or coat a hot corn dodger. Thickening okra, meaty greens, and creamy long-simmered field peas would be listed. The metallic notes of molasses (treacle) or cane syrup, the mellow caramel or woody flavors in bourbon, or the foxy tastes of muscadine or scuppernong wine are givens. Other listings might appeal to memories of fried chicken fresh from a cast-iron skillet, a salted watermelon in July, the promise of green beans from the garden, shelling pecans in anticipation of pies and pralines, or maybe Cajun "pig's ears" (crisply fried ear-shaped pastries served with lots of cane syrup).

Southern flavors beg for specific ingredients and are ample with the year-round presence of smoky and meaty tastes from barbecue to the cured meats that flavor food. Liquid smoke, smoked paprika, and smoked salt and pepper are more present as the Southern palate evolves. Preferred Southern fruits are juicy and vibrant, ranging from jammy and floral to luscious and creamy. Vegetables are sulfurous and grassy and not simply a background for meaty flavors. In between are elements that are spicy, herbaceous, and marine. Citrus, mint, and vanilla are never far away and ready to amplify.

One of the more challenging aspects of talking about the Southern palate is the dogmatism, which many apply to clichés and stereotypes about Southern ingredients and what Southern food is. Written records about Southern food going back to the Colonial and Antebellum periods demonstrate how little we can rely on our assumptions. Between 1750 and 1900, Southern ingredients included rose water from the Middle East and Mediterranean, some of America's first cultivated daikon radish, the Bambara groundnut brought from Senegambia, small local oranges and wild palm fruits, and wild Ogeechee "limes," clabber milk, watermelon molasses, and almost clear honey from basswood blossoms. There was no pimento cheese, collards were not ubiquitous, and even the mustard greens most Southerners are familiar with today were not the same. There were indeed no cola cakes or marshmallows on sweet potato casseroles. The South was not always a landscape defined in the American mouth and mind by vast swaths of culinary monoculturalism.

On the contrary, the American South is a region with a consistent paradox; remarkably unified across its microregions due to the expansion of colonial settlements and slavery with replicating patterns upheld by tradition, but with a marked diversity as well, owing to new circumstances. The distinct ethnicities that settled in specific areas, the power of local economies, and geography opened the way to particular ingredients and limited others. As Southerners moved into other regions in the twentieth century, they took portable ingredients and gave up others. Out of convenience, African Americans on the West Coast traded the blue crab (Callinectes sapidus) for the Dungeness variety (Metacarcinus magister) in their gumbos. Simultaneously, certain pockets of the South like the Mississippi Delta (nicknamed by some as "the most Southern place on earth") were also where Mexican, Lebanese, Syrian, Ashkenazi Jewish, and Cantonese cultures mixed with many others to make tamales, stir-fried collards, and cola brisket as Southern as any food from the two hundred years prior.

The best thing we can do is appreciate the layers of time, people, stories, and meaning more than the grocery lists of Southern ingredients. Instead, we should ask why. The why leads into the future, preserving the planet by conserving certain crops and foraged foods. The why asks how we can maintain cultures that produce the food and the community systems that make these foods possible, such as harvesting rice or sorghum or picking wild persimmons in the fall. Southern ingredients are best defined by their function and purpose. The Southern way, with hospitality, resourcefulness, celebration, and survival, undergird the legends and myths behind its storied staple ingredients.

MYTH, MEANING, AND COMMUNITY

Speaking of Southern food is a dance between praise and critique. To many, even within America, Southern food is delicious and decadent, but at the same time, some consider it unhealthy and intellectually unchallenging. In popular culture, the South and its food are often painted with too broad a brush. Some Southern points of interest offer little jars of moonshine and canned "roadkill." In contrast, others take home bags of benne (sesame) wafers labeled in elegant flourishes, and heirloom vegetable seeds surround replica punch bowls at historic plantation homes or living history sites. The South itself is very much self-aware of the push-pull between competing stereotypes about Southern history and identity. The vernacular culture of the South is sometimes depicted as plebeian, hard-scrabble, tobacco-road, make-do folk and, on the other side of the tracks, outrageous (exploitative) patrician ostentation. In the middle is a homely, simple, and unfussy world with a tinge of funky, informal, and fried. The real world and the places that exist in memory, myth, and mystique sit side by side on the Southern table.

To be Southern is to master a culinary vocabulary that seems like it evolved in an unbroken circle, but it has as many layers as some of our cakes. We name our food after moments, people, and corruptions of words—Sally Lunn, Hoppin' John, Limping Susan. We say, Hot Brown or Red-Eye Gravy, expecting strangers to understand what we mean. Southern words are so natural to me; putting them into a glossary seems ridiculous, but my work is not only to translate but amplify. Our material culture includes the rice mortar and pestle, the hominy grindstone, the biscuit beater, the soda bottle (pricked at the top and rusty to allow hot garden pepper vinegar to trickle out), deviled egg platters, crystal cake domes, and barbecue pits dug in the ground.

Southerners are dynamic eaters, cooks, and entertainers. We brunch at fine-dining establishments at inns and old cotton mills, and many start their days with a biscuit sandwich, often at fast-food joints (a new gathering place after the general stores popular in previous generations closed). We publish synagogue, church, and community cookbooks and swear by recipes from the glossy magazines *Southern Living* and back issues of *Ladies' Home Journal*. We pass down heirloom recipes on index cards, but we never really write down the secret—we whisper it—knowing somebody might forget it one day. We celebrate with food spreads at autumn tailgate parties, winter oyster roasts, spring cotillions, and summer barbecues and reunions.

The politics of Southern food is omnipresent, baked in from the beginning. Southern food is soaked in Native removal, racial caste and social justice, gender roles, ability issues, sexuality, and class. Once upon a time, white landholding males, with both political ambitions and money earned from enslaving others, held barbecues, fish fries, and "stews" prepared by enslaved cooks. These feasts, intended only for other white people, encouraged voters to support them. Such votes eventually led to compromises, conflicts, and the Civil War, tearing the United States apart. Our ability to appreciate the newfound zeal for Southern food means confronting these realities head-on. These aren't just recipes; they are the pleasure and pain of millions of women, men, and children who have come before and the heritage and legacy of millions to come.

A PERSONAL JOURNEY

My place in this mosaic is complex. I am from our American capital of Washington, DC, and from Maryland, where Frederick Douglass and Harriet Tubman were born and grew to resist chattel slavery. I live in Virginia, the origin place of branches of both sides of my family, and I am a product of the Great Migration of African Americans escaping the repressive Jim Crow regime in the Deep South. My mother and father were born in Ohio and in Washington D.C., on the borders of the former states that composed the Confederacy, and our roots are in the Southern states of North Carolina, South Carolina, Georgia, Alabama, and Tennessee. Family history tells me that thanks to the domestic trade in enslaved people and other migrations, marriages, and mayhem, we also have descendants in Mississippi, Florida, Arkansas, Louisiana, Kentucky, and Texas. I am African American, and the non-Native part of my family has lived in the South since the seventeenth century.

In 2012, along with my late partner, Jacob Dillow, I took thousands of photographs, interviewed dozens of people, and drove thousands of miles from Maryland to Texas for a project called the Southern Discomfort Tour. A lifetime of little dips and dives into what many people might think of the South became a curated effort to see the places where Southern food and my family began—where they arrived from West and Central Africa and Western Europe and where I encountered my deep and distant kin, the Native people of this land. You can read about the South, but—as much as my American identity has been shaped by the South—smelling, touching, and tasting it were essential for me to understand it enough to write this book.

The journey took me to Weaver D's Delicious Fine Foods in Athens, Georgia—where the band R.E.M. got their iconic album title *Automatic for the People*—as well as The Grit, a rare Southern vegetarian restaurant, which closed in October 2022. I had my first mind-blowingly fresh Creole tomato in Louisiana, saw sorghum molasses being made in a Mennonite community in Tennessee, explored the remains of the rice fields at plantations in South Carolina, saw fresh, verdant fields of rice on the way to Arkansas, ate barbecue in Texas, and tasted kudzu honey in Mississippi. I've had juicy peaches from Chilton County, Alabama, and I've learned that I like fried peanuts over boiled ones. I've seen the chaotic love of a hungry crowd for boudin sausage and cracklings in a store in Louisiana Cajun country, watched people pull catfish and bass wriggling out of the water in Kentucky, and seen piles of steamed crabs from the Eastern Shore of Maryland down to Savannah, Georgia. I've eyed heaps of fresh okra, heirloom collards, and shiny new jars of chow chow in the Carolinas. I am lucky.

As a food writer, these extraordinary new memories collide with older ones. My grandmother showed me how to pick and savor honeysuckles, priming me to savor chef Bill Smith's honeysuckle sorbet years later in Chapel Hill, North Carolina. I loved picking yellow-meat watermelons and pecans on my grandfather's farm in South Carolina, only to later make yellow tomato and watermelon sorbet at Thomas Jefferson's Monticello near Charlottesville, Virginia. I became fascinated with historic cooking at the age of seven; later in life, I had the magical experience of exploring Southern heirloom vegetable gardens with my friends and colleagues at Colonial Williamsburg and cooking in historical kitchens to teach visitors the beginning of Southern cuisine. My journeys flooded me with memories of my first church dinner on the grounds and family reunions, where I learned a whole vocabulary from my parents and grandparents to describe foods that told stories themselves.

We are nothing without the Southern woman—not just our mothers and aunties, but rebels and innovators, warriors, bartenders, and writers. Modern-day culinary masters include bakers Cheryl Day and Erika Council, Sandra A. Gutierrez; chefs Mashama Bailey, Ashleigh Shanti, Edna Lewis, Leah Chase, and Mildred "Mama Dip" Council; television pioneers like Lena Richard and Nathalie Dupree; authors like Fannie Flagg; master growers like Ira Wallace; academics such as Marcie Cohen Ferris and Ronni Lundy; and journalist-scholars like Toni Tipton Martin. Thousands of activists, growers, chefs, and entrepreneurs sit at the forefront while "many thousands gone," in the words of the spiritual, were Native innovators of outdoor feasts, enslaved women, the indentured, mill workers, coal miners, wives, and domestics.

We are also nothing without our iconoclasts, our marginalized, and our often forgotten. I am a gay man in a long line of Queer men—among them Eugene Walter, Craig Claiborne, Bill Neal, Bill Smith, John Martin Taylor, and Damon Lee Fowler—who have dared encapsulate the South in book form. We join the preservationists—Dr. David Shields, Crystal Wilkinson, Sallie Ann Robinson, Nancie McDermott, Wesley Greene, Peter Hatch, and chefs BJ Dennis, Kevin Mitchell, Michael Moore, and the late Pableaux Johnson—on the list of people who refuse to keep this circle unbroken. We are the reason why it's unbroken.

Our cuisine, with its grits and black-eyed peas (black-eye beans), crab cakes, red rice, and endless variations on the staple foods of the region, casts a spell that, if you're lucky, gets passed down through the shared acts of snapping string beans at the table and chewing cane on the back porch. My journey and this book inherently celebrate Southern food's memory keepers and practitioners—because the library of this knowledge would be closed without them. I am grateful to share this volume to whet your appetite and passion for home cooking in the American South. Enjoy and share, and welcome to our Southern family.

ICON LEGEND

V	Vegetarian
VE	Vegan
DF	Dairy-free
GF	Gluten-free
-30	30 minutes or less
-5	5 ingredients or less

BREADS, BISCUITS & BREAKFASTS

MY MOTHER'S FLOUR

I've often told the story of guarding my Alabama maternal grandmother's light bread (everyday white bread) in military gear at age seven. I had a toy compass, helmet, and toy weaponry to ensure nobody would take "my bread," even though she made it for found family and community. Since none of that gear would work, I used my tears, which usually won my small loaf that I enjoyed with hot butter and peach jam. My Virginia paternal grandmother made her holiday time rolls so good that it was incumbent on all of us to have the family recipe. Nobody would be able to say we didn't have it on hand.

While both my grandmothers relied on tradition and good fortune, my mother, Pat, became the best baker of them all, and she might have been the first person in the family to marry tradition with science. According to family legend, her maternal grandfather, who passed away at the Tuskegee University hospital in Alabama a few years before my mother was born, made the best biscuits and yeast rolls in all of Alabama. Gospel truth must have imparted some of his cooking spirit to her. My mother never used flour milled from hard winter wheat (the basis for "Northern" type bread), but always from the softer, Southern-based brands. She constantly reminded me not to overknead the dough so that "the gluten won't get cooked" by the warmth of my hands. In my mother's kitchen, "lukewarm" was never a guess: There was always a thermometer ready to gauge when the scalded milk was right where it needed to be—the perfect temperature for the yeast to proof.

Mom was a bread connoisseur, but as far as I can remember, she never made a sourdough or boule—those came from good bakeries or specific stores. Instead, she was a devotee of the Southern "light touch," and as delicious as crusty breads might be, they were simply not in her repertoire. Soft flours promised tender, flaky results, and self-rising flours promised quick breads, like buttermilk, Cheddar, and drop biscuits; potato and icebox rolls; hotcakes and waffles; sandwich bread and banana bread, and every delicacy her creativity could muster and the occasion demanded. My mother's cakes and custom pies, which she sometimes sold to people in our community, were art. She was a master at decoration and icing, and I never tried to learn that art from her, because what she did was simply magic. All you needed to hear was, "Oh, Pat!" from the corner of the room as someone beheld her baking, and you understood you were in for something ambrosial. This is the legacy those of us born into Southern heritage revere, recipes from family members that we can never exactly get right, but that always remain a testament to the skill and craft in our veins.

YEAST ROLLS

V

One of the key skills of the Southern home cook is the perfection of these rolls. People will know "store-bought" from the real thing. They are often made with potato in some variations. Note that they are also known as "dinner" rolls, served at dinner on church grounds or at a formal meal, and they are distinct from buttermilk biscuits, which are not usually associated with a formal meal.

PREPARATION TIME: 30 MINUTES, PLUS 1–3 HOURS RISING TIME
COOKING TIME: 20 MINUTES
MAKES: 12 ROLLS

1 packet (7 g) active dry yeast (2 ¼ teaspoons)
4 tablespoons (60 g) unsalted butter, melted, plus more for the bowl and brushing the rolls
½ teaspoon plus ¼ cup (50 g) sugar
4 tablespoons warm water
4 cups (520 g) all-purpose (plain) flour
1 teaspoon fine salt
1 cup (8 fl oz/240 ml) whole milk, warm
1 egg

1 In a small bowl, dissolve the yeast and ½ teaspoon of the sugar in the warm water. Let it sit for about 5 minutes until the mixture becomes frothy. Grease a large bowl with butter.
2 In a large bowl, combine the flour, remaining ¼ cup (50 g) sugar, and salt. In a separate bowl, mix the melted butter, warm milk, and the egg. Pour the yeast and milk mixtures into the dry ingredients, stirring until a dough forms.
3 Transfer the dough to a floured surface and knead for about 10 minutes, until it becomes smooth and elastic. Place the dough in the greased bowl, cover with a damp cloth, and let it rise in a warm place until doubled in size, 1–2 hours.
4 Once the dough has risen, punch it down and divide it into 12 equal portions. Shape each portion into a ball and place them 1–2 inches (2.5–5 cm) apart on a greased baking sheet. Cover the rolls with a cloth and let them rise until doubled, another 30–45 minutes.
5 Preheat the oven to 375°F (190°C/Gas Mark 5).
6 Brush the tops of the rolls with additional melted butter and bake for 15–20 minutes, until they are golden brown.
7 Let the rolls cool slightly before serving.

STORAGE: Store airtight at room temperature for up to 4 days.

CALAS

V

Consider calas as the rice cousins to flour beignets, a Louisiana staple made by the Afri-Creole women of New Orleans. These vendors sold calas hot on the street, complete with street calls that added to the music and local color of the city. They are eaten hot with powdered sugar and sometimes drizzles of cane syrup for breakfast.

PREPARATION TIME: 20 MINUTES, PLUS 2 HOURS RISING TIME
COOKING TIME: 20 MINUTES
SERVES: 4–6

- ¼ cup (2 fl oz/60 ml) warm water
- 1 packet (7 g) active dry yeast (2 ¼ teaspoons)
- ½ teaspoon plus ¼ cup (50 g) sugar
- ½ cup (4 fl oz/120 ml) whole milk
- 2 eggs, beaten
- 1 teaspoon pure vanilla extract
- 2 cups (320 g) cooked long-grain rice
- 1 cup (130 g) all-purpose (plain) flour
- 1 teaspoon kosher salt or ½ teaspoon fine salt
- ¼ teaspoon ground cinnamon
- ¼ teaspoon ground nutmeg
- Vegetable oil, for frying
- Powdered (icing) sugar, for dusting
- Cane syrup (optional), for serving

1 In a small bowl, combine the warm water, yeast, and ½ teaspoon of the sugar. Stir briefly and allow the mixture to sit until it becomes frothy, about 5 minutes.

2 In a medium bowl, whisk together the milk, beaten eggs, and vanilla. Pour the yeast mixture into the milk mixture and stir to combine.

3 In a large bowl, combine the cooked rice, flour, remaining ¼ cup (50 g) sugar, the salt, cinnamon, and nutmeg. Gradually add the milk/egg mixture to the dry ingredients, mixing until a thick batter forms. Cover the bowl with a damp cloth and let it rise in a warm place until the batter has doubled in size, about 2 hours.

4 Pour 4 inches (10 cm) oil into a deep heavy-bottomed pot and heat to 375°F (190°C). Line a plate with paper towels and have near the stove.

5 Working in batches to avoid overcrowding, drop 2 tablespoons of batter for each cala into the hot oil and fry, turning occasionally, until the calas are golden brown and cooked through, 3–4 minutes. Transfer the calas to the paper towels to drain any excess oil.

6 Serve the calas hot, dusted with powdered (icing) sugar and a drizzle of cane syrup, if desired, for a traditional taste.

BEIGNETS

V

Going to Café Du Monde in New Orleans' French Quarter and seeing the ground littered with powdered sugar is the most beautiful mess you'll ever see. This recipe helps you bring home this tasty square doughnut without waiting in line—and yes, you do need that much powdered sugar, so enjoy. Beignets are best served immediately with coffee, especially chicory coffee.

PREPARATION TIME: 2 HOURS (INCLUDES DOUGH RESTING TIME)
COOKING TIME: 20 MINUTES
MAKES: 12–15 BEIGNETS

1 packet (7 g) active dry yeast (2 ¼ teaspoons)
½ cup (4 fl oz/120 ml) warm water
4 cups (520 g) all-purpose (plain) flour
¼ cup (50 g) sugar
½ teaspoon fine salt
2 eggs, beaten
1 cup (8 fl oz/240 ml) whole milk
4 tablespoons (60 g) unsalted butter, at room temperature
Vegetable oil, for frying
Powdered sugar, for dusting

1 In a small bowl, dissolve the yeast in the warm water and let sit for 5 minutes or until frothy.

2 In a large bowl, combine the flour, sugar, and salt. Create a well in the center and pour in the yeast mixture along with the beaten eggs and milk. Mix until a sticky dough forms. Gradually incorporate the softened butter, kneading until the dough is smooth and elastic, 5–7 minutes.

3 Cover the dough with a damp cloth and let it rise in a warm place until it has doubled in size, 1–1 ½ hours.

4 Once risen, punch the dough down and transfer it to a lightly floured surface. Roll the dough out to about a ¼-inch (66 mm) thickness and cut it into squares or rectangles, roughly 2–3 inches (5–7.5 cm) on each side.

5 Pour 2 inches (5 cm) oil into a deep fryer or heavy-bottomed pot and heat to 350°F (177°C). Line a baking sheet with paper towels and have near the stove.

6 Working in batches to avoid overcrowding, carefully drop a few pieces of dough into the hot oil and fry, turning occasionally, until the beignets puff up and turn golden brown, about 2 minutes per side. Use a slotted spoon to remove them to the paper towels to drain.

7 While still warm, dust the beignets generously with powdered sugar.

FLOUR DUMPLINGS

V -5

Flour dumplings, a favorite in Northern European cuisine, found a special home in the South where the one-pot meal morphed into dozens of dishes as the three foundational cultures—Native American, Western, and Central African—merged. The dumplings were popped into a stew, and they added a special treat that soaked up the best essences of the broth. In some locations, people had to pray the flour was clean and sound, which made chicken and flour dumplings—a perfect Sunday dinner—extra special because it meant that quality flour had been acquired.

PREPARATION TIME: 15 MINUTES
COOKING TIME: 30 MINUTES
SERVES: 4–6

2 cups (260 g) all-purpose (plain) flour
1 tablespoon baking powder
1 teaspoon fine salt
¾ cup (6 fl oz/180 ml) whole milk
1 egg, beaten

1 Sift together the flour, baking powder, and fine salt into a large bowl. In a separate bowl, whisk together the milk and beaten egg until well combined. Gradually pour the wet ingredients into the dry ingredients, stirring gently until a soft dough forms. Be careful not to overmix, as this can make the dumplings tough.

2 Bring a large pot of salted water or stock (if using) to a gentle boil over medium heat.

3 Using a spoon or your hands, form the dough into small balls or drop the dough by spoonfuls into the simmering liquid, making sure they are spaced apart or they'll stick together and not cook evenly. Cover the pot and simmer the dumplings until they are cooked through and have a light, fluffy texture, 15–20 minutes. (Avoid lifting the lid too often during cooking, as this can cause the dumplings to become dense.)

4 Once cooked, remove the dumplings from the pot with a slotted spoon and transfer them to a serving dish. (The dumplings can be made a few hours in advance and serve with your stew of choice; or you can cook the dumplings directly in the stew.)

ICEBOX ROLLS

V

These rolls got their name because they were often set to rise in the refrigerator (an option I give you in this recipe). Like many Southerners, my family called them "potato rolls," and we had them at every holiday and life-cycle event. Southern wheat flours or "soft flours" are preferred to other varieties that are closer to bread flour. A home cook is lauded for bread that has the "light touch" and is airy and soft and can sop up gravy, Pot Likker (PAGE 266), and meat juices. These rolls can be used to make a quick sandwich with ham or chicken, or served alongside salad or other picnic dishes.

PREPARATION TIME: 30 MINUTES, PLUS 2 HOURS RISING TIME
COOKING TIME: 16–20 MINUTES
MAKES: 48 ROLLS

7 cups (910 g) all-purpose (plain) flour
1 tablespoon instant yeast
1 cup (8 fl oz/240 ml) whole milk
12 tablespoons (6 oz/170 g) unsalted butter
¾ cup (150 g) plus 1 teaspoon sugar
2 teaspoons fine salt
2 cups (500 g) cooled mashed boiled potatoes (from about 4 russet or Maris Piper potatoes)
2 eggs, beaten
½ cup (4 fl oz/120 ml) warm water
Cooking spray, for the bowl
Softened butter, for the pan
1 egg yolk
2 teaspoons heavy (whipping) cream

1 In a large bowl, combine the flour and yeast, stirring to blend. Set aside.

2 In a medium saucepan, heat the milk and butter over low heat, stirring frequently, until the butter melts. Add the sugar and salt and stir until dissolved. Remove from the heat and let cool to room temperature.

3 In a stand mixer fitted with the dough hook, combine the cooled milk mixture, flour mixture, potatoes, beaten eggs, and water and mix on low speed until it comes together and is thoroughly integrated, about 3 minutes. Increase the speed to medium and mix until you have a smooth dough, another 7 minutes.

4 Transfer the dough to a lightly floured surface. Sprinkle the top of the dough with flour and do a final kneading of the dough, shaping it into a block and tucking the edges of the dough to the bottom center, creating a smooth, taut ball.

5 Lightly spray a large bowl with cooking spray. Add the dough and turn to coat with oil, then turn it seam-side down. Cover with a tea towel or plastic wrap and let rise in a warm place until doubled in size, about 1 hour.

6 Lightly butter a 13 × 18-inch (33 × 46 cm) sheet pan (aka half-sheet).

7 Turn out the dough onto a lightly floured surface and divide into 48 equal portions (about 45 g each). Shape into balls and arrange in the prepared pan, in 8 rows, so they just barely touch each other. (You also have the option to cover and refrigerate until ready to use, up to 1 day.) Allow the rolls to rise in a warm place until doubled in size, about 1 hour.

8 When you are ready to bake, preheat the oven to 400°F (200°C/Gas Mark 6).

9 In a small bowl, stir together the egg yolk and heavy (whipping) cream to make an egg wash. Lightly brush the tops of the rolls with the egg wash.

10 Bake for 16–20 minutes, until golden brown.

11 Let cool on a wire rack for 5 minutes before serving. Serve warm.

STORAGE: Store airtight at room temperature for up to 4 days.

RICE BREAD

GF V

Born in the rice-growing regions of North Carolina, South Carolina, and Georgia, Southern rice breads were simple ways to use leftover rice and at the same time use a local product in place of the more expensive wheat flour. Rice bread was a hallmark part of the famed Carolina rice kitchen, created at the culinary crossroads of British and West African foodways.

PREPARATION TIME: 20 MINUTES, PLUS 1 HOUR RISING TIME
COOKING TIME: 45-50 MINUTES
MAKES: ONE 9 X 5 (23 X 13 CM) LOAF

1 packet (7 g) active dry yeast (2 ¼ teaspoons)
¼ cup (2 fl oz/60 ml) warm water
1 cup (8 fl oz/240 ml) buttermilk
4 tablespoons (60 g) unsalted butter, melted, plus more for the bowl and pan
1 egg
2 ½ cups (210 g) cooled mashed cooked long-grain rice
¼ cup (50 g) sugar
1 teaspoon kosher salt or ½ teaspoon fine salt

1 In a small bowl, dissolve the yeast in the warm water and let sit for about 5 minutes until it becomes frothy
2 Grease a large bowl and a 9 x 5-inch (23 x 13 cm) loaf pan with butter or oil.
3 In a medium bowl, whisk together the buttermilk, melted butter, and egg. Gently stir the yeast mixture into the buttermilk mixture.
4 In a large bowl, mix the mashed rice with the sugar and salt. Add the buttermilk/egg mixture, mixing until a smooth, slightly sticky dough forms.
5 Transfer the dough to the greased bowl, cover with a damp cloth, and let it rise in a warm place until it roughly doubles in size, about 1 hour. (Rice dough is denser than regular dough, but the rise should still be noticeable.)
6 Once the dough has risen, punch it down and shape it into a loaf. Place the dough in the greased loaf pan, cover it, and allow it to rise again for about 30 minutes.
7 Meanwhile, preheat the oven to 375°F (190°C/Gas Mark 5).
8 Bake for 45–50 minutes, until the crust is golden brown and the bread sounds hollow when tapped.
9 Let the bread cool in the pan for 10 minutes before turning it out onto a wire rack to cool completely.

STORAGE: Store airtight at room temperature for up to 4 days.

BUTTERMILK BISCUITS

V -5

The pride of Southern foodways, the buttermilk biscuit done right is the perfect accompaniment for everything from peach preserves and marmalades to ham, chicken, pork chops, and even chocolate gravy. Note they are generally a quick bread, just one element on a Southern breakfast table already groaning with delicious fare.

PREPARATION TIME: 20 MINUTES
COOKING TIME: 16–18 MINUTES
MAKES: 8 BIG BISCUITS

2 cups (260 g) all-purpose (plain) flour
2 teaspoons baking powder
1 teaspoon fine salt
8 tablespoons (4 oz/115 g) cold unsalted butter, cut into pieces
¾ cup (6 fl oz/180 ml) cold buttermilk or whole milk

1 Preheat the oven to 425°F (220°C/ Gas Mark 7).

2 In a large bowl, whisk together the flour, baking powder, and salt. Add the cold butter and toss quickly to coat the pieces with flour. Using a pastry blender or two table knives, cut the butter into the flour, until the mixture is very crumbly, with visible butter bits no larger than peas.

3 Make a well in the center of the flour and pour in the buttermilk. Using a large spoon or a spatula, quickly stir in big circles, pulling the flour into the buttermilk to make a shaggy dough.

4 Dump the dough onto a lightly floured surface. Dust your hands with flour and use them to quickly shape it into a mound. Press to flatten it to a thick round and then fold it in half. Flatten it again and fold it again.

5 Quickly pat the dough out into a round that is ½–¾ inch (13 mm to 2 cm) thick. Using a 2-inch (5 cm) round biscuit cutter, press the cutter straight down without twisting it to punch out biscuits. Arrange the biscuits in a 9-inch (23 cm) cake pan or cast-iron skillet. Gather the scraps, pat out, and cut out more biscuits.

6 Bake for 16–18 minutes, until the biscuits have risen and are golden brown.

7 Transfer straight out of the skillet to a serving basket or bowl lined with a napkin. Cover with the napkin and serve hot.

FRIED BISCUITS

V

Biscuit culture in the South, like cornbread culture, is often mistaken for being all the same end product. When most people think of Southern biscuits, they think of Buttermilk Biscuits (PAGE 25), not these fried biscuits. Sometimes known as "Maryland chicken biscuits," these biscuits often accompanied fried chicken at breakfast or a Sunday gathering, and they were usually lightly fried in the same grease as the chicken. We offer the recipe here as revival (though simplified by using vegetable oil).

PREPARATION TIME: 20 MINUTES
COOKING TIME: 15 MINUTES
MAKES: 6–8 BISCUITS

2 cups (260 g) all-purpose (plain) flour
2 teaspoons baking powder
2 tablespoons sugar
1 teaspoon fine salt
8 tablespoons (4 oz/115 g) cold unsalted butter, cubed
¾ cup (6 fl oz/180 ml) whole milk
Vegetable oil, for frying

1 In a large bowl, combine the flour, baking powder, sugar, and salt. Cut the cold butter into the dry ingredients using a pastry cutter or your fingers until the mixture resembles coarse crumbs. Gradually add the milk, stirring gently until a soft dough forms. Be cautious not to overwork the dough to maintain a light texture.

2 Turn the dough out onto a lightly floured surface and gently pat it into a ½-inch (13 mm) thickness. Using a floured 2 ½-inch (6.5 cm) biscuit cutter or the rim of a glass, cut out rounds of dough and place them on a floured sheet pan or baking sheet. Gather the scraps, pat out, and cut out more biscuits.

3 Pour 1 inch (2.5 cm) oil into a large cast-iron skillet and heat over medium heat, until it reaches 350°F (177°C) or a small piece of the batter sizzles when dropped into the oil. Line a plate with paper towels and have near the stove.

4 Working in batches to avoid overcrowding, carefully place a few biscuit rounds into the hot oil and fry until they are golden brown and crispy, 2–3 minutes on each side. Remove the biscuits with a slotted spoon to the paper towels to drain.

5 Serve hot.

DROP BISCUITS

V -30

Drop biscuits may have a reputation as the "lazy" biscuits, but they are a quicker and easier way to get into Southern biscuit making. The rough dough will give the biscuits their signature rustic appearance and texture. They are just as good as the fluffy, flaky kind, especially when you cannot wait for a biscuit for your jam or anything gravy-based.

PREPARATION TIME: 15 MINUTES
COOKING TIME: 12-15 MINUTES
SERVES: 8

2 cups (260 g) all-purpose (plain) flour
1 tablespoon baking powder
2 tablespoons sugar
1 teaspoon fine salt
8 tablespoons (4 oz/115 g) cold unsalted butter, cubed
1 cup (8 fl oz/240 ml) cold whole milk

1 Preheat the oven to 425°F (220°C/Gas Mark 7). Grease or line a baking sheet with parchment paper.

2 In a large bowl, sift together the flour, baking powder, sugar, and salt. Cut the cold butter into the dry ingredients using a pastry cutter or your fingertips, until the mixture resembles coarse crumbs.

3 Make a well in the center of the flour mixture and pour in the cold milk. Stir gently until just combined; the dough will be thick and somewhat sticky. Avoid overmixing to keep the biscuits light and fluffy.

4 Using a spoon or an ice cream scoop, drop spoonfuls of the dough onto the prepared baking sheet, spacing them about 2 inches (5 cm) apart.

5 Bake for 12–15 minutes, until the tops are golden brown and a toothpick inserted into the center comes out clean.

6 Transfer the biscuits to a wire rack to cool slightly before serving.

STORAGE: Store airtight at room temperature for up to 3 days.

SWEET POTATO BISCUITS

V

There is a bit of a controversy about these biscuits. Did Mary Randolph, the author of the first Southern cookbook, *The Virginia House-Wife*, mean white potato or sweet potato in her potato biscuits (tea buns)? The great food historian Karen Hess said it was sweet potato, while her student, master cook and cookbook author Damon Lee Fowler, said white potato. My take is that European and African Atlantic traditions blended, and climate and cultural changes led one version to be favored based on seasonality, personal preference, and local culture. White sweet potatoes were also a favorite throughout the Chesapeake region during the postbellum period. You can refrigerate the biscuits up to 1 hour before baking. Serve hot and well buttered.

PREPARATION TIME: 30 MINUTES
COOKING TIME: 1 HOUR – 1 HOUR 25 MINUTES
MAKES: 16 BISCUITS

Cooking spray
2 medium sweet potatoes (about 8 oz/225 g each)
3 cups (390 g) all-purpose (plain) flour
1 cup plus 2 tablespoons (140 g) cake flour
3 ½ teaspoons baking powder
1 tablespoon sugar
1 ½ teaspoons ground cinnamon
¾ teaspoon fine salt
¼ teaspoon baking soda (bicarbonate of soda)
14 oz (435 g) cold unsalted butter, cut into ½-inch (13 mm) cubes, plus 2 tablespoons (30 g) unsalted butter, melted, for brushing
2 cups (16 fl oz/470 ml) buttermilk, plus more as needed

1 Preheat the oven to 350°F (180°C/Gas Mark 4). Line a baking sheet with parchment and generously spray the parchment with cooking spray.

2 Peel the sweet potatoes and cut into 1-inch (2.5 cm) chunks. Place the cubes on the prepared pan and bake until fork-tender, 45–55 minutes.

3 Transfer the roasted potatoes to a bowl and mash with a potato masher. Measure out 1 ½ cups (328 g) and let cool. (Any leftovers are yours for snacking.)

4 When you are ready to bake, preheat the oven to 375°F (190°C/Gas Mark 5). Line a baking sheet with parchment paper.

5 In a large bowl, whisk together the all-purpose (plain) flour, cake flour, baking powder, sugar, cinnamon, salt, and baking soda (bicarb). Add the cold butter cubes and toss them to coat. Working quickly, cut them into the flour with a pastry blender, or pinch with your fingertips, while smearing the butter into the flour. You should have various-size pieces of butter ranging from coarse sandy patches to flat shaggy pieces to pea-size chunks, with some larger bits as well.

5 Make a well in the center of the dry ingredients, add the mashed sweet potatoes and mix with a silicone spatula just to incorporate. Add 1 ½ cups (12 fl oz/350 ml) of the buttermilk, gently mixing with the spatula; the dough will start to look shaggy. Gradually add about ½ cup (4 fl oz/120 ml) more buttermilk. Gently mix the ingredients with your hands until you have a shaggy dough.

6 Turn the dough out onto a clean work surface. Using the heel of your hand, smear the butter into the flour, then repeatedly smear, fold, and turn the dough to build its lamination, until the dough comes together in a mass. If the dough looks dry during this process, add more buttermilk, 1 tablespoon at a time, and continue folding until it comes together.

7 Flour a rolling pin and lightly dust your work surface and the top of the dough with flour. Roll the dough into a rectangle 1 inch (2.5 cm) thick. Dip the edges of a 2-inch (5 cm) biscuit cutter into flour and punch out the biscuits (do not twist the cutter, or you will compress the layers of dough and the biscuits will not rise as high) as close together as possible, making sure to dip the cutter in flour after every cut. Arrange on the prepared baking sheet, leaving about 1 inch (2.5 cm) between them. Then carefully gather the scraps together, gently roll them out again, and cut more biscuits. Brush the tops of the biscuits with the melted butter.

8 Transfer the biscuits to the oven and bake for 25–30 minutes, rotating the pan front to back halfway through for even baking, until golden brown.

9 Let cool on a wire rack for 5 minutes before serving.

STORAGE: Store airtight at room temperature for up to 1 day.

SALLY LUNN BREAD

V

You'll see this explanation in every Southern cookbook. The name of "Sally Lunn," a brioche-like bread that today mostly lives in the memory space of cookbooks, comes from an old English corruption of soleil et lune, or French for "sun and moon." Some spaces like Colonial Williamsburg, a living history museum in Williamsburg, Virginia, still offer their version of Sally Lunn—golden, lightly sweet, and airy—made in muffin tins.

PREPARATION TIME: 30 MINUTES, PLUS 1 HOUR RISING TIME
COOKING TIME: 45–50 MINUTES
SERVES: 8–10

1 cup (8 fl oz/240 ml) warm whole milk (110°F/95°C)
1 packet (7 g) active dry yeast (2 ¼ teaspoons)
1 teaspoon plus ⅓ cup (65 g) sugar
4 cups (520 g) all-purpose (plain) flour
1 teaspoon fine salt
8 tablespoons (4 oz/115 g) unsalted butter, at room temperature
3 eggs, beaten
Softened butter, for the pan

1 In a small bowl, stir together the warm milk, yeast, and 1 teaspoon of the sugar. Let sit until puffed and foaming, 5–10 minutes.
2 In a medium bowl, whisk together the flour and salt.
3 In a very large bowl, with an electric mixer, beat the remaining ⅓ cup (65 g) sugar and the butter on medium-high speed until creamy and light, 2–3 minutes. Add the eggs and beat to incorporate.
4 Add about one-third of the flour to the egg mixture and beat on low speed until most of the flour disappears. Add half the milk/yeast mixture and beat to incorporate. Add half the remaining flour, then the remaining milk/yeast mixture. Finish with the last of the flour. Switch to a big spoon or spatula to finish mixing the dough, stirring until no dry patches of flour remain. The dough will be thick, soft, and very sticky.
5 Cover the bowl of dough with a tea towel and let it sit in a warm place until doubled in size, about 1 hour. Meanwhile, generously butter a 10-inch (25 cm) tube pan or Bundt pan.
6 Using a large spoon or a spatula, deflate the dough by stirring it down, scraping down the sides and bringing it together. Pour the soft dough into the prepared tube pan, spreading it to fill the pan evenly and smoothing the top. Cover and let rise in a warm place again, until doubled in size, about 1 hour.
7 Preheat the oven to 350°F (180°C/Gas Mark 4).
8 Bake for 45–50 minutes, until the bread is rounded, firm, and golden brown.
9 Transfer to a wire rack and let cool in the pan for at least 10 and up to 15 minutes, then unmold onto a wire rack to cool completely, top-side up. Transfer to a serving plate and serve warm or at room temperature.

STORAGE: Store airtight at room temperature for up to 3 days.

BEATEN BISCUITS

Beaten biscuits are not the fluffy, pillowy biscuits most people associate with the South—those are Buttermilk Biscuits (PAGE 25). These tiny biscuits were quick to make but staled fast, eventually becoming as tough as hardtack. Beaten biscuits famously took one hundred whacks, constant folding, and steady pounding, often with a mallet, hammer, or ax handle. But because they were often prepared for last-minute guests, beaten biscuits would be made and consumed fresh, with a crisp exterior and a tender center, often with a thin slice of country ham. You can also choose to serve these hot with butter, bacon, or a dab of jam. (If baking with butter instead of lard, cut it into ½-inch/13 mm chunks.)

PREPARATION TIME: 1 HOUR
COOKING TIME: 20-25 MINUTES
MAKES: 36 TO 48 BISCUITS

4 cups (520 g) all-purpose (plain) flour
1 teaspoon fine salt
½ teaspoon sugar
¼ teaspoon baking soda (bicarbonate of soda)
12 tablespoons (6 oz/170 g) cold lard or unsalted butter
1–1 ¼ cups (8 fl oz/240 ml to 10 fl oz/295 ml) ice water
Softened lard or butter, for the baking sheet

1 In a large bowl, whisk together the all-purpose flour, salt, sugar, and baking soda (bicarb). Cut the cold lard or butter into the flour mixture using a pastry cutter or your fingertips, working quickly with a light touch, until the mixture resembles coarse crumbs.

2 Make a well in the center of the flour mixture. Quickly add 1 cup (8 fl oz/240 ml) of the ice water and stir with a wooden spoon to bring everything together into a dough. If the mixture is too dry, add another ¼ cup (2 fl oz/60 ml) ice water, or a few tablespoons more as needed, until the dough comes together.

3 Transfer the dough to a floured surface, flour your hands, and press the dough together into a rough ball. Flatten it out a little and then fold it over, kneading a few turns until you have a stiff, fairly smooth ball of dough.

4 To start the beating process, use a wooden rolling pin and evenly whack the dough, flattening it out into a rectangle, roughly 8 × 10 inches (20 × 25 cm). Fold the dough into thirds, turn it over, and repeat, beating and folding, turning the dough occasionally, for at least 30 minutes. The dough will gradually become smooth and elastic, developing a slight sheen as the gluten forms.

5 Once the dough has been thoroughly beaten, preheat the oven to 375°F (190°C/Gas Mark 5). Grease a baking sheet with lard or butter.

6 Roll out the dough to about a ½-inch (13 mm) thickness and use a 1 ½–2-inch (4–5 cm) biscuit cutter to cut out rounds. Place the biscuits on the greased baking sheet and then prick each biscuit two or three times with a fork, which allows steam to escape and helps the biscuits rise evenly. Gather the scraps, reroll, and cut out more biscuits.

7 Bake for 20–25 minutes, or until the biscuits are crisp, lightly browned on top, and golden brown on the bottom. Transfer to a wire rack to cool briefly, then serve warm.

STORAGE: Store airtight at room temperature for up to 1 week.

CATHEAD BISCUITS

V -30

These biscuits aren't really made out of cat heads—they are really just meant to be "as big as a cat's head." They are particularly good fresh out of the oven, spread generously with fruit butters like apple or peach, or strawberry or blackberry jam.

PREPARATION TIME: 15 MINUTES
COOKING TIME: 12-15 MINUTES
MAKES: 9 BISCUITS

Softened butter or shortening, for the skillet
4 ½ cups (585 g) all-purpose (plain) flour
¼ cup (50 g) sugar
2 tablespoons baking powder
1 teaspoon baking soda (bicarbonate of soda)
2 ½ teaspoons fine salt
⅓ cup (68 g) vegetable shortening or lard, well chilled
8 tablespoons (4 oz/115 g) unsalted butter, 4 tablespoons cold and 4 tablespoons melted
2 cups (16 fl oz/470 ml) buttermilk

1 Preheat the oven to 450°F (230°C/Gas Mark 8). Butter or grease a 12-inch cast-iron skillet and set aside.

2 In a large bowl, stir together the flour, sugar, baking powder, baking soda (bicarb), and salt.

3 Add the cold shortening and 4 tablespoons cold butter to the flour mixture. With clean hands or a pastry cutter, combine until the mixture has a pebble-like texture.

4 Slowly add the buttermilk and mix until barely combined. At this point, the dough will have a shaggy texture.

5 Transfer the dough to a clean, floured surface and press flat with your hands until smooth and 1–2 inches (2.5–5 cm) thick. Using a 3-inch (7.5 cm) cutter or a glass, cut out rounds of dough. Gather the scraps, pat out, and cut out more biscuits.

6 Place the biscuits in the skillet and brush the tops with the melted butter. Transfer to the oven immediately.

7 Bake for 12–15 minutes, until the biscuits have risen and the tops are golden brown.

STORAGE: Store airtight at room temperature for up to 3 days.

MOTHER CORN

The South's use of corn, or maize (*Zea mays*), has been notable since the first contact between European explorers, colonists, and Native peoples. The Natchez people, direct descendants of the mound builders, pre-Columbian Native people in the Midwest and Southern United States whose mastery of the immigrant crop fueled the more extraordinary Mississippian civilizations, had forty-two dishes made from corn, many of which—hominy, cornbread, and corn soup—are still consumed. To the east, the Cherokee nation honored the Corn Mother, Selu, who sacrificed herself to feed her people. The Muscogee (Creek) and their neighbors honored the crop through the Green Corn festival, celebrating the harvest and expunging the community of the past year's sins through fasting and spiritual purification. Corn varieties were vastly more diverse for Native American Southerners than they are today because of large-scale monoculture.

Mother Corn went to West and Central Africa through the Portuguese by the sixteenth century and was a major crop along the 3,500 miles from Senegal to Angola. Through African intervention, corn was also dispersed to southern and southeastern Africa. In Kongo, it was known as *masangu Mputo*, or the "grain from the Portuguese/Europeans." Corn and cassava competed against native grains like millet and sorghum, but they also spurred a population explosion, which only enhanced the greed of the transatlantic slave trade. The similarity of Southern corn dishes can still be seen in contemporary Africa. For example, South Carolina loves its fish, shrimp (prawns), and grits, and in coastal Mozambique, fish and shellfish are often eaten with corn pap, known as *nshima*. In southern Ghana, *kenkey* and *banku* provided spongy fermented corn loaves to sop up a sauce or stew. In short, the Southern food diet was impacted by more than two hundred years of Africans consuming this crop.

Initially, much of the Colonial South's corn was of the gourdseed variety, a "dent" corn. As agricultural methods changed and the South's population pushed away from the coast into the interior, white and yellow "flint" corn dominated the region in the nineteenth century. White corn was for human consumption and yellow corn for animals, although yellow processed cornmeal is today's most recognized product. Corn was the source of hominy, hoecakes, ashcakes, cornbread (further repurposed into dressing and kush), corn pone, grits, meal for breading, roasting ears, and corn liquor. It was also used for clothing starch, pipes, dolls, cobs for smoking, shucks for shining floors, or for stuffing the pallets of the poor and the enslaved. Southerners in the seventeenth through the early twentieth century knew precisely which varieties would meet their needs.

Corn sits alongside rice and wheat as the three dominant starches of Southern foodways. Native Americans would innovate fry bread (a dish that would come to symbolize both Native identity and reservation culture), Africans would sop up new stews with biscuits and cornbreads, and Europeans and Native Americans would grow and consume rice brought from West Africa and Madagascar. In these exchanges and many others, we can see the culinary foundation of Southern food that are still being built on as new South Asian, Southeast Asian, Middle Eastern, Central American, and African immigrant communities approach the South, bringing with them both ancient and fresh perspectives and appetites.

CORN MUSH

GF V -5

Corn mush may seem extremely ordinary, but at one point in Southern culinary history, corn mush was one of the most versatile starch bases available to Southerners. It was eaten with gravy, fried chicken, fish, beans, greens and pot likker, and game. In Louisiana, this dish was known as coush-coush, a term of Senegambian origin, and was eaten with plenty of butter and cane syrup.

PREPARATION TIME: 10 MINUTES
COOKING TIME: 40 MINUTES
SERVES: 4

2 cups (16 fl oz/470 ml) whole milk
1 cup (130 g) white or yellow cornmeal
1 teaspoon fine salt
2 tablespoons (30 g) unsalted butter

1 In a large saucepan, bring the milk and 4 cups (32 fl oz/950 ml) water to a gentle boil over medium-high heat.

2 Once the mixture is boiling, gradually add the cornmeal, whisking constantly to prevent lumps from forming. Reduce the heat to low and continue to cook, stirring frequently, until the mixture thickens and the cornmeal is tender, 20–25 minutes.

3 Add the salt and butter to the mixture, stirring until the butter is fully melted and incorporated. Taste and adjust the seasoning if necessary. The corn mush should have a smooth and creamy texture.

4 Serve hot.

HUSH PUPPIES

V

The embrace of native Southern field corn, the use of lard, and the continuity of the fritter from West Africa to America made this beloved side dish possible. According to culinary historian Robert Morse, hush puppies were also known in some parts of the Carolinas as "redhorse bread," made to accompany a river fish popular with enslaved cooks during the Antebellum period. Popular legend has it that the quick fried snack acquired its name from being used to feed hungry puppies looking for a treat. And there was a recent hypothesis that hush puppies were used to distract the dogs that were on the trail of the escaping enslaved, but this is utterly false.

Hush puppies have a history of being served with fried fish, barbecue, and spicy stews as the center of nineteenth-century social events, where the skills of Black cooks flourished. In keeping with that tradition, serve hush puppies with fried seafood, coleslaw, fried chicken, barbecue, and the like.

PREPARATION TIME: 15 MINUTES
COOKING TIME: 20 MINUTES
SERVES: 4–6

1 cup (120 g) white cornmeal
½ cup (65 g) self-rising flour (see NOTE)
1 tablespoon sugar
1 teaspoon fine salt
½ cup (80 g) finely chopped onion
½ cup (4 fl oz/120 ml) whole milk
1 egg
Vegetable oil or lard, for frying

---

1 In a large bowl, mix the cornmeal, self-rising flour, sugar, salt, and onion.

2 In a medium bowl, whisk together the milk and egg until well combined. Gradually add the wet ingredients to the dry ingredients, stirring until just combined (do not overmix).

3 Pour 5 inches (23 cm) oil into a large deep pot and heat to 350°F (177°C). Line a plate with paper towels and have near the stove.

4 Working in batches to avoid overcrowding, use a spoon or small ice cream scoop to carefully drop 1-tablespoon portions of the batter into the hot oil and fry until the hush puppies are golden brown and cooked through, 3–4 minutes on each side. Transfer the hush puppies to the paper towels to drain.

5 Serve hot and fresh.

NOTE: If you don't have self-rising flour, add 1 teaspoon baking powder to the batter.

VARIATION: Great flavor options include 1 teaspoon minced garlic, chopped fresh flat-leaf parsley, or thinly sliced scallions (spring onions). If you like, sneak in a little light beer instead of milk.

EASTERN NORTH CAROLINA HUSH PUPPIES

V

These cheese curl-shaped corn fritters are the perfect accompaniment for eastern North Carolina whole-hog barbecue, as well as Brunswick Stew (PAGE 159). They also shine alongside the southeastern North Carolina fried seafood known as "Calabash style," from the small waterside town where it originated.

PREPARATION TIME: 15 MINUTES
COOKING TIME: 20 MINUTES
SERVES: 4–6

1 cup (135 g) yellow cornmeal
½ cup (65 g) all-purpose (plain) flour
2 teaspoons baking powder
1 teaspoon fine salt
1 tablespoon sugar
Pinch of cayenne pepper
½ cup (80 g) finely chopped onion
½ cup (4 fl oz/120 ml) buttermilk
1 egg
Vegetable oil, for frying

1 In a large bowl, combine the cornmeal, flour, baking powder, salt, sugar, and cayenne. Add the onion and mix until evenly distributed.

2 In a small bowl, whisk together the buttermilk and egg until well blended. Gradually pour the wet mixture into the dry ingredients, stirring gently until a thick batter forms.

3 Pour 5 inches (23 cm) oil into a deep pot and heat to 350°F (177°C). Line a plate with paper towels and have near the stove.

4 Working in batches to avoid overcrowding, use a spoon or small scoop to carefully drop portions of the batter into the hot oil and fry each hush puppy until golden brown and crispy, 3–4 minutes on each side, turning with a spider skimmer. Transfer the hush puppies to the paper towels to drain.

5 Serve hot and fresh.

GRITS

GF V -5

Southern people love corn. It's our direct link with Native Americans—the Nanticoke, Powhatan, Tutelo-Saponi, Muscogee (Creek), Cherokee, Choctaw, Natchez, Seminole, and many others. Grits were both filling and nutritionally crucial. Lye-treated hominy, originally made from white flint corn, when consumed with beans, squash, sunflower seeds, and other staple crops, provided a nutritionally complete plant-based diet. The consumption of grits and hominy certainly helped enslaved Africans despite a relatively poor and monotonous diet based on rations. By 1880, Hickory King, a dent-type field corn variety, eclipsed flint corn varieties, and by the early twentieth century, according to Charleston-based culinary historian David Shields, the more easily treated variety was the standard milled variety for grits. Even though most grits today aren't hominy-based, it was this technique that was important to the survival of Southerners for over three hundred years after English arrival on Native shores.

What makes grits magically important is that they can absorb and transmit so many different flavors—they can hold cheese, gravy, herbs, or stock; or you can eat them plain the traditional way with salt and butter. (Just never admit to adding sugar.) You are welcome to add cheese, onions, or herbs for a more savory version.

PREPARATION TIME: 10 MINUTES
COOKING TIME: 55 MINUTES
SERVES: 4

- 4 cups (32 fl oz/950 ml) water or milk (or a combination)
- ½ teaspoon fine salt
- 1 cup (140 g) stone-ground grits
- 2 tablespoons (30 g) unsalted butter

1 In a large pot, bring the water or milk to a boil.

2 Add the salt to the boiling liquid and gradually whisk in the grits, ensuring they are well dispersed and free of lumps. Reduce the heat to low, cover, and simmer gently, stirring occasionally to prevent sticking, until the grits are tender and have absorbed the liquid, achieving a creamy consistency, 30–45 minutes.

3 Stir in the butter and serve.

HOMINY

GF V -5

Hominy is not grits. Hominy is corn treated with lye or lime in a process called nixtamalization, which for thousands of years, thanks to Native American innovation, has made field corn more easily digestible and nutritious by enhancing the essential amino acid, lysine. When soaked and boiled, hominy becomes more like beans or couscous. When ground up, it becomes hominy grits. Starchy, filling, plain, and versatile, hominy shines in soups, stews, and chilis.

PREPARATION TIME: 5 MINUTES, PLUS OVERNIGHT SOAKING
COOKING TIME: 2 HOURS 10 MINUTES
SERVES: 4

1 cup (170 g) dried hominy kernels
1 teaspoon fine salt
4 tablespoons (60 g) unsalted butter

1 Place the hominy in a fine-mesh sieve and rinse well with cold water until the water runs clear. Soak the dried hominy kernels in a large bowl of water overnight. The next day, drain and rinse the soaked hominy under cold running water.

2 In a large pot, bring 4 cups (1 liter) water to a boil. Add the soaked hominy and the salt. Return to a boil, then reduce the heat to a gentle simmer and cook uncovered until the hominy is tender and has expanded to a plump, chewy texture, about 2 hours. Stir occasionally to ensure even cooking and prevent sticking. If necessary, add more water to maintain the desired consistency throughout the cooking process. In the last 10 minutes of cooking, stir in the butter.

3 Serve warm.

VARIATION: If using an electric or stovetop pressure cooker, cook at high pressure for 40 minutes. Once finished, quick-release the pressure and add the butter.

BUTTERMILK CORNBREAD

V

There is the traditional skillet cornbread, which is solid, crumbly, and eaten with greens and other traditional fare. Then there is this recipe—made for the kids, as many like to say. This cornbread is a Southern soul food staple, and jelly, molasses, or syrup often comes to the table to amp up its cake-like quality.

PREPARATION TIME: 20 MINUTES
COOKING TIME: 25 MINUTES
SERVES: 9

8 tablespoons (4 oz/115 g) unsalted butter
2/3 cup (130 g) granulated (caster) sugar
2 tablespoons brown sugar
2 eggs
1 cup (8 fl oz /240 ml) buttermilk
1 cup (120 g) white cornmeal
1 cup (130 g) all-purpose (plain) flour
1/2 teaspoon baking soda (bicarbonate of soda)
1/4 teaspoon kosher salt or 1/8 teaspoon fine salt

1 Preheat the oven to 375°F (190°C/Gas Mark 5). Place the butter in a 9-inch (23 cm) cast-iron skillet and set aside.
2 In a large bowl, whisk together both sugars and the eggs until light and creamy. Add the buttermilk and whisk again.
3 In a medium bowl, whisk together the cornmeal, flour, baking soda (bicarb), and salt. Add the cornmeal mixture to the egg mixture and stir until well combined.
4 Place the cast-iron skillet over medium-high heat and melt the butter until frothy. When the butter is completely melted, pour in the cornbread batter, then transfer to the oven uncovered.
5 Bake for 25 minutes, or until the cornbread has risen and is golden brown.

STORAGE: Store airtight at room temperature for up to 3 days.

SKILLET CORNBREAD

V

There is no more emblematic bread or serious test of a Southern cook's skill than their way with a cast-iron skillet and cornbread batter. Since the early nineteenth century, this has been a mainstay of Southern quick breads and the accompaniment to many Southern dishes, from beans to greens to soups, and beyond . . . but never barbecue or fried chicken, which are best served with biscuits, rolls, or wheat flour–based breads.

PREPARATION TIME: 15 MINUTES
COOKING TIME: 20-25 MINUTES
SERVES: 10

1 ½ cups (180 g) white cornmeal
1 cup (130 g) all-purpose (plain) flour
1 tablespoon baking powder
1 tablespoon sugar
½ teaspoon baking soda (bicarbonate of soda)
½ teaspoon fine salt
2 eggs, beaten
1 ½ cups (12 fl oz/350 ml) buttermilk
6 tablespoons (3 oz/85 g) unsalted butter

1 Preheat the oven to 425°F (220°F/Gas Mark 7).
2 In a large bowl, whisk together the cornmeal, flour, baking powder, sugar, baking soda (bicarb), and salt.
3 In a medium bowl, whisk together the beaten eggs and the buttermilk. Add the egg mixture to the cornmeal mixture and stir together with a large spoon, just until the flour disappears.
4 Add the butter to a 9-inch (23 cm) cast-iron skillet and heat in the oven until melted, slightly foamy, and fragrant.
5 Carefully remove the skillet from the oven and pour the batter directly into the skillet. Give it a quick stir and return it to the oven.
6 Bake for 20–25 minutes, until golden brown. Test as you would cake, by sticking a thin wooden skewer or toothpick in the center to see if it comes out clean.

STORAGE: Store airtight at room temperature for up to 3 days.

SPOONBREAD

GF V

Spoonbread or batter bread, is a custardy side dish born in the Chesapeake Bay region in the earliest cultural collisions between Native American and British. The dish spread west as Southerners migrated out of Maryland and Virginia, into the Southern midlands of Kentucky, Tennessee, Missouri, and northern Arkansas. At Colonial Williamsburg, America's largest living history museum located in southeastern Virginia, this dish is served with bacon, fried apples, and herring roe, to cater to tourists. In the South Carolina Lowcountry, this dish was alternatively known as "awendaw", named for a locality in Charleston County.

PREPARATION TIME: 15 MINUTES
COOKING TIME: 50 MINUTES
SERVES: 6

Softened butter or cooking spray, for the baking dish
2 cups (16 fl oz/470 ml) whole milk
1 cup (120 g) finely ground white cornmeal
2 tablespoons (30 g) unsalted butter, plus more for serving
3 eggs
1 teaspoon fine salt
1 ½ teaspoons sugar
1 teaspoon baking powder
1 cup (8 fl oz /240 ml) buttermilk

1 Preheat the oven to 375°F (190°C/Gas Mark 5). Grease a 9 × 13-inch (23 × 33 cm) oval baking dish.

2 In a medium saucepan, bring the milk to a gentle simmer over medium heat. Gradually whisk in the cornmeal, stirring constantly to prevent lumps. Continue to cook until the mixture thickens, about 5 minutes. Remove the saucepan from the heat and stir in the butter, allowing it to melt into the mixture.

3 In a bowl, whisk together the eggs. Temper the eggs by slowly adding a small amount of the hot cornmeal mixture, whisking constantly. Gradually add the tempered eggs back into the saucepan, whisking to combine.

4 Add the salt, sugar, baking powder, and buttermilk to the mixture, stirring until smooth. Pour the batter into the prepared baking dish.

5 Bake for 35–40 minutes, until the top of the spoonbread is golden brown and a toothpick inserted into the center comes out clean.

6 Let cool slightly before serving. Serve with plenty of butter.

CORN DUMPLINGS

V

Why were cornmeal dumplings so popular? From the time of Native American people through the seventeenth to the mid-twentieth century, when American Southerners made most meals in one big stew or soup pot, corn dumplings were an easy way to take a staple ingredient and bolster a homecooked meal without much effort. Corn was known as "common," and wheat flour as "seldom," because one was predominantly homegrown and the other had to be imported, milled, and purchased. Serve the hot corn dumplings as a side dish to any main course, or use them to sop up Pot Likker (PAGE 266) or gravy.

PREPARATION TIME: 15 MINUTES
COOKING TIME: 30 MINUTES
SERVES: 4–6

1 cup (130 g) white or yellow cornmeal
½ cup (65 g) all-purpose (plain) flour
1 tablespoon baking powder
1 teaspoon fine salt
½ cup (4 fl oz/120 ml) buttermilk
1 egg, beaten
¼ cup (25 g) finely chopped scallions (spring onions) (optional)

1 In a large bowl, whisk together the cornmeal, flour, baking powder, and salt.

2 In a medium bowl, whisk together the buttermilk and egg until well combined. Gradually pour the buttermilk mixture into the dry ingredients, stirring until a thick batter forms. Fold in the scallions (spring onions), if desired, for a more savory dumpling.

3 Bring a large pot of salted water or stock to a simmer over medium heat. Using a spoon or small scoop, carefully drop spoonfuls of the batter into the simmering liquid. Cook the dumplings for about 10–12 minutes, turning them occasionally to ensure they cook evenly and hold their shape.

4 Once the dumplings are cooked through and have a light, fluffy texture, remove them from the pot using a slotted spoon and transfer to a serving dish. Serve warm.

CRACKLIN' BREAD

Hog butchering time was one of the most important times of the year in the rural South, from Colonial times to the mid-twentieth century. As a result, there were many seasonal delicacies, including cracklin' bread. Leftover after rendering lard were the hard cracklings (also known as fried pork rinds or chicharrones), which are crunchy and rich in fat. Tucked into a hybrid corn/wheat bread, they made for a delicious variation in what was a rather monotonous diet. You can find cracklings at country stores or online, but you can also substitute homemade fried bacon chopped into small pieces.

PREPARATION TIME: 20 MINUTES
COOKING TIME: 35 MINUTES
SERVES: 8

Bacon fat or softened butter, for the skillet
1 cup (132 g) yellow cornmeal
½ cup (65 g) all-purpose (plain) flour
1 teaspoon baking powder
½ teaspoon baking soda (bicarbonate of soda)
½ teaspoon fine salt
1 cup (8 fl oz /240 ml) buttermilk
1 egg, beaten
1 cup (125 g) cracklings or chopped crisp-cooked bacon (streaky)

1 Preheat the oven to 400°F (200°C/Gas Mark 6). Grease a 10-inch (25 cm) cast-iron skillet or a baking dish with bacon fat or butter to enhance the flavor of the bread.

2 In a large bowl, combine the cornmeal, flour, baking powder, baking soda (bicarb), and salt. Stir to mix the dry ingredients thoroughly.

3 In a medium bowl, whisk together the buttermilk and beaten egg until well combined. Gradually add the wet ingredients to the dry mixture, stirring until just combined. The batter should be thick but pourable. Fold in the cracklings, ensuring they are evenly distributed throughout the batter.

4 Pour the batter into the prepared skillet or baking dish, spreading it out evenly. Transfer the skillet to the oven.

5 Bake for 35 minutes, or until the top is golden brown and a toothpick inserted into the center comes out clean.

6 Let the cracklin' bread cool slightly in the skillet before cutting it into wedges or squares.

STORAGE: Store airtight at room temperature for up to 2 days.

HOT WATER CORNBREAD (OR HOECAKES)

DF GF V VE -5 -30

This humble cornbread tells many stories. One such story is of the Native American Southern heritage—not just villages of wood palisades tucked among tidal creeks and alluvial plains, but of great civilizations with mounds and pyramids based on the cultivation of maize. This cornbread also serves as a reminder of the hardship of enslavement, a bread made quickly and cheaply when personal time and space were luxuries. Cooked on a greased broad hoe cleaned of dirt (or a griddle called a "how" in Old English), this was the primary bread made by the enslaved community for its own consumption.

PREPARATION TIME: 15 MINUTES
COOKING TIME: 15 MINUTES
SERVES: 6

2 cups (265 g) white or yellow cornmeal
1 tablespoon sugar
1 teaspoon fine salt
1 ½ cups (12 fl oz/350 ml) boiling water
¼ cup (2 fl oz/60 ml) vegetable oil

1 In a large bowl, whisk together the cornmeal, sugar, and salt. Gradually add the boiling water to the dry ingredients, stirring constantly until the mixture forms a thick batter. Let the batter rest for a few minutes to ensure the cornmeal fully absorbs the water.

2 Line a plate with paper towels and have near the stove.

3 In a large cast-iron skillet, heat the oil over medium-high heat. Once the oil is hot, spoon 3 tablespoons of batter for each patty into the skillet. Fry the patties until golden brown and crispy on both sides, 3–4 minutes per side. Transfer the cornbread to the paper towels to drain the excess oil.

4 Serve hot.

SORGHUM WHOLE WHEAT BREAD

V

The Upland South and Southern Piedmont, between the eighteenth and nineteenth centuries, embraced sorghum bicolor, a cereal grain of South African origin, that was used to make a sweet syrup. Originally known as "Guinea corn," sorghum's Southern origins lie with the many plants brought over during the time of the transatlantic slave trade. The sorghum syrup made from the sorghum grains joins the other Southern homegrown sources of sweetness: cane syrup in the Deep South, Southern Appalachian maple syrup, and a diverse range of native wildflower honeys. This very special recipe for sorghum bread was adapted courtesy of my friends and artisan bakers Cheryl and Griffith Day of Savannah, Georgia.

PREPARATION TIME: 3 ½ HOURS
COOKING TIME: 30–40 MINUTES
MAKES: ONE 9 × 5-INCH (23 × 13 CM) LOAF

- 3 ½ cups whole wheat (wholemeal) flour
- 1 tablespoon instant yeast
- 1 tablespoon kosher salt or 1 ½ teaspoons fine salt
- 4 tablespoons sorghum syrup, golden syrup (such as Lyle's), or maple syrup
- 4 tablespoons canola (rapeseed) oil
- ½ cup (4 fl oz/120 ml) whole milk
- Softened butter, for the bowl
- Cooking spray, for the pan
- 1 egg

1 In a stand mixer fitted with the dough hook, combine the flour, yeast, and salt. Add the sorghum syrup, oil, ¾ cup (6 fl oz/180 ml) water, and the milk to the flour mixture, then mix on low speed for 3 minutes. Turn the mixer to medium and mix until the dough is soft, yet firm to the touch, 7–8 minutes.

2 Turn the dough out onto a lightly floured work surface, knead a few times, and shape into a ball. Transfer the dough to a lightly buttered bowl, coating all surfaces of the dough with butter. Cover with plastic wrap and allow the dough to rise until almost doubled in size, about 2 hours, depending on the temperature of your kitchen.

3 Lightly spray a 9 × 5-inch (23 × 13 cm) loaf pan with cooking spray. Remove the dough from the bowl onto a lightly floured work surface. Using a rolling pin, roll the dough into an 8 × 10-inch (20 × 25 cm) rectangle. With the short side facing you, gently roll the dough into a log. Place the log in the loaf pan, cover with plastic wrap and allow the dough to rise until it rises about 1 inch (2.5 cm) above the rim of the pan, about 1 hour.

4 Meanwhile, preheat the oven to 350°F (180°C/Gas Mark 4).

5 In a small bowl, beat the egg with 1 tablespoon water and a pinch of salt. Set aside.

6 When ready to bake, brush the top of the loaf with the beaten egg and transfer to the oven.

7 Bake for 30–40 minutes, until the interior temperature reads 190°F (88°C) and the crust color resembles dark honey.

8 Let the bread cool in the pan on a wire rack for 5 minutes. Then invert the bread onto the rack to cool completely.

STORAGE: Store airtight at room temperature for up to 3 days.

BUCKWHEAT CAKES

V

Buckwheat was one of a number of foods that, according to Pennsylvania-based culinary historian William Woys Weaver, marked a departure from the typical foods of eighteenth-century British cuisine. Buckwheat was more popular among the less affluent, often of Dutch and German heritage, in Pennsylvania, West Virginia, and particularly in the Delaware River Valley area. Buckwheat cakes and muffins and buckwheat flour's inclusion in scrapple (a popular breakfast loaf made from pork scraps, cornmeal, and flour) all came along with the German immigrants who traveled into the South down the Great Wagon Road. The dish was written into many historical Southern cookbooks such as Marion Cabell Tyree's *Housekeeping in Old Virginia* and many others from the Upper South.

Quick starches that could be prepared at a moment's notice were an important building block of Southern hospitality. "Buckwheat cakes" are the only food mentioned in the Confederate battle tune, "Dixie." ("Buckwheat cakes and Indian batter/makes you fat or a little fatter.") Although minstrel performer Dan Emmett is credited with writing the song, some scholars have attributed different aspects of the song to similar tunes composed by other Black minstrel performers of the time.

PREPARATION TIME: 20 MINUTES, PLUS OVERNIGHT FERMENTATION TIME
COOKING TIME: 20 MINUTES
SERVES: 4–6

- 1 packet (7 g) active dry yeast (2 ¼ teaspoons)
- 1 teaspoon light brown sugar
- 2 cups (16 fl oz/470 ml) warm water
- 1 cup (120 g) buckwheat flour
- ½ cup (65 g) all-purpose (plain) flour
- 1 teaspoon fine salt
- 1 egg
- ½ cup (4 fl oz/120 ml) buttermilk
- 2 tablespoons molasses (treacle)
- Butter or vegetable oil, for the skillet

1 The night before baking, in a small bowl, dissolve the yeast and sugar In the warm water, letting it sit for about 5 minutes until it becomes frothy.

2 In a large bowl, combine the buckwheat flour, all-purpose (plain) flour, and salt. Add the yeast mixture to the dry ingredients and stir until a smooth batter forms. Cover the bowl with a cloth, and let it sit at room temperature overnight to ferment.

3 The next morning, uncover the batter and give it a good stir.

4 In a medium bowl, beat the egg, then beat in the buttermilk and molasses (treacle). Gradually fold the buttermilk mixture into the fermented batter until well combined. The batter should be thick but pourable.

5 Heat a lightly greased griddle or cast-iron skillet over medium heat.

6 Once hot, pour or ladle the batter onto the griddle to form cakes of your desired size. Cook until bubbles form on the surface of the cakes and the edges start to set, 2–3 minutes. Flip and cook the other side until golden brown, 2–3 minutes longer. Serve hot.

CORNMEAL WAFFLES

V

Here the Dutch/Germanic waffle meets maize, the staple, rustic grain of Colonial North America. They are especially good with broiled chicken or catfish.

PREPARATION TIME: 20 MINUTES
COOKING TIME: 20 MINUTES
SERVES: 4–6

- 1 cup (130 g) yellow cornmeal
- 1 cup (130 g) all-purpose (plain) flour
- 2 tablespoons sugar
- 1 teaspoon baking powder
- ½ teaspoon baking soda (bicarbonate of soda)
- ½ teaspoon fine salt
- 1 ¾ cups (14 fl oz/420 ml) buttermilk
- 4 tablespoons (60 g) unsalted butter, melted
- 2 eggs, beaten
- Melted butter, for the waffle iron

1 In a large bowl, whisk together the cornmeal, flour, sugar, baking powder, baking soda (bicarb), and salt.

2 In a medium bowl, whisk together the buttermilk, melted butter, and eggs until well combined. Gradually add the buttermilk mixture to the cornmeal mixture, stirring until just combined into a smooth batter. Avoid overmixing to keep the waffles light and fluffy.

3 Preheat a waffle iron according to the manufacturer's instructions. Lightly grease the waffle iron with a small amount of melted butter or oil to prevent sticking. Pour enough batter onto the hot waffle iron to cover the surface, then close the lid and cook until the waffles are golden brown and crisp, 4–5 minutes, depending on your waffle iron.

4 Transfer the waffles to a warm plate and serve hot.

PAIN PERDU

V -30

This original Louisiana French toast made with French bread, served well buttered and with plenty of cane syrup, is a delicacy in itself. "Pain Perdu" is French and means "lost bread," even though the bread isn't really lost, but rather repurposed.

PREPARATION TIME: 15 MINUTES
COOKING TIME: 15 MINUTES
SERVES: 4

4 eggs
1 cup (8 fl oz /240 ml) whole milk
¼ cup (50 g) sugar
Pinch of fine salt
1 teaspoon pure vanilla extract
½ teaspoon ground cinnamon
8 slices day-old French bread
Unsalted butter, for the skillet
Powdered (icing) sugar, for serving
Hot cane syrup, for serving

1 In a shallow dish, whisk together the eggs, milk, sugar, and salt. Add the vanilla and cinnamon to infuse the mixture with aromatic warmth.

2 In a large cast-iron skillet or griddle, heat a generous amount of butter over medium heat until it's sizzling but not browned. Dip slices of day-old French bread into the egg mixture, allowing each slice to soak briefly, ensuring it is well coated but not overly saturated.

3 Place the soaked bread slices onto the hot skillet and cook until golden brown on both sides, 2–3 minutes per side. Adjust the heat as needed to prevent burning while ensuring a thorough, even cook.

4 Remove the cooked pain perdu from the skillet and keep warm, while you cook the remaining slices. Serve hot with butter, a dusting of powdered (icing) sugar, and a drizzle of hot cane syrup.

VARIATION: Add 1–2 tablespoons of whiskey to the batter for a rich taste.

GRIDDLE CAKES

V

A griddle cake (or buttermilk pancake to us) was once, according to Savannah-based culinary scholar Damon Lee Fowler, not the same things as a pancake. Pancakes were more like crepes in early America, and they were a great vehicle for seasonal fruit sauces and local honey. Batter or griddle cakes, on the other hand, were a hospitable step up from the reheated leftover bacon or ham often served for breakfast, as they were served nicely hot and fresh with light, golden sorghum molasses or maple syrup.

PREPARATION TIME: 20 MINUTES
COOKING TIME: 20 MINUTES
SERVES: 4–6

2 cups (260 g) all-purpose (plain) flour
2 teaspoons baking powder
2 tablespoons sugar
1 teaspoon fine salt
1 ½ cups (12 fl oz/350 ml) buttermilk
2 eggs, beaten
4 tablespoons (60 g) unsalted butter, melted, plus more for the skillet

1 In a large bowl, sift together the flour, baking powder, sugar, and salt.

2 In another large bowl, whisk together the buttermilk, beaten eggs, and melted butter until well combined. Gradually pour the wet ingredients into the dry ingredients, stirring gently until a smooth batter forms. (Be careful not to overmix, as this can overwork the gluten and render the result tough.)

3 Heat a lightly greased griddle or cast-iron skillet over medium heat. Once hot, pour or ladle the batter onto the griddle to form cakes of your desired size. Cook until bubbles form on the surface of the cakes and the edges start to look set, 2-3 minutes, then flip and cook the other side until golden brown, 2-3 additional minutes. Serve hot.

ASHCAKES

DF GF V VE -5

If you had no griddle or broad hoe, this was your bread-making option in the cabins of American plantations from Maryland to Texas, Missouri to Florida. The ingredients are only cornmeal, salt, and water. Ashcakes were eaten with buttermilk or Pot Likker (PAGE 266), or just plain and ungarnished. Some people remembered using tulip poplar, cabbage leaves, or corn husks to protect the dough while toasting on the coals.

PREPARATION TIME: 10 MINUTES, PLUS TIME TO PREPARE A CAMPFIRE
COOKING TIME: 20 MINUTES
SERVES: 4

- 2 cups (240 g) white cornmeal
- 1 teaspoon fine salt
- About 1 ½ cups (12 fl oz/350 ml) boiling water

1 In a large bowl, whisk together the cornmeal and salt. Gradually add 1 cup (8 fl oz/240 ml) of the boiling water, stirring well. Add the remaining ½ cup boiling water as needed, until the mixture forms a thick dough. Allow the dough to cool slightly, until it can be handled comfortably. Shape the dough into 4 small flat cakes each about ½ inch (13 mm) thick.

2 Prepare a campfire or outdoor grill with a bed of hot ashes.

3 Carefully place the cakes directly on the hot wood coals ensuring they are not in direct contact with open flames. Cook the cakes until they develop a crispy outer crust on both sides and are cooked through, about 10 minutes per side.

4 Remove the ashcakes from the fire and brush off any remaining wood and ash. Serve hot.

BENNE SEED WAFERS

V

Benne seeds are a West African variety of sesame seeds that were brought to the South from the Senegambia region and Sierra Leone, during the time of the transatlantic slave trade. *Benne*, or "sesame," a word from the Wolof language of Senegambia, is an ancient West African staple. Charleston, South Carolina, was the port where over one-quarter of all enslaved Africans first set foot on American soil. Valued for the oil pressed from the seeds, benne became a Deep South crop that spread outward from Charleston and Savannah, Georgia, to the plantations and farms of the Carolinas, Georgia, Alabama, and Mississippi—where, by the 1820s, it was noted as a common garden crop of the enslaved.

Gullah-Geechee women would sell benne seed wafers, groundnut caries, coconut confections and the like among the mansions of Rainbow Row and the streets of the Battery in Charleston and the moss-lined avenues of Savannah. To this day, benne seed wafers are available in Charleston's historical market area and every museum and gift shop, but they are fantastic to make at home. (You can also buy benne seeds from online retailers based in the South.)

PREPARATION TIME: 45 MINUTES
COOKING TIME: 12-15 MINUTES
MAKES: 36 WAFERS

- 1 cup (150 g) benne seeds or white sesame seeds
- 1 cup (130 g) all-purpose (plain) flour, preferably unbleached
- ½ teaspoon baking powder
- ¼ teaspoon kosher salt or ⅛ teaspoon fine salt
- 8 tablespoons (4 oz/115 g) unsalted butter, at room temperature
- 1 cup (190 g) packed light brown sugar
- 1 egg
- 1 teaspoon pure vanilla extract

1 Position racks in the bottom third and upper thirds of the oven and preheat the oven to 350°F (180°C/Gas Mark 4). Line two or three baking sheets with parchment paper.

2 Spread the seeds in a single layer on one of the pans and toast until they have a nutty fragrance and are a light brown, about 5 minutes. Set aside to cool, then transfer to a small bowl.

3 In a medium bowl, whisk together the flour, baking powder, and salt. Set aside.

4 In a stand mixer fitted with the paddle (or in a large bowl with a hand mixer), cream the butter, brown sugar, egg, and vanilla together on medium speed until super light and fluffy, 3–5 minutes. Turn the speed down to low and add the dry ingredients in three additions, beating until just combined. Add the toasted seeds until just combined.

5 Finish mixing the dough by hand to make sure no bits of flour or butter are hiding on the bottom of the bowl and the dough is thoroughly mixed.

6 Use a small ice cream scoop or a tablespoon to form the cookies (about 1 rounded tablespoon each) and place on the prepared baking sheets, leaving 2 inches (5 cm) between them to allow for spreading.

7 Bake the cookies for 8–10 minutes, until lightly golden brown, switching racks and rotating the pans front to back halfway through.

8 Let cool completely on the pans on wire racks.

STORAGE: Store airtight at room temperature for up to 1 week or in the freezer for up to 1 month.

SWEET POTATO PONE

GF V

Pone is an English corruption of *appone*, a word of Southern Algonquin provenance, from the Powhatan paramount chiefdom in Virginia, meaning "bread." When the word pone entered the lexicon of enslaved Africans, it was especially applied to a sweet potato bake that was enjoyed on special occasions.

PREPARATION TIME: 20 MINUTES
COOKING TIME: 1 HOUR
SERVES: 8

Softened butter or cooking spray, for the pan
2 cups (100 g) grated raw sweet potatoes
1 cup (200 g) sugar
½ cup (4 fl oz/120 ml) molasses (treacle)
8 tablespoons (4 oz/115 g) unsalted butter, melted
1 teaspoon ground cinnamon
½ teaspoon ground nutmeg
¼ teaspoon ground ginger
2 eggs, beaten
1 cup (8 fl oz /240 ml) half-and-half (single cream)
1 teaspoon pure vanilla extract

1 Preheat the oven to 350°F (180°C/Gas Mark 4). Grease a 9-inch (23 cm) square pan with butter or cooking spray.
2 In a large bowl, combine the grated sweet potatoes, sugar, molasses (treacle), and melted butter. Stir until the mixture is well blended and smooth. Stir in the cinnamon, nutmeg, and ginger.
3 In a medium bowl, whisk together the eggs, half-and-half (single cream), and vanilla until fully combined. Pour the egg mixture into the sweet potato mixture, stirring well until the batter is homogenous. The mixture should be thick but pourable. Pour the batter into the prepared baking pan, spreading it evenly with a spatula.
4 Bake for 25–30 minutes, until the top is golden brown and a knife inserted into the center comes out clean. The edges should be slightly crispy, while the interior remains moist and tender.
5 Allow the sweet potato pone to cool slightly before serving.

STORAGE: Cover with plastic wrap and store in the refrigerator for up to 3 days.

VEGETABLES

THE SOUTHERN GARDEN

Because of the long, warm growing seasons—lasting six to ten months—Southern gardening and orchard traditions are foundational to the region's relationship with produce and fruit. The American South was a veritable international garden: Crops from the Americas, Africa, Europe, and Asia met and flourished. Native American Southerners had gardens made of Three Sisters (corn, beans, and summer squash and pumpkins), with varieties of sunflowers from Muscogee (Creek) and Cherokee communities. Europeans brought a host of Eurasian crops, of which herbs, turnips, cabbage, colewort (or collards), lettuce, onions, garlic, carrots, celery, beets, mustard, and the like were the most important. Enslaved Africans and those legally designated as "Free People of Color" cultivated gardens employing elaborate intercropping where African crops like black-eyed peas (black-eye beans), groundnuts, eggplants, Angolan gherkins, okra, sesame, sorghum, millet, watermelons, and muskmelons shared space with tomatoes, peanuts, hot chile peppers, and various indigenous and European crops. Black Southerners sold or bartered produce from their gardens, often using the proceeds to purchase their freedom from enslavement. Europeans quickly adopted Native crops from across the Americas and those of West and Central Africans. Between the mid-eighteenth century and the tragedy of Native removal in the nineteenth century, black-eyed peas, watermelon, sweet potatoes, rice, and bananas (in Florida) became part of Native gardens, owing to the movement of African freedom- seekers, maroons, and the enslaved into Native communities.

We should all appreciate that Southern gardens tell a story in heirloom seeds and orchard fruit of the people who have come before and their legacy. Cherokee purple tomatoes, Kentucky Wonder green beans, cowhorn okra, datil peppers, and fish peppers share space with heritage apples like Stayman Winesaps and Grimes Golden and plums like Chickasaw. Between culinary scholars and co-op seed-saving companies, chefs, and home gardeners, the American South is enjoying a renaissance of historical crops that are returning to the home and restaurant tables.

Southerners have held on to a love of displaying the beauty of their gardens, demonstrating their pride for the concept of "homeplace," a home that does not merely survive, but generates and nourishes. They continue to pass down a reverence for "making something out of nothing" from their gardens as a source of utility and resourcefulness—as sources of both sustenance and healing. Foundational Southern cooks like Edna Lewis often reminded their audience about the patience, time, and deliberate cultivation of gardens across the season that made Southern rural life so fulfilling. Ms. Lewis herself said she was heartened to see young people "go back to the land," learning old traditions and being a legacy for the future. Nearly fifty years later from the time she noted this in her iconic book *The Taste of Country Cooking,* the movement to expand and celebrate Southern gardens has only grown stronger.

SUCCOTASH

GF -30

A dish as old as the British encounter with eastern Algonquin foodways in the seventeenth century, this mixture of beans and corn retains its original name learned in Virginia's Tidewater region. Southern cooks have added onion, salt pork, fresh herbs, and other embellishments over time.

PREPARATION TIME: 10 MINUTES
COOKING TIME: 20 MINUTES
SERVES: 6

6 ears corn, husked
4 tablespoons (60 g) unsalted butter
1 ½ cups (8 oz/240 g) frozen lima beans (butter beans)
½ cup minced yellow or white onion
4 oz (115 g) salt pork (optional), cut into 4 thick pieces
2 teaspoons sugar
Fine salt and freshly ground black pepper

1 Using a sharp knife, cut the kernels off the corn cobs into a large bowl, taking care to remove any stray silks and bad kernels.
2 In a cast-iron skillet, melt 1 tablespoon of the butter over medium heat. Add the lima beans (butter beans), onion, and salt pork (if using). Cook, stirring constantly, until golden brown, about 10 minutes.
3 Stir in the corn kernels. Add enough water to cover the vegetables by ½ inch (13 mm). Add the remaining 3 tablespoons butter and the sugar. Bring to a low simmer and cook, uncovered, until hot and soft, about 10 minutes.
4 Remove the salt pork, taste, and season with salt and black pepper.

FRIED CORN

GF V -30

Fried corn is a great seasonal delicacy. Before sweet corn varieties were commonly available, people used "green corn," which was field corn in its milky state.

PREPARATION TIME: 10 MINUTES
COOKING TIME: 20 MINUTES
SERVES: 4

4 tablespoons (60 g) unsalted butter
1 tablespoon bacon (streaky) drippings (optional)
¼ cup (40 g) finely chopped yellow onion
½ teaspoon minced garlic
4 cups (660 g) fresh sweet corn kernels (from about 8 ears), rinsed and dried
1 teaspoon kosher salt or House Seasoning (PAGE 301), or ½ teaspoon fine salt
½ teaspoon freshly ground black pepper
½ teaspoon sugar
Chopped fresh chives (optional), for garnish

1 In a medium cast-iron skillet, combine the butter and bacon drippings (if using). Cook over medium heat until the butter has melted and the mixture is sizzling, about 1 minute. Add the onion and cook, stirring often, until the onions begin to brown, about 3 minutes.

2 Add the garlic and stir constantly for about 30 seconds. Add the corn, salt, black pepper, and sugar. Stir occasionally and cook until tender, 10–15 minutes.

3 Serve hot, garnished with chives, if desired.

CREAMED CORN

V

Creamed corn is a late-summer favorite and a beloved dish for a summer church "dinner on the ground" or potluck.

PREPARATION TIME: 10 MINUTES
COOKING TIME: 30 MINUTES
SERVES: 4

8 ears corn, husked
2 tablespoons sugar
1 tablespoon all-purpose (plain) flour
Fine salt and freshly ground black pepper
1 cup (8 fl oz/240 ml) heavy (whipping) cream
3 tablespoons (45 g) unsalted butter

1 Using a sharp knife, cut the kernels off the corn cobs into a large bowl, taking care to remove any stray silk and bad kernels.

2 In a large bowl, whisk together the sugar, flour, and salt and black pepper to taste. Add the corn, heavy (whipping) cream, and ½ cup (4 fl oz/120 ml) water and mix until well combined.

3 In a large cast-iron skillet, melt the butter. Add the corn mixture and reduce the heat to medium low. Cook the corn, stirring occasionally, until creamy and slightly thickened, about 30 minutes.

4 Serve warm.

MAQUE CHOUX

GF V -30

Maque choux is the Louisiana answer to succotash, marrying Native America, France, and West Africa. In Louisiana it is also known as "Indian corn."

PREPARATION TIME: 10 MINUTES
COOKING TIME: 10 MINUTES
SERVES: 8

- 4 tablespoons (60 g) unsalted butter
- ½ cup (50 g) chopped celery
- ½ cup (80 g) finely chopped onion
- ½ cup (75 g) finely chopped green bell pepper
- 1 teaspoon minced garlic
- 4 cups (660 g) cooked corn kernels
- ½ teaspoon chile flakes
- ½ teaspoon fresh thyme leaves
- Fine salt and freshly ground black pepper
- 1 cup (8 fl oz/240 ml) heavy cream or half-and-half (single cream)
- 1–2 tablespoons finely chopped fresh flat-leaf parsley

1 In a heavy-bottomed cast-iron skillet, heat the butter over medium-high heat. Once melted, add the celery, onion, bell pepper, and garlic and sauté until soft, 3–4 minutes.

2 Stir in the corn, chile flakes, thyme, and salt and black pepper to taste. Cook until the corn is cooked through, an additional 5 minutes.

3 Add the heavy (whipping) cream and cook until thickened, about 1 minute. Toss with the parsley and season with salt and black pepper.

STORAGE: Leftovers can be stored in an airtight container and refrigerated for up to 3 days.

CREOLE TOMATOES

DF GF V VE

Creole tomatoes grow in the alluvial soil of Southern Louisiana, and the seedlings are traditionally transplanted to home gardens each year on Good Friday. They are unbelievably delicious when seasoned simply with salt and pepper. The ingredients in this salad—cane vinegar, a by-product of Louisiana sugarcane, along with fresh thyme, oregano and Creole seasoning—makes it taste like Louisiana in a bowl.

PREPARATION TIME: 20 MINUTES, PLUS 4–6 HOURS MARINATING TIME
COOKING TIME: 5 MINUTES
SERVES: 8

3 lb (1.4 kg) large red heirloom tomatoes, thickly sliced
4 scallions (spring onions), thinly sliced
2 tablespoons chopped fresh flat-leaf parsley
1 cup (8 fl oz/240 ml) extra-virgin olive oil
¾ cup (6 fl oz/180 ml) cane vinegar
1 tablespoon dark brown sugar
1 teaspoon Pepper Vinegar (PAGE 288)
1 teaspoon grated lemon zest
1 celery stalk, thinly sliced
2 large cloves garlic, thinly sliced
2 teaspoons chopped fresh oregano leaves (or dried oregano)
½ teaspoon chopped fresh thyme
1 teaspoon fine salt or House Seasoning (PAGE 301)
1 teaspoon Creole Seasoning (PAGE 299)

1 In a large heatproof bowl, combine the tomatoes, scallions (spring onions), and parsley. Set aside.

2 In a heavy-bottomed medium saucepan, combine the olive oil, cane vinegar, brown sugar, Pepper Vinegar, lemon zest, celery, garlic, and all the herbs and seasonings. Cook over medium-low heat, stirring occasionally, until the sugar and salt dissolve, about 1 minute.

3 Pour the warm marinade over the tomato mixture and toss to coat. Refrigerate for at least 4 hours and up to 6 hours before serving.

STORAGE: Store airtight in the refrigerator for up to 3 days.

SOUTHERN TOMATO SALAD

DF GF V VE -30

Because the South generally has a growing season of six or more months, dozens of varieties of heirloom tomatoes are cultivated in home gardens. Each carries with it a story, set of uses, cultural contexts, and aesthetic value. The stories may not always be accurate or clear, for example the Cherokee Purple is associated with a gifting from the Cherokee to a white family just before the Trail of Tears. The Plate de Haiti has a more traceable narrative, back to the days of the Haitian Revolution and the exodus of refugees from Hispaniola. The gardens at Thomas Jefferson's Monticello and Colonial Williamsburg, both in Virginia, cultivate the Large Red and Brandywine tomatoes. These were some of the earliest tomatoes to find popularity in American gardens, some as food and others as ornamental plants. The Spanish, West Africans, French, and Native American peoples all embraced this gift originally from Mexico's Central Valley. No other region in American cuisine embraced it more before the age of mass immigration to the United States (1880–1930) than the American South. Tomato salad really captures the raw glory of Southern tomatoes beyond just a bit of salt on a fresh slice. It can even be swapped as the centerpiece of a tomato salad sandwich, spooned onto homemade light bread.

PREPARATION TIME: 20 MINUTES
SERVES: 4

2 cups sliced tomatoes, preferably a sweet heirloom variety
2 scallions (spring onions), thinly sliced
1 tablespoon chopped fresh basil
1 teaspoon kosher salt or House Seasoning (PAGE 301), or ½ teaspoon fine salt, plus more to taste
3 tablespoons extra-virgin olive oil
1 tablespoon fresh lemon juice
1 clove garlic, minced
Freshly ground black pepper

1 In a large bowl, mix together the tomatoes, scallions (spring onions), basil, and salt. Set the bowl aside and let the tomatoes marinate for about 15 minutes.

2 In a small bowl, whisk together the olive oil, lemon juice, and garlic until well combined. Pour the olive oil dressing over the marinated tomatoes and toss until everything is fully incorporated.

3 Season with black pepper and more salt to taste. If not serving right away, store airtight in the refrigerator.

TOMATO ASPIC

DF

This is a colorful centerpiece of any old-school posh Southern luncheon. Molded, chilled, and meant to impress, it's worth a try at least once.

PREPARATION TIME: 15 MINUTES, PLUS 6 HOURS REFRIGERATION TIME
COOKING TIME: 25 MINUTES
SERVES: 10

Vegetable oil, for the mold
2 tablespoons unflavored gelatin powder
¼ cup (2 fl oz/60 ml) cold water
¼ cup (2 fl oz/60 ml) boiling water
4 cups (32 fl oz/950 ml) tomato juice
1 tablespoon minced white onion
1 teaspoon House Seasoning (PAGE 301)
1 teaspoon sugar
1 teaspoon kosher salt or ½ teaspoon fine salt
1 teaspoon Worcestershire sauce
½ teaspoon Kitchen Pepper (PAGE 301)
2 bay leaves
2 tablespoons fresh lemon juice
Chopped fresh flat-leaf parsley, for garnish

1 Brush a 10-inch (25 cm) mold (that can hold at least 6 cups) with oil. Set aside.

2 In a small bowl, sprinkle the gelatin over the cold water and let stand for 5 minutes. Whisk in the boiling water until the gelatin is dissolved.

3 In a large saucepan, stir together the tomato juice, onion, House Seasoning, sugar, salt, Worcestershire sauce, Kitchen Pepper, bay leaves, and lemon juice. Bring to a boil over medium-high heat, then reduce the heat and simmer for 15 minutes, stirring occasionally.

4 Pour the mixture through a fine-mesh sieve set over a bowl. Stir in the gelatin.

5 Pour the mixture into the prepared mold and refrigerate until set, about 6 hours. Garnish with parsley before serving.

STORAGE: Cover tightly with plastic wrap and store in the refrigerator for up to 3 days.

PAN-FRIED EGGPLANT

V

Eggplant (aubergine) made its way into American cuisine as "Guinea squash," a term for eggplants of African origin that were introduced into American gardens in the time of the transatlantic slave trade. Fried eggplant goes back to the earliest Southern cookbooks from Virginia, Maryland, South Carolina, Kentucky, and Georgia, showing an early union of Western European and African cuisines, flavors, and cooking techniques.

PREPARATION TIME: 20 MINUTES, PLUS 1 HOUR STANDING TIME
COOKING TIME: 20 MINUTES
SERVES: 6

- 2 large eggplants (aubergines), sliced into rounds ½ inch (14 mm) thick
- Fine salt
- 1 ¼ cups (10 fl oz/300 ml) buttermilk
- ¾ cup (100 g) self-rising flour
- ½ cup (65 g) white or yellow cornmeal
- Freshly ground black pepper
- Vegetable oil, for frying

1 Evenly sprinkle both sides of the eggplant (aubergine) slices with salt. Place on top of layered paper towels and allow them to sit for 30 minutes. Rinse the eggplant well and pat dry.

2 In a large bowl, place the eggplant slices and cover generously with the buttermilk. Toss to coat, then let stand for another 30 minutes.

3 In a deep dish or bowl, combine the flour, cornmeal, a generous pinch of salt, and black pepper to taste. Drain the eggplants from the buttermilk and dredge in the flour mixture.

4 Line a plate with paper towels and have near the stove. In a large cast-iron skillet, add enough oil to lightly cover the bottom of the pan. Heat the oil over medium-high heat until sizzling.

5 Working in batches to avoid overcrowding, add the eggplant slices and fry until well browned on both sides, about 2 minutes per side. Transfer to the paper towels to drain.

6 Serve right away.

TOMATO PIE

V

Tomato pie is not pizza or a Southern answer to pizza. Food historian David Shields traced this savory pie's roots back to a meat-based version enjoyed in 1830s South Carolina. The modern version shows up at luncheons, family reunions, and picnics, filled with sliced tomatoes layered with mayonnaise, Cheddar, Parmesan cheese, and fresh basil. Like its simpler cousin, the tomato sandwich, it's a beloved summertime treat throughout the modern South.

PREPARATION TIME: 45 MINUTES
COOKING TIME: 1 HOUR
SERVES: 6–8

- Pastry for a 9-inch (23 cm) single-crust pie (see PAGE 382)
- 2 lb (910 g) heirloom tomatoes
- 1 teaspoon fine salt, plus more
- 1 cup (15 g) loosely packed fresh basil leaves, coarsely chopped
- 3 scallions (spring onions), finely chopped
- ¾ cup (165 g) mayonnaise
- 1 ½ cups (6 oz/170 g) grated sharp Cheddar cheese
- ½ cup (35 g) crumbled soda crackers, such as saltines or cream crackers
- ¼ cup (23 g) grated Parmesan or Romano cheese
- ⅓ cup (20 g) finely chopped fresh flat-leaf parsley
- 2 tablespoons extra-virgin olive oil
- Freshly ground black pepper

1 Preheat the oven to 375°F (190°C/Gas Mark 5). Line a deep-dish 9-inch (23 cm) pie dish with the pie pastry, trim, and crimp the edges.

2 Line the pie shell (pastry case) with crumpled parchment paper. Fill the parchment-lined pie shell with pie weights or dried beans. Bake until the edges are dry and lightly browned, about 15 minutes.

3 Carefully remove the parchment and pie weights. Return the crust to the oven and bake until the bottom is dry and lightly browned, about 5 minutes. Leave the oven on, but reduce the oven temperature to 350°F (180°C/Gas Mark 4).

4 Meanwhile, line a baking sheet with paper towels. Core the tomatoes and slice them crosswise into slices ¼ inch (6 mm) thick to make around 3 cups sliced tomatoes. Halve each slice crosswise and arrange on the lined baking sheet. Sprinkle the salt on top and set aside for 10 minutes.

5 In a small bowl, combine the basil and scallions (spring onions).

6 In a medium bowl, combine the mayonnaise and half of the Cheddar. Add one-third of the basil/scallion mixture and stir well. Set the mayo mixture aside.

7 In a small bowl, combine the crumbled crackers with the remaining Cheddar, the Parmesan, and parsley. Stir to incorporate.

8 Carefully arrange a layer of tomato slices in the pie shell, fitting them in snugly. Sprinkle with 1 tablespoon of the olive oil, salt and black pepper to taste, and one-third of the basil/scallion mixture. Repeat with another layer of tomatoes, then salt and black pepper, the remaining 1 tablespoon olive oil, and the remaining basil/green onion mixture. Mound the remaining tomatoes in the center of the pie. Spread the mayo/Cheddar mixture over the tomatoes, covering them evenly. Sprinkle the cracker/parsley mixture over the pie, covering the filling completely.

9 Bake until bubbling, firm, and lightly browned, 35–40 minutes. Transfer to a wire rack to cool completely.

STORAGE: Cover with plastic wrap and store in the refrigerator for up to 5 days.

FRIED GREEN TOMATOES

V -30

Thanks to the Fannie Flagg novel *Fried Green Tomatoes at the Whistle Stop Cafe*, this humble early- to mid-summer delicacy became a popular culture hit. I remember my Alabama grandmother used to cook bacon, then fry the tomatoes in the bacon fat, and she would have a sword fight with the popping grease as she turned the tomatoes. When served with biscuits, this was a staple summer morning breakfast for her.

PREPARATION TIME: 20 MINUTES
COOKING TIME: 10 MINUTES
SERVES: 4–6

4 green tomatoes, cut into slices 1/4 inch (6 mm) thick
1/2 cup (4 fl oz/120 ml) buttermilk
1/2 cup (65 g) yellow cornmeal
1/4 cup (32 g) all-purpose (plain) flour
1 teaspoon fine salt or House Seasoning (PAGE 301)
1/4 teaspoon garlic powder
1/4 teaspoon onion powder
Pinch of cayenne pepper
Freshly ground black pepper
Vegetable oil, for frying
1/4 cup (2 fl oz/60 ml) bacon fat (optional)

1 Add the sliced green tomatoes to a medium bowl, pour the buttermilk over the top, and toss to combine. Let sit for 30 minutes.

2 Meanwhile, in a large bowl, combine the cornmeal and flour.

3 Line a baking sheet with parchment paper and have at the ready. Remove the tomatoes from the buttermilk marinade, then season with the salt, garlic powder, onion powder, cayenne, and black pepper to taste. Dredge each tomato slice into the cornmeal/flour mixture, making sure to coat each side well. Lay the coated slices on the lined baking sheet and let rest for 10 minutes.

4 Line a plate with paper towels and have near the stove. In a large cast-iron skillet, add enough oil to lightly cover the bottom. If you'd like, flavor it with the bacon fat. Heat the oil over medium-high heat.

5 Working in batches to avoid crowding, add the tomatoes to the hot oil and cook, turning halfway through, until golden brown, 2–3 minutes per side. Repeat until all your slices are fried and golden. Drain on the paper towels. Serve hot.

CUCUMBER SALAD

DF GF V VE

Cucumber salad is a Southern staple dish that makes hot summer family reunions, picnics, church dinner on the grounds, and Sunday dinners bearable.

PREPARATION TIME: 10 MINUTES, PLUS 1 HOUR 30 MINUTES RESTING TIME
SERVES: 4

1 lb (450 g) cucumbers, very thinly sliced
1 teaspoon kosher salt or ½ teaspoon fine salt
½ red onion, thinly sliced
¼ cup (2 fl oz/60 ml) apple cider vinegar or white wine vinegar
2 teaspoons superfine (caster) sugar
1 teaspoon finely chopped minced fresh chervil or flat-leaf parsley
Freshly ground coarse black pepper
Chile flakes

1 Set a colander over a bowl or dish and add the cucumbers. Sprinkle the cucumbers with the salt and let rest for 30 minutes for the cucumbers to drain. Gently pat the cucumbers dry to remove any additional moisture.

2 In a medium bowl, toss the cucumbers with the onion, vinegar, sugar, chervil, and black pepper and chile flakes to taste. Cover and refrigerate for 1 hour before serving.

SAUTÉED SCALLIONS

GF V -5 -30

Sautéed scallions (spring onions) are an excellent condiment or garnish for other vegetables like greens or starches such as potatoes, rice, cornbread dressing, and even meat dishes.

PREPARATION TIME: 5 MINUTES
COOKING TIME: 6 MINUTES
SERVES: 4–6

4 bunches scallions (spring onions)
3 tablespoons (45 g) unsalted butter
Fine salt

1 Prepare the scallions (spring onions) by removing any yellow stems, trim off and discard the roots. Wash under cold water and shake until still slightly wet (any residual water will help with steaming).

2 In a cast-iron skillet, melt the butter over medium-high heat until it foams lightly. Reduce the heat to medium and add the scallions. Cover and cook, turning once, until the tops appear tender and green and the whites still have a fairly crisp texture and a glossy slightly browned look, about 6 minutes total. Be careful to not overcook.

FRESH CROWDER PEAS

DF GF -5

Crowder peas, black-eyed peas (black-eye beans), red field peas, purple eyes, and pink hull peas are the same genus and species of cowpea. They just had different sizes, colors, and forms coming into the American South from West Africa in the seventeenth century. This dish was one of President Thomas Jefferson's favorites. Serve warm over a bed of rice.

PREPARATION TIME: 15 MINUTES
COOKING TIME: 4 HOURS 45 MINUTES
SERVES: 6

1 smoked ham hock (8 oz/225 g)
1 medium onion, diced
2 bay leaves
2 lb (910 g) fresh shelled crowder peas, or other field peas
1 tablespoon kosher salt or 1 ½ teaspoons fine salt
1 teaspoon freshly ground black pepper

1 In a heavy-bottomed medium pot, combine the ham hock, onion, and bay leaves. Add enough water to cover the ham hock by 2 inches (5 cm). Bring to a boil over medium heat. Reduce to a gentle simmer, cover, and cook until the hock meat is completely tender and falling off the bone, about 4 hours.

2 Once the ham hock reaches the desired tenderness, bring back to a boil and add the peas, salt, and black pepper, then reduce to a simmer and cook until the peas are tender, 30–45 minutes. (Add additional water if needed to ensure the peas are covered while cooking, and that there is still enough after cooking to cover the peas.)

3 Drain any excess liquid from the peas before serving.

SOUTHERN STRING BEANS

GF

Pole or bush string beans, cooked with smoked meat until the meaty flavor is in every bite, is a traditional Sunday dinner delicacy in the South. (This recipe uses a rich meaty broth to deliver that same flavor to the finished beans.) Sometimes the beans are mixed or cooked with new potatoes. They go well with sliced fresh tomato and scallions (spring onions) and with Skillet Cornbread (PAGE 45) or rice.

PREPARATION TIME: 1 HOUR 10 MINUTES
COOKING TIME: 1 HOUR 45 MINUTES
SERVES: 4

1 tablespoon (15 g) unsalted butter
½ cup (80 g) diced yellow or red onion
1 clove garlic, minced
½ cup (60 g) chopped cooked smoked bacon (streaky) or 1 cup (100 g) chopped smoked turkey
2 cups (16 fl oz/470 ml) chicken stock, ham stock, or Pot Likker (PAGE 266)
1 lb (450 g) green beans, ends trimmed and cut into 1-inch (2.5 cm) pieces
1 teaspoon chile flakes
Fine salt or House Seasoning (PAGE 301)
Freshly ground coarse black pepper

1 In a large heavy-bottomed pot, heat the butter over medium-high heat until melted and slightly frothy. Add the onion, garlic, bacon (streaky), and chicken stock. Bring to a boil and stir to combine. Reduce the heat to low, cover, and simmer until the liquid has deepened in flavor, about 45 minutes.

2 Reduce the heat, add the green beans and chile flakes, cover, and simmer over low until the green beans are soft and well seasoned, 45–60 minutes. (Check the green beans regularly to ensure they do not overcook.)

3 Season with salt and black pepper to taste before serving.

BRAISED VIDALIA ONIONS

GF V

Sweet braised, creamy Vidalia onions (often touted as an onion you can eat like an apple) make an excellent side dish to turkey, ham, game, or roasts. Arguably one of Georgia's most famous edible crops, Vidalias go back to the 1930s in Southeast Georgia when a farmer planted them instead of "hot onions," in his sandy coastal plain soil. The marketing campaign for the onion caught on in the 1940s through the 1970s, when the Vidalia onion was established. In 1990, it was named the state vegetable of Georgia, and over 200 million pounds of Vidalias are distributed each year.

PREPARATION TIME: 15 MINUTES
COOKING TIME: 40 MINUTES
SERVES: 6

2 tablespoons (30 g) unsalted butter
3 tablespoons honey
5 medium Vidalia onions (about 1 ½ lb/740 g total), thinly sliced
¼ cup chicken stock
½ teaspoon fine salt or House Seasoning (PAGE 301)
⅛ teaspoon ground mace
⅛ teaspoon Kitchen Pepper (PAGE 301)
½ cup (4 fl oz/120 ml) heavy (whipping) cream

1 In a large Dutch oven (casserole dish), melt the butter over medium heat. Add the honey and stir until well incorporated. Add the onions, stock, salt, mace, and Kitchen Pepper and bring to a boil. Reduce the heat, cover, and simmer for 15 minutes to meld the flavors.

2 Uncover and cook, stirring occasionally, over medium-high heat until the liquid has almost evaporated and the onions are soft and jammy, about 20 minutes.

3 Stir in the heavy (whipping) cream and cook until the sauce has thickened, 3–5 minutes. Serve warm.

BRAISED CABBAGE

GF V

Braised greens like cabbage are central to Southern and Caribbean foodways. Their popularity in the South came via the union of European households and African cultures; for the latter, a one-pot dish of greens seasoned with smoked or salted meat and eaten with cornbread was a simple and staple meal. Cabbage was planted in North American colonies as early as the sixteenth century. It was essential in the Upper South, where cooler temperatures in the fall and winter made it a resilient plant.

PREPARATION TIME: 10 MINUTES
COOKING TIME: 35 MINUTES
SERVES: 6–8

8 tablespoons (4 oz/115 g) unsalted butter
1 medium yellow onion, chopped
1 cup (8 fl oz/240 ml) chicken or vegetable stock, plus more as needed
1 teaspoon apple cider vinegar
1 ½ teaspoons fine salt
½ teaspoon House Seasoning (PAGE 301)
½ teaspoon garlic powder
½ teaspoon chile flakes
½ teaspoon freshly ground black pepper
1 head green cabbage (2–3 lb/910 g to 1.4 kg), cored and sliced

1 To a large cast-iron skillet over medium heat, add the butter. Once the butter is melted, add the onion and cook, stirring occasionally, until translucent, 2–3 minutes. Add the stock and vinegar and stir well.

2 In a small bowl, mix together the salt, House Seasoning, garlic powder, chile flakes, and black pepper, then add the mixture to the skillet. Reduce the heat to low, cover, and simmer, stirring occasionally, for 10 minutes to blend the flavors. (If the broth evaporates completely, add a bit more chicken stock to prevent the cabbage from drying out and sticking to the skillet.)

3 Add the cabbage, cover, and cook until the cabbage is fork-tender, about 18 minutes. Serve warm.

STORAGE: Store airtight in the refrigerator for up to 4 days.

BLACK-EYED PEAS

DF GF

The black-eyed pea (black-eye bean) is a legume with ancient origins in West Africa, in the area where contemporary northern Nigeria, Chad, and Niger meet in the Sahel region. It was brought to North America during the transatlantic slave trade in the seventeenth century. Originally called cowpea, it was a fodder crop that also fed my ancestors. Black-eyed peas stewed on their own with rice, okra, or greens, black-eyed pea fritters, and many other dishes were found not only in the South but across the African diaspora in the Americas. Black-eyed peas spread through forced human migration outward from the Chesapeake, Lowcountry, and Lower Mississippi Valley to the rest of the South. Despite claims that black-eyed peas were "discovered" by Confederate soldiers during the Civil War, recipes for this legume were found in many historic Southern cookbooks. These are best served over hot rice, Corn Mush (PAGE 83), or with greens and cornbread on New Year's Day. (If you want to make a vegetarian version, replace the bacon (streaky) and bacon fat with 1 tablespoon vegetable oil.)

PREPARATION TIME: 10 MINUTES, PLUS 1 HOUR OR OVERNIGHT SOAKING TIME
COOKING TIME: ABOUT 3 HOURS
SERVES: 6

- 1 lb (450 g) dried black-eyed peas (black-eye beans)
- 8 oz (225 g) thick-cut bacon (streaky), chopped, or 1 smoked ham hock
- 1 large yellow onion, finely chopped
- 1 celery stalk, finely chopped
- 1 clove garlic, minced
- 1 bay leaf
- 2 teaspoons dried thyme
- 8 cups (2 qt/1.9 liters) chicken or vegetable stock
- ½ teaspoon cayenne pepper
- Fine salt and freshly ground black pepper

1 Rinse and sort the black-eyed peas (black-eye beans), making sure to discard any shriveled or split peas. Add the peas to a large pot and add cold water to cover by 4 inches (10 cm). Let soak overnight. (If you need to make them the same day, cover in boiling hot water and let soak for 1 hour, then follow the recipe.)

2 Line a plate with paper towels and have near the stove. Add the bacon (streaky) to a large cold Dutch oven and set over medium-high heat. Cook, stirring occasionally, until browned and crispy, 5–7 minutes. Remove to the paper towels to drain and set aside.

3 In the same Dutch oven still over medium-high heat, add the onion, celery, garlic, bay leaf, and thyme and sauté until the vegetables are tender, 3–5 minutes. Pour in the stock, and season with the cayenne, salt, and black pepper to taste. Add the reserved bacon and stir to combine. Bring to a boil, then reduce to a high simmer and cook for 1 hour.

4 Drain the soaking peas, rinse, and add to the broth. Reduce the heat to low, partially cover, and simmer the peas, stirring occasionally, until the broth thickens and the beans are soft and tender, 1–1 ½ hours. (Add more stock or water if the mixture becomes dry.)

5 Discard the bay leaf, taste, and adjust the seasoning before serving.

CREAMY BUTTER BEANS

GF V

MacArthur "Genius Grant" awardee Rhiannon Giddens and her former band, the Carolina Chocolate Drops, popularized a Southern string band tune, "Cornbread and Butterbeans." It reminded people of the old pan-Southern meal consisting of cornbread and tender butter beans (lima beans) that had cooked all day in a cast-iron Dutch oven (casserole dish).

PREPARATION TIME: 15 MINUTES, PLUS 1 HOUR SOAKING TIME
COOKING TIME: 2 HOURS
SERVES: 12

- 1 lb (450 g) dried lima beans (butter beans)
- ½ large onion, diced
- 1 teaspoon garlic powder
- 1 teaspoon dried thyme
- 1 teaspoon freshly ground black pepper
- ¼ teaspoon chile flakes
- 2 bay leaves
- 8 tablespoons (4 oz/115 g) salted butter
- 1 cup (150 g) diced ham (optional)

1 Sort and rinse the beans; discard any shriveled, broken beans or debris. Place the beans in a large saucepan with enough water to cover the beans by 2 inches (5 cm) and bring to a boil over high heat. Remove the pot from the heat, cover with a lid, and let the beans rest for at least 1 hour, or until they are plump and well soaked.

2 Drain and rinse the beans again, then return to the pot and cover with more water. Return the bean pot to a boil, then reduce the heat to low. Add the onion, garlic powder, thyme, black pepper, chile flakes, bay leaves, and butter and stir well to combine. Leave the beans to simmer, stirring occasionally and adding more water as necessary, until the beans are very tender, about 2 hours.

3 Once the beans are tender, add the ham, if using, and let them warm all the way through. Remove the pot from the heat and serve warm.

STORAGE: Store airtight in the refrigerator for up to 4 days.

TEXAS CAVIAR

DF GF V VE -30

This contemporary black bean and black-eyed pea (black-eye bean) salad is salvation for Southern vegans and vegetarians. It was created in 1940 by cookbook author Helen Corbitt, who was originally from New York. She created this dish while working at the Houston Country Club. It is jokingly compared to caviar because of the visual similarity of black-eyed peas to fish eggs, yet it's incomparably cheap to make. Nevertheless, it's a great addition to any party with crackers, chips, and crudités.

PREPARATION TIME: 25 MINUTES
SERVES: 10

- 2 cans (15 oz/425 g each) black beans, drained and rinsed
- 2 cans (15 oz/425 g each) black-eyed peas (black-eye beans), drained and rinsed, or 3 cups (515 g) cooked black-eyed or other field peas
- 2 ½ cups (425 g) fresh white corn kernels, cooked
- 1 can (4 oz/114 g) chopped mild green chiles
- 1 medium red bell pepper, finely chopped
- 1 medium green bell pepper, finely chopped
- 1 small red onion, minced
- 1 jalapeño pepper (optional), seeded and finely chopped
- 1 ½ cups (112 g) finely chopped fresh flat-leaf parsley leaves
- ½ cup (4 fl oz/120 ml) apple cider vinegar or red wine vinegar
- ½ cup (4 fl oz/120 ml) extra-virgin olive oil
- 2 teaspoons superfine (caster) sugar
- 1 teaspoon kosher salt or House Seasoning (PAGE 301), or ½ teaspoon fine salt
- ½ teaspoon garlic powder
- ½ teaspoon freshly ground coarse black pepper

1 In a large bowl, combine the black beans, black-eyed peas (black-eye beans), white corn, green chiles, both bell peppers, red onion, jalapeño (if using), and parsley.

2 In a screw-top jar, combine the vinegar, olive oil, sugar, salt, garlic powder, and black pepper. Shake well until combined.

3 Pour the dressing over the bean mixture, then toss until well combined and evenly coated.

4 Serve immediately or refrigerate until ready to serve.

STORAGE: Store airtight in the refrigerator for up to 1 week.

KILT GREENS

DF GF

This recipe shows the Appalachian way with greens. It's really simple, though it requires attention and a careful eye. The springtime ended the months of want, when there were no fresh vegetables. As soon as they could be gathered, fresh greens like edible foraged lettuces, sprouts, and ramps (wild garlic)—here replaced by scallions (spring onions)—were incredibly welcome.

PREPARATION TIME: 30 MINUTES
COOKING TIME: 15 MINUTES
SERVES: 4–6

6 slices bacon (streaky)
6 scallions (spring onions), cut into 1-inch (2.5 cm) pieces
2 lb (910 g) leaf lettuce (romaine, Bibb, or black-seeded Simpson) or young greens (dandelion greens or watercress), torn into bite-size pieces
2 tablespoons apple cider vinegar
1/8 teaspoon kosher salt
Freshly ground black pepper

1 Line a plate with paper towels and set near the stove. Add the bacon (streaky) to a cold cast-iron skillet and cook over medium heat until the fat is rendered and the bacon is crispy, 10–15 minutes. Remove the bacon to the paper towels to drain and when cool enough to handle, crumble or chop.

2 Add the scallions (spring onions) to the bacon fat in the hot skillet and sauté until soft, 2–3 minutes.

3 Working in batches, add the greens and sauté for 2–3 minutes, adding more each time the previous batch shrinks in size. Carefully add the vinegar (it will splatter), and stir quickly to coat the greens. Gently toss and season with the salt and black pepper to taste. Top with the reserved crumbled bacon.

MESS OF GREENS

DF GF

A "mess" or meal of greens just refers to various types of greens brought together to make one big pot. This dish comes from the days when you picked over your greens in the late autumn and spring, looking for enough healthy tender leaves to make a satisfying supper.

PREPARATION TIME: 20 MINUTES
COOKING TIME: 1 ½ HOURS
SERVES: 8

FOR THE BROTH:
½ lb (225 g) smoked turkey wings or legs, or 1 split ham hock
2 yellow onions, halved
2 cloves garlic, smashed and peeled
6 cups (48 fl oz/1.4 liters) chicken stock

FOR THE GREENS:
3 lb (1.4 kg) collard greens, mustard greens, or turnip greens
1 medium yellow onion, minced
2 tablespoons apple cider vinegar
2 teaspoons fine salt
2 teaspoons freshly ground black pepper
2 teaspoons chile flakes
1 teaspoon sugar

1 Make the broth: In a large soup pot, combine the smoked turkey, onion halves, garlic, and chicken stock. Bring to a boil over high heat. Reduce the heat and simmer until the liquid reduces to about 4 cups (32 fl oz/950 ml), 30–45 minutes. Strain and return the liquid to the pot; discard the turkey legs/wings and cooked vegetables.
2 Prepare the greens: Thoroughly clean the greens, remove the stems and midribs, and cut the leaves into a chiffonade or tear to your preferred size.
3 Bring the broth to a gentle simmer and stir in the minced onion, vinegar, salt, black pepper, chile flakes, and sugar. Add the greens to the pot one handful at a time, letting them wilt before adding more to the pot. Cook until tender, 30–45 minutes.
4 Adjust the seasonings as needed. Serve hot.

STORAGE: Store airtight in the refrigerator for up to 4 days.

OKRA CAKES

DF GF V

These cakes are another form of vegetable fritter that will hopefully expand the repertoire of Southern okra dishes in your kitchen. They make a fun alternative to hush puppies or fried okra as a side dish.

PREPARATION TIME: 20 MINUTES
COOKING TIME: 20 MINUTES
SERVES: 6

2 cups (265 g) yellow cornmeal
2 teaspoons baking powder
½ teaspoon kosher salt or House Seasoning (PAGE 301) or ¼ teaspoon fine salt, plus more to taste
1 egg, beaten
1 ½ cups (12 fl oz/350 ml) cold water
8 oz (225 g) fresh okra, cut into slices ¼ inch (6 mm) thick
½ teaspoon chile flakes
1 clove garlic, mashed into a paste
¼ cup (2 fl oz/60 ml) vegetable oil, for frying
Freshly ground black pepper

1 In a large bowl, whisk together the cornmeal, baking powder, and salt.

2 In a medium bowl, beat together the egg and cold water. Add the beaten egg to the cornmeal mixture and whisk until combined. Add the okra, chile flakes, and garlic and stir to combine. If the batter is too thick, add more water as needed.

3 Line a plate with paper towels and have near the stove. In a 10-inch (25 cm) cast-iron skillet, heat the oil over medium heat.

4 Working in batches to avoid over-crowding, scoop and drop ¼ cup (60 ml) of the batter into the hot oil per cake. Use a spatula to flatten the pancake so it has an even surface. Cook each cake until it's browned and bubbles start to form on the surface, 2–3 minutes. Flip and cook until lightly browned on the second side, 2–3 minutes. Transfer to the paper towels to drain and season with salt and black pepper.

5 Serve hot.

CORN, TOMATOES, AND OKRA

GF V

A skillet dish of fresh corn, tomatoes, and okra—made around July or August—is what summer and the South are supposed to taste like. A few fresh herbs tossed in to flavor the vegetables, like parsley or a touch of basil—grown by some for good luck—makes the celebration more vibrant.

PREPARATION TIME: 15 MINUTES
COOKING TIME: 35 MINUTES
SERVES: 6

4 tablespoons (60 g) unsalted butter
1 large onion, chopped
1 large green bell pepper, chopped
2 cloves garlic, minced
2 cups (360 g) chopped red heirloom tomatoes
Kernels from 4 ears corn
1 cup (115 g) thinly sliced fresh okra
3 sprigs fresh flat-leaf parsley
2 sprigs fresh basil
1 teaspoon kosher salt or House Seasoning (PAGE 301), or ½ teaspoon fine salt

1 In a large cast-iron skillet, melt the butter over medium-high heat. Add the onion, bell pepper, and garlic and cook, stirring constantly, until tender and the onion is slightly translucent, 5–7 minutes.

2 Add the tomatoes and bring to a boil. Reduce the heat to low and simmer until the tomatoes are soft and mostly cooked, about 15 minutes.

3 Add the corn kernels, okra, parsley, basil, salt, and pepper and return to a boil, stirring well. Reduce the heat and simmer until the corn is tender, about 15 minutes. Remove the wilted herb sprigs before serving.

BOILED OKRA

DF GF V VE -5 -30

Okra is best eaten when the pods are young, small, and tender and not overcooked. These pods of this African cultigen are at their peak when they are fresh, before they become woody, fibrous, and less mucilaginous. Serve hot as a side dish.

PREPARATION TIME: 10 MINUTES
COOKING TIME: 15 MINUTES
SERVES: 4

1 lb (450 g) fresh small tender okra pods, washed and stems trimmed
Water or Pot Likker (PAGE 266), enough to cover the okra
Fine salt and freshly ground black pepper
Butter (optional), for serving

1 In a large pot, combine the okra pods and add water or Pot Likker to cover by 2 inches (5 cm). Bring to a boil and add a generous pinch of salt. Reduce the heat to medium and simmer uncovered until the okra pods are tender but still slightly firm, 8–10 minutes.

2 Drain the okra and season with additional salt and black pepper to taste. If desired, stir in some butter. Serve hot.

RICE, THE QUEEN OF THE TABLE

Southern rice is part of my origin story. Nine generations ago, a Mende woman from a rice-growing village in the south of Sierra Leone was enslaved in a war in the late 1760s, and she was put on a ship bound for Charleston. She had a daughter, and her daughter had a daughter named Nora. Nora had Hester, Hester had Josephine, Josephine had Mary, Mary had Hazel, and Hazel had Pat. One day, I asked Pat about the best thing she ever made. She said, "A little Black boy named Michael, I baked him low and slow." That family tree, going across the Atlantic, is how I became an American.

In the South, where my family blossomed, a meal could begin with an amuse-bouche of rice fritters, be followed by rice bread, and continue with a rice salad, before a piping hot soup over rice, before a main course of Hoppin' John with a side dish of fried rice, followed by a decadent sweet dessert of rice pudding. Such a meal is unlikely, but to be honest, being a Gullah-Geechee descendant, it's my idea of heaven. I could eat rice daily; it's my perfect food. In the American South, rice plays many roles on the stage of the table. "The Queen," as rice was known in the antebellum South, stars as everything in the Southern culinary mind from grain to sweet, with occasional performances as an ersatz vegetable.

Southern rice is predominantly enjoyed in its long-grain form. People from the Lowcountry like each grain to be separate, plump, distinct, and "dryish." Others like it clumpy, ready for gravy, or to become rice and sugar at breakfast or as the base for pudding. Savory or sweet, rice conveniently was a quick, filling choice and for many an alternative to wheat or corn. Two rice species came to the American South in the late seventeenth century: *Oryza glabberima* and *O. sativa.* The first was indigenous to Western Africa and the latter was from Eastern Asia. Both varieties were brought through the transatlantic trade; one from Madagascar and another from the Rice Coast, from Senegal and Gambia to Sierra Leone and Liberia. With rice came coiled baskets for fanning, hand-carved mortars and pestles for hulling, and millennia of experience embodied in African women and men, in their knowledge of shaping the land and directing the water in the fields. Heirloom varieties in the Lowcountry, the most famous of which were "Carolina Gold" and "Carolina White," made rice planters wealthy as their chattel knew misery in the fields; Charleston, South Carolina, became the number one port for North America's slave trade from Africa.

Rice plantations could be found from coastal North Carolina through the Lowcountry region and the southernmost area of the lower Mississippi Valley. Despite it being primarily a cash crop, rice was grown domestically across the South from Maryland to Texas. From the Chesapeake Bay to the Carolinas and Georgia to Louisiana and Mississippi, Africans were acknowledged as rice cultivators in each area over several centuries. Today, rice fields can be seen in the lower Mississippi Valley and southern Louisiana, where the rice harvest still means time for celebration. Rice has helped bring other communities to culinary prominence, from Caribbean and Latin rice and pea dishes, to Nigerian jollof rice and Viet-Cajun fusions.

RED RICE

GF

Red rice (also known as tomato pilau/perloo) is the South's connection to the family of jollof rices from West Africa. Tellingly, it was also called mulatto rice or Spanish rice by others. Due to the influence of Africa, it is meant to be flavorful, soft, and "dry"—rather than mushy—with every grain on its own. Finishing the rice in the oven avoids burning and scorching in the skillet. Its Louisiana cousin is jambalaya, another Afri-Creole rice dish.

PREPARATION TIME: 10 MINUTES
COOKING TIME: 1 HOUR
SERVES: 6

- 3 slices bacon (streaky), chopped
- 4 tablespoons (60 g) salted butter
- 1 large onion, finely diced
- 1 medium green bell pepper, finely diced
- 2 celery stalks, finely diced
- 1 clove garlic, minced
- 1 can (6 oz/170 g) tomato paste (tomato puree)
- 1 ½ teaspoons House Seasoning (PAGE 301)
- 1 teaspoon sugar
- Freshly ground black pepper
- 2 cups (16 fl oz/470 ml) chicken stock
- 1 cup (185 g) long-grain white rice
- Finely chopped fresh flat-leaf parsley, for garnish

1 Preheat the oven to 350°F (180°C/Gas Mark 4). Line a plate with paper towels and have near the stove.

2 In a large cast-iron skillet, cook the bacon (streaky) over medium-high heat, stirring occasionally, until crispy, about 5 minutes. Using a slotted spoon, transfer the bacon to the paper towels to drain; reserve the bacon drippings in the pan.

3 To the same skillet, add the butter and melt over medium-high heat. Add the bell pepper, celery, and onion and cook, stirring occasionally, until translucent, 3–4 minutes.

4 Stir in the garlic and cook until fragrant, about 30 seconds. Stir in the tomato paste (puree), House Seasoning, sugar, and pepper to taste and cook for 1 more minute.

5 Add the bacon, chicken stock, and rice and bring to a boil. Reduce the heat to medium-low and simmer, uncovered, stirring occasionally, for 9 minutes. Cover the skillet with a heatproof lid and transfer to the oven.

6 Bake until the rice is tender, 30–40 minutes, stirring every 15 minutes.

7 Fluff the rice with a fork, garnish with parsley, and serve warm.

CHORIZO DIRTY RICE

DF GF -30

This is an adaptation of a recipe from *The New Southern-Latino Table* by Sandra A. Gutierrez, an author of Guatemalan heritage who grew up and still lives in North Carolina. Her books affirm the growing and deepening heritage of Latinos in the South. Dirty rice is a Southern classic built on chicken livers and rice, and this version uses chorizo for extra flavor.

PREPARATION TIME: 10 MINUTES
COOKING TIME: 20 MINUTES
SERVES: 4

2 teaspoons vegetable oil
½ cup (75 g) finely chopped green bell pepper
½ cup (50 g) finely chopped celery
½ cup (80 g) finely chopped red onion
¼ cup (14 g) finely chopped jalapeño pepper, seeded and deveined
1 large clove garlic, finely chopped
½ teaspoon chili powder
8 oz (225 g) loose fresh Mexican chorizo
½ cup (105 g) minced chicken livers
Fine salt and freshly ground black pepper
¼ cup (2 fl oz/60 ml) dry sherry
3 ¼ cups (520 g) cooked long-grain white rice
¼ cup (20 g) finely chopped fresh flat-leaf parsley (leaves and tender stems)

1 In a deep sauté pan, heat the oil over medium-high heat. Add the bell pepper, celery, onion, and jalapeño and cook until the vegetables soften, 4–5 minutes.

2 Add the garlic and cook for 1 minute. Stir in the chili powder and cook for 1 minute. Add the chorizo and chicken livers and cook until the livers are no longer pink, 3–4 minutes. Season with salt and black pepper and cook, stirring well, for 2 minutes. Add the sherry and stir well, scraping up the browned bits at the bottom of the pan. Cook until most of the liquid has evaporated, about 2 minutes.

3 Stir in the cooked rice and combine well—there should be no white grains of rice left. Transfer to a serving platter and garnish with parsley.

RICE DRESSING

DF GF

This Louisiana-style holiday dressing is a great alternative to cornbread or stale wheat bread dressing, and it's gluten-free.

PREPARATION TIME: 15 MINUTES
COOKING TIME: 50 MINUTES
SERVES: 8

½ lb (225 g) loose sage- or spicy pork sausage meat
1 medium green bell pepper, diced
3 celery stalks, diced
½ cup diced scallions (spring onions)
2 cloves garlic, minced
½ lb (225 g) ground chicken (mince) or chicken livers
2 cups (370 g) long-grain white rice
4 ½ cups (36 fl oz/1 liter) chicken stock
2 teaspoons Creole Seasoning (PAGE 299)

1 In a large cast-iron skillet, cook the pork sausage over medium-high heat, stirring occasionally to break up the meat, until browned, about 10 minutes.

2 Carefully drain the excess grease from the pan, then add the green pepper, celery, scallions (spring onions), and garlic to the sausage and sauté until the onions are translucent and softened, 5–7 minutes.

3 Add the ground chicken (mince) or chicken livers, rice, stock, and Creole Seasoning and stir until well combined. Cover and simmer over medium heat until the liquid is absorbed and the rice is cooked, about 30 minutes.

STORAGE: Store airtight in the refrigerator for up to 3 days.

VARIATION: Use more traditional loose boudin sausage in place of the pork sausage.

LIMPING SUSAN

GF

This is another classic Southern way with okra, often jokingly referred to as Hoppin' John's sibling. Limping Susan is a staple dish of the Carolina rice kitchen, and one of the oldest versions of this recipe is from Sarah Rutledge's 1847 book *The Carolina Housewife.* (If you are ever asked in a trivia game, okra stewed like this served over grits is called Limping Kate.)

PREPARATION TIME: 40 MINUTES
COOKING TIME: 45 MINUTES
SERVES: 4

4 slices thick-cut bacon (streaky)
2 lb (910 g) shrimp (prawns), peeled and deveined, tails-on
2 tablespoons (30 g) unsalted butter
3 tablespoons vegetable oil
1 medium yellow onion, diced
2–3 cloves garlic, minced, to taste
2 cups (230 g) thinly sliced okra, fresh or thawed frozen
1 teaspoon fresh lemon juice
1 cup (185 g) long-grain white rice
2 cups (16 fl oz/470 ml) chicken stock
Fine salt and freshly ground black pepper

1 Line a plate with paper towels and have near the stove. In a large cast-iron skillet, cook the bacon (streaky) over medium heat, turning occasionally, until crispy, about 5 minutes. Transfer to the paper towels to drain. When cool enough to handle, chop and set aside.

2 In the same skillet, sear the shrimp (prawns) in the bacon fat until just barely seared, 3–4 minutes. Remove the shrimp to a plate and set aside.

3 In the same skillet, melt the butter over medium heat. Once melted, pour in the oil and stir. Stir in the onion and garlic and cook, stirring occasionally, until soft and translucent, about 4 minutes.

4 Add the okra and cook until softened, about 4 minutes. Stir in the lemon juice and cook until fragrant, about 15 seconds. Add the rice and stir to coat in the seasonings. Cook until the onions start to brown, about 3 minutes.

5 Pour in the chicken stock and season with salt and black pepper. Turn up the heat and bring to a boil, stirring often to ensure the mixture doesn't stick to the bottom of the pan. Reduce the heat to low, cover, and cook until the rice is soft and tender, 20–25 minutes. During the last 5 minutes of cooking, uncover and fluff the rice, add the shrimp and chopped bacon and stir in with a fork. Serve warm.

GREEN RICE

GF V

Green rice is an herb pilaf/pilau/perloo that is an excellent dish served with lighter fare like roast chicken, fish, shellfish, and vegetarian entrées.

PREPARATION TIME: 10 MINUTES
COOKING TIME: 30 MINUTES
SERVES: 6

4 teaspoons extra-virgin olive oil
4 teaspoons unsalted butter
1 cup (100 g) finely chopped scallions (spring onions)
1 ½ cups (280 g) long-grain white rice
1 cup (60 g) finely chopped fresh flat-leaf parsley
⅛ teaspoon cayenne pepper
1 bay leaf
3 cups (24 fl oz/710 ml) chicken stock, plus more if needed
Fine salt and freshly ground black pepper

1 In a large heavy-bottomed saucepan, melt the olive oil and butter over medium heat. Add the scallions (spring onions) and cook until soft and translucent, about 1 minute. Stir in the rice and parsley and let cook for about 45 seconds.

2 Add the cayenne and bay leaf, pour in the chicken stock, and bring to a boil. Reduce the heat to low, cover, and simmer until the liquid has evaporated and the rice is tender, about 20 minutes.

3 Discard the bay leaf and season to taste with salt and black pepper.

SEPHARDIC PINK RICE

DF GF V VE

This is the traditional rice side dish of Sephardic Jewish immigrants who came from Rhodes and other parts of the former Ottoman Empire and settled in Montgomery, Alabama, and Atlanta, Georgia. It dances well with everything from Mediterranean vegetables and grilled salmon to Greek meatballs and marinated chicken seasoned with oregano or basil.

PREPARATION TIME: 15 MINUTES
COOKING TIME: 40 MINUTES
SERVES: 4

1 cup (185 g) long-grain white rice
2 tablespoons vegetable oil
1 tablespoon extra-virgin olive oil
1 small yellow onion, diced
2 cups (16 fl oz/470 ml) vegetable or chicken stock
¼ cup (2 fl oz/60 ml) tomato sauce
1 teaspoon kosher salt or ½ teaspoon fine salt
½ teaspoon freshly ground black pepper or Kitchen Pepper (PAGE 301)

1 Rinse the rice under cold running water until the water runs clear. Drain well.

2 In a medium pot with a tight-fitting lid, combine the rice, vegetable oil, olive oil, and onion. Stir to coat the rice and cook over medium-high heat, stirring often, until the rice is lightly toasted and the onions are translucent, about 3 minutes.

3 Stir in the stock, tomato sauce, salt, and black pepper. Bring to a boil, then cover, reduce the heat to low, and simmer until the rice is tender, about 20 minutes. (Check the mixture periodically and add water if the rice starts sticking to the pan.) Turn off the heat, stir with a fork, and replace the lid. Remove from the heat and let stand, covered, for 15 minutes. Serve warm.

RICE SALAD

DF GF V VE -30

Southerners have potato salad, macaroni salad, cracker salad, and rice salad—and the list keeps going. Rice salad made this way is a contemporary light side dish that works great with vegetarian, vegan, chicken, and fish or seafood meals.

PREPARATION TIME: 15 MINUTES
SERVES: 6

FOR THE VINAIGRETTE:
4 tablespoons extra-virgin olive oil
2 tablespoons white wine vinegar
1 tablespoon fresh lemon juice
1 teaspoon coarsely ground black pepper
1 teaspoon garlic powder
1 teaspoon onion powder
1 teaspoon House Seasoning (PAGE 301) or curry powder
1 teaspoon sugar

FOR THE SALAD:
3 cups (480 g) cooked long-grain white rice, warmed
1 medium tomato, finely chopped
1 medium carrot, finely chopped
1 celery stalk, finely chopped
½ medium green bell pepper, finely chopped
½ cup (50 g) thinly sliced scallions (spring onions)

1 Make the vinaigrette: In a small bowl, whisk together the olive oil, vinegar, lemon juice, black pepper, garlic powder, onion powder, House Seasoning, and sugar until well combined.

2 Make the salad: In a large bowl, combine the warm rice, tomato, carrot, celery, bell pepper, and scallions (spring onions). Pour the vinaigrette over the rice and vegetables and stir until everything is well combined.

3 Serve warm or chilled.

NO LIVERS DIRTY RICE

DF

Dirty rice is a Louisiana no-waste dish that has become pan-Southern thanks to the popularity of the Bojangles and Popeyes fast-food chains. Here is a homemade version that omits the traditional chicken livers in favor of ground meat (mince).

PREPARATION TIME: 10 MINUTES
COOKING TIME: 25 MINUTES
SERVES: 6

1 tablespoon vegetable oil or bacon fat
1 lb (450 g) ground beef (mince)
1 lb (450 g) ground pork or chicken (mince)
¾ cup (112 g) diced green bell pepper
¾ cup (120 g) diced yellow onion
¼ cup (25 g) diced celery
2 teaspoons minced garlic
1 tablespoon dried oregano
2 teaspoons dried thyme
1 ½ teaspoons fine salt
Freshly ground black pepper
Cayenne pepper
¼ cup (32 g) all-purpose (plain) flour
2 cups (16 fl oz/470 ml) chicken stock
3 bay leaves
5 cups (800 g) cooked long-grain rice
2 tablespoon finely chopped fresh flat-leaf parsley

1 In a large cast-iron skillet, heat the oil over medium-high heat. Once hot, add the ground meat (meat) and cook, stirring occasionally, until the meat begins to brown, 5–7 minutes.

2 Stir in the bell pepper, onion, celery, garlic, oregano, thyme, salt, and black pepper and cayenne to taste. Cook, stirring occasionally, until the vegetables are tender, 5–7 minutes. Add the flour and mix well, making sure that the flour coats the meat entirely.

3 Add the stock and bay leaves. Scrape the bottom of the pan to loosen the browned bits and simmer for 5 minutes. Gently fold in the rice and parsley and simmer for an additional 5 minutes. Remove the bay leaves before serving.

CRAB FRIED RICE

DF GF

This is Southern fried rice at its absolute best. It's also a great way to use any leftover crab before it can go bad or lose its peak flavor. It makes a great treat for breakfast or brunch.

PREPARATION TIME: 15 MINUTES
COOKING TIME: 30 MINUTES
SERVES: 4

4 slices thick-cut bacon (streaky), diced
1 medium green bell pepper, chopped
1 celery stalk, chopped
1 medium yellow onion, chopped
1 large or 2 medium cloves garlic, minced
1 lb (450 g) crabmeat, chopped
3 cups (480 g) cooked long-grain rice
1 teaspoon kosher salt or ½ teaspoon fine salt, plus more to taste
1 teaspoon freshly ground black pepper, plus more to taste

1 In a sauté pan or Dutch oven (casserole dish) with a tight-fitting lid, cook the bacon (streaky), stirring frequently, over medium-high until the bacon is crisp and the fat is rendered, 5–7 minutes.
2 Add the bell pepper, celery, and onion and sauté, stirring frequently, until the veggies are softened and golden, about 5 minutes.
3 Add the garlic and crabmeat and sauté, tossing, until the crab is hot all the way through and lightly browned, about 5 minutes.
4 Add the cooked rice and toss it until it's well coated and the crab is evenly distributed. Season the mixture with the salt and pepper and stir well. Reduce the heat to medium-low, cover, and let the rice steam gently for about 10 minutes.
5 Taste and adjust the seasonings as desired. Toss well and serve hot.

VARIATION: In place of the salt and pepper, you can use 1 teaspoon finely ground crab-boil seasoning, such as Old Bay, or more to taste. You can also add 1–2 dashes of soy sauce and rice vinegar if you like.

POTATO SALAD

DF GF V

A mayonnaise-based potato salad is absolutely indispensable for outdoor events and family gatherings in Southern culture. It appears at nearly every life event where fried chicken, ham, barbecue, fried fish or seafood, gumbo, or Brunswick stew take center stage. Potato salad bears the signature style of the cook and the family in Southern culture.

PREPARATION TIME: 25 MINUTES, PLUS AT LEAST 1 HOUR REFRIGERATION TIME
COOKING TIME: 20 MINUTES
SERVES: 10

1 teaspoon kosher salt or ½ teaspoon fine salt
6 medium russet (baking) potatoes, peeled and cut into ½-inch (13 mm) pieces
4 eggs, hard-boiled, peeled, and chopped
½ cup (145 g) chopped dill pickles or bread and butter pickles
2 tablespoons pickle juice
½ cup (80 g) finely minced or grated yellow onion
½ cup (75 g) finely diced yellow bell pepper
½ cup (75 g) finely diced red bell pepper
1 celery stalk, finely chopped
1 cup (220 g) mayonnaise, such as Duke's
4 tablespoons yellow or brown mustard
1 tablespoon fresh lemon juice
1 teaspoon sugar
½ teaspoon celery seed
½ teaspoon House Seasoning (PAGE 301) or seasoned salt
½ teaspoon sweet paprika, plus more for garnish
Freshly ground coarse black pepper

1 Bring a large pot of water to a boil over medium-high heat.

2 Add the salt and potatoes and cook until fork-tender, about 10 minutes. Drain the potatoes in a colander and return the cooked potatoes to the pan. Lightly mash the cooked potatoes just two or three times, to crush but still keep them in pieces; do not overmash! You want to do just a little mashing, which will make the potato salad creamy and help blend with the mayonnaise mixture, but you still want pieces of potato.

3 In a large bowl, combine the eggs, pickles, pickle juice, onion, bell peppers, celery, mayonnaise, mustard, lemon juice, sugar, celery seed, House Seasoning, paprika, and pepper to taste. Mix well before gently folding in the cooked potatoes.

4 Refrigerate for at least 1 hour, and up to 1 day. Garnish with an extra dash of paprika and serve chilled.

STORAGE: Store airtight in the refrigerator for up to 3 days.

VARIATION: Add 1 tablespoon chopped jarred pimentos, if you like.

COLLARD GREEN EMPANADAS

The collard green is one of the South's most versatile vegetables and it perfectly fits in with global dishes involving rice, sautés, and stuffed foods, like these collard green empanadas. Adapted from a recipe shared by my friend and cookbook author Sandra A. Gutierrez, these empanadas reflect the constant innovations of Latin American Southerners, re-creating the foods of Mexico and Central America in the contemporary South.

PREPARATION TIME: 30 MINUTES
COOKING TIME: 15 MINUTES
MAKES: 16 EMPANADAS

2 tablespoons vegetable oil, plus more for frying
2 slices bacon (streaky), chopped
½ cup (80 g) finely chopped yellow onion
4 large cloves garlic, finely chopped
8 oz (225 g) collard greens, Swiss chard, or kale, finely chopped
8 oz (225 g) cream cheese, at room temperature
½ teaspoon cayenne pepper
16 thawed frozen empanada discs

1 Line a plate with paper towels and have near the stove. In a large cast-iron skillet, heat the oil over medium-high heat. Add the bacon (streaky) and cook until crisp, stirring often, about 7 minutes. Leaving the bacon fat in the pan, remove to the paper towels to drain. Once cool, crumble into small pieces and set aside.

2 Add the onion and cook for 2 minutes. Add the garlic and cook for 20 seconds. Working in batches, add the collards, making sure to stir them quickly so the garlic doesn't burn. Reduce the heat to low and cook the collards until wilted, about 8 minutes. Remove from the heat and let cool for 10 minutes.

3 In a large bowl, combine the cooled collards, bacon, cream cheese, and cayenne and stir well to combine.

4 On a work surface, separate the empanada discs (keep them covered with a towel so they don't dry out). Place a heaping 4 tablespoons of the filling on one-half of each disc, leaving a ½-inch (13 mm) border. Fold the discs in half over the filling and press the edges firmly with the tines of a fork to seal.

5 Fit two large baking sheets with wire racks. Pour 2 inches (5 cm) oil into a large heavy-bottomed pot or Dutch oven (casserole dish) and heat to 350°F (177°C).

6 Working in batches to avoid over-crowding, carefully slide the empanadas into the hot oil and fry them until golden, 3–4 minutes, turning them over halfway through. Use a slotted spoon to transfer the empanadas to the prepared racks.

7 Serve hot.

STORAGE: Store airtight in the refrigerator for up to 3 days.

CHINESE MISSISSIPPI COLLARD GREENS

DF V VE

The lower Mississippi Valley and the Mississippi Delta are historically culturally diverse, including large numbers of mainland Chinese who arrived in the 1870s. They swapped collards for bok choy, used crawfish in place of crabs, and found many other ways to meld southern China and the American South. These collards are based on a recipe from Sally and Gilroy Chow, a family whom I met and interviewed at the 2005 Smithsonian Folklife Festival.

PREPARATION TIME: 30 MINUTES
COOKING TIME: 20 MINUTES
SERVES: 4

- 2 ½–3 lb (1.1–1.4 kg) collard greens
- 2 tablespoons oyster sauce or vegan oyster sauce
- 2 tablespoons peanut or vegetable oil
- 2 tablespoons thinly sliced scallions (spring onions)
- 3 cloves garlic, minced
- ½ teaspoon sugar
- ¼ teaspoon chile flakes (optional)
- Fine salt and freshly ground black pepper

1 Set up a large bowl of ice and water. Trim out the stems and midribs of the collard greens and cut the leaves into ribbons.
2 Bring a large pot of water to boil. Working in two or three batches, blanch the collards for 1 minute (begin counting after the water returns to a boil). Immediately transfer the greens to the ice water to cool. Drain well, then squeeze out the excess water with your hands. Spread the greens on tea towels and pat them dry (excess water will cause the oil in the wok to spit).
3 In a small bowl, stir together the oyster sauce with 2 tablespoons water. Set aside.
4 Heat a wok over medium-high heat until a drop of water evaporates on contact. Add the oil and swirl to coat the bottom. Add the scallions (spring onions) and garlic and stir-fry until aromatic, about 30 seconds. Add the collards and stir-fry for 1 minute. Stir in the oyster sauce mixture, sugar, and chile flakes (if using). Reduce the heat to medium-low and allow the greens to cook, stirring occasionally, until the greens are wilted and glossy, another 3–4 minutes. Season to taste with salt and black pepper.
5 Transfer the greens to a plate and serve.

CINNAMON BAKED CUSHAW

GF V

The "pumpkin" of my enslaved ancestors' world, the cushaw (*Curcubita argyrosperma*), was brought from the West Indies by way of Mexico in the eighteenth century. The plant spread from the Chesapeake to Texas, and the pulp and seeds of this cucurbit were happily adopted into the diet of the enslaved and poor whites of the Piedmont and Southern highlands. It was baked from late summer to early winter as a substitute for sweet potatoes, hence its nickname as the "sweet potato pumpkin." Baking, boiling, drying into pumpkin leather, and sometimes pickling were traditional methods of preparation.

PREPARATION TIME: 20 MINUTES
COOKING TIME: 1 HOUR 10 MINUTES
SERVES: 8

Softened butter, for the baking dish
2 ½–3 lb (1.1–1.4 kg) cushaw, seeded, peeled, and cut into 1-inch (2.5 cm) chunks
2 teaspoons ground cinnamon
½ teaspoon ground nutmeg
½ cup (95 g) dark brown sugar
6 tablespoons (3 oz/90 g) unsalted butter, sliced
¾ cup (6 fl oz/180 ml) heavy (whipping) cream
¼ cup (2 fl oz/60 ml) half-and-half (single cream)
Fine salt and freshly ground black pepper

1 Preheat the oven to 400°F (200°C/Gas Mark 6).
2 Coat a 9 × 13-inch (23 × 33 cm) baking dish generously with butter and evenly arrange the cushaw chunks along the bottom.
3 In a small bowl, stir together the cinnamon, nutmeg, and brown sugar until well incorporated. Sprinkle the mixture over the cushaw, making sure each piece is well coated. Lay the slices of butter over the cushaw. Pour the heavy (whipping) cream and half-and-half (single cream) over the top. Season with salt and black pepper to taste. Cover the dish with foil.
4 Bake until tender, about 1 hour. Uncover and bake until lightly browned on top, another 10 minutes.
5 Serve hot.

STORAGE: Store airtight in the refrigerator for up to 3 days.

CANDIED SWEET POTATOES

GF V

Candied sweet potatoes or yams sit at the intersection of all the foundational cultures of the South. The sweet potato originally comes from early Mesoamerica, and appeared in numerous colors. The varieties most common in the American South during slavery were white-fleshed sweet potatoes, which many enslaved people used in similar ways to West African yams, an entirely different species of tuber. By the seventeenth and eighteenth century, both tubers were staple parts of the African-Atlantic diet. The orange- and yellow-fleshed types, such as Beauregard, Georgia Jet, and Porto Rico, became more common after the Civil War, and beginning in the mid-twentieth century, began being marketed as "yams." Throughout their history, sweet potatoes have been cooked in sugar, originally in molten cane juice during sugar-making season.

PREPARATION TIME: 10 MINUTES
COOKING TIME: 1 HOUR
SERVES: 4–6

2 lb (910 g) sweet potatoes, peeled and cut into rounds ½ inch (13 mm) thick
¾ cup (145 g) dark brown sugar
¼ cup (50 g) granulated (caster) sugar
2 teaspoons ground cinnamon
1 teaspoon ground nutmeg
¼ teaspoon fine salt
2 tablespoons pure vanilla extract
8 tablespoons (4 oz/115 g) unsalted butter, cut into chunks
4 tablespoons orange juice or water
Marshmallows (optional)

1 Preheat the oven to 350°F (180°C/Gas Mark 4).

2 In a medium pot, combine the sweet potatoes, both sugars, cinnamon, nutmeg, salt, vanilla, and butter and stir until the potatoes are well coated. Add the orange juice and stir to combine. Transfer to a 9 × 13-inch (23 × 33 cm) baking dish. Cover the dish with foil.

3 Bake until the sweet potatoes are tender, about 1 hour. (If you choose, add marshmallows to the top for the last 5–10 minutes and allow them to lightly brown.)

VARIATION: In the South Carolina Lowcountry, it's common to add about a cup of canned crushed pineapple to the potatoes before baking. If you choose to add it, omit the sugar.

SAUTÉED SQUASH

GF V -30

The bright yellow summer squash—we preferred the crookneck or straight-neck varieties—were sunshine on a plate. Once squash plants started to bloom and become pollinated, they were prolific, and if you had a good year they could become too much to handle. In the past, most summer squash was preserved by cutting and drying in slices and also canning—both methods have been continued by homesteaders today. Home cooks also got very creative and filled Southern tables with things like grilled squash, squash pie, squash bread, and squash salad—until the bugs or weather declared the season over.

PREPARATION TIME: 5 MINUTES
COOKING TIME: 20 MINUTES
SERVES: 4

2 tablespoons (30 g) unsalted butter
2 tablespoons vegetable oil
1 teaspoon minced garlic
1 cup (160 g) diced red onion or Vidalia onion
2 lb (910 g) summer squash, such as yellow squash and/or zucchini (courgettes), cut into ¼-inch (6 mm) slices or cubes
½ teaspoon fresh thyme
Fine salt and freshly ground black pepper

1 In a large cast-iron skillet, heat the butter and oil over medium heat until hot. Add the garlic and onion and cook, stirring occasionally, until translucent, 5–7 minutes.

2 Add the squash, thyme, and salt and black pepper to taste and sauté over medium-high heat, stirring occasionally, until golden brown and tender, about 5 minutes.

3 Reduce the heat to medium and cook until the squash is fragrant and very tender, for an additional 5 minutes.

SQUASH PUDDING

V

Squash puddings are a type of Southern dish that date back to the early nineteenth century, with recipes appearing in old Southern cookbooks for squash or cymling (pattypan squash) just after the Civil War. This version uses yellow crookneck squash, and is much enjoyed in West Virginia.

PREPARATION TIME: 15 MINUTES
COOKING TIME: 1 HOUR 10 MINUTES
SERVES: 6–8

Softened butter, for the baking dish
3 ½ cups (475 g) diced peeled yellow squash
½ cup (4 fl oz/120 ml) whole milk
¼ cup (50 g) sugar
1 egg, beaten
2 tablespoons (30 g) unsalted butter, melted
2 teaspoons fresh lemon juice
½ teaspoon kosher salt or ¼ teaspoon fine salt
½ teaspoon freshly ground coarse black pepper or Kitchen Pepper (PAGE 301)
1 cup (130 g) self-rising flour

1 Preheat the oven to 350°F (180°C/Gas Mark 4). Generously grease a 9 × 13-inch (23 × 33 cm) baking dish with butter.
2 In a large saucepan fitted with a steamer basket, fill with water to just below the steamer basket and bring to a boil. Add the squash to the steamer, cover, and cook until very tender, about 7 minutes. Transfer it to a large bowl and once cooled, mash to a rough consistency.
3 In a large bowl, combine the milk, sugar, egg, melted butter, lemon juice, salt, and black pepper. Gradually sift the flour into the mixture, then fold the mashed squash into the bowl until the batter is smooth. Pour the batter into the greased baking dish.
4 Bake until the pudding is golden brown and a toothpick in the center comes out mostly clean, about 1 hour. Let cool for about 10 minutes before serving.

STORAGE: Store airtight in the refrigerator for up to 3 days.

VIRGINIA FRIED APPLES

GF V -5

An essential Virginia breakfast dish and side dish is fried apples—they are sautéed in clarified butter or bacon fat and kept plain or seasoned with your choice of Kitchen Pepper (PAGE 301) or cinnamon. This recipe is inspired by the grande dame of Southern cooking, the late Edna Lewis of Freetown, Virginia. It's best to use a mixture of apple varieties of various textures and flavors.

PREPARATION TIME: 10 MINUTES
COOKING TIME: 25 MINUTES
SERVES: 4–6

- 3–4 tablespoons (45 to 60 ml) clarified butter or bacon (streaky) fat
- 6 medium apples (about 2 lb/910 g total), cored, peeled, and sliced into eighths
- ⅓ cup (65 g) superfine (caster) or brown sugar
- Pinch of Kitchen Pepper (PAGE 301) or ground cinnamon (optional)

1 In a medium cast-iron skillet, melt the butter or bacon fat over medium heat. Once it's hot and sizzling, add the apples in one layer. Cover the skillet, reduce the heat to medium-low, and cook until the apples begin to soften, 5–8 minutes.

2 Uncover, sprinkle the sugar and Kitchen Pepper or cinnamon (if using) over the apples, then cook, stirring occasionally, until they give up their juices, 10–15 minutes. (Add water if the pan seems to be getting too dry.) The apples are done when they are soft and fragrant, slightly jammy, and somewhere between a light and medium amber color.
Serve warm.

SOUPS, STEWS & CASSEROLES

THE ONE POT

To an outsider, the Southern love of soups and stews may seem out of place, especially in a part of the country known for its heat and humidity. Yet the one-pot meal or composite dishes is a product of the region's triple heritage coming from agrarian Native American, West and Central African, and Western European cultures. Across such a wide range of backgrounds, a pot brimming with whatever was seasonally available was eaten with the staple starch, whether it was corncakes or hominy, rice or fufu, bread or porridge. In some form, each of these patterns would eventually imprint on how Southerners would eat over the next four centuries.

Of course, the South has areas where snow is a given, or bone-chilling air can give you a reason for a hot meal in a steaming bowl. At the same time, Native American and African traditions often meant cooking outdoors, weather permitting. While winters might suggest cooking chicken and dumplings, creamy oyster soups, or stews based around a hunt or livestock culling, Southerners also had many reasons to break a sweat and self-cleanse with a stew in the warmer months. During many picnics and barbecues, community-sized pots boiled away in the shade with growing crowds of neighbors standing by with plates. Brunswick or burgoo stew were prepared by small teams of cooks rather than individuals, as were dishes like Frogmore stew and crab or crawfish boils where shellfish, sausage, corn, and potatoes were designed to feed not just families, but whole communities. In the Lowcountry, meanwhile, seasonal vegetables and ingredients—black-eyed peas (black-eye beans), field peas, okra, greens, peanuts, eggplant (aubergine), sesame seeds (or benne), and other staple vegetables—always came to the table sautéed, stewed, or in soups to be served over rice. Southern Louisiana and the Chesapeake likewise had similar traditions, putting she-crabs or their charcuterie (andouille or country ham) into their soups and stews. Of course, we can't forget soups based on seasonal produce like collards, sweet corn, peanuts, and tomatoes. But the form changed with the season; a summer soup might rely on fresh okra, while a winter vegetable soup might use dried.

Another piece of the one-pot tradition is the casseroles and platters of side dishes, which are staples of family gatherings, dinners on the grounds, parties, repasts, and reunions. Macaroni and cheese (also known as macaroni pie), sweet potato casseroles, Southern fried rice, or cornbread dressing are very heavy, tradition-bound sides. A whole family exists of long-cooked rice dishes, including jambalaya, purloos and pilaus, bogs, and hashes, all stewed for hours and used to make feasts and political rallies legendary. Whether they were prepared by stew-masters or domestic matriarchs, these dishes offered long cooked-in flavor and ambrosial scents, making memories that have lasted generations.

SOUTHERN VEGETABLE SOUP

DF GF V VE

This soup perfectly captures the seasonal flavors of the Southern summer in one bowl. It freezes beautifully for when you want to enjoy those same tastes in the winter.

PREPARATION TIME: 10 MINUTES
COOKING TIME: 40 MINUTES
SERVES: 4

1 bag (16 oz/450 g) green beans, frozen or fresh
½ head green cabbage, chopped
6 medium carrots, peeled and chopped
1 bag (16 oz/450 g) frozen okra, cut into ¼-inch (6 mm) slices
1 medium onion, chopped
1 can (28 oz/794 g) crushed tomatoes
1 teaspoon sugar
½ teaspoon kosher salt or ¼ teaspoon fine salt, plus more if needed
⅛ teaspoon ground white pepper
1 sprig fresh thyme
6 cups (1.4 liters) water or vegetable stock

1 In a large pot, combine all the ingredients and bring to a boil over medium-high heat. Reduce the heat and simmer until all the vegetables are tender, about 30 minutes.

2 Season with more salt as needed and serve warm.

STORAGE: Store airtight in the refrigerator for up to 4 days.

SOUTHERN BAKED BEANS

DF

The Southern way with baked beans is extra punchy and tangy and sweeter than traditional baked beans from New England, where they are long-cooked with salt pork and a bit of molasses (treacle). Southern baked beans were meant to pair with barbecue—tomato, mustard, brown sugar, and smoky flavors—not as a standalone dish. For many families, they are merely doctored canned beans, but here is a homemade version where you can adjust the sharper and saltier flavors as you like. These baked beans are a barbecue or picnic staple.

PREPARATION TIME: 20 MINUTES
COOKING TIME: 3 HOURS 40 MINUTES
SERVES: 8–10

4 cups (560 g) dried navy (haricot) beans
8 oz (225 g) bacon (streaky), chopped
1 large onion, finely chopped
1 clove garlic, minced
1 cup (9 oz/260 g) tomato paste (tomato puree)
½ cup (4 fl oz/120 ml) tomato-based barbecue sauce
¼ cup (2 fl oz/60 ml) cane syrup
¼ cup (50 g) brown sugar
2 tablespoons brown mustard
1 tablespoon Worcestershire sauce
2 teaspoons liquid smoke
1 teaspoon smoked paprika
1 teaspoon freshly ground black pepper
1 teaspoon House Seasoning (PAGE 301)
2 cups (16 fl oz/470 ml) low-sodium chicken stock

1 Preheat the oven to 325°F (160°C/Gas Mark 3).
2 Rinse and sort the navy (haricot) beans, then place them in a large pot. Add water to cover the beans by 2 inches (5 cm) and bring the pot to a boil. Reduce the heat to a simmer and cook the beans until tender, about 1 hour.
3 Line a plate with paper towels and have near the stove. In a medium Dutch oven (casserole dish), cook the bacon (streaky) over medium heat, stirring occasionally, until crispy, about 10 minutes. Remove the bacon with a slotted spoon to the paper towels to drain.
4 In the same pan, sauté the onion, stirring occasionally, until soft and translucent, about 5 minutes. Add the garlic and cook for 1 minute until fragrant. Stir in the tomato paste (tomato puree), barbecue sauce, cane syrup, and brown sugar, mixing well until combined. Add the brown mustard, Worcestershire sauce, liquid smoke, smoked paprika, black pepper, and House Seasoning. Stir everything together, then pour in the chicken stock and bring the mixture to a gentle simmer.
5 Drain the cooked beans and transfer them to a 9 × 13-inch (23 × 33 cm) baking dish. Pour the sauce over the beans, stirring gently to ensure everything is well coated. Sprinkle the reserved bacon over the top of the beans. Cover with the baking dish with foil.
6 Bake until very soft and flavorful, about 2 hours.
7 Remove the foil and continue baking for an additional 30 minutes, allowing the sauce to thicken and the top to caramelize slightly.
8 Let the beans cool for a few minutes before serving.

STORAGE: Store airtight in the refrigerator for up to 4 days.

COWPEA SOUP

DF GF V VE

Black-eyed peas (black-eye beans), red field peas, whippoorwill peas (also known as cowpeas) and the like make an excellent hearty Southern soup with deep African roots. This soup can be meatless and incredibly satisfying. The appearance of the cowpea in cookbooks thirty-five years before the Civil War is likely because by then, three generations of the slaveholding class had enjoyed soups like these since childhood, and they had become a nostalgic part of their acculturation in the Deep South.

PREPARATION TIME: 45 MINUTES
COOKING TIME: 1 HOUR 15 MINUTES
MAKES: ABOUT 3 QUARTS (3 LITERS)

- 2 tablespoons extra-virgin olive oil
- 1 medium red onion, chopped
- 2 cloves garlic, chopped
- Kosher salt or House Seasoning (PAGE 301)
- ½ teaspoon cayenne pepper
- 1 teaspoon Kitchen Pepper (PAGE 301)
- 1 ½ lb (680 g) collard greens, stems and midribs removed, leaves very thinly sliced
- 2 cups (360 g) chopped heirloom tomatoes or 1 can (14.5 oz/411 g) diced (chopped) tomatoes
- 2 teaspoons dried marjoram
- 2 cups (325 g) cooked or canned black-eyed peas (black-eye beans) or cowpeas
- 4 cups (32 fl oz/950 ml) vegetable stock or Pot Likker (PAGE 266)

1 In a large Dutch oven (casserole dish), heat the olive oil over medium-high heat. Add the onion and garlic and cook, stirring occasionally, until translucent and fragrant, about 6 minutes.

2 Add a pinch of salt, the cayenne, and Kitchen Pepper. Add the collards and cook until limp, 4–5 minutes.

3 Reduce the heat to medium low, add the diced tomatoes and marjoram and cook slowly, over medium-low heat, stirring occasionally, until the tomatoes break down into a sauce, about 15 minutes.

4 Add the black-eyed peas (black-eye beans) and stock and simmer until the flavors are well combined, about 45 minutes.

STORAGE: Store airtight in the refrigerator for up to 4 days.

PEANUT SOUP

Peanut soup is a quiet marriage of English cream broth with West African groundnut stew. This recipe was clearly adapted for the taste of elite whites, rather than being a direct introduction from African culture. Its roots are in southeastern Nigeria, Senegambia, Angola, and central and southern Ghana, where groundnut stews and soups are staples. It was also known in the Lowcountry as groundnut soup, and it was recorded as such in Sarah Rutledge's *The Carolina Housewife*.

Peanuts are South American in origin and were brought across the Atlantic to Africa by the Portuguese. In Central Africa, they spread quickly due to their similarity to the Bambara groundnut, which looks similar to the peanut and produces an edible underground legume, similar to a cowpea. The peanut was versatile and could be made into soups and sauces, eaten on its own, and made into sweets. It also provided great animal fodder and spread across West and Central Africa, diversifying on the way.

Early Southern terms for the peanut included *pinder* (in KiKongo *mpinda*) and *nguba* (from the word in KiMbundu, from Angola), which eventually became the term "goober." Well established in the South, peanuts were found in the archaeological remains of eighteenth-century enslaved quarters in the Chesapeake . . . long before the peanut became more popular in the North. This was thanks to their introduction by Haitian emigrés, and after the Civil War veterans came home singing a popular folk song, "goodness how delicious eatin' goober peas."

PREPARATION TIME: 20 MINUTES
COOKING TIME: 40 MINUTES
SERVES: 4–6

4 tablespoons (60 g) unsalted butter
1 small onion, finely chopped
3 cloves garlic, minced
2 celery stalks, finely chopped
½-inch (2.5 cm) piece fresh ginger, grated
3 tablespoons all-purpose (plain) flour
2 quarts (1.9 liters) chicken or ham stock
1 can (15 oz/425 g) crushed tomatoes (optional)
2 cups (512 g) creamy peanut butter
½ teaspoon cayenne pepper
Fine salt and freshly ground black pepper
1 ¾ cups (14 fl oz/420 ml) light (single) cream
Cooked white rice, for serving
Chopped roasted peanuts, for garnish

---

1 In a large pot, heat the butter over medium heat. Add the onion and cook, stirring occasionally, until softened, about 5 minutes. Stir in the garlic, celery, and ginger and cook until fragrant, about 2 minutes. Stir in the flour until well incorporated. Add the stock and crushed tomatoes (if using), and stir while bringing to a boil.

2 Meanwhile, in a small bowl, whisk together the peanut butter, cayenne, and salt and black pepper to taste until combined.

3 Stir the peanut butter mixture and light (single) cream into the soup and cook until it's fully incorporated and thickened, about 35 minutes. Taste and adjust the seasoning if needed. If the soup is too thick, you can thin it with a bit more stock or touch of water.

4 Serve the soup over rice in bowls, and garnish with the peanuts.

STORAGE: Store airtight in the refrigerator for up to 4 days.

RED BEANS AND RICE

DF GF

The classic Monday dish of south Louisiana, red beans and rice, has its roots in Haiti. After the arrival of Haitian planters and the many enslaved from Saint-Domingue, the dish became a mainstay of New Orleans cuisine. Why a Monday dish? Prepared in the days when kitchens and laundries shared the same building, this was the set-it-and-forget-it dish of the antebellum work week.

PREPARATION TIME: 30 MINUTES, PLUS OVERNIGHT SOAKING TIME
COOKING TIME: 2–3 HOURS
SERVES: 6–8

- 1 lb (450 g) dried red beans
- 2 tablespoons vegetable oil
- 1 large onion, finely chopped
- 1 medium green bell pepper, finely chopped
- 2 celery stalks, finely chopped
- 4 cloves garlic, minced
- 1 smoked ham hock
- 1 lb (450 g) andouille sausage, sliced
- 6 cups (48 fl oz/1.4 liters) chicken stock
- 2 bay leaves
- 2 teaspoons Creole Seasoning (PAGE 299)
- 1 teaspoon sweet paprika
- ½ teaspoon cayenne pepper
- Fine salt and freshly ground black pepper
- 4 cups (640 g) cooked white rice
- 4 scallions (spring onions), chopped, for garnish
- Chopped fresh flat-leaf parsley, for garnish
- Hot sauce (optional)

1 Rinse and sort the red beans, then soak them in water overnight. Drain and rinse the beans.

2 In a large pot, heat the oil over medium heat. Add the onion, bell pepper, and celery and sauté until softened, about 5 minutes. Add the garlic and cook for 1 minute.

3 Add the smoked ham hock, andouille sausage, and drained beans to the pot. Pour in the chicken stock and add the bay leaves, Creole Seasoning, paprika, and cayenne. Stir well and bring to a boil. Reduce the heat to low, cover, and simmer, stirring occasionally, until the beans are tender and the mixture has thickened, 2–3 hours. Season with salt and black pepper to taste.

4 Remove the ham hock, shred the meat, and return it to the pot. Serve the red beans over the rice. Garnish with the scallions (spring onions) and parsley. Add hot sauce if desired.

STORAGE: Store airtight in the refrigerator for up to 4 days.

HOPPIN' JOHN

DF GF

Hoppin' John, a pilau/perloo based on cowpeas, is a signature dish of the Lowcountry that consists of rice cooked with field peas in one pot. In other parts of the United States, some people make it with black-eyed peas (black-eye beans), but the original dish utilized the red or brown field pea common to the region. (They are all cowpea species.) Hoppin' John's etymology or folklore is debated by scholars. It does though belong to an ancient family of rice and legume dishes going back millennia in Africa that came through the enslaved communities of the rice and cotton plantations of the Lowcountry and Sea Islands. In Senegal—where its ancestor is made without pork—this dish is called *ceeb u niebe* (rice and cowpeas) and in Ghana it's known as *waakye*. In Louisiana, it arrived directly from Africa and was known in Creole cuisine as *jambalaya au congri*. These dishes join similar dishes from across the African Atlantic.

PREPARATION TIME: 15 MINUTES, PLUS OVERNIGHT SOAKING TIME
COOKING TIME: 1 HOUR 30 MINUTES
SERVES: 6

- 1 cup dried red field peas
- 1 cup (185 g) long-grain white rice (parboiled is okay)
- 4 slices bacon (streaky), chopped
- 1 medium onion, finely chopped
- 1 medium green bell pepper, finely chopped
- 2 celery stalks, finely chopped
- 2 cloves garlic, minced
- 1 teaspoon dried thyme
- 1 teaspoon smoked paprika
- ½ teaspoon cayenne pepper
- Fine salt and freshly ground black pepper
- 3 cups (24 fl oz/710 ml) Pot Likker (PAGE 266)

1. Rinse the red field peas and soak them in a bowl of cold water overnight.
2. Rinse the rice under cold running water until the water runs clear. Drain well.
3. In a large pot, cook the bacon (streaky) over medium-high heat, stirring occasionally, until crispy, about 10 minutes.
4. Add the onion, bell pepper, celery, and garlic and sauté until the vegetables soften, about 8 minutes.
5. Stir in the thyme, smoked paprika, cayenne, and salt and black pepper to taste. Drain the peas and add to the pot, along with the Pot Likker. Bring to a boil, reduce the heat, cover, and simmer for 45 minutes.
6. Stir in the rice, cover, and cook until the rice is tender and the liquid absorbed, about 20 minutes.
7. Adjust the seasoning if needed. Serve warm.

STORAGE: Store airtight in the refrigerator for up to 4 days.

BEAN SOUP: BLACK, RED, AND WHITE

DF GF

The Southern love of beans comes from Native American agriculture. Pinto, red kidney, and black beans, indigenous to Central America, spread to the American South, where African chefs grew and prepared them in soups, stews, and pilaus. Though Southern food is often characterized as meat-centric, this soup is a classic Southern dish, and can easily be made vegetarian by substituting vegetable stock for the beef stock.

PREPARATION TIME: 10 MINUTES
COOKING TIME: 30 MINUTES
SERVES: 4

- 2 teaspoons olive oil or vegetable oil
- 1 medium onion, chopped
- 2 cloves garlic, smashed and peeled
- 1 can (28 oz/794 g) whole peeled tomatoes
- 1 can (15.5 oz/439 g) navy (haricot) beans, drained and rinsed
- 1 can (15.5 oz/439 g) black beans, drained and rinsed
- 1 can (15.5 oz/439 g) red kidney beans, drained and rinsed
- 1 can (14.5 oz/411 g) beef stock
- ¾ teaspoon dried basil
- 1 teaspoon kosher salt or House Seasoning (PAGE 301) or ½ teaspoon fine salt
- ½ teaspoon freshly ground black pepper
- 2 teaspoons apple cider vinegar (optional)
- 2 tablespoons finely chopped fresh flat-leaf parsley

1 In a large saucepan, heat the olive oil over medium-high heat. Add the onion and garlic and cook, stirring, until tender, 3–4 minutes.

2 Add the tomatoes, all the beans, stock, basil, salt, and black pepper and bring to a boil. Reduce the heat and simmer for 20 minutes, until the flavors are well combined.

3 Stir in the vinegar (if using) and parsley before serving.

STORAGE: Store airtight in the refrigerator for up to 4 days.

HAMBONE SOUP

GF

Southerners wasted no part of the country ham. It was almost always eaten down to the bone. Then hambone soup was a classic Monday dish, meant to use up the remainder of a Sunday ham. Serve hot with Skillet Cornbread (PAGE 45).

PREPARATION TIME: 15 MINUTES
COOKING TIME: 1 HOUR 25 MINUTES
SERVES: 6

2 tablespoons vegetable oil
1 large onion, diced
4 tablespoons (60 g) unsalted butter
4 medium carrots, finely chopped
4 celery stalks, sliced thinly
5 cloves garlic, finely minced
6 cups (48 fl oz/1.4 liters) chicken stock
1 meaty ham bone
2 cups (330 g) diced ham
2 cans (15 oz/425 g each) Great Northern beans, drained and rinsed
3 bay leaves
2 sprigs fresh thyme
½ head green cabbage, shredded
Fine salt or House Seasoning (PAGE 301) and freshly ground black pepper

1 In a large Dutch oven (casserole dish), heat the oil over medium heat. Add the onion and cook, stirring often, until the onions start to caramelize, about 10 minutes.

2 Add the butter and continue to cook until soft and fragrant, about 5 minutes.

3 Add the carrots, celery, and garlic and cook, stirring often, until the carrots soften, about 10 minutes.

4 Deglaze the pan with a few splashes of the stock, making sure nothing is sticking to the bottom. Add the remaining chicken stock, the ham bone, ham, beans, bay leaves, and thyme. Stir well. Cover the pot and simmer over low heat until the ham bone has released its flavor into the soup and the beans have broken down, about 45 minutes.

5 Remove the lid, add the cabbage, and simmer again uncovered until soft, about 15 minutes.

6 Season with salt and black pepper as needed before serving.

STORAGE: Store airtight in the refrigerator for up to 4 days.

TURTLE SOUP

GF

Southerners of the elite class once indulged in different varieties of turtle soup. King among these was Maryland terrapin, popular from the mid-nineteenth to the mid-twentieth century. (During the early Colonial period, however, terrapin was provided as a protein for enslaved and indentured servants, so much so that they refused to work.) Terrapin stew, dressed with sherry and served with roasted terrapin eggs, was on many plantation tables from Baltimore and Annapolis in Maryland south to Charleston in South Carolina.

Generally, there were two types of turtle soup, white and red—one milk- or cream-based and another tomato-based. This recipe is the latter. (From the Lowcountry to Florida, cooks prepared turtle soup with cooter, a variety of freshwater turtle frequently spotted in the rice fields.)

If turtle isn't for you, you can make mock turtle soup with chicken. Serve hot with crusty bread.

PREPARATION TIME: 30 MINUTES
COOKING TIME: 2 HOURS
SERVES: 6

4 tablespoons (60 g) unsalted butter
1 large onion, finely chopped
2 celery stalks, finely chopped
1 medium green bell pepper, finely chopped
4 cloves garlic, minced
2 lb (910 g) farmed snapping turtle meat or 1 ½ lb (680 g) boneless chicken breast or thigh, chopped
4 cups (32 fl oz/950 ml) chicken stock
1 cup (8 fl oz/240 ml) tomato puree (passata)
2 bay leaves
1 teaspoon dried thyme
1 teaspoon paprika
1 teaspoon cayenne pepper
1 teaspoon Kitchen Pepper (PAGE 301)
Fine salt and freshly ground black pepper
½ cup (4 fl oz/120 ml) dry sherry
Juice of 1 lemon
2 hard-boiled eggs, finely chopped
Chopped fresh flat-leaf parsley, for garnish

1 In a large heavy-bottomed pot, melt the butter over medium-low heat. Add the onion, celery, and bell pepper and cook until they become tender and fragrant, about 10 minutes. Add the garlic, allowing it to meld with the softened vegetables for 1 more minute.

2 Add the turtle meat, stirring to coat it evenly. Cook until the meat starts to brown slightly, releasing its unique flavors into the base of the soup, 5–10 minutes.

3 Pour in the chicken stock and tomato puree (passata), stirring well to combine. Add the bay leaves, thyme, paprika, cayenne, Kitchen Pepper, and salt and black pepper to taste. Bring the soup to a gentle simmer, cover, and cook slowly until the turtle meat is tender and the flavors have fully developed, 1–1 ½ hours.

4 Discard the bay leaves. Pour in the dry sherry, stirring to incorporate its deep, aromatic notes into the soup, and simmer for 10 minutes.

5 Just before serving, add the lemon juice and stir in the hard-boiled eggs, allowing them to enrich the soup's texture and flavor.

6 Ladle the soup into bowls, garnishing each serving with a sprinkle of parsley.

STORAGE: Store airtight in the refrigerator for up to 3 days.

PINE BARK STEW

DF GF

This tomato-red fish stew was named for the pine wood, bark, and needles that were used to cook it, deep in the South Carolina woods. It was there that people gathered for fish fries, political rallies, church dinners, camp meetings, revivals, and reunions. Pine bark stew was prepared by the gallon and served over rice in the same way as hash, bog, and other stews made to feed mass crowds. (You can use any variety of freshwater fish here, such as catfish, trout, rockfish, bream, or perch.)

PREPARATION TIME: 20 MINUTES
COOKING TIME: 45 MINUTES
SERVES: 6

- 8 oz (225 g) thick-cut bacon (streaky), coarsely chopped
- 3 medium red or white potatoes, peeled and cubed
- 1 medium onion, chopped
- 1 tablespoon fresh thyme or 1 teaspoon dried thyme
- 1 teaspoon fine salt
- ½ teaspoon freshly ground black pepper
- ½ teaspoon cayenne pepper
- 2 lb (910 g) freshwater fish fillets
- 5 cups (40 fl oz/1.2 liters) boiling water
- 3 plum or Roma tomatoes, cored and finely chopped, with juices
- 3 scallions (spring onions), chopped
- ¼ cup (15 g) chopped fresh flat-leaf parsley

1 Heat a Dutch oven (casserole dish) or a large pot over medium heat until hot. Scatter in the bacon (streaky) and cook, stirring to avoid burning, until the bacon pieces are fragrant and nicely browned, 2–3 minutes. Transfer the bacon to a small bowl, leaving the bacon fat behind in the pan. Once cooled, crumble the bacon and set aside.

2 Add the potatoes and onions to the pot and cook, stirring occasionally, until the onions are shiny and softened, about 2 minutes. Add the thyme, salt, pepper, and cayenne and stir well.

3 Spread the onions and potatoes out into an even layer that covers the bottom of the pot. Carefully place the fish fillets on top of the cooked potatoes and onions. Slowly pour the boiling water over the fish, to avoid disturbing the fillets.

4 Return the soup to a boil. Reduce the heat and simmer gently, uncovered and stirring occasionally, until the fish is cooked through and the vegetables have flavored the broth, about 30 minutes.

5 Add the tomatoes, stirring gently to combine everything. Let the cooked fish break into large pieces and cook until the potatoes are tender, about 10 minutes. Stir in the reserved bacon and scallions (spring onions).

6 Transfer the stew to a serving bowl, sprinkle with the parsley, and serve hot.

STORAGE: Store in airtight container in the refrigerator for up to 4 days.

OYSTER AND BENNE SOUP

Oyster and benne or sesame soup is an old Charleston soup first recorded in Sarah Rutledge's 1847 book *The Carolina Housewife*. Once again, Europe, Africa, and Native America meet in one Southern dish.

PREPARATION TIME: 10 MINUTES
COOKING TIME: 30 MINUTES
SERVES: 4

1 pint (450 g) shucked oysters, packed in their liquor
3 tablespoons (45 g) unsalted butter
1 medium onion, chopped
3 cups (24 fl oz/710 ml) whole milk
1 cup (8 fl oz/240 ml) half-and-half (single cream)
2 tablespoons toasted sesame seeds (benne)
Fine salt and freshly ground black pepper
Crackers, for serving

1 Pour the liquor from the oysters into a small bowl and set aside.
2 In a large saucepan, melt the butter over medium heat. Add the onion and sauté until translucent, about 10 minutes.
3 Add the oyster liquid and cook until half reduced, about 10 minutes.
4 Reduce the heat to low and slowly stir in the milk and half-and-half (single cream). Add the oyster meats and sesame seeds and continue to simmer until the edges of the oysters have curled, about 10 minutes.
5 Remove the pot from the heat and season with salt and black pepper.
6 Serve hot with crackers.

STORAGE: Store in an airtight container in the refrigerator for up to 3 days.

OYSTER BISQUE

Bisques are part of the elegant arm of Savannah and New Orleans cuisine—oyster, shrimp (prawns), crab, or crawfish and these smooth and creamy subtly spiced soups go well with fresh crusty French bread.

PREPARATION TIME: 15 MINUTES
COOKING TIME: 50 MINUTES
SERVES: 4–6

2 dozen shucked oysters, with their liquor
4 tablespoons (60 g) unsalted butter
1 medium onion, finely chopped
2 celery stalks, finely chopped
1 medium carrot, finely chopped
4 cloves garlic, minced
¼ cup (30 g) all-purpose (plain) flour
½ cup (4 fl oz/120 ml) dry white wine
4 cups (32 fl oz/950 ml) seafood or chicken stock
2 cups (16 fl oz/470 ml) heavy (whipping) cream
1 cup (8 fl oz/240 ml) whole milk
1 bay leaf
1 teaspoon fresh thyme leaves
½ teaspoon cayenne pepper, plus more to taste
¼ teaspoon ground mace
Fine salt and ground white pepper
1 tablespoon fresh lemon juice
¼ cup (15 g) chopped fresh flat-leaf parsley
Oyster crackers or crusty bread, for serving
Hot sauce (optional), for serving

1 Roughly chop the oysters and transfer them to a small bowl. Store the liquor in a separate bowl and set both bowls aside in the refrigerator.

2 In a large pot, melt the butter over medium heat. Add the onion, celery, and carrot and sauté until soft and translucent, 8–10 minutes.

3 Add the garlic and cook, stirring occasionally, until fragrant, 1–2 minutes. Sprinkle the flour over the vegetables, stirring to combine, and cook for 3–4 minutes to incorporate. Gradually pour in the white wine and stir constantly until the mixture is smooth. While stirring, slowly add the stock, then stir in the reserved oyster liquor, heavy (whipping) cream, and milk.

4 Add the bay leaf, thyme, cayenne, mace, and salt and white pepper to taste. Bring the mixture to a gentle simmer over medium heat and cook, stirring occasionally, until the bisque thickens slightly, 20–25 minutes.

5 Discard the bay leaf. Blend the bisque until smooth using an immersion blender. (Alternatively, transfer the bisque in batches to a stand blender and puree until smooth, then return it to the pot.) Stir in the chopped oysters and simmer until the oysters are just cooked through, 5–7 minutes. Add the lemon juice and chopped parsley. Taste and adjust the seasoning with additional salt, white pepper, or cayenne if desired.

6 Ladle the bisque into bowls and serve accompanied by oyster crackers or crusty bread. Pass hot sauce at the table if desired.

STORAGE: Store airtight in the refrigerator for up to 3 days.

PEANUT AND OYSTER SOUP

GF

Sarah Rutledge's publication *The Carolina Housewife* is the inspiration for this recipe, based on her groundnut and oyster soup. Over and over, we see in Southern soups a blend of native ingredients, Native American know-how, English cooking techniques, and West African flavor profiles. In particular Senegambians love groundnuts, mollusks, spices, and pepper!

PREPARATION TIME: 15 MINUTES
COOKING TIME: 30 MINUTES
SERVES: 4–6

- 2 tablespoons bacon fat or peanut oil
- 1 small onion, finely chopped
- 2 cloves garlic, minced
- ½ teaspoon minced fresh ginger
- ½ cup (75 g) unsalted roasted peanuts, finely ground
- 4 cups (32 fl oz/950 ml) chicken or vegetable stock
- 2 cups (16 fl oz/470 ml) canned coconut milk
- 2 dozen shucked oysters, with their liquor
- ¼ cup (65 g) creamy peanut butter
- 1 cup (8 fl oz/240 ml) half-and-half (single cream)
- ½ teaspoon House Seasoning (PAGE 301)
- ½ teaspoon Kitchen Pepper (PAGE 301)
- ¼ teaspoon cayenne pepper
- Chopped fresh flat-leaf parsley, for garnish
- Thinly sliced scallions (spring onions), for garnish

1 In a large pot, heat the bacon fat over medium heat. Add the onion and sauté until softened, about 5 minutes. Add the garlic and ginger and cook until fragrant, 2–3 minutes. Stir in the ground peanuts and toast slightly in the pan. Add the stock and simmer until the mixture is smooth, about 10 minutes.

2 Stir in the coconut milk, oyster liquor, peanut butter, and half-and-half (single cream) and bring to a boil. Add the oysters, reduce to a simmer, and cook until the oysters turn opaque, 3–4 minutes. Season with House Seasoning and Kitchen Pepper, being careful not to overseason. Remove the pot from heat and let mellow for 5–7 minutes.

3 Stir in the cayenne and serve hot, garnished with parsley and scallions (spring onions).

STORAGE: Store airtight in the refrigerator for up to 3 days.

SHE-CRAB SOUP

This elegant soup is beloved by Marylanders, Virginians, South Carolinians, and Georgians. It is particularly important to what the Slow Food movement calls the "Blue Crab Nation," the estuaries and tidal waters of the Southeastern Atlantic Coast. She-crabs or sooks, rich in roe, are complemented by cream, delicate spices, and quality sherry. (To acquire she-crab roe, buy from a Southern fish market in season or special order online.)

PREPARATION TIME: 15 MINUTES
COOKING TIME: 40 MINUTES
SERVES: 4

1 lb (450 g) fresh lump or claw crabmeat, from blue crabs
4 tablespoons (60 g) unsalted butter
1 small onion, minced
¼ cup (25 g) finely chopped celery
¼ cup (35 g) finely chopped carrots
2 cloves garlic, minced
¼ cup (35 g) all-purpose (plain) flour
4 cups (32 fl oz/950 ml) crab or chicken stock
1 cup (8 fl oz/240 ml) heavy (whipping) cream
1 cup (8 fl oz/240 ml) whole milk
½ teaspoon Kitchen Pepper (PAGE 301)
¼ teaspoon cayenne pepper
Kosher salt and finely ground white pepper
½ cup (4 fl oz/120 ml) dry sherry
½ cup (30 g) fresh she-crab roe
Finely chopped fresh flat-leaf parsley or chives, for garnish

1 Carefully pick through the crabmeat to ensure no bits of shell or cartilage remain. Set aside.
2 In a large heavy-bottomed pot, melt the butter over medium heat. Add the onion, celery, carrots, and garlic and sauté until softened, 5–7 minutes.
3 Sprinkle the flour over the vegetables, stirring to coat evenly. Cook for 2–3 minutes. Gradually whisk in the stock, ensuring no lumps form. Simmer until slightly thickened, 10–15 minutes.
4 Stir in the heavy (whipping) cream and milk. Allow the soup to simmer gently for an additional 5 minutes, stirring occasionally.
5 Add the Kitchen Pepper, cayenne, salt, and white pepper to taste. Stir in the dry sherry, reserved crabmeat, and roe. Adjust the seasoning to taste. Reduce the heat to low and for 5 minutes to heat through, taking care not to boil again once the crab is incorporated.
6 Ladle soup into bowls and garnish with parsley or chives. Serve hot.

STORAGE: Store airtight in the refrigerator for up to 3 days.

CONCH CHOWDER

DF GF

Whether it is real conch or whelk, when stewed into a hearty soup or chowder, conch has a specific regional heritage—from the Lowcountry to Florida to the Bahamas. Conch chowder is a Florida favorite and the pride of Key West, where different restaurants vie to present the best version of this local favorite. It is one of those dishes that is meant to bring people together, to feed a crowd.

PREPARATION TIME: 20 MINUTES
COOKING TIME: 2 HOURS
SERVES: 8

- 2 cans (15 oz/425 g each) conch, pounded to tenderize and chopped into small pieces (about 2 cups)
- 2 tablespoons vegetable shortening or bacon fat
- 2 cups (320 g) diced onion
- 2 cups (200 g) diced celery
- 1 cup (150 g) diced green bell pepper
- 1 cup (130 g) diced peeled carrot
- 1 clove garlic, minced
- 3 quarts (2.8 liters) seafood stock or water
- 4 medium white potatoes, peeled and cut into small cubes
- 1 can (10.75 oz/305 g) tomato puree (passata)
- 1 can (6 oz/170 g) tomato paste (tomato puree)
- 3 tablespoons minced fresh oregano
- 3 tablespoons minced fresh basil
- 2 bay leaves
- Fine salt and freshly ground black pepper
- Hot sauce (optional), for serving

1 In a large soup pot, bring the conch and 8 cups (1.9 liters) water to a boil over high heat. Cook until the conch is slightly tender, about 15 minutes. Drain and set the conch and the soup pot aside.

2 In a large cast-iron skillet, melt the shortening over medium heat. Stir in the onion, celery, bell pepper, carrot, and garlic and sauté until softened, about 8 minutes.

3 Transfer the cooked vegetables to the soup pot. Add the drained conch, seafood stock, potatoes, tomato puree (passata), tomato paste (tomato puree), oregano, basil, and bay leaves and stir to combine. Bring to a boil over medium-high heat. Reduce the heat, cover, and simmer until the conch is tender and the potatoes are fork-tender, about 1 ½ hours.

4 Discard the bay leaves before serving. Add salt and black pepper to taste and serve with hot sauce if desired.

STORAGE: Store airtight in the refrigerator for up to 4 days.

CRAB, SHRIMP, AND OKRA GUMBO

DF

The classic shellfish and okra gumbo of New Orleans and Mobile, Alabama, reminds us how many global paths it took to get us to this dish—not only through France and Spain, but also Senegal, Dahomey (modern-day Benin), and Angola, and via stews thickened and seasoned by dried sassafras leaves by the indigenous Choctaw and Chitimacha. According to court documents transcribed by one of early Louisiana's greatest historians, Dr. Gwendolyn Midlo Hall, gumbo is mentioned as early as 1764, when two women of Mandinka origin—Comba and Louison—made it available for sale. By the time of the Louisiana Purchase, references to gumbo trickle into the American consciousness, with gumbo feasts becoming political events. The term *gumbo* has come to mean a cultural mix, an inclusive stew, or a blending with many colors, flavors, and ingredients. Gumbo is the South.

PREPARATION TIME: 30 MINUTES
COOKING TIME: 1 HOUR 30 MINUTES
SERVES: 8

- ½ cup (4 fl oz/120 ml) vegetable oil
- ½ cup (65 g) all-purpose (plain) flour
- 1 large yellow onion, finely chopped
- 1 medium green bell pepper, finely chopped
- 2 celery stalks, finely chopped
- 4 cloves garlic, minced
- 6 cups (48 fl oz/1.4 liters) seafood stock
- 1 can (14.5 oz/411 g) diced (chopped) tomatoes
- 2 bay leaves
- 1 teaspoon dried thyme
- 2 teaspoons Creole Seasoning (PAGE 299)
- ½ teaspoon cayenne pepper (optional)
- Fine salt and freshly ground black pepper
- 1 lb (450 g) fresh okra, sliced
- 1 lb (450 g) fresh crabmeat
- 1 lb (450 g) large shrimp (prawns), peeled and deveined
- ¼ cup (15 g) chopped fresh flat-leaf parsley
- 4 scallions (spring onions), thinly sliced
- Cooked white rice, for serving

1 In a large heavy-bottomed pot or Dutch oven (casserole dish), heat the oil over medium-high heat. Gradually whisk in the flour. Cook, stirring constantly, until the roux is dark brown in color, 20–25 minutes (see Brown Roux, PAGE 282).

2 Add the onion, bell pepper, and celery to the roux. Sauté until the vegetables are tender and the onion translucent, about 10 minutes.

3 Add the garlic and cook for 2 minutes. Gradually whisk in the seafood stock, making sure there are no lumps. Add the diced tomatoes, bay leaves, thyme, Creole Seasoning, cayenne (if using), and salt and black pepper to taste. Bring the mixture to a boil, then reduce the heat and let it simmer for 30 minutes.

4 In a medium Dutch oven (casserole dish), sauté the okra over medium-high heat until it is tender, about 10 minutes. (This step reduces the okra's natural mucilage, preventing a slimy texture in the finished gumbo.)

5 Add the cooked okra, crabmeat, and shrimp (prawns) and cook until the shrimp are pink and opaque, 5–7 minutes.

6 Taste and adjust the seasoning with salt and black pepper as needed. Garnish with parsley and scallions (spring onions) and serve over rice.

STORAGE: Store airtight in the refrigerator for up to 4 days.

CATFISH STEW

DF

Catfish are easily the South's favorite fish. They were the most widespread freshwater fish, and there were saltwater varieties in the Lowcountry and Tidewater. Native Southerners across the region prized them, as did West Africans, and European Southerners would come to appreciate them, especially the white and blue varieties. The first Southern cookbook, Mary Randolph's *The Virginia House-Wife*, has a stew of curried catfish—one assumes those heavy spices were meant to mask the slightly earthy flavor of wild catfish.

PREPARATION TIME: 5 MINUTES
COOKING TIME: 1 HOUR 10 MINUTES
SERVES: 6

4 slices thick-cut bacon (streaky), chopped
1 medium onion, chopped
½ cup (75 g) chopped green bell pepper
1 can (28 oz/794 g) diced (chopped) tomatoes
2 cups (400 g) diced peeled white potatoes
4 tablespoons tomato paste (tomato puree)
2 tablespoons Worcestershire sauce
1 teaspoon hot sauce
1 teaspoon apple cider vinegar
1 teaspoon House Seasoning (PAGE 301)
1 teaspoon kosher salt
½ teaspoon freshly ground black pepper
½ teaspoon Kitchen Pepper (PAGE 301)
½ teaspoon dried thyme
1 lb (450 g) catfish fillet, cut into ½-inch (13 mm) pieces

1 In a large heavy-bottomed saucepan, fry the bacon (streaky) over medium-high heat until the fat is rendered, about 3 minutes.

2 Add the onion and bell pepper and cook until softened, about 5 minutes. Reduce the heat and add the diced tomatoes, potatoes, tomato paste (puree), 1 cup (8 fl oz/240 ml) water, Worcestershire sauce, hot sauce, vinegar, House Seasoning, salt, black pepper, Kitchen Pepper, and thyme. Cover the pot and simmer for 30–40 minutes to blend the flavors.

3 Add the fish, cover again, and cook until the fish is opaque and the tomatoes have broken down, about 20 minutes. Taste and adjust the seasoning as preferred.

STORAGE: Store airtight in the refrigerator up to 3 days.

MARYLAND CRAB SOUP

Maryland, and in particular the Chesapeake Bay region, has its own delicious okra and crab stew. Although the recipe calls for cayenne pepper, the Maryland fish pepper was often the heirloom chile of choice for Chesapeake seafood cookery. Whatever chile you use, this is one of the best ways to make use of blue crabs at the height of their summer season.

PREPARATION TIME: 30 MINUTES
COOKING TIME: 40 MINUTES
SERVES: 4–6

2 tablespoons (30 g) unsalted butter
1 large yellow onion, finely chopped
2 cloves garlic, minced
2 tablespoons all-purpose (plain) flour
4 cups (32 fl oz/950 ml) chicken or crab stock
1 lb (450 g) fresh okra, sliced into rounds
1 lb (450 g) fresh crabmeat (from blue crabs), picked through for shells
1 can (14.5 oz/411 g) diced (chopped) tomatoes, drained
1 teaspoon seafood seasoning, such as Old Bay
1 teaspoon paprika
⅛ teaspoon finely ground cayenne pepper
Fine salt and freshly ground black pepper
2 scallions (spring onions), thinly sliced, for garnish
Cooked white rice, for serving

1 In a large Dutch oven (casserole dish), melt the butter over medium heat. Add the onion and garlic and sauté until translucent and fragrant, 3–4 minutes.

2 Sprinkle the flour over the onion/garlic mixture. Stir constantly to cook the raw flour without letting it brown too much, 1–2 minutes. Gradually pour in the stock, stirring constantly with a whisk to avoid lumps. Add the sliced okra and cook until tender, about 10 minutes. Stir in the crabmeat, diced tomatoes, seafood seasoning, paprika, cayenne, and salt and black pepper to taste. Bring to a simmer and cook until the flavors have melded and the crab is firm and opaque, 15–20 minutes.

3 Serve hot with rice, and garnish with the scallions (spring onions).

STORAGE: Store airtight in the refrigerator for up to 3 days.

KENTUCKY BURGOO

DF

Burgoo is Kentucky's version of a hunter's stew, much like Brunswick Stew (PAGE 159). Here pork, lamb, and chicken take the place of wild game like venison and squirrel. Serve piping hot with warm buttered cornbread.

PREPARATION TIME: 20 MINUTES
COOKING TIME: 2 ½ HOURS
SERVES: 12

- 3 tablespoons vegetable oil
- 3 lb (1.4 kg) boneless pork shoulder, cut into large pieces
- 3 lb (1.4 kg) lamb stew meat, cut into large pieces
- 3 bone-in, skinless chicken thighs, cut into large pieces
- 1 medium green bell pepper, finely chopped
- 1 large onion, finely chopped
- 2 celery stalks, chopped
- 2 cloves garlic, minced
- 4 cups (32 fl oz/950 ml) chicken stock
- 4 cups (32 fl oz/950 ml) beef stock
- 6 tablespoons Worcestershire sauce
- 1 can (28 oz/794 g) crushed (finely chopped) tomatoes
- 2 large potatoes, peeled and cut into ½-inch (13 mm) chunks
- 2 ¾ cups (16 oz/450 g) corn kernels, fresh or frozen
- 1 can (15 oz/425 g) lima beans (butter beans), drained and rinsed
- 2 bay leaves
- 1 teaspoon paprika
- Fine salt and freshly ground black pepper

1 In a large Dutch oven (casserole dish), heat the oil over medium-high heat.

2 Working in batches to avoid over-crowding, brown the pork, lamb, and chicken until golden brown on all sides, about 10 minutes. Remove the browned meat to a plate and set aside.

3 Reduce the heat to medium, add the bell pepper, onion, celery, and garlic and sauté, stirring occasionally, until softened and fragrant, 5–7 minutes.

4 Return the meat to the pot and pour in the chicken stock, beef stock, and Worcestershire sauce. Stir well to combine. Add the crushed tomatoes, potatoes, corn, lima beans (butter beans), bay leaves, paprika, and salt and black pepper to taste. Stir to combine and bring to a rolling boil. Reduce the heat to low and simmer for at least 2 hours to develop and meld the flavors.

5 Taste and adjust seasonings as needed before serving.

STORAGE: Store airtight in the refrigerator for up to 4 days.

VARIATION: Add 2 cups (230 g) sliced okra for the last 30 minutes of cooking.

GUMBO Z'HERBES

DF V VE

Gumbo z'herbes is a Lenten, and therefore meatless, gumbo. Made with nine types of greens, it can include radish leaves or cress or carrot tops. In this version, the greens are readily available ones.

PREPARATION TIME: 30 MINUTES
COOKING TIME: 1 HOUR 30 MINUTES
SERVES: 6–8

½ cup (4 fl oz/120 ml) vegetable oil
½ cup (65 g) all-purpose (plain) flour
1 cup (160 g) chopped onion
1 cup (100 g) chopped celery
1 cup (150 g) chopped green bell peppers
4 cloves garlic, minced
8 cups (1.9 liters) vegetable or chicken stock
1 bay leaf
2 teaspoons Creole Seasoning (PAGE 299)
½ teaspoon cayenne pepper
1 cup (60 g) chopped beet leaves
1 cup (95 g) shredded cabbage
1 cup (60 g) chopped collard greens
1 cup (100 g) chopped scallions (spring onions)
1 cup (60 g) chopped kale
1 cup (60 g) chopped mustard greens
1 cup (60 g) chopped fresh flat-leaf parsley
1 cup (35 g) chopped spinach
1 cup (35 g) chopped Swiss chard leaves
1 cup (60 g) chopped turnip greens
Fine salt and freshly ground black pepper
Hot sauce (optional), for serving
Cooked white rice, for serving

1 In a large pot, heat the oil over medium heat. Gradually whisk in the flour to make a roux, stirring constantly until it reaches a medium brown color, 15–20 minutes (see Brown Roux, PAGE 282).
2 Add the onion, celery, bell peppers, and garlic to the roux. Stir frequently, until the vegetables are soft, 5–7 minutes.
3 Gradually pour in the stock, stirring constantly to incorporate it into the roux. Add the bay leaf, Creole Seasoning, and cayenne. Bring the mixture to a boil, then reduce the heat and simmer uncovered, stirring occasionally, for 30 minutes to deepen the flavors.
4 Add the beet leaves, cabbage, collard greens, scallions (spring onions), kale, mustard greens, parsley, spinach, Swiss chard, and turnip greens to the pot. Stir well to combine and season with salt and black pepper. Simmer the gumbo uncovered until everything is tender and the flavors have come together, another 30–40 minutes. Taste and adjust the seasoning as needed.
5 Spoon over rice in individual bowls.

STORAGE: Store airtight in the refrigerator for up to 4 days.

DUCK AND SAUSAGE GUMBO

DF

The important thing about gumbo is that it's not just one soup. Rather, it's a category of Creole and Cajun soups that changes according to the roots of the people. The historic populations of Louisiana were of Native American, West and Central African, French and French Canadian, Spanish, German, Filipino, and British origins, each adding to the cultural stew. Gumbos also change seasonally, depending on what's available in nature, or according to religious observances and community connections. A gumbo recipe can be based on the season of the year, what is available from the market, the garden, or the wild, and takes into account life-cycle events or the religious calendar you follow.

PREPARATION TIME: 30 MINUTES
COOKING TIME: 2 HOURS
SERVES: 8–10

1 cup (8 fl oz/240 ml) vegetable oil
1 cup (130 g) all-purpose (plain) flour
1 large duck (4–5 lb/1.8–2.3 kg), cut into breasts, thighs, legs, and wings
Fine salt and freshly ground black pepper
1 large onion, finely chopped
1 medium green bell pepper, finely chopped
2 celery stalks, finely chopped
4 cloves garlic, minced
1 lb (450 g) andouille sausage, sliced into rounds ½-inch (13 mm) thick
8 cups (1.9 liters) chicken stock
1 can (14.5 oz/411 g) diced (chopped) tomatoes
2 bay leaves
1 teaspoon dried oregano
1 teaspoon sweet paprika
1 teaspoon dried thyme
½ teaspoon cayenne pepper
4 scallions (spring onions), sliced, plus more for garnish
¼ cup (20 g) chopped fresh flat-leaf parsley, plus more for garnish
Cooked white rice, for serving

1 In a large heavy-bottomed pot or Dutch oven (casserole dish), heat the oil over medium heat. Gradually whisk in the flour, stirring constantly to avoid lumps. Cook the roux, stirring constantly to ensure it does not burn, until it turns a dark brown color, similar to chocolate, 20–30 minutes (see Brown Roux, PAGE 282).

2 Meanwhile, season the duck pieces with salt and black pepper. In a large cast-iron skillet, brown the duck pieces skin-side down over medium-high heat until the skin is crispy and golden, about 8 minutes. Remove from the pan and set aside.

3 Once the roux reaches the desired color, add the onion, bell pepper, and celery and sauté, stirring constantly, in the roux until they are softened, 5–7 minutes.

4 Add the garlic and cook for 2 minutes. Add the browned duck pieces and andouille sausage to the pot. Stir in the chicken stock, diced tomatoes, bay leaves, oregano, paprika, thyme, and cayenne and bring the mixture to a boil. Reduce the heat to low and simmer, uncovered, until the duck is tender and the flavors are well developed, 1 ½–2 hours. Skim off any excess fat that rises to the surface during cooking.

5 Taste the gumbo and adjust the seasoning with salt and black pepper as needed. Stir in the sliced scallions (spring onions) and parsley just before serving.

6 Ladle the gumbo over rice in bowls, and garnish with additional scallions and parsley, if desired.

STORAGE: Store airtight in the refrigerator for up to 4 days.

OKRA SOUP

GF V

This okra soup is a signature dish of the Tidewater South, ranging from Maryland to Georgia. Okra, which came from West Africa via the Afro-Caribbean world, unites the South with the rest of the African Atlantic. It is without a roux, and although it can be made with proteins (see the VARIATION), it works perfectly as a meatless dish.

PREPARATION TIME: 20 MINUTES
COOKING TIME: 55–60 MINUTES
SERVES: 6

- 2 tablespoons vegetable oil or bacon fat
- 1 large onion, chopped
- 1 medium green bell pepper, chopped
- 3 cloves garlic, minced
- 2 cups (330 g) corn kernels, fresh or frozen
- 1 cup (180 g) diced red heirloom tomatoes
- 1 can (28 oz/794 g) diced (chopped) tomatoes
- 4 cups (32 fl oz/950 ml) vegetable or chicken stock
- Fine salt and freshly ground black pepper
- 2 tablespoons (30 g) unsalted butter
- 2 ½ cups (290 g) thinly sliced okra
- ½ teaspoon cayenne pepper
- Cooked white rice, for serving

1 In a large Dutch oven (casserole dish) or heavy-bottomed soup pot, heat the oil over medium-high heat. Add the onion, bell pepper, and garlic and sauté, stirring occasionally, until translucent, about 5 minutes.

2 Add the corn, fresh tomatoes, canned tomatoes, stock, and salt and black pepper to taste. Reduce the heat to low, cover, and simmer for 30–35 minutes, until the flavors are well combined.

3 Meanwhile, in a medium saucepan, melt the butter over medium heat. Add the okra, cayenne, and salt and black pepper to taste. Sauté, stirring often, until soft, about 5 minutes. Remove from the heat and set aside.

4 Once the broth has finished cooking, add the okra, taste, and add additional seasoning as preferred. Cover and cook over medium heat until the okra is soft and imbued with the broth, 10–15 minutes.

5 Enjoy with a spoonful of rice in each bowl.

STORAGE: Store airtight in the refrigerator for up to 4 days.

VARIATION: About 1 cup (235 g) diced raw beef or chicken makes a great addition. Add to the broth before adding the okra.

OKRA GUMBO

DF

The word *gumbo* is not an African word and neither is *okra*. The English word okra is from the cluster of Igbo dialects from present-day Southeastern Nigeria—*okwuru* and *okro,* for example *Ki-ngumbo* is from Angola and refers to the same ancient vegetable domesticated in Africa long ago.

In Louisiana, gumbo is a marriage of a classic French roux-based soup with the okra stews of West and Central Africa, and is a clear example of how these cultures melded across communities. Some people—though definitely not native Louisianans—use both filé gumbo (which is dried powdered sassafras leaves from the Choctaw culture) and okra in the same recipe, even though those are two very different seasonal varieties of gumbo.

PREPARATION TIME: 20 MINUTES
COOKING TIME: 1 HOUR 50 MINUTES
SERVES: 6

- 1 teaspoon extra-virgin olive oil
- 1 lb (450 g) boneless, skinless chicken thighs, chopped
- 12 oz (340 g) andouille sausage, cut into ¼-inch (6 mm) slices
- ½ cup (4 fl oz/120 ml) vegetable oil
- ½ cup (65 g) all-purpose (plain) flour
- 1 medium green bell pepper, chopped
- 1 medium onion, chopped
- 1 celery stalk, chopped
- 3–4 cloves garlic, to taste, minced
- 2 tablespoons Creole Seasoning (PAGE 299)
- 6 cups (48 fl oz/1.4 liters) chicken stock
- 3 large bay leaves
- 12 oz (340 g) fresh okra, cut into ¼-inch (6 mm) slices
- ¼ cup (15 g) chopped fresh flat-leaf parsley
- Fine salt and freshly ground black pepper
- Cooked white rice, for serving

1 In a large frying pan, heat the olive oil over medium-high heat. Add the chicken and sausage and cook until browned on both sides, about 10 minutes. Remove the meat to a plate and set aside.

2 In a large heavy-bottomed soup pot, heat the vegetable oil over medium heat. Add the flour and cook, stirring constantly, to make a dark brown roux, 20–30 minutes (see Brown Roux, PAGE 282).

3 Add the bell pepper, onion, celery, and garlic and stir until well combined. Cover and cook until the vegetables are softened, about 5 minutes.

4 Add the browned chicken and sausage and cook for 1 minute. Add the Creole Seasoning, chicken stock, and bay leaves, scraping the browned bits from the bottom of the pan. Reduce the heat, cover, and cook until the vegetables and meat are tender and the sauce is rich and full-bodied, at least 1 hour.

5 Stir in the okra and parsley and cook until the okra is tender, 15–20 minutes.

6 Season with salt and black pepper to taste, then serve over rice.

STORAGE: Store airtight in the refrigerator for up to 4 days.

MACARONI PIE

V

Macaroni pie is not saucy or soupy macaroni and cheese with bread crumbs on top; it is custardy and has semi-solid body to it. It was a dish with definitive plantation kitchen origins, with some attributing its popularity to James Hemings, a Paris- trained gourmet chef who labored for some time in the original kitchen at Monticello—Thomas Jefferson's main estate in Virginia—where he was enslaved.

PREPARATION TIME: 15 MINUTES
COOKING TIME: 1 HOUR 15 MINUTES
SERVES: 8

Softened butter, for the pie dish
Kosher salt
1 ½ cups (127 g) penne pasta
4 tablespoons (60 g) unsalted butter
4 tablespoons all-purpose (plain) flour
2 cups (16 fl oz/470 ml) half-and-half (single cream)
1 cup (115 g) shredded extra sharp Cheddar cheese
½ cup (45 g) grated Parmesan cheese
1 teaspoon garlic powder
1 teaspoon onion powder
½ teaspoon House Seasoning (PAGE 301)
½ teaspoon freshly ground black pepper or Kitchen Pepper (PAGE 301)
½ teaspoon sugar
⅛ teaspoon cayenne pepper (optional)
4 eggs

1 Preheat the oven to 350°F (180°C/Gas Mark 4). Grease a 9-inch (23 cm) pie dish with butter and set aside.
2 In a large pot of salted boiling water, cook the pasta until just tender according to the package directions. Drain well and transfer to a large bowl.
3 In a saucepan, melt the butter over medium heat. Whisk in the flour to form a smooth roux. Cook, stirring constantly, until the roux begins to turn golden, 1–2 minutes. Gradually pour in the half-and-half (single cream), whisking constantly to prevent lumps. Cook the mixture, stirring frequently, until it thickens and comes to a gentle boil, 5–7 minutes.
4 Reduce the heat to low. Add the Cheddar and Parmesan to the saucepan, stirring until the cheese is melted and the sauce is smooth. Season with the garlic powder, onion powder, House Seasoning, black pepper, sugar, and cayenne (if using). Pour the cheese sauce over the cooked pasta in the bowl, stirring gently to coat the pasta evenly.
5 In a small bowl, beat the eggs. Gradually stir the beaten eggs into the macaroni mixture until well combined. Transfer the macaroni mixture to the greased pie dish, spreading it out evenly.
6 Bake until the top is golden brown and the center is set, 40–45 minutes.
7 Let the pie cool for about 10 minutes before slicing and serving.

STORAGE: Store airtight in the refrigerator for up to 4 days.

CORNBREAD DRESSING

In the South we have dressing, not stuffing. Usually that dressing is made from stale bread and cornbread. Sometimes it contains giblets, ham, sausage, mushrooms, oysters—usually parcooked and thrown in for good measure. I add carrots to my cornbread dressing and others add bits of kale or turnip greens. This is a basic recipe, meant to serve as a background for a classic Southern holiday favorite like roast turkey, ham, or chicken.

PREPARATION TIME: 20 MINUTES
COOKING TIME: 1 HOUR
SERVES: 8

- Softened butter or oil, for the baking pan
- One 8-inch (20 cm) square pan yellow cornbread
- 8 slices day-old white bread or toasted bread
- 8 tablespoons (4 oz/115 g) unsalted butter or ½ cup (4 fl oz/120 ml) vegetable oil
- 1 large onion, finely chopped
- 2 celery stalks, finely chopped
- 4 cups (32 fl oz/950 ml) chicken stock
- 2 eggs, beaten
- 2 teaspoons Poultry Seasoning (PAGE 299)
- 1 teaspoon dried sage
- 1 teaspoon fine salt or House Seasoning (PAGE 301)
- ½ teaspoon freshly ground black pepper or Kitchen Pepper (PAGE 301)

1 Preheat the oven to 350°F (180°C/Gas Mark 4). Grease a 9 × 13-inch (23 × 33 cm) baking pan with butter or oil.

2 Crumble the cornbread and white bread into a large bowl, ensuring they are broken into small, even pieces.

3 In a frying pan, melt the butter over medium heat. Add the onion and celery and sauté, stirring occasionally, until they are tender and translucent, about 10 minutes.

4 Add the vegetables to the bowl with the crumbled bread. Slowly pour in the chicken stock, mixing gently until the bread mixture is moistened but not too wet. The consistency should be soft but still hold together in clumps.

5 In a separate bowl, beat the eggs, then mix them into the bread mixture. Add the Poultry Seasoning, sage, salt, and black pepper, and stir everything together until well combined. Transfer the dressing to the prepared baking dish, spreading it out evenly.

6 Bake until the top is golden brown and crispy, 45–50 minutes. If you prefer a moist dressing, cover it with foil during the first half of baking.

7 Let the cornbread dressing cool slightly before serving.

STORAGE: Store airtight in the refrigerator for up to 3 days.

VARIATION: Sauté 1 cup (138 g) loose sage sausage or hot sausage meat, rendering the grease. Remove the sausage and set aside to add to the dressing. Leaving the sausage grease in the pan, melt the butter to sauté the onion and celery and proceed with the recipe.

VARIATION: Add 1 cup (275 g) small cubed raw vegetables—carrots, bell pepper, mushrooms, etc.—to the eggs before combining them with the bread mixture.

VARIATION: Chopped cooked meat or crab is an easy add, but use no more than 1 cup (230 g for chopped meat and 130 g for crabmeat). Stir it in when you mix all the ingredients together to bake.

VARIATION: Add one or two 8 oz (225 g) cans of oysters, including the oyster liquid, when you mix up the batter, and bake as directed.

SOUTHERN FRIED RICE

DF

Southern-style fried rice is the result of generations of cooks using leftovers to make a fun, hearty meal. You can use bits of country ham, black-eyed peas (black-eye beans), or bell pepper—even throw in half a cup of okra if you like. There are no rules, and it's up to the cook to decide what to include. This pairs well with dishes like the Chinese Mississippi Collard Greens (PAGE 110) or the Fried Pork Chops (PAGE 219).

PREPARATION TIME: 15 MINUTES
COOKING TIME: 20 MINUTES
SERVES: 6

- 2 tablespoons vegetable oil or bacon fat
- 1 medium onion, finely chopped
- 2 celery stalks, finely diced
- 1 medium green bell pepper, diced
- 2 cloves garlic, minced
- 2 eggs, lightly beaten
- 1 cup (140 g) diced cooked chicken
- 1 cup (165 g) diced cooked ham
- ½ cup (80 g) cooked black-eyed peas (black-eye beans)
- 2 cups (320 g) cooked long-grain white rice, chilled
- 1 tablespoon soy sauce
- ½ teaspoon House Seasoning (PAGE 301)
- ¼ teaspoon freshly ground black pepper
- ¼ teaspoon paprika
- ¼ teaspoon cayenne pepper
- 2 scallions (spring onions), thinly sliced

1 In a large frying pan or wok, heat the oil over medium-high heat. Add the onion, celery, bell pepper, and garlic and stir-fry until the vegetables are tender, 3–4 minutes.

2 Push the vegetables to one side of the pan. Pour the beaten eggs into the other side and scramble until cooked through. Add the diced chicken, ham, and black-eyed peas (black-eye beans) and stir to combine with the vegetables and eggs. Add the chilled rice, breaking up any clumps. Cook, stirring frequently, until the rice is heated through and starting to brown slightly, 5–6 minutes.

3 In a small bowl, mix together the soy sauce, House Seasoning, black pepper, paprika, and cayenne. Pour the sauce over the rice mixture and stir to combine, ensuring everything is evenly coated. Continue to cook, stirring occasionally, until the rice is well heated and the flavors have blended, 2–3 minutes. Add the scallions (spring onions) and stir in until the rice is flavored with their aroma, 4–5 minutes.

4 Serve warm.

KUSH

During the Antebellum period, there were two dishes known as kush. On the eastern seaboard of the South, kush was a cornbread hash, the forerunner to Southern cornbread dressing. This style of kush spread across the region with the domestic trade through enslaved people. Meanwhile, in Louisiana, the Acadians used the term "coush-coush" to describe their Senegambian-influenced morning corn porridge. This dish demonstrates a clear link between ancestral African knowledge and the American South.

PREPARATION TIME: 10 MINUTES
COOKING TIME: 30 MINUTES
SERVES: 4–6

- 4 tablespoons (60 g) lard, shortening, or bacon fat
- 2 white or yellow onions, roughly chopped
- 1 teaspoon kosher salt or ½ teaspoon fine salt
- 1 teaspoon chile flakes
- 1 teaspoon rubbed sage
- ½ teaspoon dried thyme
- ½ teaspoon dried rosemary
- 4 tablespoons chopped country ham or smoked turkey (optional)
- One 9-inch (23 cm) pan day-old cornbread, crumbled
- ½ cup (4 fl oz/120 ml) ham stock or Pot Likker (PAGE 266)

1 In a large cast-iron skillet or Dutch oven (casserole dish), melt 2 tablespoons of the lard over medium-high heat. Once melted, add the onions and sauté until they are translucent, 5–7 minutes. Add half of salt, chile flakes, and dried herbs.

2 As the onions begin to turn clear, add the ham (if using) and add the remaining 2 tablespoons lard to the pan. Slowly stir the crumbled cornbread into the skillet until all of it is completely incorporated. Add the remaining salt, chile flakes, and dried herbs. Add the ham stock, then turn the heat to low and cook, stirring frequently, until the stock has been fully absorbed. (Do not allow the kush to burn.)

3 Serve warm.

BRUNSWICK STEW

Brunswick stew is a hunter's stew that originally featured squirrel. Whether it can still be called Brunswick stew if it's not made with squirrel—and whether it is still primarily made with squirrel—is only the beginning of the arguments that swirl around this dish. Was "Uncle Jimmy Mathews," the innovator of the dish, Black or white? (The term "Uncle" was usually reserved for an elderly Black man.) Which town of Brunswick—Virginia, North Carolina, or Georgia? Stale bread or crackers or none? Okra? It all depends on preference and taste—and thus the debates will never end.

PREPARATION TIME: 10 MINUTES
COOKING TIME: 1 HOUR 30 MINUTES
SERVES: 6

4 tablespoons (60 g) unsalted butter
1 large yellow onion, chopped
3 cloves garlic, minced
2 cans (14.5 oz/411 g each) diced (chopped) tomatoes
4 cups (32 fl oz/950 ml) chicken stock
4 cups (680 g) shredded cooked chicken
3 medium potatoes, diced
3 cups (495 g) corn kernels, fresh or frozen
2 cups (500 g) canned lima beans (butter beans)
2 tablespoon barbecue sauce, chili sauce (such as Heinz), or ketchup
2 tablespoons Worcestershire sauce
1 tablespoon sugar
½ teaspoon cayenne pepper
Fine salt and freshly ground black pepper

1 In a Dutch oven (casserole dish), melt the butter over medium-high heat. Add the onion and sauté until softened, about 5 minutes.

2 Stir in the garlic, diced tomatoes, stock, chicken, potatoes, corn, lima beans (butter beans), barbecue sauce, Worcestershire sauce, sugar, cayenne, and salt and black pepper to taste. Bring to a rolling boil. Reduce the heat to medium-low and simmer, stirring occasionally, until the beans and potatoes are tender, about 1 ½ hours.

3 Taste and season with your preferred seasonings and serve hot.

STORAGE: Store airtight in the refrigerator for up to 4 days.

FISH & SHELLFISH

TO FISH AND TO TRAP

Fishing as a sport and for food has been a cornerstone of the American South for thousands of years. In a region where the professional angler is celebrated, there are large commercial freshwater fisheries that supply catfish and other species, ingredients central to its cuisine. The Southern Ancestors gorged themselves across the yearly cycle of seasonal fisheries. Blessed with the Chesapeake Bay and Eastern shore, the Outer Banks and Pamlico Sound, the Lowcountry inlets, the Gulf Coast, the Mississippi River, plus dams and mill ponds and hundreds of tributaries, the South is known for the harvest its waters hold.

Fish were harvested by the thousands from the anadromous (saltwater living, freshwater breeding) species such as rockfish, herring, and shad to prize catches like catfish (of which the massive blue catfish is king), mullet, croaker, drum, bream (sunfish), trout, and bass. The earliest Southerners roasted their fish on green sapling grills and on coals and let them bubble away in pots with corn, fruit, and venison until falling apart. Europeans fried their fish in butter, Africans fried theirs in palm oil, but both traditions came together and solidified in the South, as did fish fries and shellfish barbecues between Native and African cultures.

The South also has a rich culture of trapping crab, crawfish, shrimp (prawns), snapping turtles, and at one time—almost to the point of extermination—the Diamondback terrapin (considered the catch of the elite). Gullah-Geechee perfected hand-cast netting, while other communities mastered dredging for oysters and noodling (catching fish or turtles in muddy water with bare hands). Southerners also innovated with oyster roasts, fish fries, and boils where shellfish like crab and crawfish were cooked with spices, corn, and potatoes. In addition, the shrimping culture of Vietnamese immigrants has shaped an industry and pioneered an irresistible Viet-Cajun style that has spread across the Gulf Coast. Southern social culture reveres time spent around spreads of newspaper strewn across picnic tables where the mastered rituals of shucking oysters or breaking down blue crabs or sucking the fat from crawfish heads has enabled family connections across centuries and helped build up Southern small-town life.

FRIED FISH

-30

Fish fries and Friday fish dinners are a deep part of Southern life, especially the Black Southern experience. Although most recipes require that the fish fillets be dredged in seasoned flour, it is preferable to season the protein and not the batter for a fried dish. Using this method, the oil stays cleaner, the unseasoned coating has less of a burned taste, and the seasoned pop comes with the first bite.

PREPARATION TIME: 15 MINUTES
COOKING TIME: 15-20 MINUTES
SERVES: 4

- 4 catfish fillets (3–5 oz/85–140 g each)
- 1 teaspoon House Seasoning (PAGE 301) or fine salt
- 1 teaspoon freshly ground coarse black pepper, plus more to taste
- ½ teaspoon garlic powder
- ½ teaspoon paprika
- ¼ teaspoon cayenne pepper (optional, for heat)
- 1 cup (130 g) white or yellow cornmeal
- ½ cup (65 g) all-purpose (plain) flour
- 1 cup (8 fl oz/240 ml) buttermilk
- Vegetable oil, for frying
- Kosher or sea salt
- Lemon wedges, for serving
- Pepper Vinegar (PAGE 288) or hot sauce, for serving

1 Rinse the fish fillets under cold water and pat dry with paper towels. Cut into half if desired. Season the fish with the House Seasoning, black pepper, garlic powder, paprika, and cayenne (if using).

2 Set up a dredging station in two shallow bowls: In one bowl, mix together the cornmeal and flour. Pour the buttermilk into the second bowl. Dip each piece of fish into the buttermilk, allowing any excess to drip off. Then coat each piece well in the flour/cornmeal, pressing gently to adhere the coating.

3 Pour about 1 inch (2.5 cm) oil into a large Dutch oven (casserole dish) and heat over medium-high heat to 350°F (177°C). Line a plate with paper towels and have near the stove.

4 Working in batches to avoid overcrowding, carefully place the coated fish fillets into the hot oil. Carefully place into the hot oil and fry, turning once, until medium golden-brown and crispy, 3–4 minutes per side. Adjust the heat as needed to maintain the oil temperature. Use tongs or a slotted spoon to remove the fish pieces to the paper towels to drain. Sprinkle the outside with a little salt and coarse black pepper.

5 Serve the fried fish hot, with lemon wedges and your choice of hot sauce or Pepper Vinegar.

FROG LEGS

"As any Creole or Acadian will tell you, Louisiana frogs' legs are better than even France knows about," wrote Peter S. Feibleman, author of Time-Life's classic cookbook *American Cooking: Creole and Acadian*, a signature volume on south Louisiana foodways. Crawfish are for the masses, but the taste for frog legs, born in France but enhanced by the bayou, marks a true Louisianan. Serve the frog legs hot, garnished with lemon wedges and fresh parsley if desired. They pair well with coleslaw, cornbread, and a tangy dipping sauce.

PREPARATION TIME: 15 MINUTES, PLUS AT LEAST 2 HOURS MARINATING TIME
COOKING TIME: 15 MINUTES
SERVES: 4

2 cups (16 fl oz/470 ml) buttermilk
2 tablespoons hot sauce
1 tablespoon sweet paprika
1 teaspoon garlic powder
1 teaspoon onion powder
½ teaspoon cayenne pepper
12 pairs frog legs, cleaned and trimmed
1 cup (130 g) all-purpose (plain) flour
1 cup (130 g) white or yellow cornmeal
1 teaspoon fine salt
½ teaspoon freshly ground coarse black pepper
Vegetable oil, for frying
Lemon wedges, for squeezing
Chopped fresh flat-leaf parsley, for garnish

1 In a large bowl, combine the buttermilk, hot sauce, paprika, garlic powder, onion powder, and cayenne. Submerge the frog legs in the mixture, ensuring they are fully coated. Cover and refrigerate for at least 2 hours, preferably overnight, to tenderize and flavor the meat.

2 In a shallow dish, mix together the flour, cornmeal, salt, and black pepper. Remove the frog legs from the buttermilk marinade, allowing excess to drip off. Dredge each leg in the flour and cornmeal mixture, pressing gently to ensure an even coating.

3 Pour 1 inch (2.5 cm) oil into a large Dutch oven (casserole dish) and heat over medium-high heat to 350°F (177°C). You can test the temperature by dropping a small bit of the flour mixture into the oil; it should sizzle and float to the top. Line a plate with paper towels and have near the stove.

4 Working in batches to avoid overcrowding, carefully place the coated frog legs in the hot oil. Fry until golden brown and cooked through, 3–4 minutes per side. The meat should be tender and the coating crispy. Use a slotted spoon to transfer the frog legs to the paper towels to drain.

5 Serve the frog legs hot, garnished with lemon wedges and parsley if desired.

SALMON CROQUETTES

DF

Salmon croquettes made from canned salmon are an endearing dish for many Southern and soul food palates. Here is a fresher version that still satisfies nostalgic cravings.

PREPARATION TIME: 20 MINUTES
COOKING TIME: 20 MINUTES
SERVES: 12

1 lb (450 g) salmon fillets, skinned
Fine salt and freshly ground black pepper
1 cup (210 g) mashed potatoes
½ cup (55 g) fine dried bread crumbs, plus more for dredging
¼ cup (20 g) finely chopped fresh flat-leaf parsley, plus more for garnish
¼ cup (40 g) finely chopped red onion
1 clove garlic, minced
1 teaspoon Dijon mustard
1 teaspoon grated lemon zest
2 eggs, beaten
Vegetable oil, for frying
Lemon wedges, for squeezing

1 Preheat the oven to 400°F (200°C/Gas Mark 6). Line a baking sheet with parchment paper.

2 Place the salmon fillets on the lined pan and season with salt and pepper. Bake until the salmon is firm and cooked through, 12–15 minutes. Remove from the oven and let cool slightly.

3 In a large bowl, flake the cooked salmon into small pieces using a fork. Add the mashed potatoes, bread crumbs, parsley, red onion, garlic, mustard, and lemon zest. Season with salt and black pepper. Mix until well combined.

4 Set up a dredging station in two shallow bowls: Put the beaten eggs in one and some fine dried bread crumbs in a second.

5 To make the fritters, scoop about 2 tablespoons of the mixture per croquette and shape it into a small oval patty or ball. Place them on a baking sheet lined with parchment paper.

6 Line a plate with paper towels and have near the stove. Pour 1 inch (2.5 cm) oil into a large skillet and heat over medium heat to 350°F (177°C).

7 Working in batches to avoid crowding, dip each croquette first into the beaten egg, then coat evenly with the bread crumbs. Carefully place into the hot oil and fry, turning once, until golden brown and crispy, 3–4 minutes per side. Transfer the croquettes to the paper towels to drain. Serve hot with lemon wedges and additional parsley.

STORAGE: Store airtight in the refrigerator for up to 2 days.

SEARED RED SNAPPER

DF GF

Many popular saltwater fish appear in Southern kitchens, including grouper, whiting, flounder, pompano, drum, and the gorgeous and vibrant red snapper. It's vital to give red snapper its due beyond being fried, which Southerners certainly do well, and demonstrate how tasty its fillets are. In this recipe, snapper fillets are highly seasoned, seared with a Cajun spice mix, and then baked—I resist the temptation to say blackened—to perfection.

PREPARATION TIME: 15 MINUTES
COOKING TIME: 20 MINUTES
SERVES: 4

2 tablespoons Cajun seasoning
1 teaspoon garlic powder
1 teaspoon onion powder
½ teaspoon paprika
½ teaspoon dried thyme
Fine salt and freshly ground black pepper
4 skin-on red snapper fillets (about 2 lb/910 g total)
2 tablespoons extra-virgin olive oil
1 lemon, cut into wedges, for squeezing
Chopped fresh flat-leaf parsley, for garnish

1 Preheat the oven to 400°F (200°C/Gas Mark 6).

2 In a small bowl, combine the Cajun seasoning, garlic powder, onion powder, paprika, thyme, and salt and pepper to taste.

3 Pat the red snapper fillets dry with paper towels. Rub the Cajun seasoning mixture evenly on both sides of the fillets.

4 In a cast-iron skillet or ovenproof frying pan, heat the olive oil over medium-high heat. Once hot, add the red snapper fillets skin-side down and sear until the skin is crispy and lightly browned, 2–3 minutes. Use a fish spatula to carefully flip the fillets and transfer the skillet to the oven.

5 Bake until the fish flakes easily with a fork, 12–15 minutes.

6 Let the fish rest for a few minutes before serving. Serve hot with lemon wedges and fresh parsley.

FISH AND GRITS

GF

For many Lowcountry Gullah-Geechee folks, fish and grits was far more known and popular than shrimp (prawns) and grits. Both were breakfast foods based on whatever the first catch of the day was. Having seen for myself in coastal Africa similar dishes of prepared corn mashes and ferments, served alongside fried fish and stewed, grilled shrimp, and lobsters, I know there is much history lost to the ages about these two dishes. It offers a link to the generation exiled from their homelands so long ago.

PREPARATION TIME: 15 MINUTES
COOKING TIME: 50 MINUTES
SERVES: 4

1 cup (140 g) stone-ground grits
Fine salt and freshly ground black pepper
4 fillets (about 1 lb/450 g total) fish, such as trout, catfish, or tilapia
2 tablespoons extra-virgin olive oil
2 cloves garlic, minced
1 medium lemon, thinly sliced
1 cup (150 g) cherry tomatoes, halved
½ cup (4 fl oz/120 ml) white wine or fish stock
½ cup (4 fl oz/120 ml) heavy (whipping) cream
Chopped fresh flat-leaf parsley, for garnish

1 In a medium saucepan, bring 4 cups (32 fl oz/950 ml) water to a boil. Gradually whisk in the grits. Reduce the heat to low and simmer, stirring occasionally, until the grits are thickened and tender, about 20 minutes. Season with salt and black pepper to taste. Cover and set aside, keeping warm.

2 Meanwhile, season the fish fillets with salt and black pepper.

3 In a large cast-iron skillet, heat the olive oil over medium-high heat. Add the fish fillets and cook, turning once, until golden brown and cooked through, 3–4 minutes per side depending on thickness. Remove the fish from the skillet and set aside.

4 Using the same skillet, add the garlic and lemon slices and sauté until fragrant, 1–2 minutes. Add the tomatoes and cook until they start to soften, about 2 minutes. Pour in the wine, scraping up any browned bits from the bottom of the skillet, and simmer for 2–3 minutes to slightly reduce. Stir in the heavy (whipping) cream and continue to simmer until the sauce thickens slightly, another 2–3 minutes.

5 To serve, spoon a generous amount of the warm grits onto each plate. Top with a fish fillet and spoon the creamy sauce over the fish. Garnish with parsley and serve immediately.

BAKED SHAD

GF -5

Shad was once one of the most popular fishes in the Southern culinary repertoire. American shad show up in the early watercolors of John White, who depicted the daily life of Native American groups of Southern Algonquins like the Powhatan Paramount Chiefdom and natives of Pamlico Sound in North Carolina. They harvested shad and other fish at twilight, using small fires to attract them.

In the spring, shad runs along the entire Atlantic Coast. This means that thousands of shad and other anadromous species return to their freshwater birthplaces to spawn, after a life in salt and brackish water. Yet some shad runs have been devastated by overharvesting, damming, runoff pollution, and construction initiatives. Today, shad are better managed, with Virginia tribal nations like the Mattaponi and Pamunkey taking an active role in their preservation, as the fish have a sacred role in their culture. Baked shad, broiled shad, corned shad, and shad roe were delicacies that once united North and the South, while planked shad was a spring dish anticipated across the country. Serve with roasted vegetables or a side salad. (Be warned that diners should consume shad carefully, as they tend to have many bones. If possible, have your fishmonger debone the shad for you.)

PREPARATION TIME: 20 MINUTES
COOKING TIME: 40 MINUTES
SERVES: 4

Softened butter, for the baking dish
2 whole shad (about 4 lb/1.8 kg each), cleaned and scaled
Fine salt and freshly ground black pepper
4 tablespoons (60 g) unsalted butter, melted
1 lemon, thinly sliced
Handful of fresh herbs, such as flat-leaf parsley or dill, for garnish

1 Preheat the oven to 375°F (190°C/Gas Mark 5). Butter a baking dish large enough to hold the fish.

2 Rinse the shad under cold water and pat dry with paper towels. Season the inside and outside of the fish with salt and black pepper.

3 Place the shad in the prepared baking dish. Brush the melted butter over the fish, making sure to coat both sides. Place the lemon slices inside the cavity of the fish, and arrange some on top.

4 Cover the baking dish with aluminum foil and bake until tender, about 30 minutes.

5 Uncover the dish and continue baking until the fish is fully cooked and easily flakes with a fork, 10–15 minutes.

6 Carefully remove from the oven, garnish with fresh herbs, and serve hot.

FROGMORE STEW

DF GF

Frogmore stew is not actually a stew, but rather a type of seafood boil where shellfish, meat, and vegetables are cooked together. Yet it was so-named by Richard Gay of Frogmore, a community near St. Helena Island, South Carolina. It may have been invented in a Gullah-Geechee fish camp in the 1960s, and it first appeared in print in 1977. It mixes potatoes, smoked sausage, corn, and shrimp (prawns) that, after being steamed together, are spread across a newspaper or butcher paper–covered table.

PREPARATION TIME: 15 MINUTES
COOKING TIME: 40 MINUTES
SERVES: 6

2 lb (910 g) new red potatoes
1 lb (450 g) smoked sausage, cut into 2-inch (5 cm) pieces
6 ears corn, husked and cut into thirds
4 lb (1.8 kg) peeled and deveined large shrimp (prawns)
Seafood seasoning, such as Old Bay
Fine salt and freshly ground coarse black pepper
2 lemons, halved
Melted butter, for serving

1 Bring a large pot of water to a boil over high heat.
2 Add the potatoes and cook until tender, 15–20 minutes.
3 Add the sausage and corn and cook for another 5 minutes. Stir in the shrimp (prawns) and cook until they are pink and cooked through, 3–5 minutes.
4 Drain and transfer to a large serving platter or bowl. Season with seafood seasoning, salt, and black pepper to taste. Squeeze the lemon halves over everything and drizzle with melted butter.

SHRIMP AND GRITS

GF

Shrimp (prawns) and grits is an old Charleston breakfast dish, which, according to culinary historian David Shields, appears in print after the Civil War, notably in the *Charleston Courier* in 1888. There the writer explains that shrimp gravy is paired with hominy grits—notably not on top, but served alongside them. Cookbook author Blanche Rhett put shrimp and hominy grits on the map of Charleston, South Carolina, in her 1930 volume *200 Years of Charleston Cooking*. According to Shields, Rhett's version was "derived from the celebrated African American chef William Deas." The late chef Bill Neal then popularized the dish with heirloom grits at his Chapel Hill restaurant, Crook's Corner, in the 1980s. People today tend to prefer the dish with cheesy grits, presented here.

PREPARATION TIME: 15 MINUTES
COOKING TIME: 40–45 MINUTES
SERVES: 4

- 1 cup (140 g) stone-ground grits
- Fine salt and freshly ground black pepper
- 1 lb (450 g) peeled and deveined large shrimp (prawns)
- 2 tablespoons (30 g) unsalted butter
- 2 cloves garlic, minced
- 1 cup (8 fl oz/240 ml) chicken or vegetable stock
- 1 cup (8 fl oz/240 ml) heavy (whipping) cream
- 1 cup (138 g) chive-flavored cheese, such as Boursin
- 2 tablespoons chopped fresh flat-leaf parsley, for garnish
- Lemon wedges, for squeezing

1 In a medium saucepan, bring 4 cups (32 fl oz/950 ml) water to a boil. Gradually whisk in the grits, reduce the heat to low, and simmer, stirring occasionally, until the grits are thickened and tender, 20–25 minutes. Season with salt and black pepper to taste, cover, and keep warm.

2 Meanwhile, season the shrimp (prawns) with salt and black pepper.

3 In a large cast-iron skillet, melt the butter over medium-high heat. Add the shrimp and garlic, stirring until the shrimp are pink and cooked through, 2–3 minutes per side. Remove the shrimp from the skillet and set aside.

4 In the same skillet, pour in the stock and bring it to a simmer while scraping up any browned bits from the bottom of the pan. Stir in the heavy (whipping) cream and simmer until the sauce slightly thickens, 5–7 minutes.

5 Reduce the heat to low and stir in the chive-flavored cheese until smooth and fully melted.

6 To serve, spoon a generous portion of warm grits onto each plate. Arrange the cooked shrimp on top and drizzle with the cheese sauce. Garnish with parsley and serve immediately with lemon wedges on the side for squeezing over the shrimp.

SHRIMP-STUFFED MIRLITONS

The tropical squash known in south Louisiana as mirliton can commonly be found in food markets catering to Latin American and Afro-Caribbean communities, where it is often labeled as chayote and christophene. It used to be a common garden vegetable in south Louisiana and parts of the Gulf Coast, and it was a beloved element of the old French Market in New Orleans. This dish links Louisiana with its other relatives in the cultures and cuisines of the Caribbean basin and Latin America, where the African Atlantic also incorporated indigenous foods into a new Afri-Creole cuisine. This is an adaptation of the recipe from the 1971 Time-Life cookbook *American Cooking: Creole and Acadian* by Peter S. Feibleman to remind a new audience of its tasty importance.

PREPARATION TIME: 45 MINUTES
COOKING TIME: 1 HOUR 35 MINUTES
SERVES: 10

4 mirlitons, chayotes, or christophenes (8 oz/225 g each)
½ lb (225 g) large shrimp (prawns), peeled and deveined
1 ½ teaspoons fine salt
1 teaspoon sugar
1 cup (140 g) chopped thick-cut bacon (streaky)
13 tablespoons (6 ½ oz/185 g) unsalted butter
½ cup (80 g) diced onion
½ cup (75 g) diced green bell pepper
½ teaspoon Creole Seasoning (PAGE 299)
2 cloves garlic, minced
½ teaspoon freshly ground black pepper
½ teaspoon sweet paprika
¼ teaspoon dried thyme
¼ teaspoon dried oregano
1 teaspoon Louisiana-style hot sauce, such as Tabasco, or hot pepper vinegar
2 tablespoons chopped fresh flat-leaf parsley
¼ teaspoon chile flakes (optional)
Softened butter, for the pan
1 cup (56 g) fresh bread crumbs, from French or Italian bread

1 Bring a large pot of water to boil for the mirlitons (enough water so they will be completely submerged).

2 Carefully drop in the mirlitons and cook, uncovered, until they are soft enough to pierce with a knife, about 45 minutes.

3 Meanwhile, in a bowl, the shrimp (prawns), 1 teaspoon of the salt, the sugar, and enough cool water to cover. Let sit until the salt and sugar dissolve, about 10 minutes.

4 Line a plate with paper towels and set near the stove. In a large frying pan, cook the bacon (streaky) over medium heat until crispy, about 10 minutes. Use a slotted spoon to remove the bacon to the paper towels. Drain most of the bacon fat from the pan, leaving about 1 tablespoon.

5 In the same pan, melt 1 tablespoon of the butter over medium-high heat. Add the onion and bell pepper and sauté until the vegetables are softened, 3–4 minutes. Season with Creole Seasoning. Stir in the garlic and cook until fragrant, about 1 minute.

6 Drain the shrimp, add to the pan, and season with the remaining ½ teaspoon salt, the black pepper, paprika, thyme, oregano, hot sauce, parsley, and chile flakes (if using). Cook the shrimp until pink and cooked through, 2–3 minutes per side. When cool enough to handle, chop in a food processor or by hand.

7 Preheat the oven to 375°F (190°C/Gas Mark 5). Grease a sheet pan with some softened butter.

8 When cool, drain the mirliton and halve them lengthwise, remove the seeds, and hollow out to make shells around about ¼ inch (6 mm) thick, setting aside the pulp. Invert the shells to drain any excess liquid. Set the shells open-side up in the sheet pan.

9 In a blender or food processor, puree the mirliton pulp until smooth. On the stovetop or in the microwave, melt 4 tablespoons (60 g) of the butter and set aside.

10 In a 12-inch (30 cm) cast-iron skillet, cook the mirliton puree over medium heat until almost dry, about 15 minutes.

11 Add the remaining 8 tablespoons (115 g) butter to the skillet, then stir in the shrimp mixture.

12 Dividing evenly, spoon the shrimp filling into the mirliton shells and top each with bread crumbs. Drizzle the melted butter over the crumbs.

13 Bake the shells until the filling is warmed through, about 30 minutes.

14 Serve hot.

SHRIMP PILAU

DF GF

There are countless versions of "pee-laaws" or "perloos" built on chicken, cowpeas, shrimp (prawns), oysters, crab, eggplant—whatever is on hand. These are rice pilaf dishes from the Lowcountry, and they go from simple to layered in flavor and taste. Shrimp rice or shrimp pilau is one of the most popular dishes of the South, born of the collision between the colonizing French kitchen and the exiled cuisines of West and Central African peoples. The shrimp merges with the tomato, bell pepper, and rice to make the dish sing.

PREPARATION TIME: 15 MINUTES
COOKING TIME: 50 MINUTES
SERVES: 4

2 cups 370 g) long-grain white rice
2 tablespoons vegetable oil or bacon fat
1 medium onion, finely chopped
2 cloves garlic, minced
3 cups (24 fl oz/710 ml) chicken or shrimp stock
1 medium red bell pepper, diced
1 medium tomato, diced
1 lb (450 g) peeled and deveined large shrimp (prawns)
2 teaspoons Kitchen Pepper (PAGE 301)
¼ teaspoon cayenne pepper, or to taste
Fine salt and freshly ground black pepper

1 Rinse the rice under cold running water until the water runs clear. Drain well.

2 In a large saucepan, heat 1 tablespoon oil over medium heat. Add the onion and cook until softened, 3–4 minutes. Add the garlic and cook for 1 more minute until fragrant.

3 Stir in the rice and coat well with the onion and garlic mixture. Pour in the stock and bring to a boil. Reduce the heat to low, cover, and simmer until the rice is tender and the liquid is absorbed, 15–20 minutes.

4 Meanwhile, in a large cast-iron skillet, heat the remaining 1 tablespoon oil over medium-high heat. Add the bell pepper and cook until slightly softened, 2–3 minutes. Stir in the tomato and cook for another 2 minutes. Add the shrimp (prawns) and cook until they turn pink and opaque, 3–4 minutes. Season with the Kitchen Pepper, cayenne, and salt and black pepper to taste. Stir well to combine.

5 Once the rice is cooked, fluff it gently with a fork, then stir in the shrimp and vegetable mixture. Cover the saucepan and simmer over low heat for another 5 minutes to allow the flavors to meld together.

FRIED SHRIMP

This recipe for fried shrimp (prawns) borrows from various fried shrimp traditions from the Gulf Coast, plus the Calabash style of the small namesake town in southeastern North Carolina. In this recipe, instead of seasoning the dredging flour, we season the shrimp and the egg/buttermilk mixture to prevent burning and discoloration of the shrimp crust. (We also butterfly the shrimp, slicing open the top so it fans out ever so slightly, making them especially pretty once fried.) Once the shrimp come out of the oil, they get a dusting of extra seasonings for a final pop of flavor. Serve the shrimp with lemon wedges and pair with your favorite dipping sauce like cocktail sauce or tartar sauce.

PREPARATION TIME: 25 MINUTES
COOKING TIME: 15 MINUTES
SERVES: 4

- ½ teaspoon freshly ground coarse black pepper
- ½ teaspoon garlic powder
- ½ teaspoon House Seasoning (PAGE 301)
- ½ teaspoon paprika
- ½ teaspoon seafood seasoning, such as Old Bay
- ¼ teaspoon cayenne pepper (optional, for extra heat)
- 1 lb (450 g) peeled and deveined large shrimp (prawns), butterflied
- 1 cup (130 g) self-rising flour
- 2 eggs
- 1 cup (8 fl oz/240 ml) buttermilk or evaporated milk
- Vegetable oil, for frying
- Lemon wedges, for squeezing

1 In a small bowl, stir together the black pepper, garlic powder, House Seasoning, paprika, seafood seasoning, and cayenne (if using). Mix the seasoning mixture well.

2 In a large bowl, toss the shrimp (prawns) with half of the seasoning mixture.

3 Set up a dredging station in two shallow bowls: In one bowl, spread the flour. In a second bowl, whisk together the eggs and buttermilk until well combined. Season the egg/buttermilk mixture with the remaining seasoning.

4 Pour ½ inch (13 mm) oil into a large cast-iron skillet or frying pan and heat over medium-high heat. Line a plate with paper towels and have near the stove.

5 Meanwhile, coat each shrimp by first dredging it in the flour making sure it's evenly coated. Then dip it into the egg/buttermilk mixture, ensuring each one is fully covered.

6 Working in batches to avoid overcrowding, carefully add the coated shrimp into the hot oil one at a time. Fry the shrimp, turning with tongs, until they turn light golden brown all over, 2–3 minutes on each side. Remove the shrimp to the paper towels to drain.

7 Serve with lemon wedges for squeezing.

PICKLED SHRIMP

DF GF

Pickled shrimp (prawns) have a long heritage in the South as a posh party hors d'oeuvre served with cocktails. They found their way into other party dishes, from deviled eggs to shrimp salad and other brunch and party favorites. The virtue of pickled shrimp is they are classy, artful, and flavorful, and have a quick payoff for the labor invested in the briny flavor they deliver.

PREPARATION TIME: 25 MINUTES, PLUS 8–12 HOURS PICKLING TIME
SERVES: 8

- 2 cups (16 fl oz/470 ml) sherry vinegar or red wine vinegar
- 1 ¼ cups (10 fl oz/300 ml) extra-virgin olive oil
- ¼ cup (2 fl oz/60 ml) fresh lemon juice
- 3 tablespoons sugar
- 2 teaspoons fine salt
- 1 teaspoon freshly ground black pepper
- 3 lb (1.4 kg) medium shrimp (prawns), cooked and peeled
- 2 cups (320 g) very thinly sliced onion
- 2 cups (250 g) very thinly sliced lemons (sliced crosswise)
- ½ cup (80 g) very thinly sliced shallots
- ½ cup (30 g) chopped fresh flat-leaf parsley, plus more for garnish
- 10 bay leaves

1 In a nonreactive medium bowl, whisk together the vinegar, olive oil, lemon juice, sugar, salt, and black pepper.

2 In a large glass jar or bowl, arrange a layer of shrimp (prawns), then sprinkle on a layer of sliced onions, a few lemon slices, some shallots, parsley, and 2 bay leaves. Continue layering the ingredients in this way, ending with a layer of shrimp. Carefully pour the dressing over the shrimp, covering them completely. Seal the jar, or cover the bowl tightly with plastic wrap, and refrigerate for 8–12 hours.

3 To serve, transfer the shrimp to a serving bowl or platter using a slotted spoon. Arrange some of the lemon slices and onions over the shrimp, and garnish with chopped parsley. Serve chilled.

STORAGE: Store airtight in the refrigerator for up to 3 days.

STEAMED SHRIMP

DF GF

Steam-and-peel shrimp (prawns) are a great spread-the-table-with-newspaper treat, and are a staple of backyard cookouts. The most important part of this recipe is a highly flavored shrimp boil liquid to infuse the shrimp during the very brief time they spend in the pot. (The Old Bay brand is used throughout the South for seasoning the boil liquid.) Note that cooking shrimp too long will make them way too tough.

PREPARATION TIME: 35 MINUTES
COOKING TIME: 40 MINUTES
SERVES: 6

3 lb (1.4 kg) large shrimp (prawns), deveined but peels-on (tails okay, too)
1 tablespoon fine salt
1 tablespoon sugar
1 can (12 fl oz/355 ml) light beer
5 medium lemons, 1 sliced, 4 cut into wedges for serving
1 yellow onion, halved
3 tablespoons pickling spice
4 tablespoons seafood seasoning, such as Old Bay, plus more for serving
2 cloves garlic, minced
4 tablespoons (60 g) unsalted butter (optional), melted

1 In a large bowl, combine the shrimp (prawns), salt, and sugar and add cool water to cover. Set aside for 30 minutes.

2 Meanwhile, pour 1 inch (2.5 cm) water into a large pot. Add the beer, lemon slices, onion, pickling spice, and seafood seasoning. Bring to a boil, then turn down to a simmer, cover, and simmer for 30 minutes for the flavors to meld.

3 Place a steamer basket in the pot and return the water to a boil over medium-high heat. Drain the shrimp and layer them so they fit comfortably in the steamer basket. Evenly sprinkle the garlic over the shrimp.

4 Cover the pot and steam the shrimp until they are pink and cooked through, 5–7 minutes. Remove the pot from the heat and carefully transfer the steamed shrimp to a serving dish. (You can also refrigerate to chill and serve later.)

5 If desired, drizzle the melted butter over the hot shrimp. Season with more Old Bay and serve with the lemon wedges.

CRAWFISH JAMBALAYA

DF GF

Jambalaya—the iconic rice dish of southern Louisiana—has room for chicken, crab, and crawfish (the star of the swamp). Also known as "mudbugs," the earthy, swampy flavor of crawfish tends to dance well with spicy flavors, and both flavors are absorbed fully by the rice. This classic Creole and Acadian rice dish is a meal in and of itself.

PREPARATION TIME: 15 MINUTES
COOKING TIME: 55 MINUTES
SERVES: 6

2 tablespoons vegetable oil
1 medium onion, diced
1 medium green bell pepper, diced
2 celery stalks, diced
3 cloves garlic, minced
1 teaspoon smoked paprika
1 teaspoon dried thyme
½ teaspoon cayenne pepper, or to taste
½ teaspoon freshly ground black pepper
½ teaspoon fine salt
1 cup (185 g) long-grain white rice
2 cups (16 fl oz/470 ml) chicken stock
1 can (14.5 oz/411 g) diced (chopped) tomatoes, with juices
½ lb (225 g) andouille sausage, sliced
1 lb (450 g) crawfish tails, peeled and deveined
2 scallions (spring onions), chopped, for garnish
Chopped fresh flat-leaf parsley, for garnish

1 In a large cast-iron skillet or Dutch oven (casserole dish), heat the oil over medium heat. Add the onion, bell pepper, and celery and sauté until softened, 5–7 minutes. Stir in the garlic, smoked paprika, thyme, cayenne, black pepper, and salt and cook until fragrant, about 8 minutes.

2 Add the rice and stir to coat with vegetables and spices and to lightly toast, about 1 minute. Pour in the stock and diced tomatoes, stir well to combine, and bring to a boil. Reduce the heat to low, cover, and simmer until the rice is tender and most of the liquid is absorbed, about 25 minutes.

3 Meanwhile, heat a medium frying pan over medium-high heat. Add the andouille sausage and cook until it's browned and heated through, about 10 minutes. Remove from the heat.

4 Once the rice is cooked, gently fold in the crawfish tails and cooked andouille sausage slices. Cover and let sit, off the heat, for 5 minutes.

5 Serve hot, garnished with chopped scallions (spring onions) and parsley.

CRAWFISH PIE

Hank Williams famously sang, "Jambalaya and a crawfish pie and a filé gumbo / 'Cause tonight, I'm gonna see my ma chère amie, oh / Pick guitar, fill fruit jar and be gay, oh / Son of a gun, we'll have big fun on the Bayou."

Crawfish pie is probably the most palatable and plebian way to enjoy crawfish (aka mudbugs), the freshwater cousin of the lobster. People also enjoy crawfish boiled with spices, made into a bisque, smothered as in an étouffée, or cooked into a jambalaya. This is a portable and tasty way to enjoy the mudbug, relying on the starch to hold the meat together with everything else.

PREPARATION TIME: 30 MINUTES
COOKING TIME: 45 MINUTES
MAKES: 6 PIES

FOR THE FILLING:
2 tablespoons (30 g) unsalted butter
½ cup (80 g) finely chopped onion
½ cup (50 g) finely chopped celery
½ cup (75 g) finely chopped green bell pepper
2 cloves garlic, minced
1 lb (450 g) crawfish tails, peeled and deveined
¼ cup (33 g) all-purpose (plain) flour
1 cup (8 fl oz/240 ml) seafood or chicken stock
½ cup (4 fl oz/120 ml) heavy (whipping) cream
1 tablespoon Worcestershire sauce
1 teaspoon Cajun seasoning
Fine salt and freshly ground black pepper
2 tablespoons chopped fresh flat-leaf parsley
1 tablespoon chopped scallions (spring onions)

FOR THE CRUST:
2 sheets (9 ¾ × 10 ½ inches/25 × 27 cm) store-bought frozen puff pastry, thawed
1 egg, beaten

---

1 Make the filling: In a large cast-iron skillet, melt the butter over medium heat. Add the onion, celery, bell pepper, and garlic and sauté until softened, about 5 minutes. Add the crawfish tails and cook until they start to turn pink, 2–3 minutes.

2 Sprinkle the flour over the crawfish mixture and stir well to combine. Cook for 2 minutes, stirring constantly. Gradually add the stock, stirring constantly to avoid lumps. Stir in the heavy (whipping) cream, Worcestershire sauce, Cajun seasoning, and salt and black pepper to taste. Cook until the mixture thickens, 5–7 minutes. Remove from the heat and stir in the parsley and scallions (spring onions). Let the filling cool slightly while you prepare the pastry.

3 Preheat the oven to 400°F (200°C/Gas Mark 6). Line a baking sheet with parchment paper. Set out six 3 ½ oz (100 ml) ramekins.

4 Make the crust: On a lightly floured surface, roll out the pastry to roughly 13 × 12 inches. Cut out 3 rounds about 6½ inches (15 cm) in diameter. Repeat with the second each sheet for a total of 6 large rounds. Then cut out 6 rounds about 3½ inches (9 cm) in diameter for the pie tops. Line each pie mold with one large round of puff pastry, pressing gently to fit and leaving about ¼ inch (6 mm) overhang.

5 Dividing evenly, spoon the crawfish filling into the pastry-lined molds. Brush the edges of the pastry with beaten egg. Place a small puff pastry round over each pie and press the edges to seal. Brush the tops of the pies with egg wash.

6 Place the pies on the lined baking sheet and bake for 20–25 minutes, until the pastry is golden brown and puffed.

7 Let cool for a few minutes before serving.

CRAWFISH ÉTOUFFÉE

Acadian or Cajun people were settlers of New France (Canada) who had initially emigrated from western and southwestern France. They then migrated to south Louisiana in exile in the 1750s from Nova Scotia after being expelled by the British. Thousands of Acadians were dispersed across the Atlantic world with around three thousand arriving in the Bayou Country, where African and Native American maroons (communities of enslaved people seeking their freedom in the wilderness) helped them adjust to a very different life.

This Acadian dish illustrates the rustic style of their traditional cooking—built on roux, onions, stock, homemade charcuterie, and garden produce. Étouffée means "smothered," and it joins a family of one-pot dishes in Southern foodways of smothered proteins, usually served with their gravy over rice.

PREPARATION TIME: 30 MINUTES
COOKING TIME: 1 HOUR
SERVES: 6

- 8 tablespoons (4 oz/115 g) unsalted butter
- ½ cup (65 g) all-purpose (plain) flour
- 1 large onion, finely chopped
- 1 cup (100 g) thinly sliced scallions (spring onions), plus more for garnish
- 1 medium green bell pepper, finely chopped
- 2 celery stalks, finely chopped
- 4 cloves garlic, minced
- 2 cups (16 fl oz/470 ml) seafood or chicken stock
- 1 can (14.5 oz/411 g) diced (chopped) tomatoes, drained
- 2 tablespoons tomato paste (tomato puree)
- 1 tablespoon Worcestershire sauce
- 1 teaspoon hot sauce
- 1 teaspoon sweet paprika
- ½ teaspoon cayenne pepper
- Fine salt and freshly ground black pepper
- 1 lb (450 g) crawfish tails, peeled and deveined
- 2 tablespoons chopped fresh flat-leaf parsley
- Cooked white rice, for serving

1 In a large heavy-bottomed pot, melt the butter over medium heat. Gradually sprinkle in the flour, stirring constantly to create a roux. Cook the roux (see Brown Roux, PAGE 282), stirring frequently, until it turns a deep golden-brown color, 15–20 minutes.

2 Add the onion, scallions (spring onions), bell pepper, celery, and garlic and cook, stirring often, until the vegetables are softened, 5–7 minutes.

3 Pour in the stock, stirring constantly to incorporate. Add the diced tomatoes, tomato paste (puree), Worcestershire sauce, hot sauce, paprika, and cayenne. Season with salt and black pepper to taste. Bring the mixture to a simmer, then reduce the heat to low and simmer uncovered, stirring occasionally, until the flavors meld together and the sauce thickens slightly, 20–30 minutes.

4 Add the crawfish tails to the pot and stir gently to combine. Cook until the crawfish are heated through, 5–7 minutes.

5 Remove the pot from the heat and stir in the parsley. Taste and adjust the seasoning if needed.

6 Serve hot over rice and garnish with scallions.

SHRIMP CREOLE

DF

Shrimp Creole is a simple satisfying dish from Louisiana. It's made with shrimp (prawns) smothered in a tomato-based Creole sauce—complete with bell pepper, celery, and onion—plus a bit of garlic and hot pepper.

PREPARATION TIME: 15 MINUTES
COOKING TIME: 30 MINUTES
SERVES: 4

1 lb (450g) peeled and deveined large shrimp (prawns)
Fine salt and freshly ground black pepper
A pinch plus 1 teaspoon paprika
2 tablespoons extra-virgin olive oil
1 medium onion, finely chopped
1 medium green bell pepper, finely chopped
2 celery stalks, finely chopped
3 cloves garlic, minced
2 tablespoons all-purpose (plain) flour
1 can (14.5 oz/411 g) diced (chopped) tomatoes
1 can (6 oz/170 g) tomato paste (tomato puree)
1 cup (8 fl oz/240 ml) chicken or vegetable stock
1 teaspoon dried oregano
1 teaspoon dried thyme
1 bay leaf
Cooked white rice, for serving
Chopped fresh flat-leaf parsley (optional), for garnish

1 Season the shrimp (prawns) with salt, black pepper, and a pinch of paprika. Set aside.

2 In a large cast-iron skillet or Dutch oven (casserole dish), heat the olive oil over medium heat. Add the onion, bell pepper, and celery and cook, stirring, until the vegetables are softened, 5–7 minutes.

3 Add the garlic and cook for another minute until fragrant. Sprinkle the flour over the vegetables and stir to coat evenly, cooking for 1–2 minutes to remove the raw flour taste. Stir in the diced tomatoes, tomato paste (tomato puree), and the stock. Add the 1 teaspoon paprika, the oregano, thyme, and bay leaf. Bring the mixture to a simmer, then reduce the heat to low, cover the skillet, and simmer, stirring occasionally, until the sauce has thickened and the flavors have melded, 15–20 minutes.

4 Add the seasoned shrimp to the skillet. Cook, stirring occasionally, until the shrimp are pink and cooked through, 5–7 minutes. Taste and adjust seasoning with salt and pepper if needed. Discard the bay leaf from the sauce.

5 Serve over rice and garnish with parsley, if desired.

BROILED OYSTERS

For those who do not like the flavor or texture of raw oysters, broiled (grilled) oysters offer a taste and feel more similar to shrimp scampi. Although this recipe is for the broiler, it works just as well on an outdoor grill with flames and wood amplifying the flavor. Some like to add a little crisp bacon or serve with garlic butter or Pepper Vinegar (PAGE 288).

PREPARATION TIME: 25 MINUTES
COOKING TIME: 10 MINUTES
SERVES: 4

4 tablespoons (60 g) unsalted butter, melted
2 cloves garlic, minced
4 tablespoons grated Parmesan cheese
4 tablespoons fine dried bread crumbs
1 tablespoon chopped fresh flat-leaf parsley
12 fresh oysters
Lemon wedges, for squeezing

1 Preheat the broiler (grill) to high heat. Line a baking sheet or a broiler pan with foil.
2 In a small bowl, combine the melted butter and garlic. In another small bowl, mix together the Parmesan, bread crumbs, and parsley.
3 Shuck the oysters and arrange them on the half shell on the lined pan. Brush the melted butter mixture generously over each oyster and sprinkle with the Parmesan/bread crumb mixture.
4 Place the baking sheet under the broiler and cook for 4–5 minutes, or until the bread crumbs are golden brown and the edges of the oysters begin to curl.
5 Let cool for 1–2 minutes, then serve hot, with lemon wedges for squeezing.

FRIED OYSTERS

DF -30

For chef Edna Lewis, fried oysters were a Christmas season breakfast treat in the Virginia Piedmont. For others, it was a lunch or brunch delicacy enjoyed at the tables of the elite. Baltimore, Maryland; Norfolk, Virginia; Calabash, North Carolina; Charleston, South Carolina; Savannah, Georgia; Mobile, Alabama; Southern beach towns; and coastal Mississippi and Louisiana all boast fantastic fried oysters. Some versions of this recipe prefer cracker meal as the coating for frying. Serve hot with lemon wedges, tartar sauce, cocktail sauce, and/or hot sauce.

PREPARATION TIME: 15 MINUTES
COOKING TIME: 15 MINUTES
SERVES: 10

1 lb (450 g) shucked oysters, drained of liquor
Vegetable oil, for frying
2 eggs, beaten
1 teaspoon kosher salt or ½ teaspoon fine salt
½ teaspoon freshly ground coarse black pepper
½ teaspoon paprika
1 cup (130 g) all-purpose (plain) flour
1 cup 130 g) white or yellow cornmeal

1 Pat the shucked oysters with paper towels to dry.
2 Pour 2 inches (5 cm) oil into a Dutch oven (casserole dish) and heat over medium-high heat until it reaches 350°F (177°C). Line a plate with paper towels and have near the stove.
3 In a medium bowl, season the beaten eggs with the salt, black pepper, and paprika. In another medium bowl, mix the flour and cornmeal together. Dredge each oyster in the eggs, then in the flour/cornmeal mixture, ensuring they are evenly coated.
4 Working in batches, carefully place the coated oysters into the hot oil, turning gently, until they are crispy and medium golden brown in color, 2–3 minutes per side. Use tongs or a slotted spoon to transfer the oysters to the paper towels to drain excess oil.
5 Serve hot.

CREAMED OYSTERS

-30

Creamed oysters, often served in pastry shells, are a favorite party dish in Mobile, Alabama, and other coastal ports of the deep South.

PREPARATION TIME: 10 MINUTES
COOKING TIME: 15 MINUTES
SERVES: 4

3 tablespoons (45 g) unsalted butter
2 dozen shucked oysters, with their liquor
2 tablespoons all-purpose (plain) flour
1 cup (8 fl oz/240 ml) whole milk
½ cup (4 fl oz/120 ml) heavy cream
Fine salt and ground white pepper
Dash of Worcestershire sauce
Dash of hot sauce (optional)
Chopped fresh chives or flat-leaf parsley, for garnish

1 In a saucepan, melt the butter over medium heat. Add the drained oysters and cook, stirring, until the edges curl slightly, 2–3 minutes.
2 Sprinkle flour over the oysters, stir to combine, and let cook for 1–2 minutes. Gradually pour in the reserved oyster liquor, the milk, and heavy (whipping) cream, stirring constantly to avoid lumps. Season with salt and white pepper to taste, the Worcestershire sauce, and hot sauce (if using). Bring to a gentle simmer and cook, stirring occasionally, until the sauce thickens and the oysters are heated through, 5–7 minutes.
3 Remove from the heat and adjust the seasoning if necessary. Serve hot, garnished with chives or parsley.

SHRIMP PASTE

DF -30

Shrimp (prawns) paste is an elegant party favorite, especially important to the cuisines of the southern Atlantic Coast and Gulf. In Charleston, South Carolina, it is a breakfast treat and is great with savory Benne Seed Wafers (PAGE 58), rice crackers, and the like.

PREPARATION TIME: 15 MINUTES
MAKES: 1 CUP (295 G)

½ lb (225 g) cooked peeled shrimp (prawns), roughly chopped
¼ cup (40 g) chopped onion
2 tablespoons mayonnaise
1 tablespoon fresh lemon juice
½ teaspoon Worcestershire sauce
¼ teaspoon fine salt

In a food processor. combine all the ingredients and pulse until smooth and uniform in texture, 2–3 minutes.

STORAGE: Store airtight in the refrigerator until ready to use or for up to 1 week.

POMPANO STUFFED WITH SHRIMP

Pompano en papillote was one of the signature dishes illustrative of the French heritage of Creole cooking. The fish was cooked inside an inflated paper envelope and served with crab or shrimp (prawns) and oyster sauce. A favorite dish of visitors to the French Quarter in New Orleans, it was allegedly born at the famous Antoine's (founded in 1840) to honor a balloonist. Here there is no parchment paper, and instead of a shellfish sauce, the shrimp is stuffed directly into the pompano itself.

PREPARATION TIME: 30 MINUTES
COOKING TIME: 25 MINUTES
SERVES: 4

1 lb (450 g) shrimp (prawns), peeled, deveined, and chopped
1 cup (55 g) fresh bread crumbs
½ cup (45 g) grated Parmesan cheese
¼ cup (15 g) chopped fresh flat-leaf parsley
3 cloves garlic, minced
Grated zest and juice of 1 lemon
Fine salt and freshly ground black pepper
¼ cup (2 fl oz/60 ml) olive oil, plus more for drizzling
2 whole pompano fish (about 1 lb/450 g each), scaled and cleaned
Fresh herbs, such as thyme or dill, for garnish
Lemon wedges, for squeezing

---

1 Preheat the oven to 375°F (190°C/Gas Mark 5). Line a baking sheet with parchment paper.

2 In a large bowl, combine the chopped shrimp (prawns), bread crumbs, Parmesan, parsley, garlic, lemon zest, lemon juice, and salt and pepper to taste. Add the ¼ cup olive oil and mix well.

3 Lay the pompano on the prepared baking sheet and stuff each fish generously with the shrimp mixture, pressing gently to fill evenly. Drizzle with a little more olive oil.

4 Bake until the fish is cooked through and flakes easily with a fork, 20–25 minutes.

5 Garnish with fresh herbs and serve hot, accompanied by lemon wedges for squeezing.

SOFT-SHELL CRABS

Soft-shell crab season is a frantic time (usually April to September) when molting whole blue crabs command high prices. The season, which is longer in Gulf Coast waters than in the Chesapeake Bay, sends fishermen competing to deliver the best soft shells. "Tender busters" (crabs in the process of molting) are preferred to "paper shells" (crabs that have begun to harden after molting). There are also "peelers" (crabs that will molt in a short period of time and are rushed to market). Deep-fried, broiled, baked, grilled, and fried and stuffed between buns (a "spider sandwich"), soft-shell crabs will always have a fan club. Enjoy these crispy, flavorful Southern-style soft-shell crabs as a delicious appetizer or main dish.

PREPARATION TIME: 12 MINUTES, PLUS UP TO 1 HOUR MARINATING
COOKING TIME: 45 MINUTES
SERVES: 4

4 soft-shell crabs, cleaned
1 cup (8 fl oz/240 ml) buttermilk
1 teaspoon garlic powder
1 teaspoon paprika
1 teaspoon fine salt
½ teaspoon cayenne pepper
1 cup (130 g) yellow cornmeal
1 cup (130 g) all-purpose (plain) flour
Vegetable oil, for frying
Chopped fresh flat-leaf parsley (optional), for garnish
Lemon wedges, for squeezing

1 Rinse the crabs under cold water and pat them very dry with paper towels.

2 In a large shallow bowl, combine the buttermilk, garlic powder, paprika, salt, and cayenne. Mix well to evenly distribute the seasonings. Place the crabs in the buttermilk, making sure they are fully submerged. Refrigerate the crabs for 30 minutes to 1 hour, to tenderize and add flavor.

3 Remove the crabs from the buttermilk, allowing any excess to drip off. In a shallow bowl, mix the cornmeal and flour together. Dredge each crab thoroughly in the cornmeal mixture, ensuring they are evenly coated on all sides.

4 Pour 1 inch (2.5 cm) oil into a large cast-iron skillet or frying pan and heat over medium-high heat to 350°F (177°C). Line a plate with paper towels and have near the stove.

5 Working in batches to avoid overcrowding, carefully place the crabs into the hot oil and fry them, turning gently, until golden brown and crispy, 3–4 minutes per side. Remove the crabs from the oil with a slotted spoon or tongs to the paper towels to drain.

6 Serve the soft-shell crabs hot, garnished with fresh parsley, if desired, and lemon wedges on the side for squeezing over the crabs before eating.

MARYLAND STUFFED CRAB

One of the more creative presentations in Chesapeake and Deep South cuisine is seeing a platter of empty crab carapaces stuffed with a croquette-like filling. In some places, there were once metal ramekins specifically designed to mimic the form of the crab carcass, just to send these to table the way connoisseurs once preferred. They are still a favorite on the Gulf Coast and along the south Atlantic Coast.

PREPARATION TIME: 30 MINUTES
COOKING TIME: 20 MINUTES
SERVES: 6

Crabmeat from 6 large blue crabs (1 lb/450 g total), crab shells reserved if available
1 cup (55 g) grated fresh bread crumbs
½ cup (110 g) mayonnaise
3 tablespoons whole milk
2 tablespoons minced green bell pepper
2 tablespoons chopped fresh flat-leaf parsley
1 tablespoon fresh lemon juice
1 tablespoon mustard powder
1 tablespoon Worcestershire sauce
1 teaspoon seafood seasoning, such as Old Bay
Fine salt and freshly ground black pepper
Melted butter, for brushing
Lemon wedges, for squeezing

1 Place the picked crabmeat in a large bowl.
2 In a separate bowl, combine the bread crumbs, mayonnaise, milk, bell pepper, parsley, lemon juice, mustard powder, Worcestershire sauce, and seafood seasoning. Mix everything thoroughly until the ingredients are well incorporated.
3 Use a spatula to fold the bread crumb mixture into the bowl of picked crabmeat, ensuring it's evenly distributed. Season with salt and black pepper to taste.
4 Preheat the oven to 375°F (190°C/Gas Mark 5).
5 Place the crab shells or 5-ounce (150 ml) ramekins on a baking sheet. Spoon the crab mixture into clean crab shells or into individual ramekins for serving. Brush the tops with melted butter.
6 Bake until the tops are a lightly browned and the filling is heated through, 15–20 minutes.
7 Serve with lemon wedges for squeezing.

CRAB CAKES WITH RÉMOULADE SAUCE

DF -30

Crab cakes, or crab croquettes, go back in the Southern experience to at least the eighteenth century when they were sold by hawkers—often Black women—in the streets of Baltimore and Annapolis in Maryland, and in Williamsburg in Virginia. Crab cakes are filled out with crumbs or stale bread and pepped up with different additions per locality or the chef's style. In his classic 1971 Time-Life volume, *American Cooking: Southern Style*, author Eugene Walter called crab cakes "a dish almost as beloved by true Southerners as fried chicken."

To present that original "Maryland crab cake" here would be too controversial for more than one reason. Some people do not accept Maryland—foundational to Southern culture and history—as part of the story of Southern cuisine. Also, many consider rémoulade indispensable to serving crab cakes, and it's not commonly used in the Chesapeake Bay and Delmarva South. Rémoulade sauce is more traditional in the Deep South, like Savannah, Georgia. To add to the controversy, crab cakes are sacred to different families and communities, so the amount of breading, the techniques used, and the amount of seasoning vary up and down the south Atlantic Coast. So in short, this is my recipe, with Maryland roots, up for debate.

PREPARATION TIME: 20 MINUTES
COOKING TIME: 10 MINUTES
SERVES: 4

FOR THE CRAB CAKES:
1 lb (450 g) fresh lump crabmeat, picked over for bits of shell and cartilage
1 cup (56 g) grated fresh white bread crumbs
1 egg, lightly beaten
4 tablespoons finely chopped white onion
4 tablespoons finely chopped red bell pepper
4 tablespoons mayonnaise
1 tablespoon finely chopped fresh flat-leaf parsley
1 tablespoon Worcestershire sauce
2 teaspoons Dijon mustard
½ teaspoon seafood seasoning, such as Old Bay
½ teaspoon ground white pepper
⅛ teaspoon cayenne pepper
Fine salt and freshly ground coarse black pepper
6 tablespoons clarified butter or lard, for frying

FOR THE RÉMOULADE SAUCE:
½ cup (110 g) mayonnaise
1 tablespoon Dijon mustard
1 tablespoon tomato paste (tomato puree) or chili sauce (such as Heinz)
1 tablespoon chopped capers
1 tablespoon chopped gherkins
1 tablespoon chopped fresh flat-leaf parsley
1 tablespoon fresh lemon juice
Fine salt and freshly ground black pepper

1 Make the crab cakes: In a large bowl, combine the crabmeat, bread crumbs, egg, onion, bell pepper, mayonnaise, parsley, Worcestershire sauce, mustard, seafood seasoning, white pepper, and cayenne. Gently fold the mixture together until well combined. Be careful not to break up the crabmeat too much. Season with salt and black pepper. Cover and refrigerate for at least 30 minutes to help firm up the mixture.

2 When ready to cook, form the crab mixture into 8 patties about ½ inch (13 mm) thick.

3 Line a plate with paper towels and have near the stove. In a large cast-iron skillet, heat the clarified butter over medium-high heat. Carefully place the crab cakes in the skillet and cook until golden brown and crispy, 3–4 minutes per side. Remove from the skillet to the paper towels to drain.

4 Make the rémoulade sauce: In a small bowl, whisk together the mayonnaise, mustard, tomato paste (tomato puree), capers, gherkins, parsley, and lemon juice until smooth. Season with salt and black pepper to taste.

5 Arrange the crab cakes on a serving platter and serve with rémoulade sauce on the side.

MARYLAND STEAMED CRAB

DF GF -5

The crab feast is Maryland's greatest contribution to American cuisine, a part of the Old South, from the seventeenth century tobacco plantation South through to the present day. Crabs eaten this way are a big part of the culture in the Chesapeake Bay region and Delmarva (southern Delaware and the eastern shores of Maryland and Virginia). They can be found all the way down the South Atlantic coast and in parts and pieces of the Gulf, most notably South Carolina, Georgia, and Louisiana. Once cooked, serve the crabs immediately on a newspaper-covered surface with mallets, nutcrackers/crab crackers, and—if you want—melted butter, lemon wedges, and additional seafood seasoning on the side.

PREPARATION TIME: 35 MINUTES
COOKING TIME: 25 MINUTES
SERVES: 8

12 cups (3 qt/2.8 liters) lager-style beer (National Bohemian is popular)
4 cups (32 fl oz/950 ml) apple cider vinegar
2 large onions, quartered
2 cups (230 g) seafood seasoning, such as Old Bay
24 live blue crabs (about 8 lb/3.6 kg)

---

1 In a large pot, combine the beer, vinegar, onion, and seafood seasoning with 1 cup (8 fl oz/240ml) water. Bring to a boil over high heat. Place a steaming rack or basket in the pot. Cover, turn the heat to medium, and cook for 20 minutes, until aromatic and flavorful.

2 Carefully add the live crabs to the steaming rack in the pot. Cover the pot with a lid and steam the crabs until they turn bright orange and are fully cooked, 20–25 minutes. You can add more seafood seasoning as they cook.

3 Remove the crabs from the pot using tongs, and transfer them to a large serving platter.

NOTE: Male crabs have a shape on their apron, or bottom shell, that looks like the Washington Monument. Female crabs have a broader shape like the US Capitol on their apron. Fertilized crabs also have delicious orange roe, which can be saved for immediate use in She-Crab Soup (PAGE 139) or other dishes.

STORAGE: The cooked crabmeat can be stored airtight in the refrigerator for 3 days.

HOW TO EAT MARYLAND STEAMED CRABS:

1 Remove the large claws and the six smaller legs, suck any meat out of the smaller legs.

2 Turn the crab over and carefully pry off the apron and set aside.

3 Turn the crab over and break off the top shelf. Do not eat the lungs, which have a spongy appearance. Throw them away with the top shell.

4 Snap the crab in half and scrape off cartilage.

5 Twist off the back fin and enjoy the meat.

6 Crack open the crab claws and enjoy the meat.

BREADED CRAB CHOP

A crab chop is a sort of crab croquette, a trompe l'oeil, which was probably designed to be served during the meatless Fridays and Lent in Catholic south Louisiana. Traditionally it was served with the claw substituting for the rib bone of the chop creating the illusion of a breaded piece of meat.

PREPARATION TIME: 20 MINUTES
COOKING TIME: 20 MINUTES
SERVES: 4

- 9 oz (250 g) fresh crabmeat, picked over for bits of shell or cartilage
- ¼ cup (23 g) grated Parmesan cheese
- 2 tablespoons chopped fresh flat-leaf parsley
- Grated zest of 1 lemon
- Fine salt and freshly ground black pepper
- ½ cup (65 g) all-purpose (plain) flour
- 2 eggs, beaten
- 1 cup (115 g) fine dried bread crumbs, preferably homemade
- Vegetable oil, for frying
- Chopped fresh flat-leaf parsley and lemon wedges (optional), for serving

1 In a medium bowl, combine the crabmeat, Parmesan, parsley, and lemon zest. Season with salt and black pepper to taste and mix gently. Divide the crab mixture into 4 equal portions and shape into flat chop shapes.

2 Set up a dredging station in three shallow bowls: one with flour, one with beaten eggs, and one with bread crumbs. Dredge each crab chop in the flour, then in beaten eggs, and finally coat with bread crumbs.

3 In a cast-iron skillet, heat 1 inch (2.5 cm) oil over medium heat. Line a plate with paper towels and have near the stove.

4 Once the oil is hot, fry the breaded crab chops, turning once, until golden brown and crispy, 3–4 minutes per side. Use tongs or a slotted spatula to transfer to the paper towels to drain.

5 Serve hot, garnished with parsley and lemon wedges if desired.

POULTRY,
MEAT &
GAME

SALT, SMOKE, FIRE, FRY

Southern animal proteins—meat, poultry, game, and fish—had to be well-preserved to beat the danger of spoilage during the six to ten months when it was too warm to leave meat out safely. In the seventeenth century, everything from hams to herring to bacon to shad were heavily salted and kept in wooden boxes and barrels, keeping with Northern European traditions, in which foods were cured for long winters and ocean voyages. Salt pork, salty country ham, and salted fish in parts of the South, like the Tidewater and the Lowcountry, are still stars of country cooking.

Native Americans in the South, enslaved Africans, and Europeans used flameless smoking with plant material (including corn cobs, deciduous hardwoods, nut hulls, recovered orchard branches, or leaves) to preserve or enhance the taste of meat and fish. Smoking meat with flame and using various seasonings would inform the cooking methods of Southern barbecue. Even the source words were remarkably similar; for example, in Africa, *babbake* in Hausa means to "grill, toast, roast" and in the Caribbean *barbacoa*, from the Taíno through Spanish, means "to smoke or grill on a wooden framework". These two perspectives, combined with livestock and fishing and hunting practices, created a unique element of Southern cuisine. Large birds and joints of meat were roasted on spit jacks (a spit turned by winding in an elite Colonial kitchen) or a tin oven (a heat-reflecting device also found in early Southern kitchens). Enslaved people, the original pitmasters, drew on their African traditions and roasted meat over holes in the earth until it was tender.

No region of American cooking fries meat and fish like the South; the repertoire goes beyond chicken. Deep-frying also added more shelf life to some proteins, especially when "fried hard," until it had a solid crust as insulation against air spoilage. For the most part, Southern cooks used lard, a by-product from hog-killing time, to fry pork chops, catfish, okra and other vegetables, soft-shell crab, oysters, crawfish tails, and even pickle chips, to the delight of eaters across the region. As Southerners reclaim traditional cooking methods like barbecuing and deep-frying, and preserve meat and fish by smoking, pickling, and drying, we look forward to seeing how the South's diversity and more significant concern for both cultural and environmental preservation will set its tables going forward.

SOUTHERN ROAST CHICKEN

GF

In Black communities, this dinner favorite was often called the "Gospel Bird."

PREPARATION TIME: 15 MINUTES
COOKING TIME: 1 HOUR 30 MINUTES
SERVES: 4

1 whole chicken (3–4 lb/1.4–1.8 kg)
6 tablespoons (85 g) softened butter or bacon fat
1 teaspoon freshly ground black pepper or Kitchen Pepper (PAGE 301)
1 teaspoon garlic powder
1 teaspoon onion powder
1 teaspoon paprika
1 teaspoon Poultry Seasoning (PAGE 299)
1 teaspoon fine salt or House Seasoning (PAGE 301)
1 Vidalia onion, quartered
1 lemon, halved
2 sprigs fresh rosemary

1 Preheat the oven to 375°F (190°C/Gas Mark 5). Set a wire rack in a large roasting pan.

2 Rinse the chicken inside and out with cold water, then pat dry with paper towels.

3 In a small bowl, combine the butter, pepper, garlic powder, onion powder, paprika, Poultry Seasoning, and salt. Rub the seasoned butter evenly over the surface of the chicken and under the skin.

4 Place the chicken breast-side up on the wire rack. Stuff the onions, lemon, and rosemary inside the cavity.

5 Roast the chicken, basting occasionally with the pan juices, until the skin is crispy and the internal temperature in the thickest part of the thigh reaches 165°F (74°C), about 1 hour 30 minutes.

6 Remove the aromatics and let the bird rest for 10–15 minutes before carving.

BARBECUED CHICKEN

DF GF

This recipe hits the essential barbecue notes—savory, smoky, and tangy.

PREPARATION TIME: 20 MINUTES, PLUS 4 HOURS MARINATING TIME
COOKING TIME: 30 MINUTES
SERVES: 4

4 tablespoons olive oil, plus more for rubbing
4 tablespoons apple cider vinegar
Juice of 1 lemon
2 cloves garlic, minced
Fine salt or House Seasoning (PAGE 301)
1½ teaspoons freshly ground black pepper
1 teaspoon smoked paprika
½ teaspoon cayenne pepper
2 whole chickens (about 3 ½ lb/1.6 kg each), cut into quarters
1 cup (8 fl oz /240 ml) barbecue sauce (homemade or store-bought)

1 In a small bowl, whisk together the olive oil, vinegar, lemon juice, garlic, salt to taste, pepper, paprika, and cayenne. Place the chicken in a large container, pour in the liquid, and marinate in the refrigerator for at least 4 hours and up to overnight. Drain the chicken, pat dry, and rub with olive oil.

2 Preheat an outdoor grill (barbecue) to medium heat (375°F/190°C).

3 Place the chicken on the grill skin-side down, cover, and cook, turning occasionally, until the skin is crispy and golden brown, 15–20 minutes.

4 Brush the chicken generously with your barbecue sauce of choice and continue to grill, occasionally basting with sauce, until the internal temperature reaches 165°F (74°C), 10–15 minutes.

CHICKEN SALAD

DF GF -30

Chicken salad is a good way to use up extra Sunday roast chicken and it is a Southern favorite for small parties or luncheons. Serve with rolls if desired; the Icebox Rolls (PAGE 22) are ideal.

PREPARATION TIME: 15 MINUTES
SERVES: 4

3 cups (420 g) diced cooked chicken
Fine salt or House Seasoning (PAGE 301)
Freshly ground black pepper
½ cup (110 g) mayonnaise, such as Duke's or Hellmann's
1 tablespoon extra-virgin olive oil
1 tablespoon Dijon or brown mustard
2 teaspoons sweet or dill pickle relish
1 teaspoon honey
¼ teaspoon onion powder
¼ teaspoon garlic powder
¼ teaspoon sweet paprika
¼ teaspoon celery seeds
Juice of 1 lemon
4 eggs, hard-boiled and finely chopped
1 celery stalk, finely diced
½ red onion, finely diced
Chopped fresh flat-leaf parsley, for garnish

1 Season the diced chicken with salt and black pepper to taste.

2 In a large bowl, whisk together the mayonnaise, olive oil, mustard, relish, honey, onion powder, garlic powder, paprika, celery seeds, and lemon juice until well combined. Add the hard-boiled eggs, celery, and red onion and toss gently to combine.

3 Add the chopped chicken to the bowl and gently fold everything together, until the chicken is evenly coated with the dressing and ingredients are well mixed. Taste and adjust the seasoning with salt or house seasoning and black pepper if needed.

4 Transfer the chicken salad to a serving bowl and garnish with parsley.

SOUTHERN FRIED CHICKEN

Fried chicken is the American South in one dish. Some prefer chicken simply salted and peppered, dredged in seasoned flour and fried. Others prefer a much more elaborately seasoned chicken with a buttermilk marinade or egg wash and crumbs. Some love it plain, others like it served with gravy, and still others like it under gravy. For others, the question is which gravy? Onion gravy, tomato gravy, or brown skillet gravy? Some like batter and some like it un-floured, some use cornmeal. The oil you use matters: It could be vegetable oil, canola (rapeseed) oil, or peanut (groundnut) oil. Edna Lewis used to flavor lard with country ham, and I knew folks who would do something similar by frying bacon in the grease at the same time.

Your way with fried chicken really depends on how good your homemade version was growing up and what you're willing to tolerate from others. This recipe is fairly malleable, and it's based on my personal family recipe. But if you want to be a purist and pare the seasonings down to salt and pepper that's okay. If you want to add other ingredients—as long as they aren't salty—that's okay, too.

However you make it, serve hot with your favorite sides like Southern Tomato Gravy (PAGE 69) or Onion Gravy (PAGE 280); rice or mashed potatoes; Potato Salad (PAGE 107), Coleslaw (PAGE 272), and Fried Biscuits (PAGE 26) or Yeast Rolls (PAGE 16).

PREPARATION TIME: 20 MINUTES, PLUS 4–12 HOURS MARINATING TIME
COOKING TIME: 25 MINUTES
SERVES: 4

FOR THE MARINATED CHICKEN:
- 1 whole chicken (4–5 lb/1.8 to 2.3 kg total), cut into 8 pieces
- 2 teaspoons kosher salt or 1 teaspoon fine salt
- 1 teaspoon sweet paprika
- 1 teaspoon Poultry Seasoning (PAGE 299)
- 1 teaspoon garlic powder
- 1 teaspoon onion powder
- ½ teaspoon freshly ground coarse black pepper
- 2 cups (16 fl oz/470 ml) buttermilk

FOR FRYING:
- Vegetable oil or lard (see NOTE)
- ¼ cup (30 g) cornstarch (cornflour)
- 2 cups (260 g) all-purpose (plain) flour
- Kosher or sea salt
- Freshly ground coarse black pepper

1 Marinate the chicken: Add the chicken pieces to a large bowl. Rub with 1 teaspoon of the kosher salt (½ teaspoon of the fine salt), paprika, Poultry Seasoning, garlic powder, onions powder, and pepper. Pour the buttermilk over them. Toss to make sure all the pieces are well coated, and sprinkle with the remaining 1 teaspoon kosher salt (or ½ teaspoon fine). Cover and refrigerate for at least 4 hours or overnight/all day (8–12 hours) for best results.

2 When ready to fry: pour 4 inches (10 cm) oil into a deep heavy-bottomed pot or Dutch oven (casserole dish) and heat over medium-high heat to 375°F (190°C) or until a breadcrumb browns up quickly when dropped in the oil. Set a wire rack in a sheet pan or line a baking sheet with paper towels and have near the stove.

3 In a shallow dish, mix together the cornstarch (cornflour), flour, and salt to taste.

4 Remove the chicken pieces from the buttermilk, allowing excess to drip off by putting on a rack with paper towels beneath. Dredge each piece thoroughly in the flour and cornstarch, making sure the chicken is well coated.

5 Working in batches to avoid over-crowding, carefully place the chicken pieces skin-side down in the hot oil. Fry until each piece is light golden brown and cooked through (with an internal temperature of 165°F/74°C), 6–8 minutes per side. Adjust the heat as needed to maintain oil temperature and prevent burning.

6 Remove the fried chicken to the wire rack or paper towels to drain excess oil. Sprinkle with salt and pepper to season.

NOTE: Try 3 parts vegetable oil and 1 part melted lard or shortening.

VARIATION: **Maryland Fried Chicken:** Serve with Milk or Pan Gravy (PAGE 274) on the side alongside Fried Biscuits (PAGE 26).

VARIATION: **Chesapeake Fried Chicken:** In the marinade, omit the salt and add 1 teaspoon seafood seasoning, such as Old Bay. In the dredging mixture, in addition to the salt and pepper, season with seafood seasoning to taste.

VARIATION: **Creole Fried Chicken:** Add 2 teaspoons Creole Seasoning (PAGE 299) to the buttermilk marinade. Take the buttermilk-drained chicken, and before frying, dip in a mixture of 2 eggs whisked with 1 cup (8 fl oz/240 ml) evaporated or whole milk, before coating in flour mixture.

VARIATION: **Kentucky Fried Chicken:** Take the buttermilk-drained chicken, and before frying, dip in a mixture of 2 eggs whisked with 1 cup (8 fl oz/240 ml) evaporated or whole milk, before coating in flour mixture.

VARIATION: **Cornmeal and flour coating:** Use 1 ½ cups (200 g) yellow cornmeal mixed with 1 ½ cups (195 g) self-rising flour.

SORGHUM-BRINED CHICKEN IN CABBAGE LEAVES

GF

This is an adaptation of a chicken dish described in one of the narratives recorded in the 1930s by the WPA (Works Project Administration), which sent interviewers and writers out to record oral histories across the United States. The WPA transformed the South in many ways by building dams and highways and maintaining forests. They also recorded and documented the lives of thousands of formerly enslaved Black Americans, plus American food habits, with special attention to Southern barbecues, fish fries, stews, and other culinary events.

PREPARATION TIME: 35 MINUTES, PLUS 4 HOURS BRINING TIME
COOKING TIME: 1 HOUR 30 MINUTES
SERVES: 4–6

- ½ cup (72 g) kosher salt or ¼ cup (72 g) fine salt
- ½ cup (4 fl oz/120 ml) sorghum syrup, golden syrup (such as Lyle's), or maple syrup
- 3 cups (24 fl oz/710 ml) chicken or vegetable stock, warmed, plus ¼ cup more for roasting
- 3 cups (24 fl oz/710 ml) cold water
- 1 whole roasting chicken (about 5 lb/2.3 kg), giblets removed, chicken thoroughly cleaned and dried
- 2 tablespoons Kitchen Pepper (PAGE 301)
- ⅓ cup (75 g) unsalted butter, lard, or vegetable shortening, at room temperature
- 2 tablespoons bacon fat
- 1 large head cabbage, with leaves pulled apart and washed

1 In a very large bowl (large enough to hold the chicken and the brine), dissolve the salt and sorghum syrup in the warmed stock. Allow the liquid to cool. Add the cold water and stir to combine. Submerge the chicken in the brine, then cover and refrigerate for 4 hours to overnight.

2 Preheat the oven to 375°F (190°C/Gas Mark 5).

3 Remove the chicken from the brine and rinse and dry thoroughly.

4 In a small bowl, mix the Kitchen Pepper with the butter and bacon fat. Massage the chicken with the seasoned butter all over, tucking some under the skin and being certain to cover the entire bird.

5 On a cutting board, spread out a layer of cabbage leaves. Place the chicken on the cabbage bed and cover with additional leaves. Use kitchen twine to tie the leaves around the chicken into a loose bundle, layering as many leaves as it takes to cover the bird.

6 Carefully transfer the cabbage-wrapped chicken to a large Dutch oven (casserole dish). Add the additional ¼ cup stock or water to the pot, cover lightly, and transfer to the oven.

7 Roast until the wings pull away easily from the chicken, the juices run clear, and a thermometer inserted into the thigh meat reads 165°F (74°C), about 1½ hours.

8 Let the chicken rest for 15 minutes before carving and serving.

CAROLINA PILAU

GF

Pilau, also pronounced perloo, is an old Lowcountry term for a one-pot rice dish. There is a whole family of pilaus based on seasonal resources. If you want a traditional old-school version, you can omit the tomatoes and use bacon fat instead of butter.

PREPARATION TIME: 20 MINUTES
COOKING TIME: 1 HOUR 45 MINUTES
SERVES: 6–8

1 whole chicken (3 ½–4 lb/1.6–1.8 kg)
2 quarts (1.9 liters) chicken or vegetable stock, or more if needed
8 tablespoons (4 oz/115 g) unsalted butter
1 large yellow onion, chopped (about 1 ½ cups)
1 ½ cups (225 g) chopped green bell pepper
1½ cups (150 g) diced celery
2 cups (370 g) long-grain white rice (parboiled is okay)
1 lb (450 g) large tomatoes, peeled and chopped, juices reserved
1 tablespoon chopped fresh thyme leaves, or 1 teaspoon dried thyme
1 teaspoon kosher salt or House Seasoning (PAGE 301), or ½ teaspoon fine salt
½ teaspoon freshly ground black pepper or Kitchen Pepper (PAGE 301)
¼ teaspoon chile flakes, or a dash of hot sauce

1 In a large pot, combine the chicken and enough stock to cover the chicken completely. Bring to a boil over medium-high heat, then boil uncovered, until the internal temperature reads 165°F (74°C), about 1 hour. Reserving the broth, transfer the chicken to a cutting board. When cool enough to handle, pull the meat off the skin and bones. Cut the meat into uniform bite-size pieces. Set aside.

2 In a Dutch oven (casserole dish), melt the butter over medium heat. Add the onion, bell pepper, and celery and cook until the onion starts to brown, about 10 minutes.

3 Rinse the rice under cold running water until the water runs clear. Drain well.

4 To the Dutch oven, add the tomatoes with their juices and the thyme, salt, black pepper, and chile flakes. Add the chicken meat, rinsed rice, and 4 cups (1 liter) of the reserved broth. Bring to a boil, then cover and turn the heat down to low. Simmer slowly, without lifting the lid, until the rice is tender and has absorbed the flavors, about 30 minutes. Serve warm.

STORAGE: Store airtight in the refrigerator for up to 3 days.

CHICKEN FRICASSEE

A fricassee is a term borrowed from the French for a dish that was fried and broken into pieces before stewing. Chicken fricassee was very popular in Colonial Virginia. It famously appeared in a delicious cream gravy at George and Martha Washington's Mount Vernon home, made by the legendary African American chef Hercules Posey.

PREPARATION TIME: 20 MINUTES
COOKING TIME: 1 HOUR
SERVES: 4

1 whole chicken (about 4 lb/1.8 kg), cut into 8 pieces
Fine salt and freshly ground black pepper
2 tablespoons (30 g) unsalted butter
2 tablespoons extra-virgin olive oil
1 medium carrot, diced
1 celery stalk, diced
1 medium onion, finely chopped
2 cloves garlic, minced
1 cup (135 g) sliced mushrooms
2 tablespoons all-purpose (plain) flour
1 cup (8 fl oz/240 ml) chicken stock
½ cup (4 fl oz/120 ml) white wine
1 bay leaf
1 teaspoon fresh thyme leaves
½ cup (4 fl oz/120 ml) heavy (whipping) cream
Chopped fresh flat-leaf parsley, for garnish

1 Season the chicken pieces with salt and black pepper.

2 In a large cast-iron skillet or Dutch oven (casserole dish), heat the butter and olive oil over medium-high heat. Add the chicken pieces and cook, turning with tongs, until browned on all sides, about 15 minutes. Remove the chicken from the pan and set aside.

3 To the same pan, add the carrot, celery, onion, garlic, and mushrooms and cook, stirring occasionally, until the vegetables are softened, 5–7 minutes.

4 Sprinkle the flour over the vegetables and cook for another 2 minutes, stirring constantly. Gradually add the chicken stock and white wine to the pan, stirring to combine and scraping up any browned bits from the bottom of the pan.

5 Return the chicken pieces to the pan. Add the bay leaf and thyme leaves. Bring the mixture to a simmer, then reduce the heat to low, cover, and cook until the chicken is cooked through and tender, 30–40 minutes.

6 Stir in the heavy (whipping) cream and cook for another 5 minutes to thicken the sauce slightly. Season with additional salt and pepper to taste.

7 Discard the bay leaf. Serve the chicken fricassee hot, garnished with chopped parsley.

CHICKEN BOG

GF

Chicken bog is a long-cooked chicken and rice dish—somewhere between a pilau/perloo and a backyard stew—from South Carolina, from the Pee Dee region in the northeast corner of the state. It may have been named for its likeness to the swampy countryside in which it was created—it should be thick and a tiny bit soupy, but not dry. Like Carolina Pilau (PAGE 211) and Pine Bark Stew (PAGE 132), chicken bog has remained a favorite to feed large crowds at social occasions, political outreach gatherings, family reunions, and the like. This recipe has been kept as close to the original versions as possible.

PREPARATION TIME: 15 MINUTES
COOKING TIME: 1 HOUR 30 MINUTES
SERVES: 6

- 1 whole chicken (3–4 lb), cut into pieces
- 1 large onion, chopped
- 3 cloves garlic, minced
- 1 teaspoon fine salt
- 1 teaspoon freshly ground black pepper
- ½ teaspoon paprika
- ½ teaspoon cayenne pepper
- 2 large bay leaves
- 1 lb (450 g) smoked sausage, sliced into rounds ¼ inch (6 mm) thick
- 2 cups (370 g) long-grain white rice, such as Carolina Gold
- 4 tablespoons (60 g) unsalted butter

1 In a large soup pot, combine the chicken pieces, 8 cups (2 qt/1.9 liters) water, the onion, garlic, salt, black pepper, paprika, and cayenne. Bring the mixture to a boil over medium-high heat. Reduce the heat to low, cover, and simmer until the chicken is tender and cooked through, about 45 minutes.

2 Once the chicken is done, remove it from the pot and set aside to cool. Strain the broth over a bowl, discarding the solids, and return the liquid to the pot, skimming off any excess fat from the surface. When the chicken is cool enough to handle, remove the skin and bones, and chop the meat into bite-size pieces.

3 In a large Dutch oven (casserole dish), cook the sausage over medium heat until it is browned and slightly crispy, 6–7 minutes. Remove the sausage from the skillet and set it aside.

4 In the same skillet, add the rice and toast it, stirring constantly to avoid over-browning, until it is lightly golden, about 2 minutes.

5 Add the rice and sausage to the pot with the chicken broth. Bring the mixture to a boil, then reduce the heat to low, cover, and simmer until the rice is tender and has absorbed most of the broth, about 25 minutes.

6 Stir in the shredded chicken and butter and cook for an additional 5 minutes, or until everything is heated through and well combined.

COUNTRY CAPTAIN

DF GF

It may read as curry, but Country Captain, a Lowcountry dish, has an origin story. In the eighteenth century, the British, through their colonial dominion in India and their exposure to the multiregional Indian cuisine, began changing their foodways. However, when this dish arrived in the American South, African hands took rice, chicken, and spices and did what they know how to do so well. The spices are not roasted or toasted, the sauce is built in ways West Africans might build their protein-based stews: fry, then stew.

PREPARATION TIME: 20 MINUTES
COOKING TIME: 1 HOUR
SERVES: 6

3 lb (1.4 kg) bone-in chicken pieces
1 teaspoon fine salt
½ teaspoon freshly ground black pepper
½ cup (65 g) all-purpose (plain) flour
¼ cup (2 fl oz/60 ml) vegetable oil
1 large onion, chopped
1 medium green bell pepper, chopped
2 cloves garlic, minced
1 tablespoon curry powder
1 teaspoon ground ginger
½ teaspoon Kitchen Pepper (PAGE 301)
¼ teaspoon cayenne pepper
1 can (14.5 oz/411 g) diced (chopped) tomatoes
½ cup (4 fl oz/120 ml) chicken stock
½ cup (75 g) golden raisins (sultanas)
Cooked white rice, for serving
Chopped fresh flat-leaf parsley, for garnish
4 tablespoons slivered almonds (optional), toasted

1 Season the chicken pieces with the salt and black pepper, then dredge in the flour.

2 In a large cast-iron skillet, heat the oil over medium-high heat. Add the chicken pieces and brown on all sides, 5–7 minutes per side. Remove from the skillet and set aside.

3 To the same skillet, add the onion and bell pepper and cook, stirring occasionally, until softened, about 5 minutes.

4 Add the garlic, curry powder, ginger, Kitchen Pepper, and cayenne, cooking for another minute until fragrant. Stir in the diced tomatoes, chicken stock, and golden raisins and bring the mixture to a simmer.

5 Return the chicken pieces to the skillet, nestling them into the sauce. Reduce the heat to low, cover, and simmer until the chicken is cooked through and tender, 40–45 minutes.

6 Serve over rice and garnish with parsley. If desired, also garnish with the slivered almonds.

CHICKEN AND DUMPLINGS

The rooster that wouldn't shut up or the hen past her laying days often turned into this Sunday dinner treat. It demanded low and slow cooking to tenderize a chicken that had strong, developed muscles and tough meat. Some may not think the carrots necessary or find them anathema, but some of us can't live without them in this dish. Soft pillowy dumplings and a stew cooked all day really hits the spot. My grandmother's secret was an onion studded with cloves that cooked with the chicken and was removed after the chicken was finished cooking. The meal had to be good and fit for a preacher—who was usually the guest for this meal.

PREPARATION TIME: 30 MINUTES
COOKING TIME: 1 HOUR 30 MINUTES
SERVES: 6

FOR THE BASE:
1 whole chicken (4 lb/1.8 kg)
8 cups (1.9 liters) chicken stock
1 large onion, chopped
3 carrots, peeled and sliced
3 celery stalks, roughly chopped
2 bay leaves
1 teaspoon dried thyme
Fine salt and freshly ground black pepper
½ cup (4 fl oz/120 ml) heavy (whipping) cream

FOR THE DUMPLINGS:
2 cups (260 g) all-purpose (plain) flour
1 tablespoon baking powder
1 teaspoon fine salt
½ teaspoon baking soda (bicarbonate of soda)
¾ cup (6 fl oz/180 ml) buttermilk
3 tablespoons (45 g) unsalted butter, melted

1 Prepare the base: Place the whole chicken in a large pot and cover with chicken stock. Add the onion, carrots, celery, bay leaves, thyme, and salt and black pepper to taste. Bring to a boil, then reduce the heat and simmer until the chicken is cooked through and tender, about 1 hour.

2 Remove the chicken from the pot and let it cool slightly before shredding the meat, discarding the skin and bones. Return the shredded chicken to the pot and stir in the heavy (whipping) cream.

3 Make the dumplings: In a bowl, combine the flour, baking powder, salt, and baking soda (bicarb). Stir in the buttermilk and melted butter until a dough forms.

4 Bring the soup to a simmer and drop in spoonfuls of the dough. Cover and cook until the dumplings are cooked through and fluffy, 15–20 minutes.

SOUTHERN PORK ROAST

DF

This braised pork roast, with apple or peach cider vinegar and sorghum molasses, is a great alternative entrée to ham, rib roast, or turkey. It goes well with Vidalia Onion Sauce (PAGE 268) and rice or mashed potatoes.

PREPARATION TIME: 20 MINUTES
COOKING TIME: 3½ HOURS
SERVES: 6

4 lb (1.8 kg) bone-in pork shoulder
4 tablespoons (60 g) bacon fat or butter
1 large onion, finely chopped
2 teaspoons fine salt or House Seasoning (PAGE 301)
1 teaspoon freshly ground coarse black pepper or Kitchen Pepper (PAGE 301)
1 teaspoon paprika
1 teaspoon dried thyme
1 teaspoon rubbed sage
½ teaspoon cayenne pepper
1 cup (8 fl oz /240 ml) chicken stock
¼ cup (2 fl oz/60 ml) apple or peach cider vinegar
¼ cup (2 fl oz/60 ml) sorghum syrup, golden syrup (such as Lyle's), or maple syrup
2 tablespoons Worcestershire sauce
2 tablespoons brown mustard

1 Preheat the oven to 325°F (160°C/Gas Mark 3).
2 Rinse the pork shoulder under cold water and pat it dry with paper towels.
3 In a small bowl, combine the bacon fat, onion, salt, black pepper, paprika, thyme, sage, and cayenne. Place the pork shoulder in a large roasting pan and rub the mixture all over the pork shoulder until evenly coated.
4 In a separate bowl, whisk together the stock, vinegar, sorghum syrup, Worcestershire sauce, and mustard. Pour the mixture over the pork shoulder, making sure to cover it well. Cover the roasting pan tightly with aluminum foil and transfer to the oven.
5 Roast the pork shoulder for 3 hours, basting it with the pan juices every hour. Remove the foil and increase the oven temperature to 375°F (190°C/Gas Mark 5), and continue roasting the pork until the exterior is browned and crispy, an additional 30 minutes.
6 Let the pork shoulder rest for 15–20 minutes before carving.
7 Transfer the pork to a cutting board and slice it into thick pieces. Pour the pan juices into a small saucepan and simmer over medium heat until slightly thickened.
8 To serve, arrange the sliced pork on a serving platter and drizzle with the reduced pan jus.

FRIED PORK CHOPS

Fried pork chops are more versatile than you might think. You can serve them on their own and enjoy with applesauce or Virginia Fried Apples (PAGE 116), smother them with gravy or Creole sauce and serve over rice, or enjoy them in a sandwich with sandwich bread or a Buttermilk Biscuit (PAGE 25).

PREPARATION TIME: 15 MINUTES, PLUS 4 HOURS MARINATING TIME
COOKING TIME: 20 MINUTES
SERVES: 4

4 bone-in center-cut pork chops, about 1 inch (2.5 cm) thick
1 teaspoon garlic powder
1 teaspoon onion powder
1 teaspoon paprika
1 teaspoon fine salt or House Seasoning (PAGE 301)
½ teaspoon freshly ground black pepper
½ teaspoon Poultry Seasoning (PAGE 299)
¼ teaspoon cayenne pepper
1 cup (8 fl oz /240 ml) buttermilk
1 egg, beaten
1 cup (130 g) self-rising flour
¼ cup (32 g) cornstarch (cornflour)
Vegetable oil, for frying

1 Place the pork chops in a shallow dish and season with the garlic powder, onion powder, paprika, salt, black pepper, Poultry Seasoning, and cayenne. Pour ½ cup (4 fl oz/120 ml) of the buttermilk over them, ensuring they are well coated. Cover the dish and refrigerate for at least 4 hours.

2 Set up a dredging station in two shallow bowls: In one bowl, whisk the remaining ½ cup (4 fl oz/120 ml) buttermilk with the beaten egg. In a second bowl, mix the flour and cornstarch (cornflour) together.

3 Set a wire rack over a baking sheet. Remove the pork chops from the buttermilk, letting any excess drip off. Dip each chop in the egg/buttermilk mixture and dredge each chop in the flour mixture, pressing firmly to ensure an even coating. Set on the rack while heating up the oil.

4 Pour ½ inch (13 mm) oil into a large cast-iron skillet and heat over medium-high heat. Line a plate with paper towels and have near the stove.

5 Once the oil is hot, carefully add the pork chops to the skillet. Fry the pork chops until they are golden brown on both sides and cooked through, 4–5 minutes per side. Remove the pork chops to the paper towels to drain. Sprinkle with a pinch of salt and black pepper when fresh out of the skillet.

6 Let the chops rest for a few minutes before serving.

VARIATION: For the old-fashioned pared-down way, skip the buttermilk marinade. Season the pork chops with the spices and set them aside for 30–60 minutes. Beat together ½ cup (4 fl oz/120 ml) milk (whole or evaporated) and 1 egg and dip the pork chops in that before dredging in the flour mixture.

SMOTHERED PORK CHOPS

Smothered pork chops are an easy step up from fried pork chops. The pan gravy isn't that difficult, you just have to be patient and attentive, and the result is magical. Southern-style smothered pork chops are best enjoyed with mashed potatoes or rice.

PREPARATION TIME: 20 MINUTES
COOKING TIME: 1 HOUR
SERVES: 4

- 4 bone-in pork chops, about 1 inch (2.5 cm) thick
- 2 teaspoons fine salt or House Seasoning (PAGE 301)
- 1 teaspoon freshly ground fine or coarse black pepper
- 1 teaspoon paprika
- ½ teaspoon garlic powder
- ½ teaspoon onion powder
- ½ cup (65 g) plus 2 tablespoons all-purpose (plain) flour
- 3 tablespoons vegetable oil
- 1 large onion, thinly sliced
- 1 medium green bell pepper, finely diced
- 2 cloves garlic, minced
- 2 cups (16 fl oz/470 ml) chicken stock
- 1 teaspoon dried thyme
- 1 teaspoon dried rosemary
- ½ teaspoon chile flakes
- 2 tablespoons (30 g) unsalted butter
- 2 tablespoons chopped fresh flat-leaf parsley

1 Season the pork chops on both sides with the salt, black pepper, paprika, garlic powder, and onion powder. In a shallow bowl, spread the ½ cup (65 g) of the flour. Dredge the pork chops in the flour, shaking off any excess.

2 In a large cast-iron skillet or Dutch oven (casserole dish), heat the oil over medium-high heat. Working in batches, add the pork chops and sear them until golden brown on both sides, 4–5 minutes per side. Remove the pork chops from the skillet and set aside.

3 To the same skillet, add the onion and bell pepper. Sauté over medium heat until the vegetables are softened and begin to caramelize, about 10 minutes.

4 Add the garlic and cook for an additional 2 minutes. Sprinkle with the remaining 2 tablespoons flour and whisk until mostly incorporated. Pour in the chicken stock, 1 cup at a time, scraping up any browned bits from the bottom of the skillet, keeping the pan gravy from getting lumpy or from burning. Stir in the thyme, rosemary, and chile flakes. Keep stirring and adjust the gravy to your taste, using any of the spices suggested earlier in the recipe.

5 Add the butter and bring the mixture to a simmer. Return the pork chops to the skillet, nestling them into the sauce. Reduce the heat to low, cover the skillet with a tight-fitting lid, and simmer the pork chops until they are tender and cooked through, 35–40 minutes. Stir occasionally, ensuring the sauce does not stick to the bottom of the skillet.

6 Arrange the pork chops on a serving plate and pour the gravy over them. Garnish with the parsley.

VARIATION: Add ½ cup (4 fl oz/120 ml) heavy (whipping) cream after the butter, then adjust the heat and keep stirring to thicken before you add the pork chops.

MADEIRA PICNIC HAM

DF GF

Madeira ham is an elegant antebellum Southern ham recipe. Adapted for the modern kitchen, it reads like a pork roast, but it is worth the effort and a delicious alternative to country ham. Here we take notes from culinary historian Nancy Carter Crump. I adapted her recipe years ago for my open-hearth demonstrations and to my tastes. When you serve, slice thin and pile high for ham biscuits.

PREPARATION TIME: 30 MINUTES, PLUS 2 DAYS BRINING TIME
COOKING TIME: 6 HOURS
SERVES: 8

FOR THE CURED PORK:

5–6 lb (2.3–2.7 kg) bone-in pork shoulder (picnic roast)
2 ½ cups (360 g) kosher salt
1 cup (200 g) turbinado (demerara) sugar
¼ cup (24 g) freshly ground coarse black pepper

FOR THE GLAZE:

4½ cups (36 fl oz/1 liter) Madeira wine
1 cup (8 fl oz/240 ml) orange juice
1 cup (200 g) turbinado (demerara) sugar
¼ teaspoon ground cloves
¼ teaspoon ground cinnamon
¼ teaspoon ground nutmeg
1 medium white or yellow onion
Whole cloves, for studding onion

1 Cure the pork: Place the pork shoulder in a deep bowl and rub with the salt, sugar, and black pepper. Cover tightly and refrigerate for 2 days.

2 When ready to cook, soak the pork shoulder in water for 1 hour, then drain well. Bring a large pot of water to a boil and cook the picnic ham for 1 hour.

3 Drain the pork and transfer to a large Dutch oven (casserole dish). Set over medium heat and pour 3 cups (24 fl oz/710 ml) of the Madeira wine over the pork and cook at a low boil for just under 1 hour.

4 Meanwhile, preheat the oven to 350°F (180°C/Gas Mark 4).

5 Prepare the glaze: In a medium saucepan, combine the remaining 1 ½ cups (12 fl oz/350 ml) Madeira, the orange juice, turbinado sugar, ground cloves, cinnamon, and nutmeg. Bring the mixture to a simmer over medium heat, stirring until the sugar has dissolved and the ingredients are well combined, about 15 minutes. Remove the Madeira glaze from the heat and let cool slightly.

6 Pour half of the Madeira glaze over the pork, making sure to cover the entire surface. Stud the onion with cloves and place in the liquid. Cover the Dutch oven and transfer to the oven.

7 Bake for 2 ½ hours, basting every 30 minutes with the remaining glaze. Uncover for the last 30 minutes of cooking to allow the surface to brown.

8 Add more Madeira glaze and bake for an additional 10 minutes to allow the glaze to just barely set.

9 Remove the "ham" from the oven and let it rest for at least 15 minutes before carving.

STORAGE: Leftover ham can be sliced and stored airtight in the refrigerator for up to 3 days.

MARYLAND STUFFED HAM

DF

Maryland stuffed ham is a beloved delicacy of southern Maryland. It consists of a butt ham that has been scored and stuffed with spicy greens. The effect of carving it and seeing the deep green, white fat, pink meat, and crispy brown outside is delectable. In St. Mary's County, they make stuffed ham sandwiches at the county fair.

PREPARATION TIME: 1 HOUR, PLUS 6 HOURS SOAKING TIME
COOKING TIME: 4 HOURS
SERVES: 10

1 large bone-in ham (10–12 lb/4.5–5.4 kg)
2 tablespoons vegetable oil
1 large onion, finely chopped
6 cloves garlic, minced
1 bunch collards, stems and midribs removed, leaves chopped
1 bunch kale, stems and midribs removed, leaves chopped
1 bunch spinach, chopped
1 tablespoon black peppercorns
1 tablespoon mustard seeds
2 teaspoons allspice berries
2 teaspoons whole cloves
1 tablespoon apple cider vinegar
1 tablespoon ground ginger
1 tablespoon mustard powder
2 teaspoons freshly ground black pepper
1½ teaspoons chile flakes (optional)
1 teaspoon ground mace
1 teaspoon fine salt
1 cup (56 g) fresh bread crumbs
2 tablespoons light brown sugar
10–12 whole cabbage leaves

1 In a large bowl, combine the ham with cool water to cover and let soak for at least 6 hours to remove excess salt. (If using an aged ham, before soaking, first use a stiff brush to scrape any mold from the ham's exterior.)

2 Drain the ham and, if necessary, trim any excess fat. Place the ham in a large pot and cover with water. Bring to a boil, then reduce the heat to low and simmer until partially cooked, about 1 hour.

3 Meanwhile, in a large skillet, heat the oil over medium heat. Add the onion and garlic, and cook, stirring, until softened, about 5 minutes. Add the chopped collards, kale, and spinach in batches, cooking until wilted, about 15 minutes. Remove from the heat and let cool slightly.

4 In a spice grinder or mortar and pestle, grind together the black peppercorns, mustard seeds, allspice berries, and cloves until finely ground. Transfer to a large bowl and mix in the vinegar, ginger, mustard powder, ground black pepper, chile flakes (if using), mace, salt, bread crumbs, and brown sugar.

5 Drain the cooled greens well, squeezing out any excess moisture. Add to the spice/bread crumb mixture and mix thoroughly until well combined.

6 Remove the ham from the pot (reserve the cooking liquid) and let it cool slightly. Carefully make deep cuts in the ham, about 2 inches (5 cm) apart and 1 inch (2.5 cm) deep, creating pockets for the stuffing. Stuff each pocket generously with the prepared stuffing mixture, pressing down firmly.

7 Wrap the entire stuffed ham with the whole cabbage leaves, securing with kitchen twine to hold everything in place.

8 Return the stuffed and wrapped ham to the pot with the cooking liquid. Add additional water if needed to cover the ham.

9 Bring the pot back to a boil, then reduce the heat to low and simmer gently, covered, until the ham is tender and fully cooked, about 3 hours.

10 Remove the stuffed ham from the pot and let it rest for 15–20 minutes before slicing.

STORAGE: Leftover ham can be sliced and stored airtight in the refrigerator for up to 3 days.

PORK LOIN AND SWEET POTATOES

DF GF

A meal like this emerged from Southern seasonality, particularly in the Upper South. By the early winter, the herbs had dried, the hogs were fattened on acorns, chestnuts, and pecans littering the ground, and the sweet potatoes had time to cure after harvesting. This dish is great as an alternative holiday meal or a special meal on other occasions.

PREPARATION TIME: 20 MINUTES
COOKING TIME: 1 HOUR 30 MINUTES
SERVES: 4

4 tablespoons (60 g) bacon fat or vegetable oil
1 lb (450 g) pork loin
1 teaspoon sweet paprika
1 teaspoon dried sage
½ teaspoon garlic powder
½ teaspoon onion powder
Fine salt or House Seasoning (PAGE 301)
Freshly ground black pepper
¼ cup (50 g) brown sugar, light or dark
2 tablespoons apple cider vinegar
½ cup (4 fl oz/120 ml) chicken stock
2 large sweet potatoes (about 1 lb/450 g total), peeled and cut into chunks
Chopped fresh flat-leaf parsley, for garnish

1 Preheat the oven to 350°F (180°C/Gas Mark 4). Grease a 9 × 13-inch (23 × 33 cm) baking dish with the bacon fat or oil.
2 Season the pork loin on all sides with the paprika, sage, garlic powder, onion powder, and salt and black pepper to taste.
3 Heat a large frying pan over medium-high heat. Add the pork loin and sear until golden brown on both sides, turning with tongs, 3–4 minutes per side. Remove from the skillet and set aside.
4 In the same pan, reduce the heat to medium. Add the brown sugar and vinegar, stirring until the sugar is dissolved and the mixture is bubbling, 5–7 minutes.
5 Add the chicken stock to the pan, scraping up any browned bits from the bottom. Bring to a simmer and cook until slightly reduced, 2–3 minutes.
6 Spread the sweet potatoes in the prepared baking dish and place the pork loin on top. Pour the vinegar mixture over the pork loin and sweet potatoes. Cover the baking dish with foil and transfer to the oven.
7 Bake until the pork loin is cooked through (reaching a temperature of 145°F/63°C) and the sweet potatoes are tender, 45 minutes to 1 hour, basting occasionally with the pan juices.
8 Let the pork rest for a few minutes before carving. Garnish with parsley.

BARBECUED SPARERIBS

DF GF -5

The central South—Memphis to Middle Tennessee through Mississippi and Alabama—has made the full barbecued sparerib rack the star of the show. These ribs slow-cooked on the grill offer an authentic taste of the region, especially when grilled over hickory or pecan chips (or wood pellets), which give them a light smoky taste.
If using a dry rub here, try the Antebellum Southern Dry Rub (PAGE 303).

PREPARATION TIME: 15 MINUTES, PLUS 5 HOURS SEASONING TIME
COOKING TIME: ABOUT 2½ HOURS
SERVES: 4

2 racks spareribs (1 ½–2 lb/680–910 g each), washed and trimmed as needed
1 cup (8 fl oz/240 ml) apple cider vinegar
Vegetable oil
Fine salt and freshly ground coarse black pepper, or dry rub of your choice
1 cup (8 fl oz/240 ml) barbecue sauce, homemade (see Memphis-Style BBQ Sauce, PAGE 298) or store-bought

1 Place the ribs in a large bowl or shallow dish and pour the vinegar over them. Let sit in the vinegar about 30 minutes, then flip over and let sit another 30 minutes. Pour the vinegar off and rub with oil, salt and black pepper (or the dry rub of your choice). Allow to preseason up to 4 hours.

2 Preheat an outdoor grill (barbecue) to medium-high heat, around 300°–325°F (149°–163°C), with a direct-heat side and an indirect-heat side.

3 Place the spareribs bone-side down on indirect side of the grill. Close the lid and cook until the ribs are tender and the meat pulls away easily from the bones, about 2 ½ hours, turning occasionally and basting with the BBQ sauce every 30 minutes. (During the last 15 minutes of cooking, apply an extra layer of sauce to the ribs for a sticky finish if desired.)

4 Let the spareribs rest for a few minutes before slicing and serving.

OVEN-BAKED SPARERIBS

DF GF

Oven-roasted meats, marinated and preseasoned, then dressed with barbecue sauce, are not uncommon in the winter and early spring. This particular dish is often made for those holidays when outdoor barbecue is not an option. You can use your rub and mop of your choice, but the New-Style Southern Dry Rub (PAGE 303) or Virginia BBQ Mop Sauce (PAGE 294) would both be good fits for this dish.

PREPARATION TIME: 15 MINUTES, PLUS AT LEAST 4 HOURS 30 MINUTES MARINATING TIME
COOKING TIME: 2 HOURS
SERVES: 4

2 racks spareribs (1 ½–2 lb/680–910 g each), washed and trimmed as needed
1 cup (8 fl oz/240 ml) apple cider vinegar
Vegetable oil
½ cup (50 g) dry rub of your choice
¾ cup (6 fl oz/180 ml) mop of your choice
½ teaspoon liquid smoke
1 cup (8 fl oz/240 ml) barbecue sauce, such as Alabama/Mississippi Sauce Beautiful (PAGE 292) or your favorite store-bought

1 In a large bowl or shallow dish, place the ribs and pour the vinegar over them. Let sit in the vinegar for about 30 minutes, then turn and marinate the other side for 30 minutes.

2 Pour the vinegar off, then rub the racks with oil and the dry rub. Allow to preseason for at least 4 hours and up to overnight.

3 Position racks in the bottom and top thirds of the oven and preheat the broiler (grill). Line two baking sheets with foil and set wire racks on top.

4 Divide the seasoned ribs between the two baking sheets. Place the ribs on the top rack one pan at a time and broil (grill) until browned, usually 3–5 minutes. Turn the ribs over and sear on the other side, about 3 minutes. Drain any fat that accumulates. Turn off the broiler and set the oven temperature to 350°F (180°C/Gas Mark 4).

5 In a small bowl, combine the mop with the liquid smoke. Paint about half of the mop over each slab of the ribs and cover with a second sheet of foil, crimping edges to seal the ribs inside. Return the ribs, one sheet on each oven rack, and bake for 35 minutes.

6 Uncrimp the foil and baste with the remaining mop, then switch racks and bake until the meat pulls back from the bone, an additional 35 minutes.

7 Uncover the ribs, brush with the barbecue sauce, and bake, basting with sauce every 5 minutes, until the ribs are well glazed, about 35 minutes. When the ribs have rested and are reasonably cool enough to handle, cut them apart with a sharp cleaver or heavy-duty knife. Baste with more of your favorite barbecue sauce before serving.

BOUDIN BLANC–STYLE BALLS

DF

Boudin blanc ("white sausage") and its sibling boudin rouge ("blood sausage") are the heart of Acadian charcuterie. Boudin blanc has a legendary role in southern Louisiana, where it's said that if someone loves their spouse more than ten pounds of boudin, true love has been attained. Though they are often enjoyed as sausage links, this recipe shows you how to shape the boudin blanc mixture into fried balls, a treat enjoyed widely throughout Louisiana. Serve it with the sauce of your choice on the side: Many people like a rémoulade (see Crab Cakes with Rémoulade Sauce, PAGE 196) or a roux-based gravy.

PREPARATION TIME: 50 MINUTES, PLUS 3 HOURS CHILLING TIME
COOKING TIME: 2 HOURS 40 MINUTES
MAKES: 20 BOUDIN BALLS

FOR THE SAUSAGE MIXTURE:
- 1 ½ lb (680 g) boneless pork shoulder, trimmed of excess fat and cut into chunks
- 8 oz (225 g) boneless, skinless chicken thighs, cut into chunks
- 4 oz (115 g) pork back fat, cut into small pieces
- 1 tablespoon vegetable oil
- 2 celery stalks, finely chopped
- 1 medium green bell pepper, finely chopped
- 1 small onion, finely chopped
- 4 cloves garlic, minced
- 2 cups (320 g) cooked long-grain white rice
- 2 tablespoons chopped scallions (spring onions), green part only
- 1 tablespoon chopped fresh flat-leaf parsley
- 1 tablespoon fine salt
- 2 teaspoons Creole Seasoning (PAGE 299)
- 1 teaspoon freshly ground black pepper
- 1 teaspoon sweet paprika
- 1 teaspoon dried thyme
- ½ teaspoon ground white pepper

FOR FRYING:
- ½ cup (60 g) all-purpose flour
- 4 eggs, beaten
- 3 cups (300 g) panko bread crumbs
- Vegetable oil, for deep-frying

1 Make the sausage mixture: In a large pot, combine the pork shoulder, chicken thighs, and pork fat and add water to cover by 1 inch (2.5 cm). Bring to a boil, then reduce to a simmer and cook until very soft, about 2 hours. Reserving the broth in the pot, remove the meat to a large bowl and let cool for 10 minutes.

2 Using a meat grinder fitted with a medium plate, grind the cooled meats until the mixture comes out smooth.

3 In a medium cast-iron skillet, heat the oil over medium heat. Add the celery, bell pepper, onion, and garlic and cook, stirring occasionally, until softened, 5–7 minutes. Remove from the heat and let cool slightly.

4 In a large bowl, combine the ground meat, 1 cup (8 fl oz/240 ml) of the reserved broth, the cooked vegetables, cooked rice, scallion (spring onion) greens, parsley, salt, Creole Seasoning, black pepper, paprika, thyme, and white pepper, adding more liquid if the mixture is too dry and isn't holding together. Mix thoroughly with a spoon, turning with a spatula until the meat is well combined and the mixture is sticky. Taste to make sure the seasoning is to your liking. Cover and refrigerate for at least 3 hours, or overnight.

5 When ready to fry: Line a baking sheet with parchment paper. Set up a dredging station in three wide shallow bowls: Place the flour in one bowl. Add the beaten eggs to second bowl. Spread the panko in the third.

6 Scoop the sausage mixture in 2-tablespoon portions and roll the balls in the flour, shaking off any excess. Dip in the eggs, letting excess drip off, and dredge in the panko, making sure they are completely coated. Lay them on the parchment paper until all the balls are dredged.

7 Line a large platter with paper towels and set next to the stove. Pour 1 inch (2.5 cm) oil into a Dutch oven (casserole dish) and heat over medium-high heat until it registers 325°F (163°C) on a deep-frying thermometer.

8 Working in batches of 5 balls at a time, fry, turning occasionally, until they are evenly browned, 3–5 minutes. Transfer to the paper towels to drain.

9 Transfer the finished balls to a serving dish and serve hot.

STORAGE: Store airtight in the refrigerator for up to 3 days or in the freezer for up to 3 months.

CHITLINS/CHITTERLINGS

DF GF

Chitterlings, the small intestine of the hog, are an old part of Southern heritage. Predominantly consumed in the cold season at hog-killing time, chitlins became commercially available during the age of packing and refrigeration. A soul food staple, they are not for everyone, but for those who love them, there is never enough hot sauce. There is however a festival in Salley, South Carolina, where hundreds of pounds of them are consumed each year, and even a dance is performed called the "Chitlin' Strut."

PREPARATION TIME: 40 MINUTES, PLUS OVERNIGHT SOAKING TIME
COOKING TIME: 4 HOURS
SERVES: 8

5 lb (2.3 kg) hog chitlins (pig intestines)
2 tablespoons vegetable oil
2 medium onions, finely chopped
4 cloves garlic, minced
1 celery stalk, finely chopped
1 medium green bell pepper, finely chopped
1 medium red bell pepper, finely chopped
2 bay leaves
1 tablespoon dried thyme
1 teaspoon chile flakes (optional)
Fine salt and freshly ground black pepper
Hot sauce and Pepper Vinegar (PAGE 288), for serving

1 Thoroughly clean the hog chitlins, rinsing them multiple times under cold running water, until they are completely clean and free of any debris. In a large bowl, cover the chitlins with cold water, refrigerate, and let soak overnight.

2 In a large pot or Dutch oven (casserole dish), heat the oil over medium-high heat. Add the onions, garlic, celery, and both bell peppers. Cook, stirring occasionally, until the vegetables are softened, 5–7 minutes.

3 Drain the soaked chitlins and rinse them again under cold water. Add the cleaned chitlins to the pot along with enough water to cover them by about 2 inches (5 cm). Stir in the bay leaves, thyme, and chile flakes (if using). Season generously with salt and black pepper.

4 Bring the mixture to a boil. Reduce the heat to low and simmer gently, uncovered and stirring occasionally, until the chitlins are tender and cooked through, 3–4 hours. (The cooking time may vary depending on the size and thickness of the chitlins.) Skim off any foam or impurities that rise to the surface. Discard the bay leaves.

5 Serve the chitlins hot, accompanied by hot sauce and Pepper Vinegar on the side for added flavor.

STORAGE: Store airtight in the refrigerator for up to 2 days.

PIG'S FEET

DF

Pig's feet have an alleged history as the scraps thrown out to the enslaved. Certainly, during the hog-killing time in the dead of winter, enslaved people may have enjoyed some pig's feet, washed and stewed all day. However, it was widely enjoyed by Southern planters and elites as a delicacy. From enslavement through to the postbellum period, grilled, braised, or baked pig's feet remained a key Southern soul food. Southern-style pig's feet are traditionally enjoyed with sides such as collard greens, Black-Eyed Peas (PAGE 83), and cornbread, creating a comforting and flavorful meal.

PREPARATION TIME: 20 MINUTES
COOKING TIME: 4 HOURS
SERVES: 6

4 lb (1.8 kg) pig's feet, cleaned and halved
1 large onion, finely chopped
4 cloves garlic, minced
3 bay leaves
1 teaspoon black peppercorns
2 teaspoons Poultry Seasoning (PAGE 299)
1 teaspoon dried thyme
1 teaspoon dried rosemary
1 teaspoon sweet paprika
1 teaspoon Kitchen Pepper (PAGE 301)
1 teaspoon fine salt
½ teaspoon cayenne pepper
½ teaspoon chile flakes
1 cup (8 fl oz/240 ml) apple cider vinegar
4 tablespoons light brown sugar
2 tablespoons tomato paste (tomato puree)
2 tablespoons Worcestershire sauce
Chopped fresh flat-leaf parsley, for garnish

1 In a large pot, combine the pig's feet, onion, garlic, bay leaves, black peppercorns, Poultry Seasoning, thyme, rosemary, paprika, Kitchen Pepper, salt, cayenne, and chile flakes. Add the vinegar and 4 cups (32 fl oz/950 ml) water, making sure the pig's feet are completely covered by the liquid.

2 Bring the mixture to a boil over medium-high heat. Once boiling, reduce the heat to low, cover the pot, and simmer until tender and fragrant about 3 hours. During this time, stir occasionally and ensure the pig's feet remain submerged, adding more water if necessary.

3 After 3 hours, add the brown sugar, tomato paste (puree), and Worcestershire sauce to the pot, stirring well to combine. Continue to simmer for an additional 45 minutes, allowing the flavors to meld and the pig's feet to become tender and succulent.

4 Once the pig's feet are fully cooked and tender, remove them from the pot and place on a serving platter. Strain the cooking liquid to remove the solids, then return the liquid to the pot. Simmer the liquid over medium heat until it reduces and thickens slightly, 10–15 minutes.

5 To serve, drizzle the reduced cooking liquid over the pig's feet and garnish with parsley.

HAM HOCKS WITH GREENS

DF GF

This recipe, drawn from Southern hard economic times, is an entire meal, enjoyed with Skillet Cornbread (PAGE 45) by small-time farmers and sharecroppers, Black and white alike. Ham hocks come from the joint that connects the foot of the hog to its leg and are full of flavor when salted and smoked, because of their high concentration of collagen and fat.

PREPARATION TIME: 20 MINUTES
COOKING TIME: 1 HOUR 45 MINUTES
SERVES: 4

2 smoked ham hocks (about 3 lb/ 1.4 kg total)
Fine salt and freshly ground black pepper
2 tablespoons vegetable oil
1 medium onion, chopped
3 large bunches collard greens, stems and midribs removed, leaves chopped
4 cups (32 fl oz/950 ml) vegetable stock or Grandma's Stock (PAGE 272)
1 tablespoon apple cider vinegar
1 ½ teaspoons light brown sugar
½ teaspoon chile flakes (optional)

1 Season the ham hocks generously with salt and black pepper.

2 In a large pot or Dutch oven (casserole dish), heat the oil over medium-high heat. Brown the ham hocks on all sides, about 5 minutes per side. Remove the ham hocks from the pot and set aside.

3 To the same pot, add the onion and cook until softened, about 5 minutes Working in batches, add the chopped collard greens to the pot, stirring until the greens begin to wilt, about 5 minutes.

4 Pour in the stock, vinegar, brown sugar, and chile flakes (if using). Stir well to combine. Return the browned ham hocks to the pot, nestling them into the greens, and bring the mixture to a boil. Reduce the heat to low, cover, and simmer gently, stirring occasionally, until the ham hocks are tender and the greens are cooked through, about 1 ½ hours.

5 Remove the ham hocks from the pot and let them cool slightly before removing the meat from the bones. Shred or chop the meat and return it to the pot with the greens. Taste and adjust seasoning with salt and black pepper if needed.

SMOKED HOG JOWL WITH GREENS

DF GF

For many Southerners, especially in the Upper South and Southern highlands, smoked hog jowl cooked with greens is a New Year's dish consumed for good luck. Southern-style hog jowl and turnip greens are best enjoyed with Skillet Cornbread (PAGE 45) or a side of Black-Eyed Peas (PAGE 83). Use the cornbread to mop up the pot likker.

PREPARATION TIME: 20 MINUTES
COOKING TIME: 2 HOURS
SERVES: 6

- 1 lb (450 g) smoked hog jowl, rinsed, dried, and cut into strips ¼ inch (6 mm) wide
- 1 large onion, finely chopped
- 2 cloves garlic, minced
- 2 cups (16 fl oz/470 ml) chicken stock
- 2 lb (910 g) fresh turnip or mustard greens, washed and chopped
- 1 teaspoon fine salt or House Seasoning (PAGE 301)
- 1 teaspoon freshly ground black pepper
- ½ teaspoon chile flakes
- 2 tablespoons apple cider vinegar
- 1 tablespoon light brown sugar

1 Set a large soup pot or Dutch oven (casserole dish) over medium heat and add the hog jowl slices. Cook until the hog jowl renders and the slices are crispy and browned, 10–15 minutes. Remove the hog jowl pieces from the pot and set them aside, leaving the rendered fat in the pot.

2 Add the onion to the pot with the rendered fat and sauté over medium heat until translucent and fragrant, about 5 minutes.

3 Stir in the garlic and cook for an additional 2 minutes, ensuring the garlic does not burn. Add 3 cups (24 fl oz/710 ml) water and the chicken stock and bring to a boil over high heat. Reduce the heat to medium-low, add the greens to the pot, and stir to ensure they are fully submerged in the liquid. Season the greens with salt, black pepper, and chile flakes and stir well to incorporate. Cover the pot with a tight-fitting lid and simmer the greens, stirring occasionally, until dark and tender, about 1 hour.

4 Return the crispy hog jowl pieces to the pot with the simmering greens. Stir in the vinegar and brown sugar, adjusting the seasoning to taste. Continue to simmer the greens and hog jowl for an additional 30 minutes, allowing the flavors to come together.

5 Once the turnip greens are tender, remove the pot from the heat and let it rest for 10–15 minutes.

6 To serve, use a slotted spoon to transfer the turnip greens and hog jowl to a serving platter, leaving most of the pot likker in the pot. Serve the pot likker separately for mopping up with cornbread.

TO RAISE AND TO HUNT

It's hard to imagine today, but before the Europeans arrived, thousands upon thousands of game animals roamed the warm, primeval Southern forests. Deer, bear, bison, wild turkey, small birds, aquatic mammals, and small game comprise a significant part of the indigenous Southern diet. These animals provided meat—and, in the case of the black bear, fat—and their skins, sinews, bones, claws, horns, etc. played numerous practical and spiritual roles. As colonists migrated from the coast into the Southern backcountry, however, native wildlife was exterminated in many areas, showing a casual disregard for the abundance and an aim to deplete resources for Native Americans, forcing them to move on. This colonization process was further aided by the introduction of domestic animals from the Old World. This spread disease and encroached upon Native settlements by grazing (as with cattle and sheep), out-reproducing (like swine), and destroying native ecosystems.

But alongside the narrative of fatal first contact is the exchange of resources that enriched the Southern way with animal proteins. The original game populations may have been depleted, and bison and elk may have been regionally exterminated, but bear, deer, turkey, small birds, and game continue to be part of Southern foodways through its hunting and conservation culture. African animals like guinea fowl, cattle, and the Guinea hog also crossed the Atlantic, and some Native American groups would breed their types of fowl and swine. Animals once let loose in the wilderness were tamed and bred to be more efficient meat sources. Over two hundred years, the South became a menagerie of Ossabaw and Choctaw hogs, Dominique chickens, Cotton Patch geese, Muscovy ducks, Gulf Coast sheep, and Bronze and White turkeys with varieties spanning the period of established rural homesteads to the heyday of the USDA (United States Department of Agriculture).

Animals that were originally stringy, unappetizing, dry-fleshed, and only meant for the one-pot stew were eventually improved to be worthy of roasting and barbecuing. Southern meat, poultry, and game were parts of a culture that valued hunting, animal husbandry, and the challenge of conquering and controlling nature (for good or for ill). Southern foodways also valued the well-spread table and abundance, life-cycle events, and celebrations where nobody left hungry and the host sought to impress. Barbecues were massive political events, and Sunday dinners and repasts solidified family connections. Both continued in different ways to shape Southern life. There is an oft-repeated myth about country hams being saved to be savored twenty- five years later at family weddings after purchase during the same child's infancy. And only in southern Louisiana can wedding vows include the declaration of a love surpassing cracklings and boudin.

CHICKEN-FRIED STEAK

South-Central Southern foodways are much more beef-oriented than the rest of the region, owing to the cattle-ranching economy of the Southern Plains. Here, cube steak gets the Southern fried chicken treatment until it's ready for gravy and mashed potatoes and rice, and since it is part of the state meal of Oklahoma, fried okra and then pecan pie for dessert.

PREPARATION TIME: 15 MINUTES
COOKING TIME: 25 MINUTES
SERVES: 4

4 cube steaks (minute steaks), ¼ inch thick (about 1 lb/450 g each)
Fine salt or House Seasoning (PAGE 301)
Freshly ground black pepper
1 cup (130 g) all-purpose (plain) flour
½ teaspoon garlic powder
½ teaspoon onion powder
½ teaspoon paprika
¼ teaspoon cayenne pepper (optional)
2 eggs
¼ cup (2 fl oz/60 ml) whole milk
Vegetable oil, for frying
2 cups (16 fl oz/470 ml) beef stock
½ cup (8 fl oz/120 ml) heavy (whipping) cream
Chopped fresh flat-leaf parsley (optional), for garnish

1 Season the cube steaks with salt and black pepper on both sides.

2 Set up a dredging station in two shallow bowls: In one bowl, combine the flour, garlic powder, onion powder, paprika, and cayenne (if using). In a second, whisk together the eggs and milk. Dredge each cube steak in the seasoned flour, shaking off any excess. Dip the steak into the egg mixture, then dredge again in the seasoned flour, pressing gently to adhere. (Reserve the dredging flour.)

3 Pour 2 inches (5 cm) oil into a large Dutch oven (casserole dish) and heat over medium-high heat until it reaches 350°F (177°C). Line a plate with paper towels and have near the stove.

4 Working in batches to avoid overcrowding, carefully place the coated cube steaks in the hot oil and fry until golden brown and crispy on both sides, 3–4 minutes per side. Remove the fried steaks to the paper towels to drain.

5 Pour off all but about 2 tablespoons of the oil from the skillet. Return the skillet to medium heat. Sprinkle 2 tablespoons of the seasoned flour mixture used for dredging into the skillet. Cook, stirring constantly, for 1 minute to make a roux. Slowly pour in the stock, whisking constantly to prevent lumps. Bring the mixture to a simmer and cook until thickened, about 5 minutes.

6 Stir in the heavy (whipping) cream and season with salt and black pepper to taste. Simmer, stirring occasionally, until the gravy is smooth and heated through, 2–3 minutes.

7 Serve the chicken fried steaks hot, topped with the gravy and garnished with parsley if desired.

TEXAS BRISKET

DF GF -5

Because the culture of home barbecue has flourished, this recipe was constructed with charcoal, a smoker, and pellet grills in mind. Despite the complexity of flavor in Texas brisket, its preparation is fairly straightforward, its flavor comes from salt, pepper, fat, and a light seasoning, rather than from heavy wood smoke. What you want to do with it in terms of sauce or mopping or rubs is really up to you; this is the skeleton recipe that helps you get the brisket ready for the table.

PREPARATION TIME: 20 MINUTES
COOKING TIME: 8–15 HOURS
SERVES: 8–10

1 packer brisket (8–10 lb/3.6–4.5 kg), untrimmed (see NOTE)
Fine salt and freshly ground coarse black pepper
2 tablespoons vegetable oil

1 Preheat a smoker or pellet grill for indirect cooking to 250°F (120°C) with oak or pecan wood chips or pellets.
2 Season the beef brisket generously with salt and black pepper on both sides. Rub both sides with the oil and set aside until smoker is ready.
3 Cook the brisket in the smoker or the pellet grill over indirect heat until seared, about 1½ hours per pound. Occasionally check the fire and temperature to ensure its not overheating or burning.
4 Once cooked, let the brisket rest for 15–20 minutes before slicing against the grain. There will be a "bark" (an outer crust on the outside of the meat) and a pink "smoke ring" just inside the edge of the bark. Slice thinly.

NOTE: A packer brisket is the whole brisket, with the flat cut and the point still attached to one another.

STORAGE: Store airtight in the refrigerator for up to 3 days.

VARIATION: Pre-rub with Texas-Style BBQ Rub (PAGE 302).

MISSISSIPPI ROAST BEEF

GF

This recipe is based on a popular 1990 slow-cooker version invented by Robin Chapman of Ripley, Mississippi. She famously reworked her family pot roast recipe in a slow cooker with ranch seasoning, pepperoncini peppers, and gravy mix. This recipe appears everywhere from church cookbooks to magazines to the internet, and underscores the dynamism of Southern foodways. Here is my interpretation made in a conventional oven.

PREPARATION TIME: 10 MINUTES
COOKING TIME: 6–8 HOURS
SERVES: 6–8

3–4 lb (1.4–1.8 kg) beef chuck roast
Fine salt and freshly ground black pepper
2 tablespoons vegetable oil
½ cup (4 fl oz/120 ml) beef stock
4 tablespoons (60 g) unsalted butter, cut into cubes
3 jarred pepperoncini peppers
2 tablespoons pepperoncini pickling liquid
1 packet (1 oz/27 g) ranch dressing mix
1 packet (1 oz/27 g) au jus gravy mix
1 teaspoon garlic powder
1 teaspoon onion powder
½ teaspoon dried dill (optional)
Chopped fresh flat-leaf parsley, for garnish

1 Season the chuck roast generously with salt and black pepper on all sides.
2 Preheat the oven to 275°F (130°C/Gas Mark 1).
3 In a large Dutch oven (casserole dish), heat the oil over medium-high heat. Sear the chuck roast on all sides until browned, 4–5 minutes per side. Remove the roast from the pan and set aside.
4 Add the beef stock to the Dutch oven and use a wooden spoon to scrape up any browned bits from the bottom of the pan. Return the chuck roast to the pan. Add the butter, pepperoncini peppers and two tablespoons of liquid, ranch dressing mix, au jus gravy mix, garlic powder, onion powder, and dried dill (if using). Cover the skillet or Dutch oven with a lid. Transfer it to the heated oven.
5 Roast the chuck roast for 6–8 hours, or until the meat is fork-tender and easily pulls apart. Once cooked, remove the Mississippi roast from the oven, and let it rest for a few minutes.
6 Slice or shred the chuck roast, and serve hot, garnished with chopped fresh parsley.

STORAGE: Store airtight in the refrigerator for up to 3 days.

GRILLADES AND GRITS

DF

Grits in one form or another are a breakfast staple in much of the South. In New Orleans they show up in grillades and grits. Grillades—pronounced gree-yahds, thin beef round steaks long-cooked in a Creole sauce—are an excellent pairing with toothsome grits. In this dish, the influences of France, West Africa, Spain, and the Americas all come together in one breakfast.

PREPARATION TIME: 20 MINUTES
COOKING TIME: 2 HOURS
SERVES: 4

1 lb (450 g) beef round steak (beef topside), cut into slices ¼ inch (6 mm) thick
Fine salt and freshly ground black pepper
Creole Seasoning (PAGE 299)
½ cup (65 g) all-purpose (plain) flour
4 tablespoons vegetable oil
1 medium green bell pepper, finely chopped
1 medium onion, finely chopped
2 celery stalks, finely chopped
3 cloves garlic, minced
1 can (14.5 oz/411 g) diced (chopped) tomatoes
1 cup (8 fl oz/240 ml) beef stock
1 teaspoon Worcestershire sauce
1 bay leaf
1 teaspoon ground thyme
Grits (PAGE 41) or 4 cups (960 g) prepared grits (see NOTE), for serving
Chopped fresh flat-leaf parsley, for garnish

1 Season the beef slices with salt, pepper, and Creole Seasoning to taste. Dredge each slice in the flour, shaking off any excess.

2 In a large cast-iron skillet or Dutch oven (casserole dish), heat 2 tablespoons oil over medium-high heat. Working in batches, sear the beef slices, turning with tongs, until well browned, 2–3 minutes per side. Transfer the browned beef to a plate and set aside.

3 In the same skillet, add the bell pepper, onion, celery, and garlic and the remaining 2 tablespoons oil if needed. Cook, stirring occasionally, until the vegetables are softened, 5–7 minutes.

4 Stir in the diced tomatoes, beef stock, Worcestershire sauce, bay leaf, and thyme and bring the mixture to a simmer. Return the browned beef slices to the skillet, nestling them into the sauce. Cover the skillet with a lid, reduce the heat to low, and simmer gently, stirring occasionally, until the beef is tender and the sauce has thickened, 1 ½–2 hours.

5 Once the grillades are cooked through and tender, discard the bay leaf. Taste and adjust the seasoning with salt and pepper if needed.

6 To serve, spoon the grillades over a bed of hot cooked grits. Garnish with parsley.

NOTE: Just cook the store-bought grits according to the package directions.

OXTAILS

DF

Southern oxtails may not be as well-known as those from the Caribbean, which are spicier and enjoyed with rice and peas, but they are equally flavorful and have a soul of their own. This recipe calls for a unique Southern ingredient, muscadine wine, a foxy, purple grape with a unique taste.

PREPARATION TIME: 30 MINUTES
COOKING TIME: 4 ½ HOURS
SERVES: 6

4 lb (1.8 kg) oxtail, cut into sections
3 tablespoons olive oil or bacon fat
1 large onion, finely chopped
2 carrots, chopped
2 celery stalks, chopped
1 medium green bell pepper, diced
4 cloves garlic, minced
2 teaspoons fine salt or House Seasoning (PAGE 301)
2 teaspoons Poultry Seasoning (PAGE 299)
1 teaspoon freshly ground black pepper
1 teaspoon sweet paprika
½ teaspoon dried thyme
½ teaspoon dried rosemary
2 bay leaves
½ teaspoon cayenne pepper
2 tablespoons tomato paste (tomato puree)
1 cup (8 fl oz/240 ml) muscadine wine (see NOTE)
4 cups (32 fl oz/950 ml) beef stock
1 tablespoon Worcestershire sauce

1 Preheat the oven to 325°F (160°C/Gas Mark 3).

2 Pat the oxtail sections dry with paper towels. In a large Dutch oven (casserole dish), heat the olive oil over medium-high heat. Working in batches, add the oxtail pieces to the hot oil, browning them on all sides. Remove the browned oxtail and set aside.

3 In the same Dutch oven, sauté the onion, carrots, celery, bell pepper, and garlic until they are softened and fragrant, 5–7 minutes.

4 Stir in the salt, Poultry Seasoning, black pepper, paprika, thyme, rosemary, bay leaves, and cayenne, cooking for an additional 2 minutes. Add the tomato paste (puree) to the pot, stirring well to coat the vegetables and spices. Pour in the muscadine wine, scraping up any browned bits from the bottom of the pot. Allow the wine to simmer and reduce by half, about 5 minutes.

5 Return the browned oxtail to the Dutch oven, nestling the pieces among the vegetables. Pour in the beef stock and 2 cups (16 fl oz/470 ml) water, ensuring the oxtail is mostly submerged. Stir in the Worcestershire sauce and bring the mixture to a simmer. Cover the Dutch oven with a tight-fitting lid and transfer to the oven.

6 Braise the oxtail until the meat is tender and falling off the bone, 3 ½–4 hours. Check the pot occasionally, adding more water if necessary to keep the oxtail mostly submerged.

7 Once the oxtail is tender, remove the Dutch oven from the oven and let it rest for 10–15 minutes. Skim off any excess fat from the surface of the braising liquid.

8 To serve, arrange the oxtail pieces on a serving platter and spoon the rich, flavorful sauce over the top.

NOTE: If you can't find muscadine, use Riesling or Gewürztraminer and add 1 tablespoon light brown sugar.

GULLAH-GEECHEE POT ROAST

DF

What makes this recipe uniquely Gullah-Geechee? The green bell pepper, subtle spicing, bay leaf, and rice all give you the soul of a Sunday dinner in Charleston, South Carolina, or Savannah, Georgia.

PREPARATION TIME: 20 MINUTES
COOKING TIME: 3 HOURS 15 MINUTES
SERVES: 6

3–4 lb (1.4–1.8 kg) beef chuck roast
Fine salt and freshly ground black pepper
2 tablespoons vegetable oil
1 medium onion, finely diced
1 medium green bell pepper, cut into small chunks
2 celery stalks, cut into small chunks
4 cloves garlic, minced
2 cups (16 fl oz/470 ml) beef stock
½ cup (90 g) chopped tomatoes
1 tablespoon Worcestershire sauce
1 tablespoon light brown sugar
1 teaspoon House Seasoning (PAGE 301)
1 bay leaf
Pinch of cayenne pepper
1 lb (450 g) white or yellow sweet potatoes (1–3), halved
Cooked white rice, for serving

1 Season the chuck roast generously with salt and pepper.

2 In a large Dutch oven (casserole dish) or heavy-bottomed pot, heat the oil over medium-high heat. Brown the chuck roast on all sides, turning with tongs, 4–5 minutes per side. Remove the roast from the pot and set aside.

3 In the same pot, add the onion, bell pepper, and celery and cook, stirring occasionally, until the vegetables are softened, about 5 minutes. Add the garlic and cook for 1 more minute until fragrant.

4 Return the chuck roast to the pot. Pour in the beef stock, tomatoes, Worcestershire sauce, brown sugar, House Seasoning, bay leaf, and cayenne. Stir to combine. Bring the mixture to a boil. Reduce the heat to low, cover, and simmer gently, stirring occasionally, until the beef is beginning to soften, about 1 ½ hours.

5 Add the sweet potatoes, pushing them down into the liquid around the roast. Cover again and continue to simmer until the roast is tender and the vegetables are cooked through, another 1 ½ hours.

6 Discard the bay leaf. Slice the pot roast and serve hot over rice, accompanied by the vegetables and plenty of the flavorful gravy.

TENNESSEE-INSPIRED SPICED BEEF ROUND

DF

Nashville spiced beef and spiced beef round are a significant parts of local Christmas tradition. Middle Tennessee had a pronounced German influence, and it was meat purveyors and butchers from German-speaking Europe that introduced these and other delicacies to postbellum (after 1865) Tennessee. As *The Nashville Union and American* noted in 1868, "We have looked over the bill of fare for the occasion, and find among other 'delicacies,' opossum, bone turkey, spiced round, venison, fish, oysters, quail, and things." Another paper noted that "beef is not as delicious prepared in any other way." Serve hot with other side dishes, or cold, thinly sliced with fresh Beaten Biscuits (PAGE 33). This recipe requires 2 weeks' advance preparation, but it's worth the effort.

PREPARATION TIME: 30 MINUTES, PLUS 2 WEEKS MARINATING TIME
COOKING TIME: 3 ½ HOURS
SERVES: 6

1 cup (144 g) kosher salt or ½ cup (144 g) fine salt
½ cup (95 g) light brown sugar
½ cup (4 fl oz/120 ml) sorghum syrup, golden syrup (such as Lyle's), or maple syrup
2 tablespoons Kitchen Pepper (PAGE 301)
1 tablespoon grated fresh ginger
1 ½ teaspoons ground allspice
1 teaspoon freshly ground coarse black pepper
1 teaspoon ground cinnamon
½ teaspoon cayenne pepper
4–5 lb (1.8–2.3 kg) beef top round (topside) roast
¼ cup (2 fl oz/60 ml) Worcestershire sauce
12 whole cloves
1 large yellow onion, peeled and halved
1 bay leaf

1 Two weeks prior to cooking, in a large bowl, combine the salt, brown sugar, sorghum syrup, Kitchen Pepper, fresh ginger, allspice, black pepper, cinnamon, and cayenne and mix well. Add the beef to the bowl and rub the mixture into all sides of the meat. Place the roast in a 2-gallon plastic freezer bag. Add the Worcestershire sauce and the bay leaf to the bag. Make sure the bag is completely sealed and shake it back and forth. Marinate in the refrigerator for 2 weeks, turning the meat over every day.

2 Preheat the oven to 275°F (130°C/Gas Mark 1).

3 Stick 6 whole cloves into each half of the onion. Reserving the marinade, transfer the meat to a large Dutch oven (casserole dish). Pour ¾ cup (6 fl oz/180 ml) of the reserved marinade down the sides of the pot. Retrieve the onion and bay leaf from the bag and tuck into the pot around the beef. Cover the pot tightly and transfer to the oven.

4 Braise until the beef is soft, fragrant, and tender and shows no resistance when tested with a large fork, about 3 ½ hours.

5 Transfer the beef to a tray and let cool to room temperature. Cover with foil or plastic wrap and refrigerate for at least 8 hours, or until the beef is completely chilled. Thinly slice to serve.

ROAST WILD DUCK

GF

Roast duck is especially dear to the coastal South. Maryland, South Carolina, Georgia, and Louisiana revere the migration of wild ducks that provision the table with a canvasback, teal, mallard, or wood duck. Serve hot with Southern-style sides such as collard greens, cornbread, or Candied Sweet Potatoes (PAGE 112).

PREPARATION TIME: 30 MINUTES
COOKING TIME: 1½ HOURS
SERVES: 6

2 wild ducks (about 3 ½ lb/1.6 kg each), plucked and cleaned
Fine salt and freshly ground black pepper
4 tablespoons (60 g) unsalted butter, melted
2 cloves garlic, minced
1 tablespoon chopped fresh rosemary
1 tablespoon chopped fresh sage
1 tablespoon fresh thyme leaves
4 slices bacon (streaky)
1 medium lemon, sliced
1 medium onion, sliced
2 cups (16 fl oz/470 ml) chicken or duck stock

1 Preheat the oven to 375°F (190°C/Gas Mark 5).

2 Season the cavity of each duck with salt and black pepper.

3 In a small bowl, mix together the melted butter, garlic, rosemary, sage, and thyme. Rub the outside of each duck with the seasoned butter mixture.

4 Turn the ducks breast-side up and drape 2 slices of bacon (streaky) over each duck. Stuff the cavity of each duck with half of the lemon and onion slices. Tie the legs of each duck together with kitchen twine.

5 Place the duck breast-side up in a on a wire rack set in a roasting pan and pour the stock into the bottom of the pan.

6 Roast the ducks, basting occasionally with the pan juices, until the skin is golden brown and crispy and the internal temperature reaches 165°F (74°C) in the thickest part of the breast, about 1 ½ hours. (If the ducks begin to brown too quickly, cover loosely with aluminum foil.)

7 Let the ducks rest for at least 10–15 minutes before carving.

OVEN-ROASTED QUAIL

GF

Some Southern poultry farmers have turned to domesticated quail and quail eggs, which are enjoying a renaissance among foodies, particularly in the Carolinas and Georgia. This is an elegant meal for special occasions and adds variety to your table, especially when paired with roasted oysters. Serve with hot grits or rice.

PREPARATION TIME: 15 MINUTES, PLUS 30 MINUTES MARINATING TIME
COOKING TIME: 45 MINUTES
SERVES: 4

- 8 whole quail (about 5 oz/140 g each), rinsed and patted dry
- ½ cup (4 fl oz/120 ml) fresh lemon juice
- 4 tablespoons (60 g) melted bacon fat or olive oil
- 4 cloves garlic, minced
- 2 tablespoons fresh rosemary, chopped
- 2 tablespoons fresh thyme, chopped
- 1 teaspoon freshly ground coarse black pepper
- 1 teaspoon paprika
- 1 teaspoon kosher salt or ½ teaspoon fine salt
- ½ teaspoon cayenne pepper
- 1 lemon, thinly sliced
- ½ cup (4 fl oz/120 ml) chicken stock
- ¼ cup (2 fl oz/60 ml) white wine
- 2 tablespoons (30 g) unsalted butter
- Chopped fresh flat-leaf parsley, for garnish

1 Lay the quail in a large shallow dish and add the lemon juice, turning several times to coat.

2 In a small bowl, combine the bacon fat, garlic, rosemary, thyme, black pepper, paprika, salt, and cayenne. Rub the mixture all over the quail, ensuring they are evenly coated. Set aside at room temperature and marinade the quail for at least 30 minutes.

3 Meanwhile, preheat the oven to 400°F (200°C/Gas Mark 6).

4 Fit a roasting rack in a large roasting pan. Set the quail on the rack and place the lemon slices around and on top of them. Pour the chicken stock and white wine into the bottom of the pan.

5 Roast the quail, basting occasionally with the pan juices, until the skin is golden brown and the meat is cooked through, 30–35 minutes.

6 Transfer the roasted quail to a serving dish and lightly tent with foil. Pour the pan juices into a small saucepan.

7 Add the butter to the pan juices and bring the mixture to a simmer over medium heat, whisking constantly until the butter is melted and the sauce has thickened, about 10 minutes.

8 Pour the sauce over the quail and garnish with parsley.

BARBECUED QUAIL

DF

In the South, some people use the term partridge for quail; even though they are not the same bird, it's a kind of shibboleth to separate Southern and Northern speakers. Once a favorite game item, quail are now farm-raised in many areas. Prized not only for their meat but also their eggs, Southerners enjoy them fried, barbecued, roasted, and smothered. Oysters and country ham complement their flavors well.

PREPARATION TIME: 15 MINUTES
COOKING TIME: 20 MINUTES
SERVES: 4

8 whole quail (about 5 oz/140 g each)
Fine salt and freshly ground coarse black pepper
¼ cup (2 fl oz/60 ml) bourbon (optional)
¼ cup (2 fl oz/60 ml) honey
¼ cup (2 fl oz/60 ml) extra-virgin olive oil
¼ cup (2 fl oz/60 ml) soy sauce
4 cloves garlic, minced
2 tablespoons Dijon mustard
1 tablespoon fresh rosemary, chopped, plus more for garnish
1 tablespoon fresh thyme leaves, plus more for garnish
Grated zest and juice of 1 lemon

1 Preheat an outdoor grill (barbecue) to medium-high heat.

2 Season the quail generously with salt and black pepper.

3 In a small bowl, whisk together the bourbon (if using), honey, olive oil, soy sauce, garlic, mustard, rosemary, thyme, lemon zest, and lemon juice.

4 Place the quail on the grill and cook, basting frequently with the marinade, until they are golden brown and cooked through, 8–10 minutes per side. During the last few minutes of cooking, continue to brush the quails with the marinade to build a sticky glaze.

5 Let the quail rest for a few minutes before serving.

6 Serve hot, garnished with fresh herbs if desired.

ROAST TURKEY

GF

Southern Thanksgiving tables often feature cornbread dressing, macaroni and cheese, potato salad, sweet potato pie or Cinnamon Baked Cushaw (PAGE 111), and turkeys that have been roasted, smoked, or, popularly deep-fried, along with any regional or ethnic treats specific to family tradition. This is an old-fashioned Southern, highly seasoned roast turkey that is perfect for a large occasion or holiday dinner.

PREPARATION TIME: 35 MINUTES
COOKING TIME: 3 HOURS
SERVES: 10

- 1 whole turkey (12–14 lb/5.4–6.3 kg), thawed if frozen
- House Seasoning (PAGE 301) or fine salt
- Freshly ground coarse black pepper
- 8 tablespoons (4 oz/115 g) unsalted butter, melted
- 1 tablespoon garlic powder
- 1 tablespoon onion powder
- 1 tablespoon sweet paprika
- 1 tablespoon Poultry Seasoning (PAGE 299)
- 1 tablespoon dried rosemary
- 1 tablespoon rubbed sage
- 1 lemon, quartered
- 1 Vidalia onion, quartered
- 1 celery stalk, chopped
- 2 cloves garlic, peeled but whole
- 4 sprigs fresh rosemary
- 4 sprigs fresh thyme
- 2 cups (16 fl oz/470 ml) chicken or turkey stock

1 Preheat the oven to 500°F (260°C/Gas Mark 10). Set a wire rack in a large roasting pan.

2 Remove the giblets and neck from inside the turkey cavity. Rinse the turkey under cold water and pat dry with paper towels. Season the cavity of the turkey generously with House Seasoning and black pepper to taste.

3 In a small bowl, mix together the melted butter, garlic powder, onion powder, paprika, Poultry Seasoning, rosemary, and sage.

4 Place the turkey breast-side up on the rack. Stuff the turkey cavity with the lemon, onion, celery, garlic cloves, rosemary sprigs, and thyme sprigs. Tie the legs of the turkey together with kitchen twine and tuck the wing tips under the body of the turkey. Brush the outside of the turkey with half of the seasoned butter mixture. Reserve the remaining butter mixture for basting. Pour the chicken or turkey stock into the bottom of the roasting pan.

5 Roast the turkey, allowing the bird to get nice and brown, for 30 minutes. Baste, then reduce the oven temperature to 325°F (160°C/Gas Mark 3) and loosely drape with parchment paper. Remember to baste every 30 minutes with the reserved seasoned butter mixture and pan juices, until the internal temperature reaches 165°F (74°C) in the thickest part of the thigh and the juices run clear, 2 ½–3 hours.

6 Once cooked through, remove the turkey from the oven and let it rest for at least 20–30 minutes before carving.

STORAGE: Store airtight in the refrigerator for up to 4 days.

FRIED RABBIT

An elder I met in Atlanta, Georgia, talked about migrating from the South to the North. He left Alabama with a shoebox full of fried rabbit, biscuits, and potato salad his grandmother made for the journey. Rabbit was once a far more common protein in the rural South, and is still enjoyed in many parts of West Virginia, but it generally lost favor because it was served too often—fried, stewed, fricasseed, or smothered.

PREPARATION TIME: 30 MINUTES
COOKING TIME: 30 MINUTES
SERVES: 4

2 whole rabbits (about 3 lb/1.4 kg each), cut into serving pieces
Fine salt or House Seasoning (PAGE 301) and freshly ground black pepper
1 cup (130 g) all-purpose (plain) flour
¼ teaspoon cayenne pepper
½ cup (4 fl oz/120 ml) buttermilk
2 eggs
1 cup (130 g) white or yellow cornmeal
Vegetable oil, for frying

1 Rinse the rabbit pieces under cold water and pat them dry with paper towels. Season the rabbit pieces generously with salt and black pepper.
2 Pour 1 inch (2.5 cm) oil into a large Dutch oven (casserole dish) and heat over medium-high heat to 350°F (177°C). Line a baking sheet with paper towels and have near the stove.
3 Set up a dredging station in three shallow bowls: In a one bowl, stir together the flour and cayenne. In a second bowl, combine the buttermilk and eggs. Spread the cornmeal in a third bowl. Dredge each rabbit piece first in the seasoned flour, shaking off any excess, then dip into the egg/buttermilk mixture, allowing any excess to drip off. Coat each piece thoroughly with the cornmeal mixture, pressing gently to adhere.
4 Working in batches to avoid overcrowding, carefully place the rabbit pieces in the hot oil and fry until golden brown on both sides and the internal temperature reads 165°F (74°C), 5–7 minutes per side. Transfer the fried rabbit pieces to the paper towels to drain.
5 Serve hot.

RABBIT STEW

DF GF

Rabbit or hare stew goes back to Mary Randolph's *The Virginia House-Wife*, drawing deeply on British roots. There would eventually be rabbits raised on many farms, but in the Colonial and Antebellum era and beyond, there were thousands of wild rabbits that often plagued the gardens that encroached upon their habitat. Rabbits or hares were part of the diet of Native American, African, and European eaters.

PREPARATION TIME: 30 MINUTES
COOKING TIME: 2 ½ HOURS
SERVES: 6

- 1 whole rabbit (2–3 lb/910 g to 1.4 kg), cut into pieces
- 1 teaspoon fine salt or House Seasoning (PAGE 301)
- 1 teaspoon Kitchen Pepper (PAGE 301)
- 3 tablespoons extra-virgin olive oil
- ½ cup (75 g) finely diced salt pork, rinsed
- 1 medium onion, finely chopped
- 2 medium carrots, peeled and sliced
- 2 celery stalks, sliced
- 4 cloves garlic, minced
- 2 cups (16 fl oz/470 ml) chicken stock
- 1 cup (8 fl oz/240 ml) Madeira wine
- 1 tablespoon tomato paste (tomato puree)
- 1 teaspoon dried rosemary
- 1 teaspoon dried thyme
- 1 bay leaf

1 Rub the rabbit with salt and Kitchen Pepper.

2 In a large Dutch oven (casserole dish) or heavy-bottomed pot, heat the olive oil over medium-high heat. Working in batches to avoid overcrowding, brown the rabbit pieces on all sides, turning with tongs, about 5 minutes per side. Remove the rabbit pieces and set aside.

3 To the same pot, add the salt pork, onion, carrots, and celery. Cook, stirring occasionally, until the vegetables are softened, 5–7 minutes. Add the garlic and cook, stirring, until fragrant, about 1 minute.

4 Return the browned rabbit pieces to the pot. Pour in the stock, Madeira, and tomato paste (tomato puree) and stir to combine. Add the rosemary, thyme, and bay leaf and season with additional salt and pepper if needed. Bring the stew to a boil. Reduce the heat to low, cover, and simmer gently, stirring occasionally, until the rabbit is tender and cooked through, 1 ½–2 hours.

5 Discard the bay leaf before serving.

VENISON STEW

DF GF

Venison was a prestige game meat for British elites. The deer were kept in private parks, and the poor were not allowed to hunt them. When the British arrived in what would become the American South, the top animal protein for Native American people was the whitetail deer, which was plentiful and freely available. Hunter's stews were a central part of a world where humans had to constantly beat back nature and game, which competed for resources and took advantage of crops. According to one scientific estimate, upon European arrival there were several hundred deer per every ten square miles. Today it is still considered a delicacy in many parts of the South, and especially in West Virginia.

PREPARATION TIME: 45 MINUTES
COOKING TIME: 2 ½ HOURS
SERVES: 10

2 tablespoons vegetable oil
2 lb (910 g) venison stew meat, cubed
1 medium onion, diced
2 cloves garlic, minced
4 cups (32 fl oz/950 ml) beef or venison stock
1 cup (8 fl oz/240 ml) red wine, such as a Shiraz or Zinfandel
2 medium potatoes, peeled and diced
3 medium carrots, peeled and sliced
1 celery stalk, diced
1 bay leaf
1 teaspoon dried thyme
1 teaspoon dried rosemary
Fine salt and freshly ground black pepper
2 tablespoons all-purpose (plain) flour (optional, for thickening)
Chopped fresh flat-leaf parsley, for garnish

1 In a large pot or Dutch oven (casserole dish), heat the oil over medium-high heat. Working in batches to avoid crowding, add the venison and sear, turning with tongs, until browned on all sides, 5–6 minutes. Repeat with the remaining venison.

2 Add the onion and garlic and cook, stirring occasionally, until the onion is translucent, 3–4 minutes.

3 Pour in the stock and red wine, scraping any browned bits from the bottom of the pot. Add the potatoes, carrots, celery, bay leaf, thyme, rosemary, and salt and pepper to taste. Bring the stew to a boil. Reduce the heat to low, cover, and simmer until the venison is tender and the vegetables are cooked through, 1 ½–2 hours.

4 If desired, mix the flour with a little water to form a slurry and stir into the stew to thicken the broth, if a thicker consistency is preferred. Simmer for an additional 10–15 minutes.

5 Discard the bay leaf before serving. Garnish with fresh parsley.

STORAGE: Store airtight in the refrigerator for up to 4 days.

POSSUM AND SWEET POTATOES

DF GF

The pairing of opossum and sweet potatoes goes back to the time of enslavement. Enslaved Africans took native game and an American vegetable and prepared it in a way that bridged Western European and Western African tastes and techniques. For many enslaved people and their descendants over the next generations, this was a key dish at holiday time. The possum was never roadkill; the best opossum had to be taken alive and fed food to clean it out before it was culled. Luckily by the winter months, the opossums were fat—and were eating more fruits and nuts and less carrion—and were thus easier to capture. The recipe is presented here not as a license to harm the Virginia opossum—a 5-pound (2.25 kg) pork roast will also work—but to remind us of the impact of time and place on Southern cuisine.

PREPARATION TIME: 15 MINUTES, PLUS 30 MINUTES MARINATING TIME
COOKING TIME: 2 ½ HOURS
SERVES: 6

1 possum (8 lb/3.6 kg), cleaned and cut into 6–8 serving pieces
½ cup (4 fl oz/120 ml) apple cider vinegar
Fine salt and Kitchen Pepper (PAGE 301)
2 tablespoons bacon fat or vegetable oil
1 medium green bell pepper, chopped
1 medium onion, chopped
2 celery stalks, chopped
2 large sweet potatoes, peeled and cut into 2-inch (5 cm) chunks
2 cups (16 fl oz/470 ml) chicken stock
2 tablespoons brown sugar or sorghum syrup
1 teaspoon dried thyme
½ teaspoon cayenne pepper

1 Preheat the oven to 350°F (180°C/Gas Mark 4).

2 In a large bowl, add the possum quarters and vinegar, turning to coat. Refrigerate for 30 minutes, then drain and wipe dry. Season the possum quarters generously with salt and Kitchen Pepper.

3 In a large Dutch oven (casserole dish) or ovenproof heavy-bottomed pot, heat the bacon fat over medium-high heat. Add the possum quarters and brown on all sides, 4–5 minutes per side. Remove the possum from the pot and set aside.

4 In the same pot, add the bell pepper, onion, and celery and cook, stirring occasionally, until the vegetables are softened, 5–7 minutes.

5 Return the possum quarters to the pot. Add the sweet potatoes, stock, brown sugar, thyme, and cayenne. Stir well to combine. Cover the pot and transfer to the oven.

6 Bake until the possum is tender and cooked through and the sweet potatoes are soft, 2–2 ½ hours.

7 Let the possum rest for a few minutes before serving.

BARBECUED MUTTON

DF

How do you bring home Kentucky lamb barbecue? Using oak, hickory, or apple chips (or wood pellets) on an outdoor grill (barbecue) or smoker, you can get the flavor pretty close. (If you don't have an outdoor grill, see the oven variation below). Serve hot with buns and Owensboro Kentucky Mutton BBQ Sauce (PAGE 284).

PREPARATION TIME: 30 MINUTES
COOKING TIME: 4–6 HOURS
SERVES: 6–8

1 mutton shoulder (4–5 lb/1.8–2.3 kg)
Fine salt and freshly ground black pepper
¼ cup (2 fl oz/60 ml) vegetable oil or bacon fat
1 ½ cups (12 fl oz/350 ml) beef stock
½ cup (4 fl oz/120 ml) fresh lemon juice
2 tablespoons Worcestershire sauce
1 tablespoon brown sugar or sorghum syrup
2 teaspoons kosher salt or House Seasoning (PAGE 301), or 1 teaspoon

1 Set up a smoker or an outdoor grill (barbecue) for low and slow cooking at 220°F (105°C).
2 Season the mutton shoulder generously with salt and black pepper.
3 In a large cast-iron skillet, heat the oil over medium-high heat. Sear the mutton on all sides, turning with tongs, until browned, 4–5 minutes per side. Remove the mutton and set aside.
4 In a small saucepan, combine the stock, lemon juice, Worcestershire sauce, brown sugar, and salt. Set the mop outside near the grill or smoker.
5 Place the mutton in the smoker or on the grill fat-side up. Cover and smoke until the mutton reads around 170°F (77°C), about 1 ½ hours per pound, using oak, hickory, and apple chips or wood pellets to produce the smoke. Mop every hour.
6 Let the mutton rest for 15–20 minutes, then shred or slice.

STORAGE: Store airtight in the refrigerator for up to 4 days.

VARIATION: To prepare in the oven, preheat the oven to 275°F (130°C/Gas Mark 1). Sear the mutton as directed and place the seared mutton in a large roasting pan. Omit the mop. Cover tightly with aluminum foil and roast until the meat is tender and easily pulls apart with a fork, 4–6 hours. Baste the mutton occasionally with the pan juices. Let rest, then shred or slice before serving.

RENDERED BACON FAT

DF GF -5

Many Southern recipes benefit from this essential homemade ingredient. (A high-quality thick-cut bacon will yield the best flavor and a higher quality of fat.) A final strain of the fat will result in a smooth, clean fat, ideal for use in future recipes.

PREPARATION TIME: 5 MINUTES
COOKING TIME: 30 MINUTES
MAKES: 1 CUP (220 G)

1 lb (450 g) thick-cut bacon (streaky), cut crosswise into ½-inch (13 mm) pieces

1 Set a large heavy-bottomed frying pan or cast-iron skillet over medium-low heat. Once the pan is warm, add the bacon (streaky) pieces in a single layer, ensuring they are not overcrowded. (Work in batches as needed to avoid overcrowding.) Line a plate with paper towels and have near the stove.

2 As the bacon begins to cook, the fat will slowly melt and accumulate in the pan. Stir the bacon occasionally to prevent sticking and to ensure even cooking. Cook slowly and gently for 20–30 minutes, allowing the fat to render out completely without burning.

3 Once the bacon is crispy and has released most of its fat, use a slotted spoon to remove it to the prepared plate. (Reserve the cooked bacon for another use.)

4 Allow the rendered fat (which should be clear and golden in color) to cool slightly in the pan before carefully pouring it through a fine-mesh sieve or cheesecloth into a heatproof container. Let the fat cool to room temperature, then cover the container tightly and store it in the refrigerator.

STORAGE: Store airtight in the refrigerator for up to 6 months.

SAUCES, SEASONINGS & PICKLES

CREOLE OR CAJUN?

The two French-speaking cultures of renown in southern Louisiana are not the same, nor are their cuisines. Outsiders often think of both Cajun and Creole cuisines as shorthand for spicy food. In the 1980s, comedian and television chef Justin Wilson's cooking show embraced the liberal use of cayenne pepper, which scandalized and enthralled audiences. Chef Paul Prudhomme was responsible for popularizing "blackening" (creating a heavily seasoned crust on redfish, chicken, and other delicacies), leaving many to believe that hot and spicy flavors might be central to either genre of cuisine. The reality of Cajun cuisine is much more born out of culture and environment.

Creole culture emerged from the urban centers of the South, combining elements of French, Spanish, West and Central African (Bamana, Wolof, Fulani, Fon, Yoruba, and Kongo civilizations), and local Native American cultures (like the Choctaw and Chitimacha), and later influences from Southern Anglo-American settlers, German, Irish, and Italian immigrants. Creole culture emerged in New Orleans and Mobile (on the Gulf Coast of Alabama), and on the sugarcane plantations and towns along the tributaries of the lower Mississippi across three centuries. Creole food brought together culinary elements of all these cultures to form a foundational cuisine.

Creole food was informed on the European side by French vegetables and livestock cooked into braises and stews, Spanish dishes like paella, Franco-German charcuterie, and touches from later immigrant communities. Upon arrival, these traditions incorporated indigenous ingredients, including crops, foraged foods, local fish and shellfish, and unique elements like filé powder ground from dried sassafras leaves. The enslaved and free cooks added African ingredients like okra, black-eyed peas (black-eye beans), and other beans to European dishes, along with cooking traditions emphasizing rice-based dishes, deep-fried proteins, and quick fritters, and seafood stews liberally flavored with heady seasonings.

In contrast, Cajun foodways are rural traditions based on what the wilderness, farms, and waters had to offer. The Acadian Diaspora comprised refugees from Nova Scotia, Canada, who came from a strong pioneering culture. The influence of Africa came through the maroons, the enslaved, and the Free People of Color who had settled in these regions. The Native Americans who had retreated to the bayous to escape persecution forged a similar bond. Cajun food, especially in the south-central part of Louisiana, is of the land and bayou; other Cajun foodways are of the Gulf Coast west of the lower Mississippi.

Although hot chile peppers—from long red cayennes to little red Tabasco peppers—are staples in both traditions, neither Creole nor Cajun cuisine is reckless with hot peppers or hot pepper sauce. Heat enhances but does not define the foodways of South Louisiana. There is tremendous pride in the craft of cooking, of how the food looks, tastes, and smells, and how the community will receive it. Cajun foodways are built around annual events, including the hog killing or boucherie, which is followed by the making of andouille sausage and ham for the year, and the cooking of pots of stew made with the pig's spine to feed the working crowd. During Mardi Gras, wandering crewes—the people who support the floats in the annual parades—work together to assemble chicken gumbo. There are festivals, dinners and dances to celebrate the seasonal harvests of crawfish, rice, sugarcane, or sweet potato, and massive brown jambalayas are prepared for large gatherings.

The Creole traditionally had calas, pain perdu, grits, grillades, tomato-based jambalaya, and various étouffées featuring saltwater fish and shellfish; the Cajun have their coush-coush, tomato-less jambalaya, and dishes featuring freshwater fish and crawfish. Sometimes, the differences are subtle, and sometimes they are more abrupt. Over time, in restaurant culture, the two cuisines have intersected and blended. They share the same "holy trinity" of onion, celery, and green bell peppers, the sofrito of southern Louisianan cuisines to which garlic, known as "the pope," is sometimes added. No words can do them justice. You just have to eat the food and feel the difference.

SMOKED PORK STOCK

DF GF

This smoky full-bodied stock makes it easier to prepare a rich base for gravies or sauces, or a cooking liquid for vegetables like string or pole beans, cabbage, potatoes, greens, and the like.

PREPARATION TIME: 15 MINUTES
COOKING TIME: 2 1/2 HOURS
MAKES: ABOUT 2 QUARTS (2 LITERS)

1–2 lb (450–910 g) smoked ham hocks or cured country ham
1 teaspoon fine salt
1 teaspoon freshly ground coarse black pepper or Kitchen Pepper (PAGE 301)
3 medium carrots, roughly chopped
3 celery stalks, roughly chopped
2 sprigs fresh thyme
1 medium onion, quartered
1 bay leaf

1 In a large soup pot, combine all the ingredients with 12 cups (3 qt/2.8 liters) water and bring to a boil. Reduce the heat to medium-low, partially cover, and simmer, skimming occasionally to ensure that the stock is clear, until the stock has reduced to about 8 cups (2 qt/2 liters), about 2 ½ hours.

2 Carefully strain the liquid and discard the solids. (If you like, pull the meat off the ham hocks and return to the stock.)

STORAGE: Store airtight in the refrigerator for 3 days, or in the freezer for up to 2 months.

POT LIKKER

DF GF

Although pot likker is usually a byproduct of making greens, and is a key Southern ingredient for many dishes, having a separate and concentrated form of pot likker is great for cooking Southern vegetables and making sauces and gravies. The role it plays in your kitchen is only limited by your creativity and how you want to layer flavor. Much like my Grandma's Stock (PAGE 272), it's meant to add just a little something extra to savory dishes.

PREPARATION TIME: 20 MINUTES
COOKING TIME: 1 HOUR
MAKES: 4 CUPS (32 FL OZ/950 ML)

1 lb (450 g) chopped collard greens, leaves and stems
1 medium onion, chopped
2 cloves garlic, minced
1 celery stalk, chopped
1 medium carrot (optional), chopped
½ lb (225 g) smoked meat (optional), such as split smoked ham hocks, smoked turkey, etc.
Water, Smoked Pork Stock (PAGE 265), or smoked turkey stock

1. In a large pot, combine the greens, onion, garlic, celery, carrot (if using), and smoked meat (if using). Add water or stock to cover by 3 inches (7 ½ cm). Bring to a boil over medium-high heat. Reduce the heat to medium-low, cover, and simmer for 1 hour to meld the flavors.
2. Strain out the solids.

STORAGE: Store in an airtight container in the refrigerator for up to 1 week.

VIDALIA ONION SAUCE

DF GF V VE -30

Sweet Georgia Vidalia onions make a fantastic onion gravy for rice, pork chops, fried chicken, and vegetables.

PREPARATION TIME: 15 MINUTES
COOKING TIME: 20 MINUTES
MAKES: ¾ CUP (6 FL OZ/180 ML)

½ teaspoon vegetable oil
1 large Vidalia onion, thinly sliced
1 teaspoon fine salt
1 tablespoon sugar, or 2 tablespoons cane syrup
1 ¼ teaspoons cornstarch (cornflour)
3 tablespoons distilled white vinegar
1 teaspoon onion powder
½ teaspoon garlic powder

1 In a small frying pan, heat the oil over medium heat. Add the onions and ¼ teaspoon of the salt. Cook until the onions are soft and caramelized, about 12 minutes, stirring briskly and adjusting the heat as needed to prevent the onions from burning. Set the onions aside to cool.

2 Once cooled, transfer the onions to a blender. Add the remaining ¾ teaspoon salt, the sugar or cane syrup, and ½ cup (4 fl oz/120 ml) water and blend until very smooth.

3 Run the onion puree through a fine-mesh sieve to remove any chunks. Return the onion puree to the skillet. Stir the cornstarch (cornflour) into a small amount of water and add to the onion puree along with the vinegar, onion powder, and garlic powder. Bring to a boil, whisking, over medium-high heat. Reduce the heat to low and simmer for 3 minutes, until incorporated.

4 Remove from the heat and let cool before storing.

STORAGE: Store airtight in the refrigerator for up to 3 days.

RAW TOMATO RELISH

DF GF V VE

The relish plate gets a boost with a fresh mix similar to chimichurri. It's great with green beans, black-eyed peas (black-eye beans), okra, and greens or even roasted meat, poultry, or fish. It will give you a pop of grassy, tangy, and peppery.

PREPARATION TIME: 15 MINUTES, PLUS 1 HOUR REFRIGERATION TIME
MAKES: 1 ½ CUPS (300 G)

1 ½ cups (270 g) finely chopped tomatoes
½ cup (80 g) chopped Vidalia onion
2 ½ tablespoons red wine vinegar
2 tablespoons finely chopped fresh flat-leaf parsley
2 tablespoons sugar
½ teaspoon House Seasoning (PAGE 301)
½ teaspoon freshly ground coarse black pepper

In a medium bowl, combine all the ingredients. Cover with plastic wrap and refrigerate for at least 1 hour before serving.

STORAGE: Store airtight in the refrigerator for up to 4 days.

SOUTHERN TOMATO GRAVY

DF

Some Southern tomato gravies are in the milk gravy family, but this one is a less rich alternative, and can be eaten with a more versatile array of foods from fried chicken to biscuits to vegetables, beef and beyond.

PREPARATION TIME: 10 MINUTES
COOKING TIME: 25 MINUTES
MAKES: ABOUT 3 CUPS (24 FL OZ/710 ML)

3 tablespoons vegetable oil or bacon fat
1 clove garlic, minced
3 tablespoons all-purpose (plain) flour
1 ⅓ cups (11 fl oz/320 ml) chicken stock
2 cups (360 g) diced seeded fresh tomatoes
½ teaspoon light brown sugar
½ teaspoon fine salt
½ teaspoon freshly ground black pepper
1 teaspoon onion powder

1 In a frying pan, warm the oil or bacon fat over medium heat. Add the garlic, stirring quickly so it does not burn. Add the flour and cook, stirring constantly, until the flour turns a pale brown, to make a roux, about 10 minutes. Once the roux becomes fragrant, whisk in the chicken stock and stir until very smooth.

2 Add the tomatoes, brown sugar, salt, black pepper, and onion powder. Reduce the heat and cook, stirring frequently, until thickened, about 10 minutes.

3 Serve hot.

GRANDMA'S STOCK

DF GF

This was my Alabama grandmother's way of not letting odds and bits go to waste. You can use frozen vegetable scraps if you like. We never really used water on its own for soups and sauces, so this was a great way to build flavor quickly and to be resourceful. You can add a few carrot tops if you wish.

PREPARATION TIME: 20 MINUTES
COOKING TIME: 3 HOURS
MAKES: ABOUT 2 QUARTS (2 LITERS)

2 lb (910 g) chicken feet, wings, or backs
1 medium white turnip, sliced into chunks
½ rutabaga (swede), cut into chunks
4 large carrots, cut into chunks
2 cups (90 g) chopped collard, kale, or mustard greens (or just the stems)
1 celery stalk, cut into chunks
2 large onions, quartered, or 1 whole onion
8 whole cloves
2 cloves garlic, smashed and peeled
1 herb bundle: fresh thyme, rosemary, sage, and flat-leaf parsley
2 teaspoons kosher salt or 1 teaspoon fine salt, plus more
1 teaspoon Kitchen Pepper (PAGE 301)

1 In a large pot, combine the chicken parts, turnip, rutabaga (swede), carrots, greens, and celery. Stud the onion with the cloves and add to the pot along with the garlic, herb bundle, salt, and Kitchen Pepper. Add cold water to cover by 3 inches (7.5 cm) and bring to a low boil. Reduce to a simmer, cover, and cook for 3 hours, until fragrant and rich in color.

2 Strain through a cheesecloth and discard the solids.

STORAGE: Store airtight in the refrigerator for 3–4 days or in the freezer for up to 3 months.

COLESLAW DRESSING

DF GF V -30

Coleslaw is a necessity for barbecue, fried fish, and picnics in the South. This basic dressing will give the coleslaw a traditional Southern taste.

PREPARATION TIME: 10 MINUTES
SERVES: 4

¾ cup (165 g) mayonnaise
2 tablespoons apple cider vinegar
1 tablespoon Dijon mustard
1–2 teaspoons sugar, to taste
¾ teaspoon celery seeds
¼ teaspoon kosher salt or ⅛ teaspoon fine salt
Freshly ground black pepper

In a medium bowl, whisk together all the ingredients until fully incorporated. Refrigerate until needed.

VARIATION: Southern Coleslaw: Toss the dressing with 2 cups shredded cabbage or coleslaw mix. Let sit for at least 30 minutes and up to 1 hour before serving.

VINAIGRETTE

DF GF V VE -30

This is a simple table dressing for fresh salads. From wild greens to domesticated lettuces, fresh salads hold an important place in Southern cuisine. This recipe hearkens back to the days of Mary Randolph and her cookbook, *The Virginia House-Wife.*

PREPARATION TIME: 5 MINUTES
MAKES: ¾ CUP (6 FL OZ/180 ML)

2 cloves garlic, minced
½ cup (4 fl oz/120 ml) extra-virgin olive oil
3 tablespoons white wine vinegar
1 tablespoon Dijon mustard
1 teaspoon sweet paprika
1 teaspoon superfine (caster) sugar
¼ teaspoon kosher salt or ⅛ teaspoon fine salt
Freshly ground black pepper, to taste

In a medium bowl, whisk together the ingredients until completely combined.

STORAGE: Store airtight in the refrigerator for up to 7 days. Shake well before using.

GAME MARINADE

DF -30

If you're going to barbecue racoon, deer, rabbit, or squirrel, you're going to need this piquant apple cider vinegar–based marinade to get that gamey taste out of it. One batch of this is sufficient for 2–3 pounds of meat, which should be marinated for about 12 hours.

PREPARATION TIME: 10 MINUTES
MAKES: 1 QUART (1 LITER)

1 ½ cups (12 fl oz/350 ml) extra-virgin olive oil
¾ cup (6 fl oz/180 ml) soy sauce
1 cup (8 fl oz/240 ml) apple cider vinegar
½ cup (4 fl oz/120 ml) fresh lemon juice
¼ cup (2 fl oz/60 ml) Worcestershire sauce
2 cloves garlic, roughly chopped
1 ½ teaspoons roughly chopped fresh flat-leaf parsley
2 tablespoons mustard powder
2 ¼ teaspoons kosher salt or 1 ⅛ teaspoons fine salt
1 teaspoon freshly ground black pepper
1 teaspoon Kitchen Pepper (PAGE 301)

In a large bowl, mix all the ingredients until well combined.

STORAGE: Store airtight in the refrigerator for up to 1 week.

MILK OR PAN GRAVY

V -5 -30

This is what Southerners call "chicken gravy," because it typically accompanies Maryland fried chicken, along with side dishes including biscuits, rice, Corn Mush (PAGE 83), waffles, and the like. You could also use it to serve with Chicken-Fried Steak (PAGE 241), Southern Fried Chicken (PAGE 204) or Fried Rabbit (PAGE 256).

PREPARATION TIME: 10 MINUTES
COOKING TIME: 20 MINUTES
MAKES: 3 CUPS (24 FL OZ/710 ML)

2 tablespoons pan drippings (from frying chicken), vegetable oil, or vegetable shortening
1 ½ tablespoons all-purpose (plain) flour, plus more as needed
2 cups (16 fl oz/470 ml) whole milk
1 teaspoon freshly ground fine black pepper
½ teaspoon fine salt or House Seasoning (PAGE 256)
Chicken or vegetable stock (optional)

1 In a frying pan, heat the drippings or oil over medium heat. Slowly add the flour, whisking constantly for 2–3 minutes until smooth. Keep whisking and slowly pour in the milk. Bring to a quick boil, being careful not to let it burn. Add the black pepper and salt and whisk until thickened.

2 Reduce the heat and simmer until it has thickened and the ingredients have melded together, 8–10 minutes. (Chicken or vegetable stock can be whisked in to thin the gravy, if it becomes too thick.)

VARIATION: Cut a small onion into slices ⅛ inch (3 mm) thick and add at the same time you add in the seasonings. Cook in the gravy for 10 minutes.

SHRIMP GRAVY

This gravy is great over rice, or over vegetables, or it can be used to give a little surf-and-turf treatment to another protein.

PREPARATION TIME: 10 MINUTES
COOKING TIME: 30 MINUTES
SERVES: 4

- 1 lb (450 g) shrimp (prawns), peeled, deveined, and roughly chopped
- 3 tablespoons extra-virgin olive oil
- ¼ teaspoon kosher salt or House Seasoning (PAGE 301), or ⅛ teaspoon fine salt
- ⅛ teaspoon freshly ground coarse black pepper
- ½ teaspoon seafood seasoning, such as Old Bay
- ½ cup diced white or yellow onion
- ½ cup diced green bell pepper
- ½ cup diced celery
- 8 ounces (225 g) mushrooms, chopped
- 3 tablespoons (45 g) unsalted butter
- 3 tablespoons all-purpose (plain) flour
- 2 cups (16 fl oz/470 ml) half-and-half (single cream)
- ½ teaspoon paprika
- 1 tablespoon fresh lemon juice

1 In a medium bowl, toss the shrimp (prawns) with 1 tablespoon of the olive oil and season with the salt, black pepper, and seafood seasoning.

2 Heat a large nonstick frying pan over medium-high heat. Add the shrimp and cook until the shrimp is light pink on both sides, about 2 minutes. Remove from the heat, transfer to a dish, and set aside.

3 In the same pan, heat the remaining 2 tablespoons olive oil over medium heat. Add the onions, bell pepper, celery, and mushrooms and sauté until softened and browned, 5–7 minutes. Remove from the heat.

4 In a large saucepan, melt the butter over medium-high heat. Whisk in the flour until smooth and cook for 7-8 minutes, stirring constantly, to make a roux. Continuing to whisk, slowly pour in the half-and-half (single cream) and cook over medium-high heat until the gravy thickens, about 10 minutes.

5 Remove from the heat and stir in the vegetables and shrimp. Stir in the paprika and lemon juice.

RED-EYE GRAVY

DF GF -5 -30

The "red eye" in the title of this gravy allegedly dates back to Tennessee in the nineteenth century, when President Andrew Jackson asked for a gravy as red as the eyes of the inebriated chef preparing his breakfast. Some people add tomato or a touch of black pepper. My grandmother served it with grits and ham.

PREPARATION TIME: 10 MINUTES
COOKING TIME: 20 MINUTES
SERVES: 4

4 large slices country ham (about 8 oz/225 g total)
¾ cup (6 fl oz/180 ml) strong black coffee

1 Reserving the trimmings, trim most of the fat from the slices of ham.
2 Heat a large cast-iron skillet over medium-high heat. Add the ham trimmings and cook until 2–4 teaspoons of fat are rendered, 4–5 minutes.
3 Add the slices of ham to the skillet and cook until browned on both sides; about 10 minutes. Once fully cooked, remove the ham from the skillet and set aside.
4 Pour the coffee into the skillet and bring to a boil, scraping any bits that are stuck to the bottom. Reduce the heat and simmer until the liquid reduces to about ½ cup (4 fl oz/120 ml), about 10 minutes.
5 Discard the rendered fat pieces. Serve the ham hot with the gravy spooned on top.

SAUSAGE GRAVY

-5 -30

Sausage gravy and Drop Biscuits (PAGE 27) are friends. Though this gravy can go with rice and corn mush, too, the greatest pairing is drop biscuits, hot and freshly cut open, with sausage gravy on top.

PREPARATION TIME: 10 MINUTES
COOKING TIME: 20 MINUTES
SERVES: 8

1 lb (450 g) loose pork breakfast sausage meat, preferably hot or sage
6 tablespoons all-purpose (plain) flour
4 cups (32 fl oz/950 ml) whole milk
1 ½ teaspoons freshly ground black pepper
¼ teaspoon seasoned salt or House Seasoning (PAGE 301) (optional)

1 Preheat a large nonstick frying pan or cast-iron skillet over medium heat for 2 minutes. Add the sausage and use a wooden spoon to break it into small pieces. Let the sausage fry until fully and evenly cooked, about 4 minutes. Evenly distribute the sausage and reduce the heat to medium.

2 Lightly sprinkle 2 tablespoons flour over the sausage and stir to fully incorporate. After about 1 minute, add the remaining 4 tablespoons flour and stir again to combine. Cook the flour and sausage for 3 minutes, uncovered, until the raw flour flavor has cooked off.

3 Adding 1 cup (8 fl oz/240 ml) at a time, whisk in the milk, making sure the ingredients are fully incorporated before adding the next cup. Let the mixture simmer for 1 minute before adding the black pepper and seasoned salt (if using). Reduce the heat to low and simmer until it begins to thicken, about 3 minutes. (The gravy will also thicken as it cools.)

4 Serve hot.

MADEIRA GRAVY

-5 -30

A good sauce for fine Southern dining, Madeira, a fortified wine from the Portuguese colonized islands off the coast of Africa, was once extremely popular in the Colonial and Antebellum South; it was a drink and ingredient meant to impress.

PREPARATION TIME: 10 MINUTES
COOKING TIME: 20 MINUTES
MAKES: 3 CUPS (24 FL OZ/710 ML)

3 tablespoons (45 g) unsalted butter
2 medium shallots, minced
¼ cup (2 fl oz/60 ml) Madeira wine
3 tablespoons all-purpose (plain) flour
About 2 ½ cups (20 fl oz/600 ml) reserved pan juices (see NOTE)
Fine salt
Freshly ground black pepper or Kitchen Pepper (PAGE 301)
Minced fresh flat-leaf parsley, for garnish

1 In a saucepan, melt the butter over medium heat. Add the shallots and cook, stirring, until translucent, about 3 minutes. Deglaze with the Madeira wine, scraping with a spatula/wooden spoon, until most of the shallots are incorporated. Slowly stir in the flour, making sure there are no visible clumps. Stir in the pan juices and cook for 2 minutes, or until golden brown.

2 Slowly bring the gravy to a boil, whisking constantly. Once the gravy has come to a boil, reduce the heat to low and whisk constantly for 3 minutes, until it begins coats the back of a spoon. Add salt and black pepper to taste. Garnish with parsley.

NOTE: Madeira gravy is especially good when made with the pan juices of a pork, beef, or lamb roast, so make sure to set them aside. (If you don't get enough juices from the roast, use chicken broth.)

ONION GRAVY

Smothered foods in the South are nothing without their gravies, made from drippings in the cast-iron skillet. The simplest version relies on traditional gravy with onions cooked in it. This is a homemade version of the gravy packets that fill many a pantry in the name of expediency.

PREPARATION TIME: 5 MINUTES
COOKING TIME: 50 MINUTES
MAKES: 2 CUPS (16 FL OZ/470 ML)

- 4 tablespoons (60 g) unsalted butter
- 2 large yellow onions, cut into rounds ½ inch (13 mm) thick
- 3 tablespoons cornstarch (cornflour)
- 3 tablespoons cold water
- 1 ½ teaspoons Worcestershire sauce
- 1 teaspoon onion powder
- 1 teaspoon dried thyme
- ½ teaspoon ground sage
- ½ teaspoon garlic powder
- 2 cups (16 fl oz/470 ml) beef or vegetable stock
- 1 beef or vegetable bouillon (stock) cube, or 1 teaspoon bouillon paste

1 In a medium saucepan, melt the butter over medium heat. Add the onions, partially cover, and cook, stirring every few minutes to prevent burning, until softened and beginning to brown, about 25 minutes.

2 Meanwhile, in a bowl, whisk together the cornstarch (cornflour) and cold water until combined. Add the Worcestershire sauce, onion powder, thyme, sage, garlic powder, and beef stock to the bowl and stir well. Refrigerate until ready to use.

3 Once the onions are reduced and translucent, deglaze the pan with the beef stock mixture, then add the bouillon (stock) cube. Bring the gravy to a boil. Reduce to a simmer and cook until the gravy has thickened enough to slowly drip off the back of a spoon, about 20 minutes.

GIBLET GRAVY

An essential traditional accompaniment to a beautifully roasted Southern turkey and dressing. Even though many Americans make their Thanksgiving gravy with giblets, it's Southerners who mastered the art of using the turkey's odds and ends.

PREPARATION TIME: 10 MINUTES
COOKING TIME: 2 HOURS
MAKES: 2 ½ CUPS (20 FL OZ/590 ML)

- Turkey giblets and neck from a whole turkey
- 2 cups (32 fl oz/950 ml) roast turkey drippings
- 4 tablespoons (60 g) unsalted butter
- ¼ cup (30 g) all-purpose (plain) flour
- ½ cup (4 fl oz/120 ml) whole milk
- 2 eggs, hard-boiled and finely chopped
- ½ teaspoon kosher salt or ¼ teaspoon fine salt
- ½ teaspoon freshly ground black pepper

1 In a large saucepan, combine the giblets, turkey neck, roast turkey drippings, and 2 cups (16 fl oz/470 ml) water. Bring to a rolling boil. Reduce the heat to medium-low and simmer until reduced by half, at least 1 ½ hours.

2 Strain the reduced stock through a fine-mesh sieve into a bowl (discard the giblets and neck).

3 In another saucepan, melt the butter over medium heat. Stir in the flour and continue to whisk for 4–5 minutes.

4 Slowly whisk in the reduced stock, bring to a boil, and cook for 3 minutes. Add the milk, continuing to stir until the mixture has thickened, 3–5 minutes.

5 Remove the saucepan from heat and stir in the chopped eggs. Season with the salt and black pepper.

BROWN ROUX

DF GF V VE -5

Roux is the most important basis of Creole, Cajun, and Gulf Coast Southern cuisine. A good roux is a mark of a great Louisiana cook. But a brown roux has versatility outside of south Louisiana and Gulf Coast cookery; it can be used as the basis for a more decadent, more complex homemade gravy or to begin a stew, especially one that uses strong-tasting meat or game.

PREPARATION TIME: 5 MINUTES
COOKING TIME: 30–40 MINUTES
MAKES: ½ CUP (ABOUT 170 G)

½ cup (4 fl oz/120 ml) vegetable oil
½ cup (65 g) all-purpose (plain) flour

1 In a seasoned cast-iron skillet or enameled frying pan, stir together the oil and flour until smooth, making sure there are no visible pockets or clumps of flour in the pan.

2 Cook over low heat, stirring constantly, until the roux has slightly thickened, about 1 minute. Continue to cook until it appears to be foaming, about 5 minutes.

3 Continue cooking, stirring frequently to prevent it from burning or clumping, until the mixture has a nutty aroma, is a light walnut brown, and begins to thicken, about 30 minutes. (If it looks like it's getting too dark, take it off the heat and keep stirring—a burned roux is a lost roux.)

STORAGE: Store airtight in the refrigerator for a few weeks.

OWENSBORO KENTUCKY MUTTON BBQ SAUCE

DF

Lamb and mutton barbecue is a uniquely Kentucky phenomenon in Southern barbecue. The bluegrass region and beyond was once home to one of the largest sheep-raising regions of the nineteenth century. Scots-Irish settlers and West African cultures with Muslim roots, from what is now Senegal and Gambia, combined to pass down the only mutton-centered meat culture in the American South. This version cuts through any gamey flavors and gives it a good piquant taste.

PREPARATION TIME: 10 MINUTES
COOKING TIME: 25 MINUTES
MAKES: 1 QUART (1 LITER)

- ½ cup (4 fl oz/120 ml) Worcestershire sauce
- ⅓ cup (80 ml) apple cider vinegar
- 2 tablespoons dark brown sugar
- 1 ½ tablespoons fresh lemon juice
- 1 tablespoon freshly ground black pepper
- 1 tablespoon kosher salt or 1 ½ teaspoons fine salt
- 1 teaspoon onion salt
- 1 teaspoon chile flakes or 2 teaspoons Pepper Vinegar (PAGE 288)
- ½ teaspoon Kitchen Pepper (PAGE 301)
- 1 clove garlic, minced

1 In a large saucepan, combine all the ingredients and 4 cups (32 fl oz/950 ml) water. Cook at a simmer over low heat, stirring frequently, for 45 minutes.

2 Remove the sauce from the heat and let sit for up to 10 minutes for the flavors to meld.

STORAGE: Store airtight in the refrigerator for up to 1 week.

VARIATION: Throw in 2 tablespoons or more of Kentucky bourbon with the other ingredients.

GEORGIA PEACH BBQ SAUCE

DF V VE

This peachy sauce is really great with barbecue chicken, turkey, and duck. You can make it from overripe peaches, or even really good canned ones out of season.

PREPARATION TIME: 15 MINUTES, PLUS 30 MINUTES REFRIGERATION TIME
COOKING TIME: 45 MINUTES
MAKES: 2 CUPS (16 FL OZ/470 ML)

4 ripe peaches (about 4 oz/115 g each) or 2 cans (15 oz/425 g) peaches
⅓ cup (80 ml) apple cider vinegar
⅓ cup (80 g) brown mustard
⅓ cup (90 g) ketchup or tomato paste
¼ cup (50 g) brown sugar
2 tablespoons soy sauce
Fine salt and freshly ground black pepper

1 If using fresh peaches, peel, pit, and chop. If using canned, drain and chop.

2 In a large bowl, mix together the peaches, vinegar, mustard, ketchup, brown sugar, ¼ cup (2 fl oz/60 ml) water, soy sauce, and salt and black pepper to taste. Cover with plastic wrap and refrigerate for at least 30 minutes, allowing the flavors to meld.

3 Pour the sauce ingredients into a medium saucepan and bring to a boil over medium-high heat. Reduce heat to low and simmer until fragrant, thickened, and darkened, about 45 minutes.

4 Remove from the heat and let the sauce come to room temperature before transferring to an airtight container or jar. If possible, let sit in the refrigerator for 2 days before using (the flavors will be deeper).

STORAGE: Store airtight in the refrigerator for up to 1 week.

NEW MOP SAUCE

DF V VE

This recipe is an updated mop drawing on contemporary flavors favored by the competitive barbecue scene throughout the South. It should be used sparingly until the last 15–20 minutes of cooking owing to the sugar content. If you want to use more of it longer without the risk of burning the meat, you can omit the brown sugar and use stock in place of apple juice.

PREPARATION TIME: 10 MINUTES
COOKING TIME: 45 MINUTES
MAKES: 2 ½ CUPS (20 FL OZ/600 ML)

3 cups (24 fl oz/710 ml) apple or peach cider vinegar
¾ cup (4 fl oz/120 ml) apple juice or low-sodium stock
2 tablespoons light brown sugar
2 tablespoons soy sauce
2 tablespoons steak or meat sauce, such as Allegro, Dale's, or A.1.
2 tablespoons yellow or brown mustard
1 teaspoon fine salt or House Seasoning (PAGE 301)
1 teaspoon freshly ground black pepper
½ teaspoon cayenne pepper
½ teaspoon chile flakes

1 In a large saucepan, combine all the ingredients with 1 cup (8 fl oz/240 ml water) and simmer over medium-high heat until all the sugar has dissolved and the sauce is hot and has reduced, 30–45 minutes.

2 Remove from the heat and let the sauce come to room temperature before transferring to an airtight container or jar.

STORAGE: Store airtight in the refrigerator for up to 3 months.

CAROLINA GOLD BBQ SAUCE

DF

With German and African American influences, this sauce is one of my favorites. The northernmost reaches of this sauce lie in Lancaster County in central South Carolina, where my family has lived for generations since the early nineteenth century. It's more brown than gold, but if you love mustardy flavors this is for you.

PREPARATION TIME: 15 MINUTES, PLUS 1 DAY REFRIGERATION TIME
COOKING TIME: 30–45 MINUTES
MAKES: 2 CUPS (16 FL OZ/470 ML)

¾ cup (6 fl oz/180 ml) apple cider vinegar
¾ cup (180 g) brown mustard
¾ cup (180 g) yellow mustard
½ cup (4 fl oz/120 ml) light sorghum syrup, golden syrup (such as Lyle's), or maple syrup
4 tablespoons light brown sugar
2 tablespoons tomato paste (tomato puree)
1 tablespoon onion powder
2 teaspoons Worcestershire sauce
1 teaspoon garlic powder
1 teaspoon fine salt
½ teaspoon freshly ground coarse black pepper or Kitchen Pepper (PAGE 301)
½ teaspoon ground white pepper
Pinch of cayenne pepper
Dash of hot sauce

1 In a small saucepan, whisk all the ingredients together with 1 cup (8 fl oz/240 ml) water until well incorporated. Set the pan over medium-high heat and bring to a boil. Reduce the heat to low and simmer for 30–45 minutes, to mellow the taste of the vinegar and the mustard.

2 Remove from the heat and let cool completely before pouring the sauce into a jar with a lid. Refrigerate for at least 1 day to allow the flavors to fully develop before using.

STORAGE: Store airtight in the refrigerator for up to 1 week.

VARIATION: **Kentucky Gold Sauce:** Omit the yellow mustard and add ¼ cup (85 g) honey and ¼ cup (2 fl oz/60 ml) bourbon.

PEPPER VINEGAR

DF GF V VE -5 -30

Pepper vinegar appears in the first Southern cookbook, Mary Randolph's *The Virginia House-Wife,* and it appears in various Southern cookbooks thereafter. I prefer it to hot sauce, and sometimes I use un-heated clear rum instead of vinegar. It joins the other hot condiments of the African Atlantic and the Americas as a foundational part of the Southern flavor profile.

PREPARATION TIME: 10 MINUTES
COOK TIME: 5 MINUTES
MAKES: 2 ½ CUPS (20 FL OZ/600 ML)

7 fresh cayenne chiles
7 small habanero chiles or bird's eye chiles
1 teaspoon kosher salt, or ½ teaspoon fine salt
2 ¼ cups (18 fl oz/530 ml) distilled white vinegar
2 large cloves garlic (optional), smashed and peeled

1 Halve the chiles lengthwise. Place them in a sterilized 1-quart (1-liter) canning jar or container and season with the salt.

2 In a small saucepan, combine the vinegar, ½ cup (4 fl oz/120 ml) water, and the garlic (if using). Bring to a boil over high heat (make sure your kitchen is well ventilated). Once boiling, remove and discard the garlic, then pour the hot liquid over the chiles.

3 Let cool completely for 3 hours before covering and placing in the refrigerator for up to 12 hours.

STORAGE: Store airtight in the refrigerator for up to 2 weeks.

DATIL PEPPER SAUCE

DF GF V VE -30

The datil is a prized heirloom pepper of the Menorcan ethnic community of Florida by way of the island of Menorca off the coast of Spain. There are over eleven thousand Menorcan descendants living in northeastern Florida, rooted in a community that started in the 1760s. Datils have a fruity, tangy taste and heat similar to that of a Scotch bonnet pepper.

PREPARATION TIME: 10 MINUTES
COOKING TIME: 20 MINUTES
MAKES: 1 CUP (8 FL OZ/240 ML)

- 3 ½ oz (100 g) fresh datil peppers
- 5 tablespoons (3 oz/85 g) tomato paste (tomato puree) or ketchup
- 2 tablespoons apple cider vinegar
- 1 tablespoon fresh lemon juice
- 1 teaspoon garlic powder
- 1 teaspoon sweet paprika
- 1 teaspoon kosher salt or ½ teaspoon fine salt

1 In a medium saucepan, combine the peppers, tomato paste (puree), vinegar, lemon juice, garlic powder, paprika, and salt. Bring to a boil over medium-high heat. Reduce the heat to low and simmer until the peppers are soft, about 20 minutes.

2 Let the sauce cool and then process in a blender with 4 tablespoons water until smooth. Add additional water if necessary.

STORAGE: Store airtight in the refrigerator for up to 2 weeks.

Ball

ALABAMA/MISSISSIPPI SAUCE BEAUTIFUL

It has many nicknames, but this is a sweet, tomato-based barbecue sauce that comes from the fertile Delta and Black Belt regions of these adjacent states. This sauce is especially good for spareribs and pork shoulders. The orange juice, peach preserves, mace, thyme, and deep umami flavors from soy and Worcestershire sauce all work together to create a flavor that goes down to the bone. Use to finish off pork or beef ribs, pork shoulder, or chicken on the grill or baste in the oven.

PREPARATION TIME: 15 MINUTES
COOKING TIME: 45–60 MINUTES
MAKES: ABOUT 2 CUPS (16 FL OZ/470 ML)

4 tablespoons (60 g) unsalted butter or margarine
1 cup (160 g) chopped onions
2 cloves garlic, smashed and peeled
2 cups (530 g) tomato paste (tomato puree) or ketchup
1 cup (8 fl oz/240 ml) orange juice
¼ cup (2 fl oz/60 ml) fresh lemon juice
2 tablespoons apple cider vinegar
2 tablespoons dark brown sugar
2 tablespoons peach preserves
1 tablespoon Worcestershire sauce
1 tablespoon sweet or smoked paprika
1 tablespoon soy sauce
1 teaspoon hot sauce
1 teaspoon chile flakes
½ teaspoon garlic powder
½ teaspoon ground mace
½ teaspoon onion powder
½ teaspoon dried thyme
3–4 bay leaves
Freshly ground black pepper

1 In a medium saucepan, melt the butter over medium heat. Add the onion and garlic and cook, stirring, until softened, about 5 minutes.

2 Add the remaining ingredients with 1 cup (8 fl oz/240 ml) water, whisking them together. Bring to a quick boil, then reduce the heat and cook at a simmer until thick enough to coat a spoon, 45–60 minutes.

3 Remove from the heat and let the sauce come to room temperature before transferring to an airtight container or jar.

STORAGE: Store airtight in the refrigerator for up to 1 week.

ALABAMA WHITE SAUCE

DF -30

One of the latest additions to the family of Southern barbecue sauces, this sauce was especially created by Bob Gibson to go with his pit-barbecued chicken at Big Bob Gibson Bar-BQ in Decatur, Alabama.

PREPARATION TIME: 10 MINUTES
MAKES: 2 CUPS (455 G)

1 ¼ cups (275 g) mayonnaise
¾ cup (6 fl oz/180 ml) apple cider vinegar
1 tablespoon freshly ground black pepper
1 tablespoon superfine (caster) sugar
1 tablespoon fresh lemon juice
1 teaspoon kosher salt or ½ teaspoon fine salt
1 teaspoon garlic powder
½ teaspoon cayenne pepper
1 teaspoon Worcestershire sauce

In a medium bowl, whisk all the ingredients together until smooth. Transfer to an airtight container.

STORAGE: Store airtight in the refrigerator for up to 2 weeks.

VIRGINIA BBQ MOP SAUCE

Virginia barbecue is as old as North Carolina barbecue, but you won't hear about it as often. Butter or lard, sage, hot pepper, onion, vinegar, spices, and even a bit of mustard and mushroom ketchup (Worcestershire sauce is a great substitute) were typical ingredients for a mop, a barbecue condiment traditionally applied with a "mop" or swab used specifically for cooking. You can add some tomato if you'd like, but that's up to you.

PREPARATION TIME: 30 MINUTES, PLUS 2 DAYS REFRIGERATION
COOKING TIME: 40–45 MINUTES
MAKES: 5 CUPS (40 FL OZ/1.2 LITERS)

⅓ cup (75 g) bacon fat or unsalted butter
1 small onion, finely chopped
2 cloves garlic, minced
1 cup (8 fl oz/240 ml) water or stock
⅓ cup (80 ml) apple cider vinegar
¼ cup (2 fl oz/60 ml) Worcestershire sauce
1 tablespoon light brown sugar
1 tablespoon brown mustard
2 teaspoons rubbed sage
2 teaspoons dry-rub style barbecue seasoning, such as Antebellum Southern Dry Rub (PAGE 303)
1 teaspoon chile flakes
1 teaspoon kosher salt or ½ teaspoon fine salt
1 teaspoon freshly ground black pepper or Kitchen Pepper (PAGE 301)

1 In a 3-quart (3-liter) saucepan, heat the bacon fat or butter over medium-high heat. Once hot, add the onion and garlic and cook until soft and translucent, about 6 minutes.

2 Add the water, vinegar, Worcestershire sauce, brown sugar, mustard, sage, barbecue seasoning, chile flakes, salt, and black pepper. Bring to a boil. Reduce the heat to low and simmer for 30–45 minutes to mellow the taste of the vinegar and mustard.

3 Remove from the heat and let the sauce come to room temperature before transferring to an airtight container or jar. Refrigerate for at least 2 days before using.

STORAGE: Store airtight in the refrigerator for up to 1 week.

ANTEBELLUM BARBECUE SAUCE

GF V

Mr. Wesley Jones is one of my favorite culinary ancestors. He was a formerly enslaved barbecue man from western South Carolina. In his narrative for the WPA (Works Project Administration), he gave us a list of the ingredients he put in his "sass." Keep in mind that for rich planters, throwing barbecues with mass quantities of food was a political way of buying votes, using their hospitality, liquor, and the labor of skilled enslaved barbecue chefs. We have a sense that some sauces—although not as many as now—contained overripe tomatoes or mustard, but Mr. Jones's sauce is extremely interesting on its own. This can be used as a light mop sauce or glaze during the last 15–30 minutes over the pit of coals, and as a dip for cooked meat.

PREPARATION TIME: 15 MINUTES
COOKING TIME: 50 MINUTES
MAKES: 2 CUPS (16 FL OZ/470 ML)

- 4 tablespoons (60 g) unsalted butter or lard
- 1 large yellow or white onion, well chopped
- 2 cloves garlic, minced
- 1 cup (8 fl oz/240 ml) apple cider vinegar
- 4 tablespoons dark brown sugar or sorghum syrup
- 1 tablespoon kosher salt or 1 ½ teaspoons fine salt
- 1 teaspoon freshly ground black pepper
- 1 teaspoon dried basil, or 1 tablespoon minced fresh basil
- 1 teaspoon rubbed sage
- ½ teaspoon crushed coriander seeds
- 1 dried cayenne chile or 1 teaspoon chile flakes

1 In a large saucepan, melt the butter over medium heat. Add the onion and garlic and sauté until translucent, 3–5 minutes.

2 Turn the heat down slightly and add the vinegar, ½ cup (4 fl oz/120 ml) water, the brown sugar, salt, black pepper, basil, sage, coriander seeds, and cayenne. Cook, stirring gently, until thickened and the sharp flavor of the vinegar is well masked, about 45 minutes.

3 Remove from the heat and let the sauce come to room temperature before transferring to an airtight container or jar.

STORAGE: Store airtight in the refrigerator for up to 1 week.

VARIATION: **Old Carolina Mustard Sauce:** Add ½ cup (120 g) brown mustard or more to taste, and a bit more sugar.

VARIATION: **"Red Sauce":** Add 2 tablespoons Worcestershire sauce and 1 can (6 oz/170 g) tomato paste (tomato puree) or 4 very ripe red or purple heirloom tomatoes (Large Red, Cherokee Purple, Brandywine, Amish Paste), cooked down for several hours on low heat into a comparable consistency.

NORTH CAROLINA EASTERN SAUCE

DF GF V VE -5

This baste and sauce is nothing like what most people expect. There is no tomato, and the sugar is here just to cut through the heat and vinegar. North Carolina mop and sauce is made for whole-hog barbecue, where wood smoke does the rest of the work. The barbecued hog, browned and crispy, is pulled apart, head to tail, and trickled with the sauce before going on a plate with Eastern North Carolina Hush Puppies (PAGE 40), coleslaw, and Brunswick Stew (PAGE 159).

PREPARATION TIME: 5 MINUTES, PLUS 24 HOURS REFRIGERATION TIME
MAKES: 2 CUPS (16 FL OZ/470 ML)

- 1 cup (8 fl oz/240 ml) distilled white vinegar
- 1 cup (8 fl oz/240 ml) apple cider vinegar
- 1 tablespoon sugar
- 1 tablespoon chile flakes
- 1 tablespoon hot pepper sauce
- 1 teaspoon fine salt
- 1 teaspoon freshly ground black pepper

In a screw-top jar, combine all the ingredients and shake well. Shaking occasionally, refrigerate the sauce for 1–2 days, making sure all of the ingredients are blended together.

STORAGE: Store airtight in the refrigerator for up to 2 months.

VARIATION: Omit the sugar and add 1 can (12 fl oz/355 ml) ginger ale. The rest of the ingredients stay the same.

WESTERN NORTH CAROLINA SAUCE

DF -30

This is also referred to as dip and is used as a condiment for barbecued pork shoulder and as a dressing for coleslaw in some parts of Western North Carolina. The main distinction/addition is the added bit of tomato.

PREPARATION TIME: 10 MINUTES
COOKING TIME: 20 MINUTES
MAKES: 2½ CUPS (20 FL OZ/590 ML)

- 2 cups (16 fl oz/470 ml) apple cider vinegar
- ⅓ cup (65 g) dark brown sugar
- ¾ cup (130 g) ketchup, or 1 can (6 oz/170 g) tomato paste (tomato puree), diluted with water to ¾ cup (180 ml)
- 1 tablespoon hot pepper sauce, or more to taste
- 1 tablespoon Worcestershire sauce
- ½ teaspoon ground white pepper
- ½ teaspoon kosher salt or ¼ teaspoon fine salt
- ½ teaspoon freshly ground black pepper

1 In a medium saucepan, combine all the ingredients and bring to a simmer over medium-high. Cover, reduce the heat to low, and continue to cook, stirring often, until the sauce has thoroughly blended, about 20 minutes. It will be rather thin.

2 Remove from the heat and let the sauce come to room temperature before transferring to an airtight container or jar.

STORAGE: Store airtight in the refrigerator for up to 1 month.

MEMPHIS-STYLE BBQ SAUCE

The people of Memphis, Tennessee love their dry rub, but they also have great sauce traditions. This is a standard rib-mop worthy of Western Tennessee and the northern Delta.

PREPARATION TIME: 10 MINUTES
COOKING TIME: 1 HOUR
MAKES: ABOUT 3 CUPS (24 FL OZ/710 ML)

4 tablespoons (60 g) unsalted butter or margarine
½ cup (80 g) minced onion
2 cups (544 g) ketchup or tomato paste (tomato puree)
1 cup (8 fl oz/240 ml) apple cider vinegar
¾ cup (140 g) dark brown sugar
4 tablespoons honey
2 tablespoons Worcestershire sauce
2 tablespoons yellow mustard
1 tablespoon chili powder
1 tablespoon garlic powder
1 tablespoon hot sauce
1 tablespoon kosher salt or 1 ½ teaspoons fine salt
1 tablespoon paprika
1 teaspoon freshly ground black pepper
½ teaspoon ground allspice
1 ⅛ teaspoons ground cinnamon

1 In a deep saucepan, melt the butter over medium-high heat. Add the onion and cook, stirring, until softened, about 5 minutes.
2 Add the remaining ingredients with ½ cup (4 fl oz/120 ml) water and bring to a boil. Reduce the heat and simmer on low, stirring until thick, 45 minutes – 1 hour.
3 Remove from the heat and let the sauce come to room temperature before transferring to an airtight container or jar.

STORAGE: Store airtight in the refrigerator for up to 3 months.

VARIATION: Use 1 teaspoon Kitchen Pepper (PAGE 301) in place of the black pepper, allspice, and cinnamon. You can also add 2 tablespoons of whisky (such as Uncle Nearest or Jack Daniels) for a spicy flavor.

CREOLE SEASONING

DF GF V VE -30

Creole seasoning is essential to contemporary southern Louisiana cuisine. Use a sprinkle of this in your New Orleans–based dishes.

PREPARATION TIME: 5 MINUTES
MAKES: GENEROUS ¾ CUP (85 G)

- 2 tablespoons granulated garlic
- 2 tablespoons (18 g) kosher salt or 1 tablespoon (18 g) fine salt
- 2 tablespoons onion powder
- 2 tablespoons paprika
- 1 tablespoon freshly ground coarse black pepper
- 1 tablespoon dried basil
- 1 tablespoon dried oregano
- 1 tablespoon dried thyme
- 1 tablespoon ground white pepper
- 1 teaspoon cayenne pepper, or more to taste
- 1 bay leaf

In a spice grinder, process the ingredients together until you have a fine powder.

STORAGE: Store airtight in a cool, dry place for up to 6 months.

POULTRY SEASONING

DF GF V VE -30

This herb and spice mixture is a great perk for roasted, fried, or grilled poultry and the sauces, gravies, and dressings that accompany it.

PREPARATION TIME: 5 MINUTES
MAKES: 2 TABLESPOONS

- 2 teaspoons ground sage
- 1 ½ teaspoons dried thyme
- 1 teaspoon dried marjoram
- ½ teaspoon ground nutmeg
- ½ teaspoon ground ginger
- ½ teaspoon freshly ground fine black pepper
- ¾ teaspoon dried ground rosemary

Combine all the ingredients and store airtight.

STORAGE: Store airtight in a cool, dry place for up to 6 months.

HOUSE SEASONING

DF GF V VE -30

A favorite with many contemporary Southern restaurants, this blend, which you can alter to your preferences, is essentially a collection of "secret ingredients," particularly in vegetable and meat dishes with simple preparations.

PREPARATION TIME: 5 MINUTES
MAKES: ¾ CUP (70 G)

4 tablespoons (36 g) kosher salt or 2 tablespoons (36 g) fine salt
2 tablespoons paprika
2 tablespoons seasoned salt or soul seasoning (can be salt-free)
2 tablespoons freshly ground coarse black pepper
1 tablespoon Kitchen Pepper (PAGE 301)
1 tablespoon garlic powder
1 tablespoon onion powder

Combine all the ingredients and store airtight.

STORAGE: Store in a cool, dry place for up to 6 months.

KITCHEN PEPPER

DF GF V VE -30

This is a Colonial and antebellum-era spice mixture that appears in many old recipe books. It adds an extra layer of flavor and fragrance that speaks to the transfer of the tastes of Medieval Europe and West Africa into Southern cooking.

PREPARATION TIME: 5 MINUTES
MAKES: ½ CUP (45 G)

2 tablespoons freshly ground coarse black pepper
1 tablespoon ground allspice
1 tablespoon ground cinnamon
1 tablespoon ground ginger
1 tablespoon ground mace
1 tablespoon ground nutmeg
1 tablespoon ground white pepper
1 teaspoon cayenne pepper

Combine all the ingredients and store airtight.

STORAGE: Store in a cool, dry place for up to 6 months.

SMOKED SALT SOUTHERN DRY RUB

DF GF V VE -5 -30

This rub, particularly good on both poultry and meats and oily fish, such as salmon, utilizes hickory- and pecan wood-smoked salts, which are now more widely available online.

PREPARATION TIME: 10 MINUTES
MAKES: 1 ¼ CUPS (120 G)

4 tablespoons freshly ground coarse black pepper
4 tablespoons garlic powder
4 tablespoons hickory- or pecan-smoked salt
4 tablespoons onion powder
2 tablespoons chili powder
2 tablespoons smoked paprika

Combine all the ingredients and store airtight.

STORAGE: Store in a cool, dry place for up to 6 months.

TEXAS-STYLE BBQ RUB

DF GF V VE -30

Some traditional Texas rubs are simply salt and pepper. This recipe is more elaborate with more of a Tex-Mex inspired barbecue flavor.

PREPARATION TIME: 5–10 MINUTES
MAKES: ABOUT 1 ¼ CUPS (120 G)

4 tablespoons (36 g) kosher salt or 2 tablespoons (36 g) fine salt
2 tablespoons freshly ground coarse black pepper
2 tablespoons smoked salt (oak or mesquite)
2 tablespoons light brown sugar
2 tablespoons onion powder
2 tablespoons garlic powder
2 tablespoons chili powder
2 tablespoons sweet or smoked paprika
1 tablespoon cayenne pepper
1 tablespoon ground cumin

Combine all the ingredients and store airtight.

STORAGE: Store in a cool, dry place for up to 6 months.

ANTEBELLUM SOUTHERN DRY RUB

DF GF V VE -30

This is my attempt at a home recipe version of a dry rub that incorporated the flavors mentioned by Mr. Wesley Jones of Spartanburg, South Carolina, that might give honor to his and many others contribution to the development of American barbecue. Mr. Jones did much of his craft without pay, having been born into the world of American slavery. He told his story to an interviewer from the Works Progress Administration in the 1930s.

PREPARATION TIME: 10 MINUTES
MAKES: GENEROUS 1 CUP (110 G)

5 tablespoons kosher salt or 2 ½ tablespoons hickory smoked salt
2 tablespoons freshly ground coarse black pepper
2 tablespoons turbinado sugar
1 tablespoon dried basil
1 tablespoon ground sage
1 tablespoon ground coriander
1 tablespoon garlic powder
1 tablespoon mustard powder
1 tablespoon onion powder
1 tablespoon cayenne pepper

Combine all the ingredients and store airtight.

STORAGE: Store in a cool, dry place for up to 6 months.

NEW-STYLE SOUTHERN DRY RUB

DF GF V VE -30

In the past few years, new ingredients that have invigorated grilling culture have come into the home kitchen through online shopping. Tomato powder, honey powder, crystallized lemon or even lemonade powder, and MSG (less stigmatized than in the past) are used by barbecue greats like chef Rodney Scott, who are shaping the new Southern 'cue culture.

PREPARATION TIME: 10 MINUTES
MAKES: 1 ½ CUPS (ABOUT 140 G)

4 tablespoons kosher salt or 2 tablespoons smoked salt (hickory-smoked preferred)
2 tablespoons freshly ground coarse black pepper
2 tablespoons brown sugar or honey powder
2 tablespoons celery salt
2 tablespoons chili powder
2 tablespoons garlic powder
2 tablespoons onion powder
2 tablespoons sweet or smoked paprika
2 tablespoons tomato powder
1–2 tablespoons lemonade powder, or 2 teaspoons crystallized lemon
1 tablespoon mustard powder
2 teaspoons cayenne pepper
1 teaspoon MSG (optional)

Combine all the ingredients and store airtight.

STORAGE: Store in a cool, dry place for up to 6 months.

BASIC RELISH PLATE

DF GF V VE -30

This platter is a necessity when salads, deviled eggs, green beans, and the like are served at Southern life-cycle events and informal parties. Our family always had one on hand during every holiday dinner.

PREPARATION TIME: 10 MINUTES
SERVES: 8–10 (OR MORE)

Sliced tomato
Scallions (spring onions), trimmed and halved lengthwise
Chow Chow (PAGE 308)
Bread and butter pickles
Pickled Watermelon Rinds (PAGE 309) (optional)
Okra Pickles (PAGE 312)
Optional adds: Olives (preferably pimento-stuffed), deviled eggs, crackers, and/or bread

Arrange all the ingredients on a platter.

JERUSALEM ARTICHOKE PICKLES

DF GF V VE

Also known as sunchoke or Jerusalem artichoke, the root of *Helianthus tuberosus* is actually the root of a type of sunflower cultivated by Native Americans long before European arrival. They were celebrated by chef Bill Smith of Crook's Corner in Chapel Hill, North Carolina, who reinterpreted heirloom recipes to create many of the restaurant's most iconic dishes, including a tomato-watermelon salad, honeysuckle sorbet, and cheese pork (aka "Southern schnitzel"). They make a great addition to the Basic Relish Plate (PAGE 304). For this recipe, you will need 4 sterilized 1-quart (1-liter) jars with tight-fitting lids (see Storing Preserves, PAGE 307).

PREPARATION TIME: 30 MINUTES, PLUS 12 HOURS SOAKING TIME AND 1 WEEK PICKLING TIME
COOKING TIME: 10 MINUTES
MAKES: 4 QUARTS (4 LITERS)

- 3 lb (1.4 kg) Jerusalem artichokes
- Juice of 3 lemons
- 4 tablespoons (36 g) kosher salt or 2 tablespoons (36 g) fine salt
- 5 cups (40 fl oz/1.2 liters) apple cider vinegar
- 2 cups (400 g) sugar
- 2 tablespoons mustard seeds
- 1 tablespoon chile flakes
- 1 ½ teaspoons whole cloves
- 1 teaspoon mustard powder
- 1 teaspoon ground turmeric
- 4 bay leaves

1 Cut the Jerusalem artichokes into ½-inch (13 mm) pieces. Place them in a large bowl of water with the lemon juice and let sit for 10 minutes.

2 In another large bowl, combine the salt with 4 cups (32 fl oz/950 ml) water and let sit until the salt is completely dissolved, about 5 minutes.

3 Drain the Jerusalem artichokes and place them in the salt brine, making sure the Jerusalem artichokes are completely submerged. Let them soak for 12 hours or overnight in a cool place.

4 In a large saucepan, combine the vinegar, sugar, mustard seeds, chile flakes, cloves, mustard powder, turmeric, and 1 cup (8 fl oz/240 ml) water. Bring to a boil over medium-high heat, then remove from the heat and let cool.

5 Meanwhile, sterilize four 1-quart (1-liter) jars (see PAGE 307).

6 Rinse the artichokes very well before packing them into the hot jars. Pour in the pickling liquid, leaving ½ inch (13 mm) of headspace. Add 1 bay leaf to each jar. Seal and refrigerate. If planning on longer storage, process the jars for 10 minutes in a boiling water bath (see Storing Preserves, PAGE 307).

7 The pickles are ready to enjoy after 1 week.

STORAGE: If processed in a water bath, the pickles will keep in a cool dark place for up to 4 months. Once opened, refrigerate and enjoy within 2–3 weeks.

STORING PRESERVES

Note that the following instructions are specifically for the pickles and preserves in this book. If you are canning something other than those recipes, please consult the USDA's Complete Guide to Home Canning for the appropriate and safe canning methods. If you don't want or need the pickles to be shelf-stable, then be sure to store in the refrigerator.

How to Sterilize Jars
Regardless of how long you plan on storing preserves, the first step is always to sterilize the jars.

Place 2 clean tea towels in the bottom of a large pot to protect the jars from overheating. Add jars open-side up and their lids, and then add enough water to cover by 6 inches (15 cm). Bring the water to a boil over high heat and maintain a boil for 10 minutes.

Meanwhile, set out 2 clean tea towels on the countertop.

Using tongs, transfer the hot jars and lids to the tea towels, placing the jars upside down to drain. Plan to fill these sterilized jars with pickles or preserves while they are still warm.

Refrigerator Storage
If you are planning on consuming the pickles or preserves within a few weeks, simply pack the warm pickles or preserves into hot sterilized jars. Let them cool to room temperature, cover, and store in the refrigerator, using them up within the time specified in the recipe.

Water-Bath Canning
Water-bath canning makes most jams, jellies, pickles, and preserves shelf-stable at room temperature for up to 1 year (though check each recipe for specific usage recommendations).

Fill the still-hot sterilized jars with the preserves, leaving about 1/2 inch (13 mm) of headspace at the top. Wipe the lids dry, then place on the jars and screw on the tops to close.

Place a rack in the bottom of a large pot, fill the pot with enough water to come about halfway up, and bring to a full simmer. Using canning tongs, carefully lower the filled jars into the water one at a time. They should be covered by 1–2 inches (2.5–5 cm) water. If necessary, add more boiling water to the top of the pot to ensure the jars are covered. Bring the pot to a rolling boil, then cover the pot and boil for the amount of time that is specified in the recipe.

Remove the pot from the heat and let the jars sit for 10 minutes before removing them from the pot. Confirm the jars are fully sealed: If you press on the lid of the jar and it pops up, then the jar is not sealed. (Store any unsealed jars in the fridge.) Let cool for at least 12 hours before storing at room temperature in a cool dark place, usually for up to 1 year.

CHOW CHOW

DF GF V VE

Chow chow is a popular Pennsylvania German relish tradition that traveled South down the Great Wagon Road. It then spread out across the South, which has dozens of traditional local homemade pickles and relishes. Along with other dishes, such as waffles and dumplings, when chow chow came South it morphed to fit local ingredients, tastes, and resources.

PREPARATION TIME: 45 MINUTES, PLUS OVERNIGHT REFRIGERATION TIME
COOKING TIME: 40 MINUTES
MAKES: 2 QUARTS (2 LITERS)

- 6 large green tomatoes
- 3 medium yellow onions
- 3 bell peppers, 1 each of red, yellow, and orange
- 1 large green bell pepper
- ½ head green cabbage
- ¼ cup (36 g) kosher salt or 2 tablespoons (36 g) fine salt
- 3 ½ cups (28 fl oz/830 ml) distilled white vinegar
- 1 cup (200 g) sugar
- 1 tablespoon mustard seeds
- 1 teaspoon celery seeds

1 Working in batches, use a food processor to finely chop all the vegetables into small pieces.

2 Transfer the vegetables to a large bowl and sprinkle with the salt. Toss until everything is evenly incorporated. Cover and refrigerate overnight.

3 The next day, drain the vegetables in a fine-mesh sieve, pressing the liquid out gently, and set aside.

4 In a large pot, combine the vinegar, sugar, mustard, and celery seeds and bring to a boil over high heat. Reduce the heat to low, cover, and simmer for 15 minutes.

5 Add the vegetable mixtures to the pot and increase the heat to high, bringing the mixture to a rolling boil. Cook for 10 minutes, stirring often to prevent sticking.

6 Meanwhile, sterilize four 1-pint (475 ml) glass jars (see PAGE 307).

7 Once the vegetables are fully cooked and still hot, transfer to the hot jars, leaving ½ inch (13 mm) of headspace. If planning on longer storage, process the jars for 5 minutes in a boiling water bath (see Storing Preserves, PAGE 307). Allow the jars to cool before sealing and storing in the refrigerator.

STORAGE: If processed in a water bath, the pickles will keep in a cool, dark place for up to 1 year. Once opened, refrigerate and enjoy within 2–3 weeks.

PICKLED WATERMELON RINDS

DF GF V VE

Southern people are the waste-not-want-not people. Why let a watermelon rind go to waste when it makes a perfectly great refreshing pickle? It's a member of the cucurbit family (melons, cucumbers, etc.), so the rinds substitute well.

PREPARATION TIME: 25 MINUTES, PLUS AT LEAST 12 HOURS PICKLING TIME
COOKING TIME: 40 MINUTES
MAKES: 2 QUARTS (2 LITERS)

2 lb (910 g) watermelon rind
1 cup (8 fl oz/240 ml) apple cider vinegar
¾ cup (145 g) superfine (caster) sugar
4 teaspoons (12 g) kosher salt or 2 teaspoons (12 g) fine salt
1 teaspoon Kitchen Pepper (PAGE 301)
1 teaspoon chile flakes
8 whole cloves

1 Using a paring knife, remove the outer layer of the green portion of the watermelon rind. Cut the trimmed rinds into 1-inch (2.5 cm) cubes and set aside.
2 In a medium saucepan, combine the vinegar, 1 cup (8 fl oz/240 ml) water, the sugar, salt, Kitchen Pepper, chile flakes, and cloves. Bring to a boil over medium-high heat and cook for 2 minutes. Add the watermelon rinds, then remove the saucepan from the heat and let rest for 35 minutes.
3 Meanwhile, sterilize two 1-quart (1-liter) glass jars (see PAGE 307).
4 Transfer the watermelon rinds to the hot jars, leaving ½ inch (13 mm) of headspace and let cool to room temperature. Cover and refrigerate. Let sit for at least 12 (and ideally 24) hours before eating. If planning on longer storage, process the jars for 10 minutes in a boiling water bath (see Storing Preserves, PAGE 307).

STORAGE: If processed in a water bath, the pickles will keep in a cool, dark place for up to 1 year. Once opened, refrigerate and enjoy within 2–3 weeks.

PIMENTO CHEESE

Pimento cheese is a contemporary Southern potluck favorite born in New York. Johan D. Frederickson, of Little Falls, New York, was credited in 1910 with the first formal recipe for what was then called "Pepper Cream Cheese." Full of creamy and savory flavors, it pairs well with everything from crackers and veggies to deviled eggs and sandwiches. Serve it as a spread on crackers and sandwiches, as a dip for vegetables, or even stuffing for olives!

PREPARATION TIME: 15 MINUTES, PLUS 1 HOUR REFRIGERATION TIME
MAKES: 2 CUPS (450 G)

8 oz (225 g) sharp Cheddar cheese, grated
4 oz (115 g) cream cheese
1 jar (4 oz/113 g) diced pimentos, drained
½ cup (110 g) mayonnaise
½ teaspoon Worcestershire sauce
½ teaspoon hot sauce
¼ teaspoon sugar
¼ teaspoon garlic powder
Pinch of cayenne pepper
Fine salt and freshly ground black pepper

In a bowl, stir everything together until well combined and creamy. Refrigerate the pimento cheese for at least 1 hour to let the flavors meld together.

STORAGE: Store airtight in the refrigerator for up to 4 days.

OKRA PICKLES

DF GF V VE

Okra pickles are small, crisp, and flavorful additions to the table. Beyond the more commonly known methods of frying, boiling, steaming, and including in soups and gumbos, pickling has been one of the best ways to make their presence felt at the table beyond the summer.

PREPARATION TIME: 45 MINUTES, PLUS 1 WEEK REFRIGERATION TIME
COOKING TIME: 10 MINUTES
MAKES: 2 PINTS (1 LITER)

4 cloves garlic, peeled but whole
2 bay leaves
2 lb (910 g) okra, very small tender pods
4–6 sprigs fresh dill
1 ½ cups (12 fl oz/350 ml) distilled white vinegar
1 tablespoon (9 g) kosher salt or 1 ½ teaspoons (9 g) fine salt
¾ teaspoon black peppercorns

1 Place 2 cloves garlic and 1 bay leaf into each of two sterilized (see PAGE 307) 1-pint (475 ml) jars. Add the okra pods, stem down, and then add the dill.
2 In a large pot, combine the vinegar, 1 ½ cups (12 fl oz/350 ml) water, and the salt and bring to a boil. Remove from the heat and stir in the peppercorns.
3 Pour the brine into each jar, making sure the okra is fully submerged and there is ½ inch (13 mm) of headspace. Allow the jars to cool before sealing and storing in the refrigerator. If planning on longer storage, process the jars for 15 minutes in a boiling water bath (see Storing Preserves, PAGE 307).
4 Refrigerate for at least 1 week before eating.

STORAGE: If processed in a water bath, the pickles will keep in a cool dark place for up to 1 year. Once opened, refrigerate and enjoy within 2–3 weeks.

PICKLED PEACHES

DF GF V VE -5

Pickled or sometimes brandied peaches utilized the South's favorite orchard fruit as a delicious relish for ham, turkey, and other baked or roasted entrees. For this recipe, you will need 5 sterilized 1-quart (1-liter) jars with tight-fitting lids (see Storing Preserves, PAGE 307).

PREPARATION TIME: 15 MINUTES, PLUS 2 DAYS PICKLING TIME
COOKING TIME: 45 MINUTES
MAKES: 5 QUARTS (5 LITERS)

4 lb (1.8 kg) peaches
4 cups (800 g) sugar
1 cup (8 fl oz/240 ml) distilled white vinegar
1 tablespoon whole cloves
5 cinnamon sticks

1 Set out a large bowl of cold water and add a dozen or so ice cubes. Bring a big pot of water to a rolling boil over high heat. Set out a platter to hold the blanched peaches.

2 When the water is boiling, drop 2–3 peaches at a time into the pot and boil for 2 minutes. Using a slotted spoon or a ladle, quickly transfer the peaches to the ice water and let them chill while you blanch the remaining peaches. Once finished, transfer the cooled peaches to the platter and gently rub the skins to peel them.

3 In a large saucepan, combine the sugar, vinegar, cloves, and 1 cup (8 fl oz/240 ml) water and bring to a boil, stirring to dissolve the sugar. Boil gently for 5 minutes, until it forms a light syrup.

4 Using a slotted spoon, carefully lower the peaches into the boiling syrup. Cook until the peaches are soft and tender, 15–20 minutes.

5 Meanwhile, sterilize five 1-quart (1-liter) jars (see PAGE 307).

6 Place a cinnamon stick into each jar. Scoop out the peaches and divide them among the hot jars, packing them in tightly. Ladle or pour hot syrup over the peaches in each jar, leaving ½ inch (13 mm) headspace. Clean the rims with a dry cloth, seal with lids, and set aside to cool to room temperature. Cover the jars and transfer to the refrigerator. If planning on longer storage, process the jars for 25 minutes in a boiling water bath (see Storing Preserves, PAGE 307).

7 Wait 2 days for flavor to develop; then open and enjoy.

STORAGE: If processed in a water bath, the peaches will keep in a cool dark place for up to 1 year. Once opened, refrigerate and enjoy within 2–3 weeks.

DESSERTS, PIES & SWEETS

SWEET SOUTHERN FLAVORS

The story of the plantation economy, from its roots in the Mediterranean to Latin America and the American South, begins with the desire to cultivate sugarcane for profit. Seen initially as a medicinal product, sugarcane cultivation centered on pleasure, quick energy, and confection across class lines. Because commercial sugarcane had a limited growing range in the historical South—predominantly along the Gulf Coast, Florida, and, most important, southern Louisiana and southeastern Texas—it was seen as a homegrown luxury. Most of the crop in the Americas would be cultivated in places like the Caribbean basin, with cultural and economic ties to the South and its reliance on racial chattel slavery. Sugarcane, along with other West Indian plantation crops like tea, coffee, and chocolate, represented economies of consumption based on afternoon tea, coffeehouses, and the making of hot chocolate that enhanced Southern beverage and hospitality culture.

Southerners heavily relied on sugar in domestic life: It was used to preserve peaches, apples, berries, and persimmons into jams, jellies, conserves, condiments, and later even some types of ham and bacon. An incredibly diverse culture of confections and desserts emerged, many of which incorporated native nuts such as pecans and black walnuts. When sugar was not available—or was not the sweetener of choice—honeybees brought by Europeans seeded widespread apiculture that took advantage of wildflowers, tupelo blossoms, clover, orange blossoms, and the like. In the eighteenth and nineteenth centuries, native corn and sorghum, domesticated in Africa, were tapped for their usefulness for syrup. Sorghum became the source of sorghum "molasses," and was predominantly grown on homesteads in the Upper South to sweeten coffee, quick breads, cakes, and pies. In a limited region of the Appalachian South, sugar maples were tapped for their sap to make syrup.

The Southern sweet tooth may be difficult for some outside the culture to understand. Some of our traditions are branded as unhealthy in a broader American diet, where ultraprocessed foods prevail and fast-food culture has negatively impacted the region. At the same time, we can't deny the craft, skill, and art employed to make these treats and the bonds of community they help forge. These sweetened foods came from a world in which heavy physical activity, outdoor living, and strenuous agricultural labor were the norm.

They were also used as a counterpoint: Sugar, molasses, and the like were paired with sour or bitter flavors to make foods more palatable, to drive their ability to enhance social pleasure, or to give a burst of energy. In the South, iced tea, baked beans, sweet potatoes, or even sauces used on meat often benefit from traditional pairings of lemon, apple cider vinegar, and heavy spices with sweeteners. These treats, while ubiquitous, were always meant to be enjoyed in balance in a life with encounters with the sour, bitter, and hard to swallow.

COCONUT CAKE

V

Coconut cake is, for many in the South, the highlight of the winter holiday season. Christmas was the time of the year when specialty ingredients like spices, citrus fruit, and coconuts made an appearance on the tables of people of modest means. Often these cakes were given as gifts, especially to children. Lots of people have fond childhood memories of these treats.

PREPARATION TIME: 45 MINUTES
COOKING TIME: 25–30 MINUTES
SERVES: 10–12

FOR THE CAKE:
Softened butter and flour, for the pans
3 cups (390 g) all-purpose (plain) flour
2 teaspoons baking powder
½ teaspoon fine sea salt
1 cup (8 fl oz/240 ml) whole milk
2 teaspoons pure vanilla extract
16 tablespoons (8 oz/225g) unsalted butter, at room temperature
2 cups (400 g) sugar
4 eggs

FOR THE ICING:
1 cup (200 g) sugar
¼ cup (2 fl oz/60 ml) light corn syrup
2 egg whites
¼ teaspoon fine salt
¼ teaspoon cream of tartar
1 teaspoon pure vanilla extract
3 ½ cups (335 g) sweetened shredded (desiccated) coconut

1 Make the cake: Preheat the oven to 350°F (180°C/Gas Mark 4). Grease and flour two 9-inch (23 cm) round cake pans.

2 In a medium bowl, whisk together the flour, baking powder, and salt. In a separate bowl, stir the milk and vanilla together.

3 In a stand mixer (or in a large bowl with a hand mixer), beat the butter on medium speed until light and fluffy, about 3 minutes. Add the sugar and beat until light and whipped, about 3 minutes. Add the eggs, one at a time, beating well after each addition, until the batter is thick and smooth.

4 Add the flour mixture to the butter/egg mixture in three additions, alternating with the milk mixture, beginning and ending with the flour. Beat on low speed after each addition until the batter is thick and smooth. Quickly scrape the batter into the prepared cake pans, dividing it evenly, and smoothing the tops.

5 Bake for 25–30 minutes, until the layers are golden, firm in the center, and pulling away from the sides of the pan.

6 Let the layers cool in the pans for 15 minutes before turning them out onto wire racks, top-side up, to cool completely.

7 Meanwhile, make the icing: Bring about 3 inches of water to an active simmer in the bottom of a double boiler or a saucepan that will accommodate a heatproof medium bowl so it will sit snugly above the water.

8 In the top of the double boiler or in the heatproof bowl, on the countertop, combine the sugar, corn syrup, ¼ cup (2 fl oz/60 ml) water, the egg whites, salt, and cream of tartar. Beat with a mixer at low speed for 1 minute, until the mixture is very foamy.

9 Place the pan or bowl of icing over the simmering water and beat at high speed until the icing becomes white, thick, and shiny, and triples in volume, 7 minutes or more. Continue beating until the frosting forms firm peaks and loses some of its shine. (This whole process could take as long as 15–20 minutes.) Remove the icing from the heat, add the vanilla, and continue beating for 2 minutes more, until the icing loses its shine.

10 To assemble the cake, place one of the cake layers on a serving plate, top-side down. Spread about one-third of the icing evenly over the cake, almost to the edge. Place the second layer over the icing, top-side up. Cover with a similar amount of icing, spreading to the edge. Use the remaining icing to cover the sides evenly.

11 Place the iced cake on a baking sheet to catch the coconut as you finish the cake. Sprinkle coconut generously all over the cake, patting coconut onto the sides and covering the icing evenly.

STORAGE: Store airtight at room temperature for up to 5 days or in the refrigerator for up to 1 week.

LADY BALTIMORE CAKE

V

Lady Baltimore cake is an early twentieth-century eponymous dessert from the Lady Baltimore Tea Room in Charleston, South Carolina. It was made popular by the 1905 novel *Lady Baltimore* by Owen Wister. Once very fashionable, this cake was often served at Christmas time. It is a classic cake of the era, with two to four layers of yellow or white butter cake enrobed in the fluffy white frosting known as boiled icing. For the filling, chopped dried figs, raisins, and pecans are stirred into a portion of the icing and spread between the layers, adding a pleasing contrast in texture and flavor.

PREPARATION TIME: 50 MINUTES, PLUS 1 HOUR RESTING
COOKING TIME: 55 MINUTES
SERVES: 10–12

FOR THE CAKE:
Softened butter and flour, for the pans
2 cups (260 g) all-purpose (plain) flour
2 teaspoons baking powder
½ teaspoon fine salt
1 cup (8 fl oz/240 ml) whole milk
1 teaspoon pure vanilla extract
4 egg whites
1 ½ cups (300 g) sugar
8 tablespoons (4 oz/115 g) unsalted butter, at room temperature

FOR THE FILLING AND ICING:
½ cup (70 g) raisins, chopped
½ cup (80 g) finely chopped dried figs
½ cup (65 g) finely chopped pecans or walnuts
3 tablespoons sherry, brandy, or orange juice
1 cup (200 g) sugar
2 egg whites
¼ cup (2 fl oz/60 ml) light corn syrup
¼ teaspoon cream of tartar
¼ teaspoon fine salt
1 teaspoon pure vanilla extract

1 Make the cake: Preheat the oven to 350°F (180°C/Gas Mark 4). Grease and flour two 9-inch (23 cm) round cake pans.

2 In a medium bowl, whisk together the flour, baking powder, and salt and stir with a fork to mix well. In a second medium bowl, combine the milk and vanilla.

3 In a third medium bowl, with an electric mixer, beat the egg whites at medium speed until they are foamy, about 1 minute. Increase the speed to medium-high and beat until the egg whites are shiny and thick and will hold firmly curled peaks. Set aside.

4 In a large bowl, with an electric mixer, cream the sugar and butter at high speed, stopping to scrape down the sides of the bowl now and then, until light and fluffy, about 5 minutes. Reduce the speed to low and carefully pour in the milk mixture, beating only until blended. Add the flour mixture to the batter all at once and beat at low speed, scraping the batter from the sides. Beat only until the flour disappears.

5 Remove the beaters and set aside. Add half the beaten egg whites and use a spatula to gently fold them into the batter. Add the remaining egg whites and gently combine them with the batter. A few streaks are fine; don't let the batter deflate. Quickly divide the batter between the two cake pans.

6 Bake for 20–25 minutes, until the cakes are golden and beginning to pull away from the sides of the pans.

7 Let the cakes cool in the pans for 5 minutes on wire racks. Then turn the cakes onto the racks top-side up to cool completely.

8 Prepare the filling: In a small bowl, combine the raisins, figs, and pecans and toss to mix well. Add the sherry and stir well. Set aside for 1 hour, or up to 1 day.

9 Make the icing: In a medium saucepan, bring 4 inches (10 cm) water to a boil.

10 In a large heatproof bowl (that can fit over the saucepan), combine the sugar, egg whites, corn syrup, cream of tartar, and salt. With a hand mixer, beat at medium speed, until the egg white mixture is foamy and incorporated, 1–2 minutes.

11 Place the bowl over the saucepan of boiling water and adjust the heat to maintain a gentle boil. Using the hand mixer, beat the sugar/egg white mixture at high speed until it thickens and swells, forming thick peaks, 10–15 minutes.

12 Transfer the bowl to the countertop, add the vanilla, and beat until incorporated, 1–2 minutes.

13 Measure out about 1 cup of the icing and add to the bowl of dried fruits and nuts and their liquid. Using a large spoon, mix until completely incorporated.

14 To assemble the cake, put one layer on a serving plate, top-side down. Cover the cake with the dried fruit-and-nut filling, spreading it to the edges of the cake layer. Cover the filling with the second layer, top-side up. Spread the fluffy white icing evenly over the top and sides of the cake. Use a table knife to swirl the icing into beautiful peaks and curls.

STORAGE: Store airtight at room temperature for up to 5 days or in the refrigerator for up to 1 week.

LOUISIANA SYRUP CAKE

V

This old-time Cajun cake, also known by its French name, *gâteau au sirop*, is flavored with southern Louisiana's favorite sweetener, Steen's cane syrup. Sugarcane, grown with the forced labor of enslaved Africans, Haitians, and African Americans made the planters of Louisiana some of the richest men and women in the country and the world. Cane syrup remains one of the most unique elements of Creole and Cajun food culture—taking the place of brown sugar, refined sugar, and maple syrup in other cuisines.

PREPARATION TIME: 35 MINUTES
COOKING TIME: 30–35 MINUTES
SERVES: 8

FOR THE CAKE:

Softened butter and flour, for the pan
2 ½ cups (325 g) all-purpose (plain) flour
1 teaspoon ground cinnamon
1 teaspoon ground ginger
¼ teaspoon ground cloves
½ teaspoon fine salt
1 ½ cups (12 fl oz/350 ml) pure cane syrup, such as Steen's
½ cup (4 fl oz/120 ml) vegetable oil
1 egg
1 ½ teaspoons baking soda (bicarbonate of soda)
¾ cup (6 fl oz/180 ml) hot water

FOR THE FROSTING:

4 tablespoons (60 g) unsalted butter, at room temperature
3 tablespoons cane syrup, such as Steen's
1 teaspoon pure vanilla extract
¼ teaspoon fine salt
2 cups (240 g) powdered (icing) sugar, sifted

1 Make the cake: Preheat the oven to 350°F (180°C/Gas Mark 4). Grease and flour a 9-inch (23 cm) round cake pan.

2 In a medium bowl, whisk together the flour, cinnamon, ginger, cloves, and salt.

3 In a large bowl, whisk together the cane syrup, oil, and egg until evenly incorporated.

4 In a small bowl, stir the baking soda (bicarb) into the hot water.

5 Stir half the flour mixture into the syrup mixture, then stir in half the baking soda mixture. Stir in remaining flour and then the remaining baking soda mixture, mixing just until the flour disappears and the batter is smooth and evenly combined. Quickly pour the batter into the prepared pan.

6 Bake for 30–35 minutes, until the cake is smooth and rounded, and beginning to pull away from the sides of the pan.

7 Let the cake cool in the pan for 15 minutes, then unmold it onto a wire rack, top-side up, to cool completely.

8 Make the frosting: In a medium bowl, with an electric mixer, beat the butter, cane syrup, vanilla, and salt at medium speed until light and fluffy, 2–3 minutes. Add the powdered (icing) sugar and beat at medium-high speed until the frosting is smooth, creamy, and well combined, about 2 minutes.

9 When the cake has cooled, spread the frosting evenly over the top and sides of the cake.

STORAGE: Store airtight at room temperature for up to 5 days or in the refrigerator for up to 1 week.

VARIATION: Fold ½ cup (60 g) chopped pecans into the batter before baking.

MISSISSIPPI MUD CAKE

V

Southern Living magazine said that this cake from the World War II era was created from thrift and was supposedly named after its appearance, which reminded people of the muddy Mississippi River bottom.

PREPARATION TIME: 25 MINUTES
COOKING TIME: 30 MINUTES
SERVES: 10–12

FOR THE CAKE:
Softened butter and flour, for the pan
16 tablespoons (8 oz/225g) unsalted butter, cut into chunks
½ cup (40 g) unsweetened cocoa powder
2 cups (400 g) granulated (caster) sugar
1 ½ cups (195 g) all-purpose (plain) flour
⅛ teaspoon fine salt
4 eggs, beaten
1 teaspoon pure vanilla extract
1 cup (125 g) chopped pecans

FOR THE FROSTING AND TOPPING:
4 cups (480 g) powdered (icing) sugar
½ cup (40 g) unsweetened cocoa powder
8 tablespoons (4 oz/115 g) unsalted butter, melted
½ cup (4 fl oz/120 ml) whole milk
1 teaspoon pure vanilla extract
4 cups (10 oz/285 g) mini marshmallows

1 Make the cake: Preheat the oven to 350°F/180°C/Gas Mark 4). Grease and flour a 9 × 13-inch (23 × 33 cm) baking pan.
2 In a small saucepan, combine the butter and the cocoa and cook over medium heat, stirring often, until smooth, 2–3 minutes.
3 In a large bowl, whisk together the granulated (caster) sugar, flour, salt, eggs, and vanilla. Add the chocolate/butter mixture and whisk to incorporate everything into a thick, smooth batter. Stir in the pecans, then quickly pour the batter into the pan.
4 Bake for 25–30 minutes, until the cake springs back when touched gently in the center and is beginning to pull away from the sides of the pan.
5 Meanwhile, make the frosting: In a large bowl, with an electric mixer, beat together the powdered (icing) sugar, cocoa, melted butter, milk, and vanilla on medium speed until incorporated, creamy, and smooth, 2–3 minutes.
6 When the cake is done, remove it from the oven, scatter the marshmallows over the top, and return the cake to the hot oven to soften the marshmallows, about 3 minutes.
7 Place the hot cake on a wire rack. Pour the frosting over the marshmallow-dotted cake, and let it cool to room temperature.

STORAGE: Store airtight at room temperature for up to 5 days or in the refrigerator. for up to 1 week.

MORAVIAN SUGAR CAKE

V

The Moravian Church is one of the earliest Protestant denominations, originating in what is now the Czech Republic. In the early eighteenth century, Moravians settled in Georgia and Pennsylvania, and in 1753 established a community in North Carolina that eventually become part of the city of Winston-Salem. This dessert is featured at the Moravian Love Feast, a special church service in which coffee or cocoa is passed and enjoyed, often by candlelight. This cake has become an ambassador for Moravian baking traditions outside of their religious rituals. The brown sugar-cinnamon topping is enticing.

PREPARATION TIME: 40 MINUTES, PLUS 2 ½ HOURS RISING
COOKING TIME: 20–25 MINUTES
SERVES: 10–12

FOR THE CAKE:
¾ cup (6 fl oz/180 ml) whole milk, warmed (110°F/43°C)
1 packet (7 g) active dry yeast (2 ¼ teaspoons)
⅓ cup (60 g) sugar
Vegetable oil, for the bowl and pan
½ cup (110 g) mashed potatoes
1 egg, beaten
⅓ cup (75 g) salted butter, melted
½ teaspoon fine salt
2 cups (260 g) all-purpose (plain) flour

FOR THE TOPPING:
½ cup (60 g) light or dark brown sugar
2 teaspoons ground cinnamon
⅓ cup (75 g) salted butter, melted

1 Make the cake: In a small bowl, stir together the warm milk, yeast, and 1 teaspoon of the sugar. Set aside for 10 minutes. Grease a large bowl with oil and set aside.

2 In a large bowl, combine the remaining sugar, mashed potatoes, egg, melted butter, and salt. Using a large spoon, stir to combine everything well. Add the milk/yeast mixture and stir to incorporate. Add the flour and stir until a dough forms and there are no dry patches of flour remaining.

3 Turn the dough out onto a lightly floured surface and knead for 10 minutes, adding a little flour if needed, until the dough becomes less sticky and is smooth and springy. Add the kneaded dough to the oiled bowl, turning to coat it evenly with the oil. Cover with a tea towel and set in a warm place to rise until puffy and doubled in size, 1–1 ½ hours.

4 Grease a 9-inch (23 cm) square baking pan with oil. Punch down the dough, releasing the air, and gently knead for 1 minute. Place the dough in the prepared pan and stretch and press to fit the pan. Cover with a tea towel and let rise again in a warm place, until puffy and doubled in size, about 1 hour.

5 Preheat the oven to 375°F (190°C/Gas Mark 5).

6 Add the topping: Use the handle of a wooden spoon or your fingers to poke holes all over the surface of the cake. In a bowl, stir together the brown sugar and cinnamon. Sprinkle the mixture generously and evenly all over the surface of the cake. Drizzle the melted butter over the brown sugar, covering it well.

7 Bake for 20–25 minutes, until the cake is puffed up and golden brown and the brown sugar and butter are bubbling.

8 Let the cake cool in the pan on a wire rack.

STORAGE: Store airtight at room temperature for up to 3 days.

MOLASSES CAKE

V

Recipes like this molasses cake signify the kind of desserts that Southerners inherited from their Colonial and antebellum forebears.

PREPARATION TIME: 20 MINUTES
COOKING TIME: 25–30 MINUTES
SERVES: 8–10

Softened butter, for the pan
1 ½ cups (195 g) all-purpose (plain) flour
1 ½ teaspoons baking powder
½ teaspoon ground cinnamon
½ teaspoon ground cloves
¼ teaspoon fine salt
1 cup (8 fl oz/240 ml) molasses (treacle)
½ cup (4 fl oz/120 ml) warm water
3 tablespoons (45 g) unsalted butter, melted

1 Preheat the oven to 350°F (180°C/Gas Mark 4). Generously grease a 9-inch (23 cm) square pan.
2 In a medium bowl, whisk together the flour, baking powder, cinnamon, cloves, and salt.
3 In a large bowl, whisk together the molasses (treacle), warm water, butter, and egg. Whisk to mix well and evenly.
4 Add the flour mixture to the wet mixture and stir until there are no dry patches of flour remaining. The batter will be thin. Pour the batter into the prepared pan.
5 Bake for 25–30 minutes, until firm, rounded, and pulled away from the sides of the pan.
6 Let the cake cool completely in the pan on a wire rack. before cutting into squares.

STORAGE: Store airtight at room temperature for up to 4 days or in the refrigerator for up to 1 week.

OCRACOKE ISLAND FIG CAKE WITH BUTTERMILK GLAZE

V

While barrier islands border a number of Southern states, including Virginia, South Carolina, and Georgia, North Carolina's barrier islands are unique in the short distance between the islands in the chain. Ocracoke Island, largest of these islands known collectively as the Outer Banks, has abundant figs central to the cuisine and atmosphere of the region. Ocracoke fig cakes, preserves, and fig-based sauces are legendary.

PREPARATION TIME: 1 HOUR
COOKING TIME: 30 MINUTES
SERVES: 10–12

FOR THE CAKE:
Softened butter and flour, for the pan
2 cups (260 g) all-purpose (plain) flour
1 teaspoon baking soda (bicarbonate of soda)
1 teaspoon ground allspice
1 teaspoon ground cinnamon
1 teaspoon ground nutmeg
1 teaspoon fine salt
3 eggs
1 ½ cups (300 g) sugar
1 cup (8 fl oz/240 ml) vegetable oil
1 teaspoon pure vanilla extract
½ cup (4 fl oz/120 ml) buttermilk
1 cup (300 g) fig jam
1 cup (130 g) coarsely chopped pecans or walnuts

FOR THE GLAZE:
½ cup (4 fl oz/125 ml) buttermilk
½ cup (100 g) sugar
4 tablespoons (60 g) unsalted butter
1 ½ teaspoons cornstarch (cornflour) or flour
¼ teaspoon baking soda (bicarbonate of soda)
1 teaspoon pure vanilla extract

1 Make the cake: Preheat the oven to 350°F (180°C/Gas Mark 4). Generously grease and flour a 10 × 4-inch (25 × 10 cm) tube or Bundt pan.

2 In a medium bowl, whisk together the flour, baking soda (bicarb), allspice, cinnamon, nutmeg, and salt.

3 In a large bowl, with a whisk or electric mixer, beat the eggs well. Add the sugar, oil, and vanilla and beat until evenly incorporated into a thick, smooth batter. Add half the flour mixture and stir until no dry patches of flour remain. Add the buttermilk and mix well. Add the remaining flour and stir until no dry patches of flour remain. Add the fig jam and the nuts, using a spatula to mix everything until evenly incorporated. Quickly scrape the batter into the prepared pan.

4 Bake for 55 minutes – 1 hour 5 minutes, until the cake has risen and is firm on top.

5 Transfer to a wire rack to cool in the pan for 15 minutes.

6 While the cake is cooling, make the glaze: In a medium saucepan, whisk together the buttermilk, sugar, butter, cornstarch (cornflour), and baking soda (bicarb). Bring to a boil over medium heat, stirring often. Cook until smooth and thickened a bit, about 3 minutes. Remove from the heat and stir in the vanilla. Cover to keep warm.

7 Unmold the cake onto a wire rack. Pour the warm glaze over the cake. Let the glazed cake cool completely, then transfer to a cake plate before slicing and serving.

STORAGE: Store airtight at room temperature for up to 5 days or in the refrigerator for up to 1 week.

BLACK WALNUT CAKE

V

Black walnuts, hickory nuts, pecans, and many other nuts were turned into candies, taffies, cakes, and breads—anything that was available and possible. Foraging and using resources at hand is a deep part of Southern foodways.

PREPARATION TIME: 30 MINUTES
COOKING TIME: 25–30 MINUTES
SERVES: 10–12

FOR THE CAKE:
Softened butter and flour, for the pans
3 cups (390 g) all-purpose (plain) flour
2 teaspoons baking powder
½ teaspoon fine salt
1 cup (8 fl oz/240 ml) buttermilk or whole milk
1 teaspoon pure vanilla extract
16 tablespoons (8 oz/225g) unsalted butter, at room temperature
1 cup (200 g) granulated (caster) sugar
1 cup (200 g) packed light brown sugar
4 eggs
1 cup (120 g) chopped black walnuts

FOR THE ICING:
1 cup (8 fl oz/240 ml) whole milk
¼ cup (35 g) all-purpose (plain) flour
16 tablespoons (8 oz/225g) unsalted butter, at room temperature
1 cup (200 g) granulated (caster) sugar
1 teaspoon pure vanilla extract
¼ teaspoon fine salt
¾ cup (90 g) finely chopped black walnuts

1 Make the cake: Preheat the oven to 350°F (180°C/Gas Mark 4). Grease and flour two 9-inch (23 cm) round cake pans.

2 In a large bowl, whisk together the flour, baking powder, and salt. In a medium bowl, combine the buttermilk and vanilla.

3 In a large bowl, with an electric mixer, beat the butter on medium speed until creamy, about 2 minutes. Add both sugars and beat until light and fluffy, about 3 minutes more. With the mixer on medium-high speed, add the eggs, one at a time, beating well after each addition, until the batter is thick and smooth.

4 With the mixer on low speed, add one-third of the flour mixture, beating until no dry patches of flour remain. Add half the buttermilk mixture and beat until incorporated. Add half the remaining flour mixture, then the remaining buttermilk, and then all the flour mixture, beating each time just to incorporate everything. Stir in the chopped black walnuts, mixing them evenly into the batter. Divide the batter between the prepared pans.

5 Bake for 25–30 minutes, until the golden brown and beginning to pull away from the sides of the pan.

6 Transfer to wire racks and let cool in the pans for 15 minutes, then unmold the cake layers onto the racks to cool completely.

7 Make the icing: In a medium saucepan, whisk together the milk and flour. Bring to a simmer over medium heat, whisking as it thickens like pudding, 2–4 minutes. Transfer to a small bowl to cool completely.

8 In a stand mixer (or in a large bowl with a hand mixer), beat the butter on high speed until light and fluffy, about 2 minutes. Add the granulated sugar, vanilla, and salt and beat until incorporated, 2–3 minutes. Add the cooled milk mixture and beat until smooth, creamy, and easy to spread, 2–3 minutes. Using a spatula or a large spoon, stir in the black walnuts, and mix well.

9 To ice the cake: place a cake layer, top-side down, on a serving plate. Quickly spread the icing over the top, using an offset spatula, spatula, or table knife to spread it to the edges. Place the second layer on the iced layer, top-side up. Scoop more icing on the top layer and spread it to the edges. Use any remaining icing to cover the sides.

STORAGE: Store airtight at room temperature for up to 5 days or in the refrigerator for up to 1 week.

CARAMEL CAKE

V

Caramel cake is the cake of both joy and sorrow. It was served at every life-cycle event from life's start to its end and in between, at dinner on the church grounds after services, or at family reunions.

PREPARATION TIME: 1 ½ HOURS
COOKING TIME: 1 HOUR
SERVES: 10–12

FOR THE CAKE:
Softened butter and flour, for the pans
1 cup (8 fl oz/240 ml) whole milk
12 tablespoons (6 oz/170 g) unsalted butter
2 cups (280 g) sifted all-purpose (plain) flour
2 ¾ teaspoons baking powder
½ teaspoon fine salt
4 eggs
2 cups (400 g) granulated (caster) sugar
1 teaspoon pure vanilla extract

FOR THE ICING:
4 cups (760 g) light brown sugar
8 tablespoons (4 oz/115 g) salted butter
½ cup (4 fl oz/120 ml) evaporated milk
1 teaspoon pure vanilla extract

1 Make the cake: Preheat the oven to 325°F (165°C/Gas Mark 3). Grease and flour two 9-inch (23 cm) round cake pans.

2 In a small saucepan, combine the milk and butter and cook over low heat, stirring occasionally, until the butter melts, 2–3 minutes. Set aside to cool to room temperature.

3 In a medium bowl, whisk together the flour, baking powder, and salt.

4 In a large bowl, with whisk or electric mixer, beat the eggs and granulated (caster) sugar on high speed until light yellow, smooth, and thick, about 3 minutes. Add the flour mixture and beat on low speed until there are no dry patches of flour remaining. Add the cooled milk mixture and the vanilla, beating until incorporated. Divide the batter between the prepared pans, smoothing with a spatula.

5 Bake for 25–30 minutes, until pale golden brown and beginning to pull away from the sides of the pan.

6 Let cool in the pans on wire racks for 10 minutes, then turn out onto the racks top-side up to cool completely.

7 Make the icing: Have the cake layers handy, ready to be frosted, so you can spread the warm frosting quickly once it is ready.

8 In a heavy medium saucepan, combine the brown sugar, butter, and evaporated milk. Bring the mixture to a boil, stirring to dissolve the sugar, melt the butter, and combine everything well. Once the mixture boils, reduce the heat to maintain a gentle boil and cook, without stirring, for 7 minutes. Remove the pan from the heat, stir in the vanilla, and let cool for 15 minutes.

9 Beat the warm icing with a wooden spoon until it thickens, 3–5 minutes.

10 Place a cake layer, top-side down, on a serving plate. Quickly pour one-third of the icing over the top and use an offset spatula (palette knife), spatula, or table knife to spread it to the edges.

11 Place the second layer on the iced layer, top-side up. Pour more icing and spread it to the edges. Pour the remaining icing around the edges and quickly spread it over the sides. (If the icing becomes too hard to spread, place the saucepan over low heat, add 1–2 spoonfuls of evaporated milk, stir to combine, and continue icing the cake.)

STORAGE: Store airtight at room temperature for up to 5 days or in the refrigerator for up to 1 week.

APPLE STACK CAKE

V

Stack cake is a classic dessert from the Southern Appalachian Mountains, in which thin layers of spiced butter cake are sandwiched together with a cooked apple filling. Dried apples, sorghum syrup, and, in some recipes, apple butter, speak to the staples that make the Southern highlands unique and distinct, and this cake remains a favorite in West Virginia. Here we've toned down the spices to allow the apples and sorghum to shine more brightly. Plan to let the completed cake sit, covered, for one day before serving.

PREPARATION TIME: 1 ½ HOURS, PLUS 1 DAY REST BEFORE SERVING
COOKING TIME: 2 HOURS
SERVES: 10–12

FOR THE CAKE:

Softened butter and flour, for the pans
4 cups (520 g) all-purpose (plain) flour
2 teaspoons baking powder
½ teaspoon baking soda (bicarbonate of soda)
½ teaspoon fine salt
¼ teaspoon ground cinnamon
¼ teaspoon ground cloves
¼ teaspoon ground nutmeg
16 tablespoons (8 oz/225 g) unsalted butter, at room temperature
1 cup (190 g) packed brown sugar, light or dark
3 eggs, beaten well
1 cup (8 fl oz/240 ml) sorghum syrup, golden syrup (such as Lyle's), or maple syrup
1 cup (8 fl oz /240 ml) buttermilk

FOR THE FILLING:

4 cups (454 g) chopped dried apples
1 cup (190 g) packed brown sugar, light or dark
¼ teaspoon ground cinnamon
¼ teaspoon ground cloves
¼ teaspoon ground nutmeg
¼ teaspoon fine salt
Powdered (icing) sugar, for garnish

1 Make the cake: Preheat the oven to 350°F (180°C/Gas Mark 4). Grease and flour two 9-inch (23 cm) round cake pans, or more if you have them (see NOTE).

2 In a large bowl, whisk together the flour, baking powder, baking soda (bicarb), salt, cinnamon, cloves, and nutmeg.

3 In a stand mixer fitted with the paddle (or in a large bowl with a hand mixer), beat the butter and brown sugar on medium speed until everything is well combined, about 4 minutes. Add the eggs and sorghum syrup and beat at medium-high speed, scraping the bowl often, to blend them well.

4 Add half the flour mixture, beating at low speed until it disappears into the batter. Add half the buttermilk, beating until blended. Add the remaining flour, beating until it disappears. Add the remaining buttermilk and beat until the batter is thick and smooth.

5 Quickly pour about 1 cup (8 fl oz/240 ml) of the batter into each of the prepared pans, using a spatula to spread it evenly in the pan.

6 Bake for 10–12 minutes, until the cakes are beginning to pull away from the sides of the pans.

7 Let the cakes cool in the pans for 10 minutes, then unmold them onto wire racks or plates top-side up and cool completely. Continue to bake until you have 6 thin cakes.

8 Make the filling: In a medium saucepan, combine the dried apples and 4 cups (32 fl oz/950 ml) water. Bring to a boil over medium-high heat. Adjust the heat to maintain a lively simmer and cook, stirring occasionally, until the apples are soft and most of the liquid has cooked away, 25–30 minutes.

9 Remove from the heat and use a potato masher to mash the apples into a fairly smooth sauce. (If the sauce is chunky, transfer to a food processor and process, pulsing until smooth.) Add the brown sugar, cinnamon, cloves, nutmeg, and salt and stir to combine everything well.

10 To assemble the cake, place one layer, top-side up, on a serving plate, saving the prettiest layer for the top of the cake. Spoon about one-fifth of the apple filling on the cake and spread it out evenly all the way to the edges. Continue filling and stacking the layers, finishing with one plain layer on top.

11 Cover the cake tightly with plastic wrap and set aside in a cool place or refrigerate for at least 1 day.

12 Before serving, bring to room temperature, and sift powdered sugar over the top layer.

NOTE: You'll be making a total of 6 thin layers, so prepare as many pans as you have, and plan to bake in several batches if need be.

STORAGE: Wrap in foil and store airtight at room temperature for up to 3 days or in the refrigerator for up to 1 week.

LANE CAKE

V

“Miss Maudie baked a Lane cake so loaded with shinny [moonshine] it made me tight,” said Scout, the main character of Harper Lee’s classic novel, *To Kill a Mockingbird*. Alabama Lane cake, invented by Emma Rylander Lane in the late 1800s, was a county fair–winning cake, originally from Georgia, that became a centerpiece dessert. The classic had expanded fame after it was published in the second issue of *Southern Living* magazine. It is the state cake of Alabama.

PREPARATION TIME: 1 ½ HOURS
COOKING TIME: 55 MINUTES
SERVES: 10–12

FOR THE CAKE:
Softened butter and flour, for the pans
3 ¼ cups (425 g) all-purpose (plain) flour
1 tablespoon baking powder
½ teaspoon fine salt
1 cup (8 fl oz/240 ml) whole milk
1 teaspoon pure vanilla extract
8 egg whites
2 cups (400 g) sugar
16 tablespoons (8 oz/225 g) unsalted butter, at room temperature

FOR THE FILLING:
8 egg yolks
1 ¼ cups (150 g) sugar
8 tablespoons (4 oz/115 g) unsalted butter, melted
1 cup (95 g) unsweetened shredded (desiccated) coconut
1 cup (145 g) raisins, chopped
1 cup (125 g) chopped pecans
½ cup (4 fl oz/120 ml) brandy, bourbon, or apple juice
1 teaspoon pure vanilla extract
⅛ teaspoon fine salt

FOR THE ICING:
1 cup (200 g) sugar
¼ cup (85 g) light corn syrup
2 egg whites
¼ teaspoon cream of tartar
¼ teaspoon fine salt
1 teaspoon pure vanilla extract

1 Make the cake: Position oven racks in the top and bottom thirds and preheat the oven to 350°F (180°C/Gas Mark 4). Grease and flour three 8-inch (20 cm) or 9-inch (23 cm) cake pans.

2 In a medium bowl, whisk together the flour, baking powder, and salt. In another medium bowl, combine the milk and vanilla.

3 In a third medium bowl, with an electric mixer, beat the egg whites at medium speed until they are foamy, about 1 minute. Increase the speed to medium-high and continue to beat the egg whites until they are thick and shiny and hold firmly curled peaks, about 5 minutes. Set aside.

4 In a large bowl, with an electric mixer, cream the sugar and butter at high speed until light and fluffy, stopping to scrape down the sides of the bowl now and then. Reduce the mixer's speed to low and carefully pour in the milk mixture, beating just to combine. Add the flour mixture to the batter all at once and beat at low speed, scraping the sides to incorporate evenly, until the flour disappears, about 5 minutes.

5 Use a spatula to add half the beaten egg whites to the batter, gently blending them into the batter. Add the remaining egg whites and gently combine them with the batter. A few streaks are fine, but don't mix so vigorously that the batter deflates. Quickly divide the batter among the three cake pans.

6 Bake for 20–25 minutes, until the cakes are golden and beginning to pull away from the sides of the pans.

7 Let the cakes cool in the pans for 5 minutes, then invert the cakes top-side up onto wire racks to cool completely.

8 Make the filling: In a medium bowl, with an electric mixer, beat the egg yolks and sugar at medium speed until thick, billowy, pale yellow, and smooth, about 7 minutes.

9 Use a spatula to scrape the egg/sugar mixture into a heavy 1 ½-quart (1.5-liter) saucepan. Set the pan over medium heat and stir in the melted butter. Cook, stirring often, until thickened and smooth and thick enough to coat the back of a spoon, 10–15 minutes.

10 Remove the filling from the heat and gently stir in the coconut, raisins, pecans, brandy, vanilla, and salt. Stir well to mix everything together into a uniformly thick, chunky filling. Let cool, briefly.

11 To assemble the cake, place one cake layer top-side down on a serving plate. Place half the filling on the cake layer, carefully spreading it out to the edges of the cake. Place the second layer top-side down on top of the filling. Spread the remaining filling over the cake layer, covering it to the edge. Place the third cake layer top-side up, covering the second layer of filling. Set aside while you make the icing.

12 Make the icing: In medium saucepan, bring about 4 inches (10 cm) of water to a boil.

13 In a large heatproof bowl (that can sit over the saucepan without touching the water), combine the sugar, corn syrup, egg whites, cream of tartar, and salt. With a hand mixer, beat at medium speed until the egg white mixture is foamy and incorporated, 1–2 minutes.

14 Place the bowl over the boiling water and adjust the heat to maintain a gentle boil. Using the hand mixer, beat the sugar/egg white mixture at high speed until it swells and forms thick peaks, 10–15 minutes. Remove the bowl from the pan and stir in the vanilla until incorporated.

15 Spread the icing on the sides and top of the cake, using a table knife to swirl into beautiful peaks and curls.

STORAGE: Store airtight at room temperature for up to 5 days or in the refrigerator for up to 1 week.

PEACH UPSIDE-DOWN CAKE

V

Sometimes Southern desserts are reactions to national trends. Thanks to the popularity of canned pineapple (most often available from the Dole fruit company), many people love pineapple upside-down cake, since the recipe was free for the taking on the can's label. Meanwhile, Southern homemakers with magazines and church cookbooks made their own delicious upside-down cake using their favorite fresh or home-canned fruit.

Peaches have been a part of Southern life since the Portuguese brought them here in the seventeenth century. It impacted all the threads: Native American, African American, and European. For starters, Native Americans loved the peach and planted peach trees in their villages between the eighteenth and early nineteenth centuries. In fact, the Cherokee and the Muscogee (Creek) developed their own cultivars. Early British Colonial law demanded that peaches be planted on farmsteads, and orchards were passed from landowner to landowner. Peaches had also been brought by the Portuguese to Central Africa very early in the seventeenth century. African Americans famously enjoyed the peach and created their own relationship with the fruit in the soul food tradition.

PREPARATION TIME: 30 MINUTES
COOKING TIME: 35–40 MINUTES
SERVES: 8–10

FOR THE PEACH TOPPING:

- 6 tablespoons (85 g) salted butter, melted
- ⅔ cup (145 g) firmly packed light or dark brown sugar
- 2 ½ cups (565 g) sliced fresh peaches

FOR THE CAKE:

- 1 ½ cups (195 g) all-purpose (plain) flour
- 1 ½ teaspoons baking powder
- ½ teaspoon fine salt
- ½ cup (4 fl oz/120 ml) buttermilk or milk
- 1 teaspoon pure vanilla extract
- 8 tablespoons (115 g) unsalted butter, at room temperature
- ¾ cup (150 g) granulated (caster) sugar
- 2 eggs

1 Preheat the oven to 350°F (180°C/Gas Mark 4).

2 Make the peach topping: Add the melted butter to a 9-inch (23 cm) round cake pan and tilt to evenly coat the pan. Sprinkle the brown sugar over the butter. Cover the bottom of the pan with the peach slices, pushing them gently into the brown sugar.

3 Make the cake: In a large bowl, whisk together the flour, baking powder, and salt. In a small bowl, combine the buttermilk and vanilla.

4 In a large bowl, with a whisk or electric mixer, beat the butter and sugar on medium speed until light and fluffy, about 2 minutes. Add the eggs and beat until the batter is thickened and smooth, about 2 minutes more. Add the flour mixture and beat on low speed until there are no dry patches of flour remaining. Add the buttermilk mixture and beat to incorporate, about 1 minute more.

5 Carefully pour the batter over the peaches, using a spatula to spread it to the edges of the pan and smooth the top.

6 Bake for 35–40 minutes, until the cake is golden brown, with the edges beginning to pull away from the sides.

7 Transfer to a wire rack to cool for 10 minutes. Loosen the edges of the cake. Place a serving plate upside down over the warm cake pan, and invert the cake onto the plate, gently lifting off the pan once you feel it drop loose. Replace any peach slices that remain in the pan.

8 Serve warm or cool completely.

STORAGE: Store airtight at room temperature for up to 5 days or in the refrigerator for up to 1 week.

HUMMINGBIRD CAKE

V

This cake of Jamaican origin became a Southern favorite in the 1970s. The logo for Jamaica's flagship airline, Air Jamaica, included an image of a native hummingbird, the red-billed streamertail, known in Jamaica as the doctor bird. As part of a publicity campaign in the late 1960s, the airline shared the recipe for this cake with newspaper food editors. Baked in a tube pan and served without icing, it was called the Doctor Bird Cake. Food editors renamed it Hummingbird Cake to help it resonate with their readers. In 1978, *Southern Living* published a reader's version of the cake, baked in layers and finished with cream cheese icing. Hummingbird Cake remains the magazine's most requested recipe ever.

PREPARATION TIME: 1 HOUR
COOKING TIME: 25–30 MINUTES
SERVES: 10–12

FOR THE CAKE:

Softened butter and flour, for the pan(s)
3 cups (390 g) all-purpose (plain) flour
2 cups (400 g) granulated (caster) sugar
1 teaspoon baking soda (bicarbonate of soda)
1 teaspoon ground cinnamon
1 teaspoon fine salt
1 ¼ cups (10 fl oz/300 ml) vegetable oil
3 eggs, beaten
2 teaspoons pure vanilla extract
2 cups (300 g) mashed ripe bananas
1 can (8 oz/227 g) crushed pineapple, undrained

FOR THE FROSTING:

8 oz (225 g) cream cheese, at room temperature
4 tablespoons (60 g) unsalted butter, at room temperature
4 cups (480 g) powdered (icing) sugar
1 teaspoon pure vanilla extract

1 Make the cake: Preheat the oven to 350°F (180°C/Gas Mark 4). Grease and flour two 9-inch (23 cm) round cake pans.

2 In a large bowl, whisk together the flour, granulated (caster) sugar, baking soda (bicarb), cinnamon, and salt.

3 In a medium bowl, whisk together the oil, eggs, and vanilla until well combined. Add the flour mixture and use a large spoon or spatula to stir until well combined. Add the bananas and the pineapple with its liquid, then stir with the spatula until well combined. Pour the batter into the prepared pan(s).

4 Bake for 25–30 minutes, or until the cake is golden brown, firm, and pulling away from the edges.

5 Let cool for 15 minutes in the pans, then loosen the sides carefully. Turn the cake layers out onto wire racks top-side up to cool completely.

6 Make the frosting: In a large bowl, with a hand mixer at medium speed, beat together the cream cheese, butter, powdered (icing) sugar, and vanilla until well combined, 2–3 minutes. Scrape the bowl and then beat at high speed until the frosting is light, fluffy, and very smooth, about 5 minutes.

7 To assemble the cake, place one cake layer top-side down on a serving plate. Spread icing evenly to the edges. Cover with the second layer, top-side up, and frost the top and sides of the cake.

STORAGE: Store airtight at room temperature for up to 5 days or in the refrigerator for up to 1 week.

COLONIAL QUEEN CAKES

V

Queen cakes were an eighteenth- and nineteenth-century sweet consisting of small cakes baked in a mold, with an appearance like petite cupcakes. During the holiday season, they were often iced and decorated, and were particularly enjoyed in the Tidewater region of Virginia.

PREPARATION TIME: 15 MINUTES
COOKING TIME: 15–20 MINUTES
MAKES: ABOUT 24 SMALL CAKES

Softened butter, for the muffin tin
1 cup (130 g) all-purpose (plain) flour
¼ teaspoon fine salt
½ teaspoon ground nutmeg or mace (optional)
4 tablespoons currants or raisins (optional)
8 tablespoons (4 oz/115 g) unsalted butter, at room temperature
½ cup (100 g) sugar
2 eggs
1 tablespoon rose water or orange flower water, or 1 teaspoon pure vanilla extract

1 Preheat the oven to 325°F (165°C/ Gas Mark 3). Grease 24 cups of a mini muffin tin.
2 In a medium bowl, combine the flour, salt, and nutmeg (if using) and stir with a fork to mix well. Stir in the currants (if using) to coat them with flour.
3 In a large bowl, with an electric mixer, beat the butter and sugar on medium speed until light and fluffy, 2–3 minutes. Add the eggs one at a time, beating well after each addition. Add the rose water and beat until the batter is thick and smooth, 1 minute more. Use a wooden spoon to mix in the flour mixture, stirring only enough to mix in the currants and make the flour disappear into the batter. Divide the batter evenly among the muffin cups, filling them to the brim.
4 Bake for 15–20 minutes, until the little cakes are golden and firm, with rounded tops.
5 Let the cakes cool in the pan for 1–2 minutes, then quickly unmold them onto a wire rack to cool completely.

STORAGE: Store airtight at room temperature for up to 5 days or in the refrigerator for up to 1 week.

KING CAKE

V

In New Orleans, everyone lives for this Mardi Gras cake, which has undergone a revival in popularity thanks to home bakers. Cultural groups in New Orleans favor different forms of king cake, but this recipe is the version that anyone in Louisiana will recognize as traditional. King Cake includes a fève or charm, tucked into the finished cake after baking. Whichever lucky guest finds the charm becomes King or Queen for that event, and is expected to bring a king cake to the next Mardi Gras season gathering.

Traditionally the fève would be a very small ceramic charm, often shaped like the Baby Jesus, or a coin. Today, commercial bakeries provide a tiny plastic baby charm, which the host can tuck into the underside of the king cake. A whole almond or pecan half serves as a simpler option, which is what this recipe calls for.

PREPARATION TIME: 1 ½ HOURS
COOKING TIME: 25–30 MINUTES
SERVES: 12–14

FOR THE CAKE:
2 packets (7 g each) active dry yeast (4 ½ teaspoons)
2 teaspoons plus ½ cup (100 g) sugar
½ cup (4 fl oz/120 ml) warm water
3 ½–4 ½ cups (455–585 g) all-purpose (plain) flour
1 ½ teaspoons fine salt
½ teaspoon ground cinnamon
½ teaspoon freshly grated nutmeg
½ cup (4 fl oz/120 ml) whole milk, warmed
5 egg yolks, beaten
8 tablespoons (4 oz/115 g) unsalted butter, at room temperature
Vegetable oil, for the bowl

FOR THE ICING AND DECORATIONS:
2 cups (240 g) powdered (icing) sugar, sifted
3 tablespoons whole milk
Colored sanding sugar in purple, green, and yellow/gold
1 pecan half or 1 whole almond

1 Make the cake: In a small bowl, combine the yeast, 2 teaspoons of the sugar, and the warm water and stir to mix well. Set aside until puffed and foamy, about 10 minutes.

2 In a large bowl, whisk together 3½ cups (455 g) of the flour, the remaining ½ cup (100 g) sugar, the salt, cinnamon, and nutmeg. Scoop out a well in the flour and pour the yeast mixture into it. Use a large spoon or spatula to stir the mixture and then add the warm milk and beaten egg yolks. Stir to incorporate until you have a very soft dough, 5–7 minutes.

3 Add the soft butter to the dough and use your hands to mix it into the dough, pressing it against the sides of the bowl to incorporate. Add another ½ cup (65 g) flour, to form a dough that is quite sticky but holds its shape. Add more flour, little by little, until you have a very soft ball of dough, more dry than sticky.

4 Turn out the dough onto a lightly floured work surface. Using floured hands, knead the dough, adding flour little by little, until the dough is soft, springy, and dry, about 10 minutes.

5 Generously grease the inside of a large bowl with oil. Place the dough in the bowl and turn to grease it evenly. Cover with a tea towel and set in a warm place to rise until the dough is dry, puffed up, and twice its original size, 1–1 ½ hours.

6 Punch the dough to release the air and then knead it gently for 1 minute. Line a large baking sheet with parchment paper.

7 Turn the dough out onto a lightly floured surface. Shape the dough into a plump cylinder, about 20 inches (50 cm) long. Move the dough to the prepared baking sheet and shape it into a large open ring, either round or oval. Cover the shaped ring with a tea towel and let it rise in a warm place until doubled in size, 1–1 ½ hours.

8 Preheat the oven to 375°F (190°C/ Gas Mark 5).

9 Bake for 25–30 minutes, until golden brown, rotating the sheet front to back halfway through.

10 Transfer to a wire rack to cool completely before icing.

11 Make the icing: In a medium bowl, whisk the powdered (icing) sugar and milk together to make a smooth, shiny, and thick but pourable icing.

12 Place the cooled cake on a wire rack over a sheet pan or parchment-lined counter surface to catch icing and sanding sugar. Use a large spoon, spatula, or whisk to spoon, drizzle, or slather icing all over the surface of the cake. Quickly sprinkle on the purple, green, and yellow/gold sanding sugars, making thin stripes or big color patches. Let stand for 15 minutes to set.

13 Transfer to a serving platter and serve at room temperature.

STORAGE: Store airtight at room temperature for up to 5 days or in the refrigerator for up to 1 week.

THE SOUTHERN LIFE CYCLE IN FOOD

Food plays a critical role in the life cycle of the American South. When a child is born, some families hold a "sip-and-see," in which a child is received by their community for the first time. When one leaves the world, a good homegoing or funeral demands an ample repast, often with the favorite dishes of the one who has passed. Between the two—a lifetime if one is lucky—there are baptisms, b'nai mitzvot, dinners on the grounds, iftars, celebration of sacred days of the Saints or the Vodun, cotillions, marriages, family reunions, and a host of other occasions and rites of passage. Seasonality, highs, and lows in life, regionality, and personal taste determine the beverages, the cakes and pies, and the emotions and spirit invested in the delicacies on the table. As the great chef and author Nathalie Dupree said, food "is the very first thing we control as an infant and the very last thing we control when we are dying." Life is bridged by food, from pot likker mashed with cornbread in toddlerhood to favorite treats left at the grave or altar brought faithfully on days of remembrance.

Southern food is emblematic of life's path and the journey through Southern identity and knowledge transfer. In our youth, some Southern kids are put to snapping beans, sorting peas, picking berries, and making forays in the garden and farmers' market, where we learn by watching and through imitation. Soon, others of us will catch our first fish, usually a sunfish or smallmouth bass, and realize that fried fish doesn't just come that way. By the time we are teenagers, some will take up the rod again, or the gun, and deer, turkey, or ducks may come to the table after a first kill. In the days when youth organizations like Jack and Jill of America and 4-H clubs were paths of socialization, food played a prominent role in raising money (Girl Scout Cookies started in the South with Juliette Gordon Low). Additionally, potlucks and organizational cookbooks (especially chapters of the Junior League) were a key part of growing up. American fraternities and sororities at colleges often have parties based around local food traditions like barbecues, cookouts, oyster roasts, crab boils, and stews, ensuring that specific tastes and flavors will be inculcated right at the time when adulthood means establishing new homes, lineages, and the passing of cookbooks to new hands as wedding gifts.

Southern people mature in food preparation by learning skills like barbecuing, baking, or making the basics for Sunday or Friday night dinner through careful tutelage from elders eager to pass on their skills, hoping that what is being taught will endure. I learned how to make the nightly iced tea, wash and sort collard greens, season flour and meat for frying, and bake biscuits from an early age. Proud is the family member who sees their youth enter competitions and have a prize cake or dish win a ribbon with the family name. Many families have a treasured handwritten family cookbook or a few appointed experts in the specific tastes and secrets key to each family's identity. There is nothing so satisfying as hearing the ones who raised you declare something you've made "Ain't half bad" or say "You've put your foot in here" (both very positive, I assure you) as they go back for seconds.

FRUITCAKE

V

This is a Southern Christmas favorite, complete with pecans, dried fruit, and other embellishments, presented here in the spirit of tradition.

PREPARATION TIME: 45 MINUTES
COOKING TIME: 2 ½ HOURS
SERVES: 14–16

Softened butter and flour, for the pan(s)
4 cups (520 g) all-purpose (plain) flour
2 teaspoons baking powder
1 teaspoon ground cinnamon
1 teaspoon ground nutmeg
¼ teaspoon ground cloves
¼ teaspoon fine salt
2 cups (450 g) chopped candied cherries, red and green
1 ½ cups (340 g) chopped candied pineapple
2 ½ cups (300 g) chopped pecans
12 oz (340 g) unsalted butter
2 cups (400 g) sugar
6 eggs
¾ cup (6 fl oz/180 ml) sherry, bourbon, or apple juice
1 teaspoon pure vanilla extract

1 Preheat the oven to 275°F (140°C/Gas Mark 1). Grease and flour a 10 × 4-inch (25 × 10 cm) tube pan or two 9 × 5-inch (23 × 13 cm) loaf pans.
2 In a large bowl, whisk together the flour, baking powder, cinnamon, nutmeg, cloves, and salt.
3 In a medium bowl, combine the candied cherries, candied pineapple, and pecans. Sprinkle ½ cup (65 g) of the flour mixture over the candied fruit and nuts. Use a wooden spoon or your hands to toss the fruit and nuts with the flour, mixing everything well.
4 In a stand mixer (or in a large bowl with a hand mixer), beat the butter and sugar on medium speed until light and fluffy, about 2 minutes. Add the eggs, one at a time, beating well after each addition, until pale yellow, creamy, and thickened.
5 Add half the remaining flour mixture, and beat at low speed until the flour disappears. Add the sherry and vanilla and beat to incorporate. Add the remaining flour mixture and beat until the flour disappears.
6 Remove the mixer bowl to the counter and add the candied fruit and nuts to the bowl. Using a spatula or a large spoon, stir the fruit and nuts into the batter to combine them evenly. Pour the batter into the prepared pan(s) and smooth the top.
7 Bake for 2–2 ½ hours for the tube pan, or 1 ½–1 ¾ hours for the loaf pans, until the cake is golden brown, firm, and beginning to pull away from the sides of the pan.
8 Let cool completely in the pan(s) on a wire rack. Remove the cooled cake from the pan and place it top-side up on a serving plate.

STORAGE: To keep the cake for up to 1 month, transfer it to a cake tin or an airtight container or wrap it tightly in foil. For longer storage, see the Spirited Fruitcake variation below.

VARIATION: **Spirited Fruitcake:** To season the cake in the classic Southern fashion, you will need cheesecloth and spirits, such as sherry, rum, or bourbon. Place a few layers of cheesecloth about the size of a tea towel in a large bowl and pour in enough of your chosen spirit to soak the cloth well. Spread the soaked cheesecloth on a cutting board and place the fruitcake on top. Gently wrap the fruitcake, enclosing it completely. Sprinkle a little more spirits on top of the cake, then place it in a cake tin or other airtight container. Sprinkle it every 3 days with your chosen spirit, until serving day. Wrapped and seasoned, it will keep for up to 2 months.

POUND CAKE

V -5

Originally based on one pound of each main ingredient (butter, sugar, flour, and eggs), pound cake is a favorite for potlucks or keeping on the table in a cake dome to have on hand for company that might stop by in the afternoon. No leavening is needed; its rise comes from the butter and sugar creamed together, and then lightened again by the vigorous beating of eggs. Every Southern family swears theirs is the best.

PREPARATION TIME: 20 MINUTES
COOKING TIME: 1 ½ HOURS
SERVES: 10–12

Softened butter and flour, for the pan
3 ½ cups (455 g) all-purpose (plain) flour
½ teaspoon fine salt
1 lb (450 g) unsalted butter, at room temperature
2 cups (400 g) sugar

1 Position a rack in the bottom third of the oven and preheat the oven to 325°F (165°C/Gas Mark 3). Generously grease and flour a 10 × 4-inch (25 × 10 cm) tube pan or two 9 × 5-inch (23 × 13 cm) loaf pans.
2 In a medium bowl, stir together the flour and salt.
3 In a stand mixer (or in a large bowl with a hand mixer), beat the butter on high speed until light and fluffy, about 2 minutes. Add the sugar and beat until smooth and very creamy, about 3 minutes. Add the eggs, one at a time, beating well after each addition, until the batter is extremely light and whipped. Add the flour mixture in three additions, beating at medium-low speed until it has disappeared into the smooth, thick batter. Quickly scrape the batter into the prepared pan(s).
4 Bake without opening the oven for about 1 ½ hours for the tube pan or 55–65 minutes for the loaf pans, until the cake has risen well, is golden brown and firm, and a skewer or a toothpick inserted in the center comes out clean.
5 Let the cake(s) cool in the pan(s) for 10 minutes, then carefully unmold onto a wire rack, top-side up, to cool completely.

STORAGE: Store airtight at room temperature for up to 5 days or in the refrigerator for up to 1 week.

COLA CAKE

V

In the 1950s, recipes for cakes with soft drinks emerged. Soft drinks were incorporated into cakes, barbecue sauces, glazed hams, briskets, and other dishes no one could have previously imagined. This cake reminds us that the cola flavor is based partly on the West African kola nut.

PREPARATION TIME: 20 MINUTES
COOKING TIME: 35 MINUTES
SERVES: 10–12

FOR THE CAKE:
Softened butter and flour, for the pan
2 cups (260 g) all-purpose (plain) flour
⅓ cup (32 g) unsweetened cocoa powder
1 teaspoon baking soda (bicarbonate of soda)
½ teaspoon fine salt
1 cup (8 fl oz/240 ml) cola soft drink, such as Coca-Cola
½ cup (4 fl oz/120 ml) buttermilk
1 teaspoon pure vanilla extract
1 cup (200 g) granulated (caster) sugar
8 tablespoons (4 oz/115 g) unsalted butter, at room temperature
2 eggs
1 ½ cups (105 g) mini marshmallows

FOR THE FROSTING:
4 cups (280 g) powdered (icing) sugar
8 tablespoons (4 oz/115 g) salted butter
¼ cup (24 g) unsweetened cocoa powder
⅓ cup (80 ml) cola soft drink, such as Coca-Cola
1 teaspoon pure vanilla extract

1 Make the cake: Preheat the oven to 350°F (180°C/Gas Mark 4). Grease and flour a 9 × 13-inch (23 × 33 cm) pan.
2 In a medium bowl, whisk together the flour, cocoa, baking soda (bicarb), and salt. In a small bowl, combine the cola, buttermilk, and vanilla and stir well.
3 In a stand mixer (or in a large bowl with a hand mixer), beat the granulated (caster) sugar and butter on medium speed until incorporated, about 2 minutes. Add the eggs, one at a time, beating until light and fluffy, 2–3 minutes.
4 With the mixer on low speed, add the flour mixture in three additions, alternating with the buttermilk mixture, beginning and ending with the flour. Beat on low speed after each addition until the batter is thick and smooth and no dry patches remain. Stir in the marshmallows. Pour the batter into the pan.
5 Bake for 30–35 minutes, until the cake is a handsome brown color, firm, and pulling away from the pan at the edges.
6 Transfer the pan to a wire rack and set aside while you make the frosting.
7 Make the frosting: Sift the powdered (icing) sugar into a large bowl.
8 In a small saucepan, melt the butter over medium heat. Add the cocoa and whisk until smooth. Remove from the heat and whisk in the cola and vanilla.
9 Pour the warm butter mixture over the powdered sugar and whisk until thick and smooth.
10 To frost the cake, quickly pour the warm icing over the warm cake, spreading to evenly cover the cake. Leave the cake on the wire rack to cool completely.

STORAGE: Store airtight at room temperature for up to 5 days or in the refrigerator for up to 1 week.

LEMON-LIME POUND CAKE

V

We Southerners love lemon-flavored desserts, and this 1953 cake is no exception. When sodas became an ingredient in Southern baking, the range of flavor for Southern cakes increased, while sparking conversation about how ingredients pioneered by human food science added to caramelization, leavening, as well as acidity and volume.

PREPARATION TIME: 35 MINUTES
COOKING TIME: 1–1 ½ HOURS
SERVES: 12

FOR THE CAKE:

Softened butter and flour, for the pan
12 ounces (340 g) unsalted butter, at room temperature
3 cups (600 g) granulated (caster) sugar
5 eggs
3 cups (390 g) all-purpose (plain) flour
½ teaspoon fine salt
¾ cup (6 fl oz/180 ml) lemon-lime soda, such as 7 Up
2 teaspoons lemon extract

FOR THE GLAZE:

1 ½ cups (180 g) powdered (icing) sugar
3 tablespoons lemon-lime soda, such as 7 Up
½ teaspoon lemon extract

1 Make the cake: Preheat the oven to 325°F (165°C/Gas Mark 3). Grease and flour a 10-inch (25 cm) Bundt pan or tube pan.

2 In a stand mixer (or in a large bowl with a hand mixer), beat the butter and sugar on medium speed until light and fluffy, 2–3 minutes. Add the eggs, one at a time, beating well after each addition, until pale yellow, creamy, and thickened. Add the flour and salt and beat on low speed until no dry patches of flour remain. Add the lemon-lime soda and lemon extract, then beat on low speed just until the batter is thick and evenly combined. Pour the batter into the prepared pan and smooth the top.

3 Bake for 1–1½ hours, until the cake is golden brown, firm and beginning to pull away from the sides of the pan.

4 Let the cake cool completely in the pan on a wire rack.

5 Make the glaze: In a medium bowl, whisk together the powdered (icing) sugar, lemon-lime soda, and lemon extract to make a smooth glaze.

6 Unmold the cooled cake and set it top-side up on a serving plate. Drizzle the glaze over the cooled cake.

STORAGE: Store airtight at room temperature for up to 5 days or in the refrigerator for up to 1 week.

PUMPKIN PIE

V

Southern pumpkin pie was historically made from winter squash/pumpkins like the cushaw, sweet potato pumpkin, Seminole cheese pumpkin, or Dutch Fork pumpkin that were more likely to thrive in Southern heat. The cushaw, favorite pumpkin of African American Southerners, spread across the South thanks to their love of the vegetable. Look for cushaw pumpkins in farmers' markets, late summer to early fall. Shaped like large crookneck squash or gourd, they have beautiful variegated green skin, and keep exceedingly well. You can halve, seed, and roast a cushaw and then scoop out and puree the flesh to use in this pie. You can also use any roasted or mashed pumpkin or canned pumpkin puree.

PREPARATION TIME: 20 MINUTES
COOKING TIME: 1 HOUR
SERVES: 8

- Pastry for a 9-inch (23 cm) single-crust pie, homemade (PAGE 382) or store-bought
- 3/4 cup (150 g) sugar
- 1 teaspoon ground cinnamon
- 1/2 teaspoon ground ginger
- 1/2 teaspoon ground nutmeg
- 1/2 teaspoon fine salt
- 2 cups (490 g) canned 100% pumpkin puree
- 3/4 cup (6 fl oz/180 ml) evaporated milk or half-and-half (single cream)
- 2 eggs, beaten
- 1/4 cup (2 fl oz/60 ml) sorghum syrup, pure cane syrup, or maple syrup

1 Position a rack in the center of the oven. Preheat the oven to 450°F (230°C/Gas Mark 8). Line a 9-inch (23 cm) pie pan with the pie pastry, trim, and crimp the edges.

2 In a small bowl, whisk together the sugar, cinnamon, ginger, nutmeg, and salt.

3 In a large bowl, whisk together the pumpkin puree, evaporated milk, eggs, and sorghum syrup. Add the sugar-spice mixture and whisk to incorporate into a thick, smooth filling.

4 Pour the filling into the pie shell (pastry case) and bake for 10 minutes. Reduce the oven temperature to 325°F (165°C/Gas Mark 3) and bake for 45–50 minutes, until the edges puff up and the center is fairly firm.

5 Transfer to a wire rack to cool completely.

STORAGE: Cover with plastic wrap and store in the refrigerator for up to 5 days.

PEANUT PIE

V

A favorite in southern Virginia, eastern North Carolina, and the coastal plain of Georgia, peanut pie is a great alternative to pecan pie. "The poor man's pecan pie" is a popular offering at the Virginia Diner, a restaurant anchored in the heart of Virginia's peanut belt.

PREPARATION TIME: 30 MINUTES
COOKING TIME: 50–55 MINUTES
SERVES: 8

Pastry for a 9-inch (23 cm) single-crust pie, homemade (PAGE 382) or store-bought
¾ cup (150 g) brown sugar, light or dark
½ cup (4 fl oz/120 ml) corn syrup, dark or light
3 eggs, beaten
5 tablespoons (85 g) salted butter, melted
1 teaspoon pure vanilla extract
¼ teaspoon fine salt
2 cups (290 g) salted dry-roasted peanuts, lightly crushed

1 Position a rack in the center of the oven. Preheat the oven to 350°F (180°C/Gas Mark 4). Line a 9-inch (23 cm) pie pan with the pie pastry, trim, and crimp the edges.

2 In a large bowl, combine the brown sugar, corn syrup, eggs, melted butter, vanilla, and salt. Whisk to incorporate everything into a smooth, thick filling. Add the peanuts and stir to mix them into the filling. Pour the filling into the pie shell (pastry case).

3 Bake for 50–55 minutes, until the filling is golden brown, puffed, and set in the center.

4 Transfer to a wire rack to cool completely before serving.

STORAGE: Cover with plastic wrap and store in the refrigerator for up to 5 days.

SWEET POTATO PIE

V

Sweet potato pie was enjoyed by Henry VIII, and it was made with what the English once termed "Spanish potatoes"—though this was nothing like the sweet potato custard-like pie made famous in the hands of Southern cooks. This was lighter and more delicately flavored. It lived in the family of Afri-Creole puddings found across the African Atlantic—with eggs and milk from European confectionary, and baking spices and flavors gleaned from the Caribbean and Africa. Like many Southern foods, it evolved to perfection in the painful antebellum era, when it became a traditional holiday treat for African Americans who grew the cane and sweet potatoes in their gardens and as field crops.

PREPARATION TIME: 25 MINUTES
COOKING TIME: 50–55 MINUTES
SERVES: 8

- Pastry for a 9-inch (23 cm) single-crust pie, homemade (PAGE 382) or store-bought
- ½ cup (100 g) granulated (caster) sugar
- ½ cup (95 g) packed brown sugar, light or dark
- ½ teaspoon ground cinnamon
- ½ teaspoon ground nutmeg
- ¼ ground cloves
- ¼ teaspoon fine salt
- 1 ¼ cups (10 fl oz/300 ml) evaporated milk or half-and-half (single cream)
- 2 eggs, beaten
- 4 tablespoons (60 g) unsalted butter, melted
- 1 teaspoon pure vanilla extract
- 1 ½ cups (300 g) mashed cooked sweet potatoes

1 Preheat the oven to 350°F (180°C/Gas Mark 4). Line a 9-inch (23 cm) pie pan with the pie pastry, trim, and crimp the edges.

2 In a medium bowl, whisk together both sugars, the cinnamon, nutmeg, cloves, and salt.

3 In a large bowl, whisk together the evaporated milk, eggs, melted butter, and vanilla. Add the sugar mixture and whisk to incorporate. Add the sweet potatoes and use a spatula or a spoon to mix everything together into a thick, smooth filling. Pour the filling into the pie shell (pastry case).

4 Bake for 50–55 minutes, until the edges puff up and pie is firm.

5 Transfer to a wire rack to cool completely.

STORAGE: Cover with plastic wrap and store in the refrigerator for up to 5 days.

PECAN PIE

V

Once known as "Illinois nuts," pecans are grown in most of the South. They are traditionally native to the Gulf Coast, the Lower Mississippi valley, and eastern Texas, with many varieties growing in Louisiana. Pecans were sold from foraged varieties in the south-central states and sold in the urban antebellum South starting in the 1830s. According to culinary historian Dr. David Shields, in the 1850s, Boone Hall plantation in South Carolina boasted over 15,000 pecan trees, making it the world's first, and at the time largest, cultivated pecan grove in the world. Thanks in large part to enslaved labor, pecan cultivation became widespread across the South, with Georgia becoming the leader in pecan production by 1870.

Pecan pie was invented in the 1880s in Texas as a pecan-egg-custard type pie, then it morphed into a syrup-based pie by the early 1900s. By the Depression, many Southern housewives were following the recipe on the back of Karo corn syrup bottles.

PREPARATION TIME: 30 MINUTES
COOKING TIME: 45–50 MINUTES
SERVES: 8

- Pastry for a 9-inch (23 cm) single-crust pie, homemade (PAGE 382) or store-bought
- 2 cups (400 g) firmly packed brown sugar, light or dark
- 3 tablespoons all-purpose (plain) flour
- 8 tablespoons (4 oz/115 g) unsalted butter
- 1 cup (8 fl oz/240 ml) whole milk
- 3 eggs
- 1 teaspoon pure vanilla extract
- 1 ½ cups (190 g) pecans, chopped or halves

1 Preheat the oven to 350°F (180°C/Gas Mark 4). Line a 9-inch (23 cm) pie pan with the pie pastry, trim, and crimp the edges.

2 In a medium saucepan, combine the brown sugar, flour, and butter. Cook over medium heat, stirring to melt the butter, until you have a thick, smooth sauce, 3–4 minutes. Let cool.

3 In a large bowl, whisk together the milk, eggs, and vanilla. While whisking, slowly pour the warm brown sugar mixture into the egg mixture, stirring to combine everything well. Stir in the pecans. Pour the filling into the pie shell (pastry case).

4 Bake for 40–50 minutes, until the filling puffs up and the center is fairly firm.

5 Transfer to a wire rack to cool completely.

STORAGE: Cover with plastic wrap and store in the refrigerator for up to 5 days.

CHESS PIE

V

Chess pie is a British legacy in the traditional Southern baking repertoire of the buttery egg custard family of desserts. As used in this pie's name, the word chess is attributed by Southern food writer Damon Lee Fowler to an antiquated term for "cheese." The making of cheeses and custards involves the thickening and curdling of milk. While this pie has no milk, the presence of cornmeal and vinegar in the batter sets the dessert apart, thickening the eggs and butter to create a luscious filling.

PREPARATION TIME: 20 MINUTES
COOKING TIME: 40–45 MINUTES
SERVES: 8

Pastry for a 9-inch (23 cm) single-crust pie, homemade (PAGE 382) or store-bought
1 ½ cups (250 g) sugar
1 tablespoon white or yellow cornmeal
¼ teaspoon fine salt
3 eggs, beaten
1 tablespoon apple cider vinegar
1 teaspoon pure vanilla extract
8 tablespoons (4 oz/115 g) unsalted butter, melted

1 Preheat the oven to 325°F (165°C/Gas Mark 3). Line a 9-inch (23 cm) pie pan with the pie pastry, trim, and crimp the edges.

2 In a medium bowl, whisk together the sugar, cornmeal, and salt.

3 In a large bowl, whisk together the eggs, vinegar, and vanilla. Add the melted butter and stir well. Whisk in the sugar mixture until you have a thick, smooth filling. Pour it into the pie shell (pastry case).

4 Bake for 40–45 minutes, until the filling is golden brown, puffed up, and set.

5 Transfer to a wire rack to cool completely.

STORAGE: Cover with plastic wrap and store in the refrigerator for up to 5 days.

LEMON CHESS PIE

V

Fresh lemon or lemon extract is a favorite flavoring in many Southern desserts. This lemon chess pie is a delicious example of that.

PREPARATION TIME: 20 MINUTES
COOKING TIME: 40–45 MINUTES
SERVES: 8

Pastry for a 9-inch (23 cm) single-crust pie, homemade (PAGE 382) or store-bought
1 ½ cups (250 g) sugar
1 tablespoon all-purpose (plain) flour
1 tablespoon white or yellow cornmeal
1 tablespoon grated lemon zest
¼ teaspoon fine salt
4 tablespoons (60 g) unsalted butter, melted
¼ cup (2 fl oz/60 ml) lemon juice (from 3 lemons)
4 eggs, beaten
½ teaspoon pure vanilla extract

1 Preheat the oven to 350°F (180°C/Gas Mark 4). Line a 9-inch (23 cm) pie pan with the pie pastry, trim, and crimp the edges.

2 In a large bowl, whisk together the sugar, flour, cornmeal, lemon zest, and salt. Add the melted butter and lemon juice and whisk to combine well. Add the eggs and vanilla and whisk to incorporate everything into a thick, smooth filling. Pour the filling into the pie crust (pastry case).

3 Bake for 40–45 minutes, until golden brown, puffed up, and set.

4 Transfer to a wire rack to cool completely.

STORAGE: Cover with plastic wrap and store in the refrigerator for up to 5 days.

COCONUT CUSTARD PIE

V

Coconut appears more frequently in Southern food, thanks to the connection the South has with the Caribbean. Coconuts have invariably been naturalized in a few Southern states—Florida, Georgia, North Carolina, and South Carolina. Historically though, coconuts were brought to the South on ships from West Africa and the Caribbean. Because of their role in the gastronomic heritage of the African Atlantic, coconut-based sweets and desserts, ranging from pies to cakes and ambrosia to candies, formed a culinary bridge from West and Central Africa to the Caribbean and Latin America, arching upward to the American South.

PREPARATION TIME: 20 MINUTES
COOKING TIME: 45–55 MINUTES
SERVES: 8

Pastry for a 9-inch (23 cm) single-crust pie, homemade (PAGE 382) or store-bought
1 cup (200 g) sugar
1 tablespoon all-purpose (plain) flour
¼ teaspoon fine salt
¾ cup (6 fl oz/180 ml) whole milk
8 tablespoons (4 oz/115 g) unsalted butter, melted
3 eggs, beaten
1 teaspoon pure vanilla extract
1 ¼ cups (125 g) sweetened shredded (desiccated) coconut

1 Preheat the oven to 325°F (165°C/Gas Mark 3). Line a 9-inch (23 cm) pie pan with the pie pastry, trim, and crimp the edges.

2 In a large bowl, whisk together the sugar, flour, and salt. Add the milk, melted butter, eggs, and vanilla and whisk to incorporate everything. Use a spatula to stir in the coconut. Pour the filing into the pie shell (pastry case).

3 Bake for 45–55 minutes, until the filling is firm, puffing up, and golden brown.

4 Transfer to a wire rack to cool completely.

STORAGE: Cover with plastic wrap and store in the refrigerator for up to 5 days.

EGG CUSTARD PIE

V

It's amazing how some Southern classic dishes have such old roots. Egg custard pie has ancient and medieval European roots. It traveled in the minds and taste memories of English immigrants to the Southeastern seaboard. Of all the many places it could have taken root, this dish morphed into a whole family of egg custard pies, which enrich the way people celebrate holidays, life-cycle events, honor their heritage, and bring people together.

PREPARATION TIME: 20 MINUTES
COOKING TIME: 45–50 MINUTES
SERVES: 8

Pastry for a 9-inch (23 cm) single-crust pie, homemade (PAGE 382) or store-bought
4 eggs
¾ cup (150 g) sugar
¼ teaspoon fine salt
1 ¼ cups (10 fl oz/300 ml) whole milk
1 teaspoon pure vanilla extract
¼ teaspoon ground nutmeg

1 Preheat the oven to 425°F (220°C/Gas Mark 7). Line a 9-inch (23 cm) pie pan with the pie pastry, trim, and crimp the edges.
2 In a large bowl, whisk the eggs well. Add the sugar and salt, whisking to dissolve the sugar and incorporate everything well. Add the milk and vanilla, whisking to combine everything well.
3 Pour the custard filling into the pie shell (pastry case) and sprinkle the nutmeg over the surface of the pie.
4 Bake the pie for 10 minutes. Reduce the oven temperature to 350°F (180°C/Gas Mark 4) and bake 30–35 minutes, until the custard filling is golden brown and set around the edges.
5 Transfer to a wire rack to cool completely.

STORAGE: Cover with plastic wrap and store in the refrigerator for up to 5 days.

KEY LIME PIE

V

One of Florida's gifts to Southern and American cuisines, this sweet-tart pie was supposedly created in late nineteenth-century Key West, Florida, at the Curry Mansion by a woman named "Aunt Sally." However, this story is disputed by Southern baker and James Beard Award–winner Stella Parks, who says the pie may have been originally created in New York City. Although the original Key lime pie had a pastry crust, graham cracker crust used here is the more common variety.

PREPARATION TIME: 30 MINUTES, PLUS 4 HOURS REFRIGERATION TIME
COOKING TIME: 15 MINUTES
SERVES: 8

FOR THE PIE:
4 egg yolks
1 ¼ cups (10 fl oz/300 ml) sweetened condensed milk
1 teaspoon grated lime zest
½ cup (4 fl oz/120 ml) Key lime juice or regular lime juice
¼ teaspoon fine salt
Graham Cracker Crust (PAGE 383) or one 9-inch (23 cm) store-bought crust

FOR THE WHIPPED CREAM TOPPING:
1 ¼ cups (10 fl oz/300 ml) heavy (whipping) cream, cold
3 tablespoons powdered (icing) sugar
1 teaspoon pure vanilla extract

---

1 Preheat the oven to 350°F (180°C/ Gas Mark 4).
2 Make the pie: In a large bowl, whisk the egg yolks well. Pour in the sweetened condensed milk and whisk to combine them evenly. Add the lime zest, lime juice, and salt and whisk to incorporate everything into a smooth, thick filling. Pour the filling into the graham cracker crust (pastry case).
3 Bake for 15 minutes, or until set.
4 Transfer to a wire rack to cool completely. Cover loosely and refrigerate for 3 hours, or as long as overnight.
5 Make the whipped cream topping: In a large bowl, with a balloon whisk or electric mixer, whip the heavy (whipping) cream at medium speed until thickened and increased in volume, 1–2 minutes. Add the powdered (icing) sugar and vanilla and continue beating until the cream is billowing and thick, holding soft peaks beautifully and easily.
6 Pile the whipped cream onto the pie filling and refrigerate for 1 hour or longer. Serve cold.

STORAGE: Cover with plastic wrap and store in the refrigerator for up to 5 days.

BUTTERMILK PIE

V

Buttermilk pie is in the chess pie family (though there isn't any cornmeal, as is typical of chess pies). It was also known to some as "desperation pie" because of its popularity during the Great Depression, when the simplest, most affordable desserts were preferred. Buttermilk, a tangy Southern staple, gives many of the South's traditional foods versatility and spunk, and the pie is experiencing a resurgence in interest among younger bakers.

PREPARATION TIME: 20 MINUTES
COOKING TIME: 40–50 MINUTES
SERVES: 8

Pastry for a 9-inch (23 cm) single-crust pie, homemade (PAGE 382) or store-bought
⅔ cup (130 g) sugar
3 tablespoons all-purpose (plain) flour
¼ teaspoon fine salt
1 cup (8 fl oz/240 ml) buttermilk
2 eggs, beaten
4 tablespoons (2 oz/60 g) unsalted butter, melted
½ teaspoon pure vanilla extract

1 Preheat the oven to 425°F (220°C/Gas Mark 7). Line a 9-inch (23 cm) pie pan with the pie pastry, trim, and crimp the edges.
2 In a medium bowl, whisk together the sugar, flour, and salt.
3 In a large bowl, whisk together the buttermilk, eggs, melted butter, and vanilla. Add the sugar mixture and whisk to incorporate everything into a smooth filling. Pour the filling into the pie shell (pastry case).
4 Bake for 10 minutes. Reduce the oven temperature to 350°F (180°C/Gas Mark 4) and bake 30–40 minutes more, until the filling is golden brown, puffed up, and set.
5 Transfer to a wire rack to cool completely.

STORAGE: Cover with plastic wrap and store in the refrigerator for up to 5 days.

SCUPPERNONG OR MUSCADINE GRAPE HULL PIE

V

Scuppernongs (*Vitis rotundifolia*) are the large, gelatinous wild Southern grapes with big seeds in the middle. When you eat them washed and fresh, you spit out the seeds, munch on the pulp, and chew the hulls. For this pie, you discard the seeds but use both the pulp and the thick grape hulls and have a juicy green (scuppernong) or purple (muscadine) pie with a sweet earthy aroma and a jammy, juicy flavor.

PREPARATION TIME: 50 MINUTES
COOKING TIME: 55–60 MINUTES
SERVES: 8

- Pastry for a 9-inch (23 cm) double-crust pie, homemade (PAGE 382) or store-bought
- 3/4 cup (150 g) sugar
- 1/4 cup (35 g) all-purpose (plain) flour
- 1/4 teaspoon fine salt
- 5 cups (460 g) scuppernong or muscadine grapes
- 1 tablespoon fresh lemon juice
- 3 tablespoons (45 g) cold unsalted butter, chopped into bits

1 Preheat the oven to 400°F (200°C/Gas Mark 6). Line a 9-inch (23 cm) pie pan with one round of pie dough, trimming to extend 1 inch (2.5 cm) beyond the edge of the pie pan.

2 In a small bowl, whisk together the sugar, flour, and salt.

3 Squeeze the pulp of grapes out of their skins and into a medium saucepan, letting the juicy pulp fall into the pan. (If needed, make a small slit on the stem end of each grape to release the pulp.) Reserve the juiced skins in a medium bowl.

4 Add 3 tablespoons water to the saucepan and bring to a gentle boil over medium-high heat. Reduce the heat to low and simmer gently until the grape pulp is softened and shiny, about 5 minutes.

5 Transfer the grape pulp and juices to a large bowl and cool. Have the saucepan handy. Using your hands, separate the large round seeds from the pulp, placing the seeded grapes back into the saucepan and leaving the seeds and juice in the bowl.

6 Strain the juice through a fine-mesh sieve back into the pan with the grape pulp, discarding the seeds. Add the reserved grape skins to the saucepan. Bring to a boil over medium-high heat and simmer to soften the skins, about 5 minutes. Add the sugar/flour mixture and lemon juice and stir to mix everything well.

7 Pour the filling into the pie shell (pastry case) and scatter the cold butter over the grape filling. Cover the grape filling with the second round of dough. Trim to fit the edges of the bottom crust, then press the crusts together firmly to seal the pie. Crimp the edges.

8 Bake for 10 minutes. Then reduce the oven temperature to 350°F (180°C/Gas Mark 4). Bake for 40–45 minutes, until the crust is golden brown and the juices are bubbling up through the crust.

9 Transfer to a wire rack to cool completely.

STORAGE: Cover with plastic wrap and store in the refrigerator for up to 5 days.

RICE PUDDING

GF V

A Southern favorite for hundreds of years, rice pudding goes back to its British origins in the Tudor era when it was an elite dish. In the antebellum period, an enslaved cook in east Texas made a meal for Sam Houston, the politician and former president of the Republic of Texas, that included hot rice pudding, a common treat in rice-growing country. This dessert enhances the classic English custard pudding with rice, which came to the South by way of Africa. It shows the love Southern home cooks have for turning leftovers, or excess, into delicacies.

PREPARATION TIME: 15 MINUTES
COOKING TIME: 50 MINUTES
SERVES: 8–10

3 cups (24 fl oz/710 ml) whole milk
1 cup (8 fl oz /240 ml) evaporated milk or half-and-half (single cream)
1 cup (185 g) long-grain white rice
1 teaspoon fine salt
4 eggs, beaten
¾ cup (150 g) sugar
1 teaspoon pure vanilla extract
½ teaspoon grated nutmeg
½ teaspoon ground cinnamon

1 In a heavy-bottomed 2-quart (2-liter) saucepan, combine both milks, the rice, and salt. Bring to a boil over medium-high heat. Stir well, reduce the heat to low, and simmer, stirring occasionally, until the rice is tender, 20–25 minutes. Remove from the heat.
2 In a medium bowl, combine the eggs and sugar. While stirring, add about 4 tablespoons of the hot rice mixture to the bowl, warming the eggs. Add 3 more scoops, stirring well each time.
3 Add the warmed egg/sugar mixture to the saucepan, stirring constantly to combine well.
4 Return the saucepan to low heat and cook gently, without boiling, stirring often to prevent the rice from sticking to the pan. Simmer and stir until the pudding is creamy and thickened, about 20 minutes.
5 Remove from the heat and stir in the vanilla, nutmeg, and cinnamon. Serve hot, warm, or at room temperature.

STORAGE: Store airtight in the refrigerator for up to 4 days.

PERSIMMON PUDDING

V

The native American persimmon, *Diospyros virginiana*, is one of the South's most important wild foraged foods. It's indigenous and was dried, baked into cornbread, and used in stews. Native American peoples enjoyed them fresh and dried, in breads and beverages, and as medicine. Europeans made persimmon puddings, raised breads, and cakes, while Africans used them in baking and also fermented them into persimmon beer. Despite its name, persimmon pudding is really a cake, which is baked and served in squares. Whipped cream or ice cream makes a lovely accompaniment.

PREPARATION TIME: 20 MINUTES
COOKING TIME: 55 MINUTES
SERVES: 10–12

Softened butter, for the pan
2 cups (260 g) all-purpose (plain) flour
1 ½ cups (300 g) sugar
1 teaspoon ground cinnamon
1 teaspoon baking soda (bicarbonate of soda)
¼ teaspoon fine salt
2 cups (520 g) persimmon pulp (see NOTE)
1 ¾ cups (14 fl oz/420 ml) milk
2 eggs, beaten
4 tablespoons (60 g) unsalted butter, melted

1. Preheat the oven to 350°F (180°F/Gas Mark 4). Generously grease a 9 × 13-inch (23 × 33 cm) pan.
2. In a medium bowl, whisk together the flour, sugar, cinnamon, baking soda (bicarb), and salt.
3. In a large bowl, whisk together the persimmon pulp, milk, eggs, and melted butter until incorporated.
4. Add the flour mixture to the persimmon mixture and stir with a spoon, until no dry patches of the flour remain and the batter is smooth. Pour the batter into the prepared pan.
5. Bake for 40–50 minutes, until the pudding is firm, puffed up a bit, and beginning to pull away from the sides of the pan.
6. Place the pan on a wire rack and cool completely. Cut into squares and serve.

NOTE: For persimmon pulp from native persimmons, remove stems and mash the soft fruits through a large sieve, capturing the seeds and scraping the outside often to capture all the thick pulp. You can also use the very ripe, soft pulp of Hachiya persimmons (*Diospyros kaki Hachiya*), the long, lantern-shaped variety of Asian persimmons, scooping it out of the skins and pureeing in a blender or small food processor to make a smooth puree. You will need about 5 Hachiya persimmons to get the 2 cups called for.

STORAGE: Store airtight in the refrigerator for up to 2 days.

OREILLES DE COCHON (CAJUN PIG'S EARS PASTRY)

V

Apart from the usual suspects of Southern foodways like cobblers, fried pies, etc., this is a popular yet rare recipe for Cajun Pig's Ears. It is a classic fried dough, and uses two of the most important resources available in South Louisiana—cane syrup and native pecans (*Carya illinoinensis*). It also shows the Acadian versatility with a cast-iron pot, important to so many iconic Acadian dishes.

PREPARATION TIME: 45 MINUTES
COOKING TIME: 20 MINUTES
MAKES: 16 PASTRIES

FOR THE DOUGH:
2 cups (260 g) all-purpose (plain) flour
2 teaspoons baking powder
1 teaspoon sugar
½ teaspoon fine salt
Pinch of ground cinnamon (optional)
¾ cup (6 fl oz/180 ml) whole milk

FOR THE TOPPING AND FRYING:
1 ½ cups (12 fl oz/360 ml) pure cane syrup
1 cup (150 g) chopped pecans
Vegetable oil, for frying

1 Make the dough: In a large bowl, whisk together the flour, baking powder, sugar, salt, and cinnamon (if using). Make a well in the center and pour in the milk. Using a large spoon, stir to make a dough.
2 Transfer to a floured surface and knead lightly until smooth. Divide the dough into 16 equal portions and shape into balls. Roll each ball into an 8-inch round and place on a baking sheet lined with parchment paper.
3 Make the topping: In a medium saucepan, heat the cane syrup over medium heat until very warm. Stir in the pecans, remove from the heat, and cover to keep warm.
4 Line a large baking sheet pan with a wire rack, or a few layers of paper towels and have near the stove. Pour 2 inches (5 cm) oil into a medium Dutch oven (casserole dish) and heat until it reads 365°F (185°C) on a deep-fry thermometer.
5 Working with one pastry round at a time, slide the pastry into the oil and insert a long-handled fork into its center. Twist the fork with a circular motion, so the round wrinkles up around the edges. Hold it in place for about 30 seconds, until it holds its shape. Turn to brown it evenly, then transfer to the wire rack or paper towels. Continue, cooking all the rounds.
6 Place the pastries on a serving plate and generously drizzle each one with warm cane syrup and pecans. Serve warm or at room temperature.

NORTH CAROLINA PEACH SONKER WITH DIP

V

This North Carolina Piedmont version of a large and hearty cobbler fit for a crowd is unique because of its dip—an icing—that is poured in the middle and tops each served portion. Sonker is a regional term for a deep-dish cobbler native to two North Carolina counties—Surry and Wilkes—where the dessert originated. Some say the term "sonker" is borrowed from Scotland, but locals have made it their signature dish. The town of Mount Airy in Surry County hosts an annual Sonker Festival and has created a "Sonker Trail," guiding visitors to eateries around the county where they can enjoy a serving of sonker complete with dip poured on top.

PREPARATION TIME: 40 MINUTES
COOKING TIME: ABOUT 1 HOUR
SERVES: 10–12

FOR THE FILLING:
- 1 ½ cups (300 g) sugar
- ⅓ cup (43 g) all-purpose (plain) flour
- 1 teaspoons ground cinnamon
- ½ teaspoon freshly grated nutmeg
- ¼ teaspoon ground cloves
- ½ teaspoon fine salt
- 9 cups (1.5 kg) chopped peeled peaches

FOR THE SONKER:
- 1 ½ recipes Southern Pie Dough (PAGE 382) or three 9-inch (23 cm) rounds storebought pie dough (shortcrust pastry)
- 8 tablespoons (4 oz/115 g) unsalted butter, melted

FOR THE DIP:
- ½ cup (100 g) sugar
- 3 tablespoons cornstarch (cornflour)
- ¼ teaspoon fine salt
- 3 cups (24 fl oz/710 ml) whole milk
- 1 teaspoon pure vanilla extract

1 Preheat the oven to 450°F (230°C/Gas Mark 8).

2 Make the filling: In a large bowl, stir together the sugar, flour, cinnamon, nutmeg, cloves, and salt. Add the peaches and toss gently to evenly coat the fruit with the sugar mixture.

3 Assemble and bake the sonker: Use 2 rounds of the dough to line (as a pastry case) the bottom and sides of a 9 × 13-inch (23 × 33 cm) baking pan, leaving 2 inches (5 cm) of overhang. Spoon the filling into the lined baking pan and spread it out into an even layer. Pour the melted butter and ⅓ cup (80 ml) water evenly over the peach filling.

4 On a floured surface, arrange the remaining round of pie crust dough alongside the remaining scraps of dough from the bottom crust. Use a rolling pin to press them together into one rectangular sheet of pastry, which will be used to cover the filling. For a crisscross patterned top crust, cut the pie dough into 6 strips 14 inches (36 cm) long and about 1 inch (2.5 cm) wide and 12 strips 10 inches (25 cm) long and 1 inch (2.5 cm) wide.

5 Place the 6 long strips lengthwise over the peach filling, then place the 12 shorter strips at right angles across the width of the pan, making a crisscross pattern with the filling showing through. Press the end of each strip firmly against the side of the bottom crust, and then fold the overhang down to enclose the strips. Press and crimp the edges to seal the crust all around the pan.

6 Bake for 10 minutes. Reduce the oven temperature to 350°F (180°C/Gas Mark 4) and continue baking for 35–40 minutes, until it is lightly browned but not yet done.

7 Meanwhile, make the dip: In a medium saucepan, whisk together the sugar, cornstarch (cornflour), and salt. Add the milk and vanilla and bring to a boil over medium-high heat, whisking to dissolve the sugar. Reduce the heat to medium and cook, stirring often, until thickened and is smooth, 3–5 minutes. Remove from the heat and use a measuring cup to set aside 1 cup (8 fl oz/240 ml) of dip. Leave the remaining dip in the saucepan and set the reserved cup of dip by the stove.

8 When the sonker has been in for the 35–40 minutes, remove it briefly to the top of the stove and pour the reserved 1 cup of dip down the center of the sonker, which will absorb most of the dip.

9 Return to the oven and bake for 10–15 minutes more, until the sonker is golden brown and the filling is thick and bubbling.

10 Let the sonker cool on a wire rack for 30 minutes.

11 Serve warm or at room temperature, topping each portion with a splash of dip.

STORAGE: Cover with plastic wrap and store at room temperature for 2–3 days or in the refrigerator for up to 5 days.

GRAPE DUMPLINGS

V

Native American people made these with cornmeal dumplings, simmering them with wild grapes such as possum grapes, fox grapes, muscadine, and scuppernongs. These native grapes were harvested at their peak sweetness and cooked into a thick jam. This is a modern adaptation worthy of our Cherokee and Choctaw ancestors.

PREPARATION TIME: 20 MINUTES
COOKING TIME: 30 MINUTES
SERVES: 6

2 cups (260 g) all-purpose (plain) flour
1 tablespoon baking powder
½ teaspoon fine salt
1 ¼ cups (250 g) sugar
4 tablespoons (60 g) cold unsalted butter, cubed
1 cup (8 fl oz/240 ml) whole milk
4 cups (370 g) wild grapes, fresh or frozen

1 In a large bowl, combine the flour, baking powder, salt, and ¼ cup (50 g) of the sugar and stir to blend the dry ingredients evenly. Cut in the cold butter using a pastry cutter or your fingers until the mixture resembles coarse crumbs. Gradually add the milk, mixing until a soft dough forms.

2 Turn the dough out onto a lightly floured surface and roll it out to about a ¼-inch (6 mm) thickness. Cut the dough into rectangles 1 × 2 inches (2.5 × 5 cm) and set them aside.

3 In a large pot, combine the grapes and 2 cups (16 fl oz/470 ml) water and bring to a boil over medium-high heat. Reduce the heat and let the grapes simmer until they begin to break down and release their juices. Stir in the remaining 1 cup (200 g) sugar and continue to simmer until the sugar is dissolved and the mixture thickens slightly, about 3 minutes.

4 Carefully drop the dough pieces into the simmering grape mixture, ensuring they are submerged. Cover the pot and cook until the dumplings are cooked through and tender, 10–15 minutes.

STORAGE: Wrap in plastic wrap and store in the refrigerator for up to 4 days.

TEA CAKES

V

The South's favorite traditional homemade cookie has an interesting history. Its roots are in the British baking tradition, and its wings are in African Americans aspiring to comfort and freedom. The tea cake was a treat from the plantation days that had a life of its own in Black culture and the relationship between Blacks and whites. It was a little something pulled together while making biscuits, a delicacy that Black grandmothers and mothers could give to their children despite the deprivations of slavery and the pains of inequality during Jim Crow. It was also a culinary endearment across lines of race and class. References to "Mammy's Tea Cakes" are standard, clearly showing the provenance of this cookie upon leaving the nineteenth century. This recipe is adapted from baker Cheryl Day.

PREPARATION TIME: 20 MINUTES
COOKING TIME: 25 MINUTES
MAKES: 24 COOKIES

- 3 cups (390 g) unbleached all-purpose (plain) flour
- ½ teaspoon baking soda (bicarbonate of soda)
- ¼ teaspoon freshly grated nutmeg
- ½ teaspoon kosher salt
- 16 tablespoons (8 oz/225 g) unsalted butter, at room temperature
- 1 ½ cups (300 g) sugar
- 2 eggs, at room temperature
- 1 tablespoon pure vanilla extract
- 1 tablespoon grated lemon zest (optional)

---

1 In a medium bowl, whisk together the flour, baking soda (bicarb), nutmeg, and salt. Set aside.

2 In a stand mixer fitted with the paddle (or in a large bowl with a hand mixer), cream the butter and sugar together until super light and fluffy and pale, 3–5 minutes. Add 1 egg at a time, mixing well after each addition, and scraping down the sides and bottom of the bowl as needed. Add the vanilla and lemon zest (if using), mixing until just combined. Add the flour mixture in three additions, mixing after each addition until just incorporated.

3 Finish mixing by hand to make sure no bits of flour or butter are hiding on the bottom of the bowl and the dough is thoroughly mixed. Remove the dough from the bowl and wrap in plastic wrap. Refrigerate until firm, about 20 minutes.

4 Position racks in the bottom and upper thirds of the oven and preheat the oven to 325°F (160°C/Gas Mark 3). Line two baking sheets with parchment paper.

5 Use a small ice cream scoop to form the cookies (about 1 rounded tablespoon each) and place on the prepared baking sheets, leaving room between them to allow for spreading.

6 Bake the cookies for 8–10 minutes, until lightly golden around the edges, switching racks and rotating the pans front to back halfway through.

7 Let cool completely on the pans on wire racks.

STORAGE: Store airtight at room temperature for up to 5 days.

PEACH FRIED PIES OR "MULE EARS"

V

This treat, mentioned by Martha McCulloch-Williams in her 1913 Tennessee cookbook, *Dishes and Beverages of the Old South*, demonstrates the ways the technique of deep-frying dovetails with desserts in Southern foodways, like fried apple or peach pies.

PREPARATION TIME: 45 MINUTES
COOKING TIME: 30 MINUTES
MAKES: 12–14 FRIED PIES

FOR THE FILLING:
3 cups (675 g) chopped peeled peaches
¾ cup (150 g) sugar
½ teaspoon fine salt
2 tablespoons fresh lemon or lime juice
2 tablespoons cornstarch (cornflour)
2 tablespoons (30 g) unsalted butter

FOR THE DOUGH:
2 ½ cups (325 g) all-purpose (plain) flour
1 teaspoon baking powder
¾ teaspoon fine salt
½ cup (100 g) vegetable shortening, chilled, or cold unsalted butter, chopped into small chunks
⅔ cup (5 fl oz/160 ml) buttermilk or whole milk

FOR ASSEMBLY:
Vegetable oil, for frying

1 Make the filling: In a large frying pan, combine the peaches, sugar, and salt. Bring to a boil over medium-high heat, then reduce the heat to low and simmer, stirring occasionally, until thickened, 3–4 minutes. Stir in the lemon juice.

2 In a small bowl, stir the cornstarch (cornflour) and 2 tablespoons water together to make a slurry. Add the cornstarch slurry to the simmering peaches. Increase the heat to high, bring to a boil, stirring often, and cook for 1 minute. Remove from the heat, add the butter, and stir until melted. Set aside to cool.

3 Make the dough: In a large bowl, whisk together the flour, baking powder, and salt. Using a pastry blender or two table knives, cut the shortening into the flour to make pea-size crumbs. Add the buttermilk and stir with a large spoon or spatula until a dough begins to form.

4 Transfer the crumbly dough to a work surface dusted with flour. Gather and quickly press it together, kneading gently and quickly to create a ball of dough. Flatten the ball into a disk, and cut the dough into 12 equal wedges, like a pie. Roll each piece into a ball, place on a baking sheet, and cover.

5 Assemble the hand pies: On a lightly floured surface, roll one ball into a 5-inch (13 cm) round, about the size of a teacup saucer.

6 Place 2 tablespoons of filling in the center of the round. Fold the dough over to make a half-moon. Wet the edges with water and press them together, then use the tines of a fork to seal them well. Continue rolling and filling pies. Cover them and refrigerate for 30 minutes.

7 Lay a wire rack on a baking sheet and set next to the stove. Pour 2 inches (5 cm) oil into a large deep pot or Dutch oven (casserole dish) and heat to 350°F (177°C) or until a cube of bread browns in 30 seconds.

8 Working in batches of 2, add the pies to the hot oil and fry until golden brown, turning once, about 2 minutes per side. Transfer to the wire rack.

9 Serve warm or at room temperature.

STORAGE: Store airtight at room temperature for up to 3 days or in the refrigerator for up to 5 days.

SOUTHERN PIE DOUGH

V -5

Traditionally, Southern bakers depended on soft wheat flour combined with lard as the standard fat for making pie pastry as well as biscuits. The richness of lard made for flaky and tender crusts, while butter provided rich flavor and was easier to make. When shortening appeared in the marketplace early in the twentieth century, Southern bakers embraced it as another option to use in place of or in combination with lard and butter. This recipe is for a basic butter pie pastry.

PREPARATION TIME: 50 MINUTES
COOKING TIME: 15–20 MINUTES
MAKES: ENOUGH FOR TWO 9-INCH (23 CM) PIE CRUSTS

3 cups (390 g) all-purpose (plain) flour
½ teaspoon fine salt
16 tablespoons (8 oz/225 g) cold unsalted butter, cubed
½ cup (4 fl oz/120 ml) ice water

1 In a large bowl, whisk together the flour and salt. Add the butter and toss quickly to coat with flour. Using your fingertips and working quickly, squeeze the butter and press it into small bits, tossing often to mix it with the flour.

2 When the flour is very crumbly, pour the ice water into the center of the bowl. Use a big spoon or spatula to quickly mix the water and flour, scooping from the edges to the center. Quickly press into a very rough ball.

3 Turn the dough out onto a lightly floured surface and knead it a few times. Cut the dough in half and shape each portion into a big disk. Wrap in plastic and refrigerate for 30 minutes or longer.

4 On a lightly floured surface, using a lightly floured rolling pin, roll out one disk into a large round about 10 inches (25 cm) in diameter. Transfer to a 9-inch (23 cm) pie pan and ease it gently into the pan, without stretching the dough. Trim the edges to leave a small overhang beyond the edge of the pie pan. Fold this overhang under and squeeze it to make a crust extending above the edge of the pan. Crimp or press with the tines of a fork.

STORAGE: Shape the dough into disks and cover with plastic wrap. Store wrapped unbaked dough in the refrigerator for up to 3 days, or in the freezer for 2 months.

GRAHAM CRACKER CRUST

V -5

This crust and other cookie crumb–based crusts became popular in the early twentieth century, as a quick and sweeter foundation for pies. They are especially popular with creamy pie fillings and as the base for classic cheesecakes.

PREPARATION TIME: 15 MINUTES
COOKING TIME: 12 MINUTES
MAKES: ONE 9-INCH (23 CM) CRUMB CRUST (PASTRY CASE)

1 ½ cups (180 g) graham cracker or digestive biscuit crumbs
¼ cup (50 g) sugar
6 tablespoons (85 g) unsalted butter, melted

1 Preheat the oven to 350°F (180°C/Gas Mark 4).
2 In a medium bowl, stir together the graham cracker crumbs and sugar. Use a spatula to stir in the melted butter until well combined.
3 Pour the crumb mixture into a 9-inch (23 cm) pie pan. Distribute the mixture evenly over the bottom and sides of the pan. Using a small flat-bottomed measuring cup, press firmly on the bottom and sides of the pan to flatten the crumbs and shape a sturdy, even crust (pastry case).
4 Bake for 10 minutes to set the crust.
5 Transfer to a wire rack and cool to room temperature before filling.

FIG PRESERVES

DF GF V VE -5

A Deep South favorite, fig preserves were the key home product made from the family fig trees, which clung to the southern exposure of the house or were in the family orchard. They are favored in eastern North Carolina, especially on Ocracoke Island in the Outer Banks, where figs are everywhere. For this recipe, you will need 5 sterilized 1/2-pint (250 ml) jars with tight-fitting lids (see Storing Preserves, PAGE 307).

PREPARATION TIME: 20 MINUTES
COOKING TIME: 1 HOUR
MAKES: 5 HALF-PINT (250 ML) JARS

3 lb (1.4 kg) fresh ripe figs, left whole
3 cups (600 g) sugar
5 lemon slices

1 In a large heavy-bottomed saucepan, combine the figs, sugar, lemon slices, and ½ cup (4 fl oz/120 ml) water. Stir gently to mix them well. Bring to a boil over medium-high heat. Reduce the heat to medium-low to maintain an active simmer and cook, stirring occasionally, until the figs are tender and the syrup has thickened and are surrounded by a nice, thick, flavorful syrup, about 1 hour.

2 While the figs are simmering, sterilize 5 half-pint (250 ml) glass jars. Let the jars cool to room temperature while the figs cook.

3 When the figs are done, remove them from the heat and divide them among the sterilized jars. Divide the syrup among them and cover tightly. If planning on longer storage, process the jars for 15 minutes in a boiling water bath (see Storing Preserves, PAGE 307).

STORAGE: If processed in a water bath, the preserves will keep in a cool dark place for up to 1 year. Once opened, refrigerate and enjoy within 2–3 weeks.

PEACH BUTTER

DF GF V VE -5

Peach, apple, and other fruit butters were one of the creative ways introduced by Germanic immigrants for preserving the most common orchard crops in the early South. Apples and peaches were required crops by law, because they were a source of sustenance for both people and animals. In a time when distillation and fermentation made things safer to drink, apple cider and peach cider were important. The fruits were also dried and made into leathers, or made into jams, jellies, sauces, and butters, which lasted a long time because of the sugar content. Spread on a hot fresh buttermilk biscuit, fruit butters are the best. For this recipe, you will need 3 sterilized 1-pint (475 ml) jars with tight-fitting lids (see Storing Preserves, PAGE 307).

PREPARATION TIME: 10 MINUTES
COOKING TIME: 45 MINUTES
MAKES: ABOUT 4 CUPS (32 FL OZ/950 ML)

6 cups (2 lb/925 g) sliced peeled peaches
1 ½ cups (300 g) sugar
½ teaspoon ground cinnamon
¼ teaspoon ground ginger
¼ teaspoon ground nutmeg

1 In a large heavy-bottomed pot, combine the peaches, sugar, ¼ cup (2 fl oz/60 ml) water, the cinnamon, ginger, and nutmeg. Bring to a boil over medium-high heat stirring to dissolve the sugar. Reduce the heat to maintain a lively simmer and cook for 10 minutes. Remove from the heat.

2 Set out a large bowl next to a blender. Transfer about one-quarter of the peach mixture to the blender and puree until very smooth. Pour into the bowl and continue, working in batches to puree the peach mixture.

3 Return the peach puree to the pot and bring to a boil over medium-high heat. Reduce the heat to maintain a lively simmer and cook, stirring often, until the peach puree thickens, darkens a bit in color, and can be mounded up on a spoon, 30–35 minutes.

4 Meanwhile, sterilize three 1-pint (475 ml) glass jars (see PAGE 307).

5 Remove the peach butter from the heat and ladle it into the hot jars, leaving ½ inch (13 mm) of headspace. Let cool to room temperature. Cover the jars and transfer to the refrigerator. If planning on longer storage, process the jars for 10 minutes in a boiling water bath (see Storing Preserves, PAGE 307).

STORAGE: If processed in a water bath, peach butter will keep in a cool dark place for up to 1 year. Once opened, refrigerate and enjoy within 2–3 weeks.

PRALINES

GF V

Pralines have roots in French cuisine, but the sweet treat blossomed into the beloved signature candy of New Orleans in the skilled hands of African American women. The French version involved almonds or hazelnuts, caramelized with sugar to make a crisp confection. Afri-Creole women used native pecans and enriched their version with butter and cream, creating an irresistible candy both creamy and crunchy, which they sold up and down the streets of the French Quarter, creating a Louisiana classic still cherished today.

PREPARATION TIME: 30 MINUTES, PLUS 45 MINUTES COOLING
COOKING TIME: 25 MINUTES
MAKES: 16–18 LARGE PRALINES

2 ½ cups (315 g) pecan halves
1 ½ cups (300 g) granulated (caster) sugar
1 ½ cups (285 g) packed dark brown sugar
½ teaspoon fine salt
2 tablespoons light corn syrup
½ cup (4 fl oz/120 ml) buttermilk
½ cup (4 fl oz/120 ml) heavy (whipping) cream
3 tablespoons (45 g) unsalted butter, at room temperature
1 teaspoon pure vanilla extract

1 Preheat the oven to 350°F (180°C/Gas Mark 4). Line a large baking sheet with parchment paper.
2 Spread the pecan halves out on the baking sheet and bake until fragrant and lightly browned, 6–8 minutes. Transfer to a plate to cool.
3 In a heavy 3-quart (3-liter) saucepan, combine the granulated (caster) sugar, brown sugar, salt, corn syrup, buttermilk, and heavy (whipping) cream. Cook gently over medium heat, stirring often, until the sugars are melted, about 3 minutes.
4 Attach a candy thermometer to the pan and bring to a boil, stirring constantly. Boil gently until the mixture reaches the soft-ball stage, about 236°F (113°C) on a candy thermometer, 5–7 minutes. Remove from the heat and cool to 220°F (104°C), 8–10 minutes.
5 Using a wooden spoon, beat in the butter and vanilla, stirring until the mixture becomes creamy and opaque. Stir in the browned pecans, then scoop out 3-tablespoon portions and place them on the baking sheet.
6 Let cool completely, about 45 minutes.
7 Serve, or wrap each praline individually in waxed paper or plastic wrap.

STORAGE: Store airtight at room temperature for up to 1 week.

SORGHUM TAFFY

GF V

Apart from penny candy like peppermints, lemon drops, and horehound (a candy flavored like root beer made from the local herb), there wasn't much for the rural Southern sweet tooth prior to World War II. But sorghum and molasses taffy go back to the antebellum period, when children enjoyed this treat in the autumn. The highlight of sugarcane or sorghum cane season was making candy at home, called a molasses pull.

PREPARATION TIME: 15 MINUTES, PLUS 20 MINUTES COOLING
COOKING TIME: 15–20 MINUTES
MAKES: 40–50 PIECES

Softened butter, for the pan
1 cup (8 fl oz/240 ml) sorghum syrup, golden syrup (such as Lyle's), or maple syrup
½ cup (100 g) sugar
1 teaspoon distilled white vinegar or apple cider vinegar
2 tablespoons (30 g) salted butter, plus more for taffy-pulling
⅛ teaspoon baking soda (bicarbonate of soda)

1 Generously grease a sheet pan or a 9 × 13-inch (23 × 33 cm) pan with butter.

2 Attach a candy thermometer to the side of a heavy-bottomed medium saucepan or small Dutch oven (casserole dish). Place a small bowl of water near the stove.

3 In the saucepan, combine the sorghum, sugar, 4 tablespoons water, and the vinegar. Bring to a boil over medium-high heat and stir to dissolve the sugar. Reduce the heat to maintain a gentle boil and cook, stirring occasionally, until it reaches 250°–266°F (121°–130°C), 15–20 minutes.

4 Test the taffy by dropping a small spoonful into the bowl of water; when you can shape the taffy mixture into a small ball that holds its shape, remove the pan from the heat. Add the butter and baking soda (bicarb) and stir to incorporate.

5 Carefully pour the hot taffy into the buttered pan. Let stand until cool enough to handle, 15–20 minutes.

6 With generously buttered hands, take a handful of taffy and pull it, folding it over and stretching it out until it becomes stiffer, lightens in color, plumps up, and hardens somewhat. Twist the taffy into thick ropes and cut it into big bite-size lengths. Wrap in wax (greaseproof) paper or parchment paper.

STORAGE: Store airtight at room temperature for up to 1 month.

BEVERAGES

THE SOUTHERN WAY WITH BEVERAGES

Teranga (teh-ran-ga) is a simple word with many connotations. From Senegal and Gambia, it is a social quality that underlies the values of many ethnic groups that would end up in Southern ports and leave a lasting impression on Southern culture. Roughly translated, it means something close to "hospitality." Many enslaved Senegambians would become a significant part of the Colonial South's domestic workforce, including cooks and servants. The word didn't survive forced assimilation that my Ancestors had to endure, but the courtly and generous mores of a casted civilization did. This warm and resilient spirit mixed with the values of others around them and gave us our world-famous "Southern hospitality."

Whether you are in Senegambia or South Carolina, the first objective of the host is to offer you refreshments as you recover from your journey. In the South, that usually starts with, "Can I get you something to drink?" Cold water, usually iced or ice cold, is the minimum offering. From spring into early fall, ice water is generally followed by iced tea, often called "the house wine of the South." Dressed with lemon, orange, or a bit of fresh mint or mint syrup—the way my Virginia grandmother preferred it—it can be cloyingly sweet or gently sweetened, depending on personal taste. And there is nothing like homemade Southern lemonade, which is often doctored according to the wizardry of the elder making it.

Ice is a common factor here, and the heat and humidity made early icehouses very popular among elites, mainly to have something to make drinks refreshing and appealing, further enhancing the experience of Southern hospitality. Many Southern households served mint juleps, or a glass of whiskey, bourbon, or gin topped off by a shard of ice (hacked off from the precious supply from a half-buried shed filled with huge hog-sized blocks of ice insulated in sawdust). Many nineteenth-century travelers to the South wrote elaborate descriptions of arriving flustered and exhausted, and having enslaved servants immediately prepare drinks and cocktails for them. For example, the journey from Montpelier (the plantation of James and Dolley Madison) to Monticello (the plantation of Thomas Jefferson), which was just one county over and is drivable today in minutes, took nine to twelve hours, and required driving up a mountain in a wooden buggy weighed down with people, luggage, and gifts.

Once they arrived at their destination, early Southerners of the Chesapeake and Lowcountry loved their sherry, toddy, syllabub, eggnog, Madeira wine, punch bobbing with tropical fruit (owing to the cultural and economic relationship with the Caribbean basin), port, and imported wine. Southern folk beverage traditions evolved into their local art. Southerners, particularly Southern women—Black, white, and Native American—brewed teas from yaupon holly to sassafras and used broths and pot likker to heal the sick. Delights like applejack and cherry bounce, blackberry wine, peach brandy, and persimmon beer appeared at public events. Bootlegging might be their finest art;

their stills set in the woods produced potent batches of clear moonshine for centuries—a product now regulated (primarily) and flavored and sold at tourist spots throughout the Upland South.

It should be noted that this isn't where the story stops. Southerners have long loved their beer, and in recent years craft breweries have helped bring life to downtown eateries in the New South. Former tobacco fields now sprout hop vines and grape vines, and the wineries of Virginia and its neighbors have come to rival those in New York and California. New Southern vineyards embrace the Norton grape, muscadines, and scuppernongs and celebrate tradition and indigenous resources. Most exciting is the number of mixologists that have risen to fame and the resurrection of Southern cocktail culture, especially in urban centers like Atlanta or New Orleans, which has been significantly driven by women and people of color. The South is rapidly moving beyond its borders through its food and drink culture, and through its creators, who have brought Southern culture to all four corners of the earth.

MINT JULEP

DF GF V VE -5 -30

Mint juleps were a common and favorite drink of the mid-nineteenth-century plantation South—even though the drink has roots in gulab, a concoction from Persia passed through to the French during the Middle Ages. To our knowledge, the first time it appeared in print was in 1839 in Lettice Bryan's *The Kentucky Housewife*, where she mentions a drink based on brandy or whiskey flavored with mint, cloves, cinnamon, or anise. The julep was so popular in the Deep South that one Northern visitor to a plantation was offered one every few hours throughout the duration of his visit, much to his annoyance. Every first Saturday in May, the julep takes the starring role as the popular beverage of the annual derby in Louisville, Kentucky. It is best served in chilled metal tumblers or heavyweight glasses.

PREPARATION TIME: 5 MINUTES
MAKES: 1 COCKTAIL

8 fresh mint leaves, plus more for garnish
¼–½ fl oz (7–15 ml) simple syrup, to taste
2 fl oz (60 ml) bourbon
Crushed ice, for serving

In a julep glass, use a metal or wooden muddler, or the end of a spoon, to press on the mint leaves to release their oils and scent. Add the simple syrup and bourbon and top with crushed ice. Stir the ice until the glass becomes chilled and frosted on the outside. Add additional simple syrup based on desired sweetness. Top the cocktail with more crushed ice as needed, and garnish with mint leaves.

FRONT PORCH LEMONADE

DF GF V VE -5 -30

Lemonade on the front porch is as Southern as you get. It is considered good manners to have something for guests to drink, especially on the front porch on a hot day, and lemonade, tea, or simply water does the trick. Serve cold.

PREPARATION TIME: 10 MINUTES
COOKING TIME: 10 MINUTES
SERVES: 10

8 medium lemons
2 cups (400 g) sugar
Ice, for serving

1 Halve the lemons and use a citrus juicer to squeeze out the juice to get 1 ½ cups (12 fl oz/350 ml). Reserve the lemon halves after juicing them.

2 In a medium saucepan, combine the sugar and 2 cups (16 fl oz/470 ml) water. Bring to a boil over high heat, stirring often until the sugar dissolves completely. Transfer to a medium bowl to cool.

3 When ready to serve, pour 7 cups (1.6 liters) water into a large pitcher (jug). Add the spent lemon halves. Add the lemon juice and sugar syrup and use a long-handled spoon to stir well. Serve the lemonade in tall, ice-filled glasses.

SUMAC LEMONADE

DF GF V VE -5 -30

Thank the students who researched the traditions of southern Appalachia for the Foxfire project for helping to preserve the lore about staghorn sumac (*Rhus typhina*). Staghorn sumac flowers from May to July, and the fruit ripens from June to September, with red berries distinguishing it from the white berries of poisonous sumac (*Toxicodenderon vermix*). In Southern Appalachia, Middle Eastern sumac (*Rhus coriaria*) was historically used as a substitute for lemon.

PREPARATION TIME: 15 MINUTES
COOKING TIME: 10 MINUTES
MAKES: 2 CUPS (16 FL OZ/475 ML) SYRUP (ENOUGH FOR 8 DRINKS)

FOR THE SUMAC SYRUP:
2 cups (400 g) sugar or 1 cup (8 fl oz/240 ml) sorghum syrup
3 tablespoons ground sumac or cracked fresh sumac berries (soaked and washed)

FOR SERVING:
Ice
1 tablespoon fresh lemon juice
Slice of lemon, for garnish

1 Make the sumac syrup: In a saucepan, combine the sugar and 2 cups (16 fl oz/470 ml) water and cook over medium heat, stirring occasionally, until the sugar has dissolved, about 5 minutes. Reduce the heat to medium-low and cook for an additional 5 minutes, until just slightly more concentrated.

2 Remove from heat and add the sumac. Let rest for 15 minutes. Strain through a fine-mesh sieve or coffee filter. (The syrup will keep for a week refrigerated.)

3 For each serving: Add ice cubes to a chilled glass. Pour ¼ cup (2 fl oz/60 ml) of the sumac syrup and the lemon juice into each glass. Garnish with lemon slices.

Ball
IDEAL

PERSIMMON BEER

DF GF V VE -5

The persimmon may be indigenous to North America, but it has twenty-one related species in Africa, which is why the persimmon joins a number of plants with edible and medicinal qualities that enslaved Africans had experience with before their arrival in America. 'Simmon beer is actually closer to a liquor, and it owes its existence to the Native American, African, and European heritage of the South. Native American people did not traditionally ferment the persimmon into alcohol, but they did make it into fruit leathers and bread, while Europeans and West Africans used it to make a fermented drink. Others used this version, which reminds me of the type my Virginia grandmother taught me to make. (Make sure all your brewing equipment, including a large pot, stirring spoon, fermentation vessel, and airlock—are thoroughly sterilized before starting this recipe, to ensure the cleanliness of your beer; see PAGE 307 for instructions on how to do so.)

PREPARATION TIME: 30 MINUTES, PLUS SEVERAL WEEKS' FERMENTATION TIME
COOKING TIME: 30 MINUTES
MAKES: 1 GALLON (3.8 LITERS)

3 lb (1.4 kg) ripe wild persimmons, lightly washed and chopped
2 cups (385 g) superfine (caster) sugar
1 packet (7 g) ale yeast
Juice of 1 lemon
4 tablespoons honey (optional)

1 In a large pot, combine the chopped persimmons and 16 cups (4 qt/3.8 liters water. Bring to a boil over medium-high heat. Reduce the heat to low and simmer for 30 minutes, allowing the persimmons to soften and release their flavors.

2 Remove the pot from the heat, then use a potato masher or immersion blender to break down the persimmons until well mashed. Add the sugar to the pot, stirring well to dissolve the sugar.

3 Allow the mixture to cool to room temperature, then strain it through a fine-mesh sieve or cheesecloth into your fermentation vessel, discarding the solids. (To prevent killing the yeast. ensure that the liquid is cooled to below 80°F/27°C before adding the ale yeast.) Sprinkle the yeast over the surface of the liquid and gently stir in to combine. Stir the lemon juice into the mixture. (For a sweeter beer, you may also add honey; stir well to incorporate.)

4 Seal the fermentation vessel with an airlock and store it in a dark, cool place, ideally between 65°–75°F (18°–24°C). Allow the mixture to ferment for 1–2 weeks, checking occasionally to ensure the fermentation process is active; you will notice bubbles forming in the airlock, as the yeast converts the sugars into alcohol.

5 After the fermentation period, carefully siphon the persimmon beer into sterilized bottles, leaving any sediment behind. Cap the bottles tightly and let them carbonate for an additional 1–2 weeks at room temperature. Once carbonation is achieved, store the bottles in a cool, dark place or refrigerate them.

6 To serve, pour the persimmon beer into chilled glasses, leaving any remaining sediment in the bottle.

SCUPPERNONG WINE

DF GF V VE -5

The scuppernong (*Vitis rotundifolia*) is a round wild grape, native to the Southeast. A variety of muscadine grape, it is fragrant and has a musky flavor, soft green to bronze in color, with thick hulls and big seeds. Its name comes from ascuponung, a native word for the grape. From the time of colonization, it was used to make a popular local wine, though it has to be carefully minded (see NOTE). It has been cultivated since historic times, and different varieties are available from nurseries. The thick skins are full of flavor, color, and scent, but they are quite a unique grape.

PREPARATION TIME: 3 HOURS, PLUS 13 WEEKS FERMENTATION TIME
MAKES: 1 GALLON (3.8 LITERS)

- 4 quarts (2 lb/910 g) scuppernong grapes, muscadine grapes, or Concord grapes, washed and stemmed
- 4 cups (32 fl oz/950 ml) boiling water, preferably filtered or distilled
- 2 ¼ cups (450 g) sugar

1 DAY 1: In a large stoneware crock or bowl, smash the grapes, being sure to keep the seeds intact. Pour the boiling water over the grapes. Loosely cover the container or bowl with a clean tea towel or cheesecloth. Leave to stand in a cool, dark place for 24 hours, undisturbed.

2 DAY 2: Stir the sugar into the grape mixture, then cover with a new clean tea towel or cheesecloth. Let stand again for an additional 24 hours in a cool, dark place.

3 DAY 3: Strain out and discard the pulp, seeds, and skins of the grapes, while trying to extract and save as much juice as possible. Lightly cover the liquid with a new cloth and let rest for an additional 3 days.

4 DAY 7: Bottle the liquid in sterilized bottles (see PAGE 307) and store in a cool dark place for 3 months before consuming.

NOTE: When making homemade wine, it is important to "burp" or degas it to release the accumulated carbon dioxide (CO_2) produced during fermentation. This process involves carefully removing the airlock, allowing the gas to escape, and then resealing the container. The frequency of burping depends on the stage of fermentation. During the initial, more active phase, it may be necessary to burp the wine once or even twice a day. As fermentation slows, the need for burping decreases accordingly.

SWEET ICED TEA

DF GF V VE -5

The "house wine" of the South first appears in 1879 in the Southern cookbook, *Housekeeping in Old Virginia* by Marion Cabell Tyree, as noted by culinary historian Damon Lee Fowler. The British had cold tea punches dating to the eighteenth century, but likely it took Southern iced tea forty years to get to a cookbook. That lag corresponds with the heart of the antebellum area and the ease with which ice became commonly available to urban elites, around the 1830s and 1840s. By the 1930s, sweet tea took its crown.

PREPARATION TIME: 15 MINUTES, PLUS REFRIGERATION TIME
COOKING TIME: 15 MINUTES
MAKES: 2 QUARTS (2 LITERS)

6 orange pekoe tea bags
1/8 teaspoon baking soda (bicarbonate of soda)
2 cups (16 fl oz/470 ml) boiling water
1–2 cups (190–380 g) superfine (caster) sugar, to taste
6 cups (48 fl oz/1.4 liters) cold water
Lemon slices and mint sprigs (optional, for garnish)

1 Place the tea bags and baking soda (bicarb) in a large glass measuring cup. Pour the boiling water over the tea bags and let steep for 15 minutes.
2 Remove the tea bags, making sure not to squeeze out any additional liquid, and pour the mixture into a 2-quart (2-liter) pitcher (jug). Add the sugar and stir until dissolved.
3 Add the cold water and refrigerate until chilled. Serve over ice; garnish with lemon slices or mint sprigs if you wish.

VARIATION: Serve unsweetened along with simple syrup to taste for those who desire it.

EGGNOG

GF V -5 -30

A Maryland minister, Jonathan Boucher, first mentioned eggnog in 1774. Eggnog was a British tradition that was particularly vibrant in the Chesapeake Bay area and Lowcountry where syllabub, rum, and brandy-spiked milk punches were beloved delicacies. Many formerly enslaved people told their WPA (Works Progress Administration) interviewers that they looked forward to libations of eggnog during plantation days. Homemade eggnog remains a holiday staple for many Southerners.

PREPARATION TIME: 15 MINUTES, PLUS CHILLING TIME
COOKING TIME: 10 MINUTES
SERVES: 6

6 egg yolks
½ cup (100 g) sugar
1 cup (8 fl oz /240 ml) heavy (whipping) cream
2 cups (16 fl oz/470 ml) whole milk
½ teaspoon freshly grated nutmeg, plus more for garnish
Pinch of fine salt
¼ teaspoon pure vanilla extract
Ice
Ground cinnamon, for garnish

1 In a heatproof medium bowl, whisk together the egg yolks and sugar until light and creamy. Set aside.

2 In a heavy-bottomed medium saucepan, combine the heavy (whipping) cream, milk, nutmeg, and salt. Bring to a rolling boil over medium-high heat, stirring often. Immediately remove the saucepan from heat (to avoid boiling over).

3 With a ladle, add 1 heaping spoonful of hot milk to the egg mixture and whisk vigorously to prevent the eggs from curdling. Repeat until all of the egg and milk are combined.

4 Return the milk and egg mixture to the saucepan, set it over medium-high heat, and cook the eggnog, whisking, until thickened slightly, 1–2 minutes.

5 Remove the saucepan from the heat, stir in the vanilla, then pour the liquid through a fine-mesh sieve into a pitcher (jug). Cover with plastic wrap and refrigerate to chill.

6 As the liquid cools, it will become thicker in consistency. If the mixture is too thick, add a few tablespoons of milk at a time, until you have reached the desired level of thickness.

7 Serve cold, over ice. Garnish it with cinnamon or nutmeg and enjoy.

VARIATION: **Baltimore Eggnog:** Spike to taste with Madeira, rye whiskey, or Jamaican rum.

VARIATION: **Kentucky Eggnog:** Spike with Kentucky bourbon.

CHAMOMILE TEA

DF GF V VE -5 -30

Much of the chamomile commercially consumed in the US comes from two European strains: Roman or English chamomile (*Chamaeleum nobile*) or German chamomile (*Matricaria retuticia*). But in the American South, a native chamomile (*Matricaria discoidea*), also known as pineappleweed, grows wild and low to the ground. It was used frequently in teas and salads, its leaves release a slightly sweet smell when crushed. Indigenous peoples have long held pineappleweed in high regard, and many today still rely on it to soothe anxiety and indigestion. When combined with lemon balm, a transplanted herb famed for its citrusy aroma, and a shard of cinnamon for color and flavor, this tea is a fragrant reminder of the many herbalist traditions that inform Southern beverages. (If you can find wild chamomile for this tea, that would be great, but conventional chamomile will also work.)

PREPARATION TIME: 5 MINUTES
COOKING TIME: 25 MINUTES
SERVES: 4

2 teaspoons dried chamomile
2 teaspoons dried lemon balm
½ cinnamon stick
Sugar or honey (optional)

1 In a large pot, bring 5 cups (40 fl oz/1.2 liters) water to a boil. Add the chamomile, lemon balm, and cinnamon stick to the pot. Remove from heat and allow to brew for 10 minutes.

2 Strain the liquid into a large pitcher through a fine-mesh sieve or coffee filter. If desired, sweeten to taste with sugar or honey.

SOUTHERN HERBALISM

A significant part of Southern food and drink culture never enters the cookbooks. Southern herbalism isn't just the practical use of cultivated and wildcrafted plants to heal ailments, to flavor food or drink, or to provide an aesthetic or aromatic flourish. Southern herbalism branches into the metaphysical and mystical parts of Southern culture. It is the secret world documented by many, from the master folklorist and author Zora Neale Hurston to the researchers of the Foxfire project, a student writing program consisting of stories from Appalachia. Herbalism occupies a space at the intersection of folk and faith healing, astrology, and the sacred knowledge of Native American, West and Central African, and Northwest European mythology.

In times when a medical doctor was difficult to find, plants like dandelion greens, spicebush (*Lindera benzoin),* American ginseng (*Panax quinquefolius*), wild ginger (*Asarum canadense),* wild violet, mullein, yarrow, rabbit tobacco, and hundreds of others were used in a range of broths, tinctures, salves, and tisanes. The seasonal foraging for these plants, as well as for specific berries, roots, and barks, sat alongside the cultivation of food, and at many times, the two were connected. Springtime was the most critical period in this traditional calendar. People planted by the phases of the moon and astrological signs; corn was seeded when the oak trees had leaves "larger than a squirrel's ear." Newly sprouted wild greens like pokeweed (*Phytolacca americana*) set off the yearly cycle of foraging. However, when consumed raw, it was toxic and needed a careful eye. For herbalists today following tradition, they must get the leaves young and free of red streaks and then boil and rinse them several times before cooking. Despite all that labor, pokeweed is very nutritious and good—but taking a chance on its toxicity can be dangerous.

Sassafras (*Sassafras albidum*) is another plant that requires careful preparation. Sassafras tea is a reddish-colored drink made from tree roots that became popular among colonists, indentured servants, and the enslaved. It was something of a spring tonic that served as an herbal panacea that supposedly "cured" colds, gout, and obesity. In a time in history when all sorts of ailments and parasites demanded that you "clean out" your system when the spring sassafras saplings appeared, sassafras remained popular until the FDA issued health warnings against its active ingredient safrole and its potential toxicity. On the other hand, sassafras is still harvested in the spring when the leaves are small, aromatic, and tender, and then dried and pounded into filé powder. The powder is harmless and is a key ingredient in the filé gumbo made across the Gulf Coast and in Southern Louisiana, as it helps to thicken the soup slightly. As a result, many have shifted to responsible and measured consumption for those who continue to utilize it.

What Southerners consume has always been tied to different types of knowledge, and what comes to the table speaks greatly of whose memories or traditions are valued along with what flavors remain enticing.

GLOSSARY

This short glossary is a brief explanation of some of the key events and eras, people, and places germane to our treatment of the American South. If you are not familiar with the region, it will help provide greater context.

EVENTS AND ERAS

Antebellum Era (roughly 1790–1865)
The period in the American South before the Civil War, during which it reached its apogee of economic power and political influence under the expansion and entrenchment of chattel slavery.

"Dinner on the Grounds"
A communal meal celebrated on the church property, traditional in the Protestant churches of the American South.

Great Migration (1910–1970)
The episodic migration of over five million African American Southerners to the Northeast, Midwest, and West Coast of the United States. They moved in masses in search of a better life outside of the authority of de facto segregation known as Jim Crow. Jim Crow was a form of systemic racial violence created after enslavement and based in white supremacy—including restrictions on voting, poor educational opportunities, no social protections, and consistent violent repression and assault.

Great Wagon Road
The historical road used during the eighteenth century, leading thousands of Scots-Irish (Ulster Scots) and German immigrants from Philadelphia to the Southern backcountry, culminating in Georgia.

Haitian Revolution (1791–1804)
The successful rebellion of enslaved people living in the prosperous French colony of Saint Domingue who, when faced with intense oppression and torturous enslavement broke free from their slaveholders to establish the world's first Black republic. The Haitian Revolution sent a wave of Black and white migration to Louisiana and the American South. It was also one of the major motivations for the sale of the remainder of New France, also known as The Louisiana Purchase.

Post-bellum Period (roughly 1865–1900)
The time period following the Civil War in the American South to the dawn of the twentieth century. The period includes emancipation, Reconstruction, the establishment of Jim Crow, and the expansion of the Industrial Age in the region.

Trail of Tears
The vernacular name for the consequence of the Indian Removal Act. In the 1830s, thousands of Native Americans, in particular the "Five Tribes," of the American South—the Cherokee, Muscogee (Creek); Seminole and Mikasuki, Choctaw, and Chickasaw—and many of their neighbors were dispossessed of sovereign lands promised them by treaty. Many endured forced exile to Indian Territory now known as Oklahoma. Many of these groups were accompanied by enslaved Africans who were their chattel, and in some cases Africans were members of said tribes.

Transatlantic Slave Trade
The forced migration of over twelve million Africans to the ports, plantation, mines, and urban centers of North, Central and South America between 1500 and 1880, during which time most were enslaved in perpetuity, thus forming the basis of the African Diaspora in the Americas.

PEOPLES

Acadians/Cajuns
A French-Canadian culture that developed in maritime Canada—descendants of peasants from western France encouraged to settle New France, mostly Nova Scotia. In 1755, many were expelled from their settlements after refusing to pledge allegiance to the British crown. This sent eleven thousand people into exile, with almost half perishing on the way to other locales. About three thousand made it to southern Louisiana, where their traditions blended with Black and Native communities to create what we call Cajun culture.

Cherokee, Choctaw, Muscogee (Creek), Nanticoke, Natchez, Powhatan, Seminole, Tutelo-Saponi
These refer to some of the major Native American nations living in the historical American South.

Creole
A word that originally meant someone born in the New World. In Louisiana, it came to mean people born in Louisiana. Later in the vernacular, it came to mean people of mixed French and Spanish descent (the main Colonial powers), as well as those of German, African, and Native ancestry.

"Maroons"
Freedom seekers during enslavement who escaped and set up communities in the wilderness of the American South, Caribbean, Latin America, and South America, where they could live independently outside of the plantation system.

Melungeons
An ethnically-mixed community dating back to the 17th century, descended from enslaved Africans, indentured European servants, and others living in Southern Appalachia and beyond. The word comes from Mbundu from Angola, "mulungo," meaning "shipmate."

Pan-Southern
Referring to either the Southern culture and presence outside of the boundaries of the traditional South, owing to migration and settlements by Southerners. Examples include the Southern areas of Ohio, Indiana and Illinois, or areas impacted by the Great Migration.

Powhatan Paramount Chiefdom
The political body formed of related tribes living in what is now Tidewater Virginia between the 1500s and 1600s. Its populace lived under the leadership and authority of the Mamanatowick, or paramount chief Powhatan, at the time of English arrival in 1607. The Mattaponi and Pamunkey were some of the more than thirty tribes under his authority.

Southern Algonquin
The Algonquin-speaking peoples and neighboring tribes living in the warmer Tidewater regions of the Chesapeake Bay, Outer Banks, and coastal plains.

PLACES

African Atlantic
The Atlantic Ocean–facing part of the African Diaspora, including North and South America, West and Central Africa, and parts of Western Europe united by the history of the transatlantic slave trade, colonialism, and migration.

Atlantic World
A historical concept for the period between 1500 to the mid-nineteenth century, describing migrations and interactions between the peoples of Africa, Europe, and the Americas.

Black Belt
The fertile plain stretching across Alabama into Mississippi where some of the best cotton-growing lands were in the Antebellum era as well as a solid stretch of counties with a plurality of Black residents.

Caribbean Basin
The region encompassing the Caribbean islands and their adjacent mainland areas—including the greater West Indies and areas along the Gulf Coast of the American South, Mexico, and northern South America.

Chesapeake Bay
The large estuary in the United States shared by Maryland and Virginia. Chesapeake is derivative of a Southern Algonquin term meaning Great Shellfish Bay. The Colonial Chesapeake region or historic "greater Chesapeake," was composed of Maryland and Virginia with some parts of neighboring southern Delaware and northeastern North Carolina settled by the cultures common to the region.

Colonial North America
The thirteen colonies under British rule facing the Atlantic on the eastern coast of what is now the United States from the seventeenth to eighteenth centuries. The Southern colonies were Maryland, Virginia, North and South Carolina, and Georgia.

Deep South
Also known as the Lower South, stretching from southeastern North Carolina through South Carolina, Georgia, Alabama, Mississippi, most of Arkansas, Louisiana, and the deep east of Texas.

Delaware River Valley
A region that includes areas along the Delaware River, reaching into New Jersey, Philadelphia, and parts of Maryland.

Delmarva South
The Eastern Shore region composed of parts of Delaware, Maryland, and Virginia.

The Delta
The region of the Mississippi River plain settled predominantly after the Civil War, known for its many cotton plantations and rich Southern cultural traditions, including the birthplace of the blues.

The French Market
The historical food market area located in New Orleans. The market was once a Native American trading post and became an important site of trade in the Colonial era. Some market buildings have been standing since the early nineteenth century.

Gulf Coast
The warm-water coast of the Southern United States facing the Gulf of Mexico, which includes the western coast of Florida, Alabama, Mississippi, Louisiana, and the eastern coast of Texas.

Lowcountry
The coastal region of the Southeast stretching from Georgetown, South Carolina, to southern coastal Georgia. The larger Gullah-Geechee Corridor includes this area, and stretches from the coastal and Sea Islands of southeastern North Carolina through South Carolina and Georgia. It continues into northeastern Florida where rice, indigo, and sea island cotton plantations flourished.

Pamlico Sound
The largest lagoon on the North American east coast, between the mainland and the Outer Banks of North Carolina.

Piedmont
The plateau area of the southeastern United States, set between the Tidewater, south Atlantic coastal plain, and the Appalachian Mountain region; characterized by rolling hills and reddish clay soils.

Rainbow Row
The historical area of Charleston, South Carolina, noted for its historical architecture and colorful pastel aesthetic. This area is close to the market area, where sweetgrass baskets, benne wafers, and other local specialties are sold.

Tidewater
The coastal plains of Maryland, Virginia, and northeastern North Carolina, plus the islands off the coast.

Upper South
The region composed of Maryland, Virginia, Kentucky, eastern and central Tennessee, West Virginia, much of North Carolina, and parts of Arkansas and Missouri.

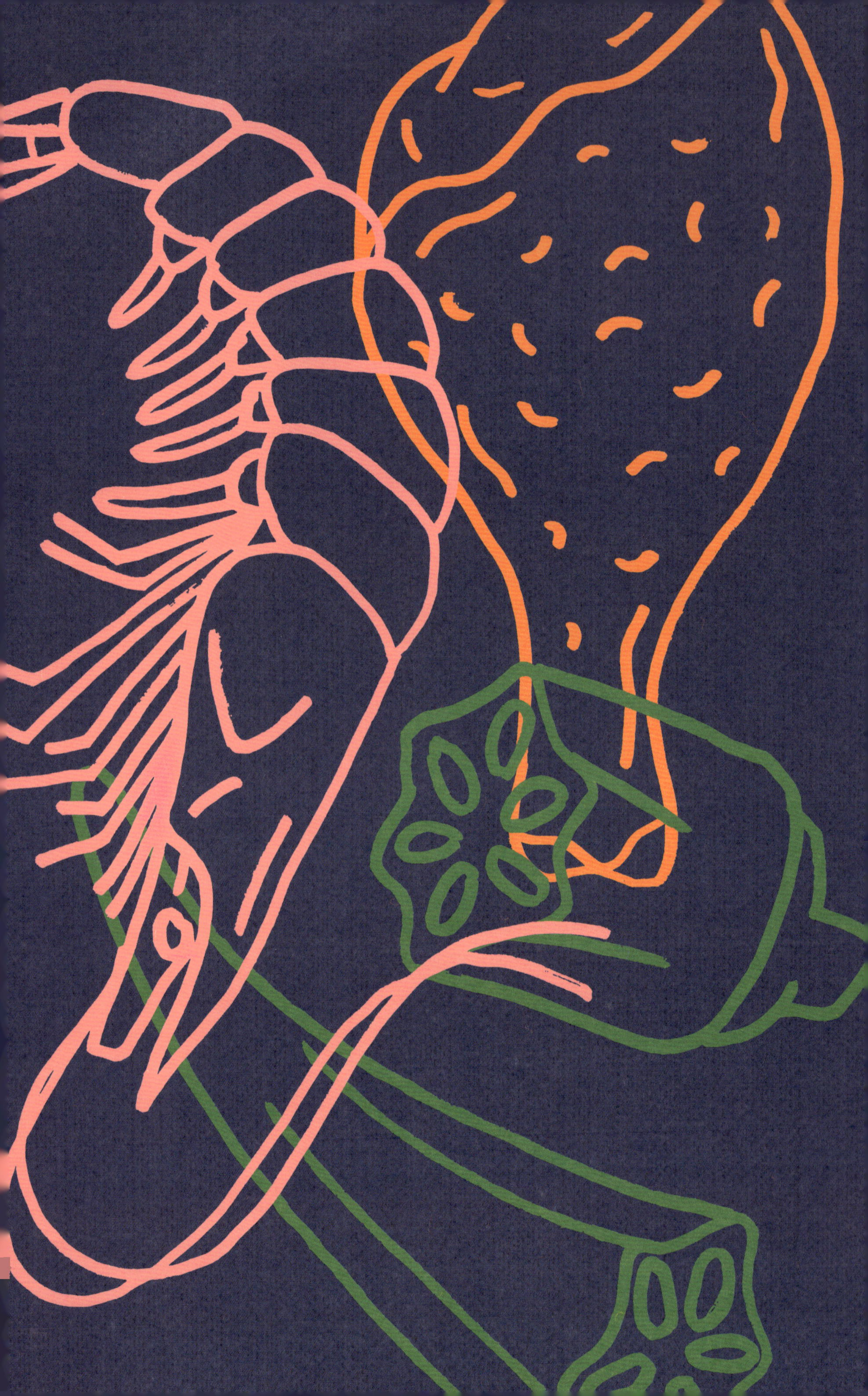

SELECTED BIBLIOGRAPHY

Bennett, Chris. *Southeast Foraging: 120 Wild and Flavorful Edibles from Angelica to Wild Plums.* Timber Press, 2015.

Bolling, Morgan, ed. *When Southern Women Cook: History, Lore, and 300 Recipes with Contributions from 70 Women Writers.* America's Test Kitchen, 2024.

Brock, Sean. *Heritage.* Artisan, 2014.

Carney, Judith Ann. *Black Rice: The African Origins of Rice Cultivation in the Americas.* Harvard University Press, 2001.

Carney, Judith Ann, and Richard Nicholas Rosomoff. *In the Shadow of Slavery: Africa's Botanical Legacy in the Atlantic World.* University of California Press, 2009.

Charles, Dora. *A Real Southern Cook in Her Savannah Kitchen.* Mariner Books, 2015.

Chase, Leah. *The Dooky Chase Cookbook.* Pelican Publishing, 1990.

Craughwell, Thomas J. *Thomas Jefferson's Crème Brûlée: How a Founding Father and His Slave James Hemings Introduced French Cuisine to America.* Quirk Books, 2012.

Crump, Nancy Carter. *Hearthside Cooking: Early American Southern Cuisine Updated for Today's Hearth and Cookstove.* University of North Carolina Press, 2008.

Day, Cheryl. *Cheryl Day's Treasury of Southern Baking.* Artisan, 2021.

Dupree, Nathalie, and Cynthia Graubart. *Mastering the Art of Southern Cooking.* Gibbs Smith, 2012.

Edge, John T., ed. *The New Encyclopedia of Southern Culture: Volume 7: Foodways.* University of North Carolina Press, 2007.

Egerton, John. *Southern Food: At Home, on the Road, in History.* Alfred A. Knopf, 1987.

Eltis, David, and David Richardson. *Atlas of the Transatlantic Slave Trade.* Yale University Press, 2010.

Ethridge, Robbie. *Creek Country: The Creek Indians and Their World.* University of North Carolina Press, 2003.

Fehribach, Paul. *The Big Jones Cookbook: Recipes for Savoring the Heritage of Regional Southern Cooking.* University of Chicago Press, 2015.

Feibleman, Peter S. *American Cooking: Creole and Acadian.* Time-Life Books, 1971.

Ferris, Marcie Cohen. *The Edible South: The Power of Food and the Making of an American Region.* University of North Carolina Press, 2014.

Ferris, Marcie Cohen. *Matzoh Ball Gumbo: Culinary Tales of the Jewish South.* University of North Carolina Press, 2005.

Fields-Black, Edda L. *Deep Roots: Rice Farmers in West Africa and the African Diaspora.* Indiana University Press, 2008.

Fowler, Damon Lee. *Classical Southern Cooking: A Celebration of the Cuisine of the Old South.* Gibbs Smith, 2008.

Gutierrez, Sandra A. *The New Southern-Latino Table: Recipes that Bring Together the Bold and Beloved Flavors of Latin America and the American South.* University of North Carolina Press, 2011.

Hatch, Peter J. *A Rich Spot of Earth: Thomas Jefferson's Revolutionary Garden at Monticello.* Yale University Press, 2012.

Hilliard, Sam Bowers. *Hog Meat and Hoecake: Food Supply in the Old South, 1840–1860.* Southern Illinois Press, 1971.

Hudson, Charles. *The Southeastern Indians.* University of Tennessee Press, 1989.

Johnson, Pableaux. *Eating New Orleans: From French Quarter Creole Cooking to the Perfect Poboy.* Countryman Press, 2005.

Lewis, Edna. *The Taste of Country Cooking.* Alfred A. Knopf, 2003.

Lewis, Edna, and Scott Peacock. *The Gift of Southern Cooking: Recipes and Revelations from Two Great American Cooks.* Alfred A. Knopf, 2003.

Lundy, Ronni. *Victuals: An Appalachian Journey, with Recipes.* Clarkson Potter, 2016.

McDermott, Nancie. *Southern Cakes: Sweet and Irresistible Recipes for Everyday Celebrations.* Chronicle Books, 2012.

McDermott, Nancie. *Southern Pies: A Gracious Plenty of Pie Recipes, from Lemon Chess to Chocolate Pecan.* Chronicle Books, 2010.

Meggett, Emily. *Gullah Geechee Home Cooking: Recipes from the Matriarch of Edisto Island.* Abrams Books, 2022.

Miller, Jim Wayne. "From Oats to Grits, Mutton to Pork: North British Foodways in Southern Appalachia" in *Cornbread Nation 3: Foods of the Mountain South,* edited by Ronni Lundy, 59-71. University of North Carolina Press, 2005.

Moss, Kay, and Katheryn Hoffman. *The Backcountry Housewife: A Study of Eighteenth-Century Foods.* Schiele Museum of Natural History, 2001.

Osseo-Asare, Fran. *Food Culture in Sub-Saharan Africa.* Greenwood Press, 2005.

Randolph, Mary. *The Virginia House-Wife,* with historical commentary by Karen Hess. University of South Carolina Press, 1984.

Robinson, Sallie Ann. *Gullah Home Cooking the Daufuskie Way: Smokin' Joe Butter Beans, Ol' 'Fuskie Fried Crab Rice, Sticky-Bush Blackberry Dumpling, & other Sea Island Favorites.* University of North Carolina Press, 2003.

Sauceman, Fred. "Of Sorghum Syrup, Cushaws, Mountain Barbecue, Soup Beans and Black Iron Skillets," in *Cornbread Nation 3: Foods of the Mountain South,* edited by Ronni Lundy, 216–225. University of North Carolina Press, 2005.

Shields, David S. *Southern Provisions: The Creation & Revival of a Cuisine.* University of Chicago Press, 2015.

Smart-Grosvenor, Vertamae. *Vibration Cooking; or The Travel Notes of a Geechee Girl.* University of Georgia Press, 2011.

Smith, Bill. *Seasoned in the South: Recipes from Crook's Corner.* Little, Brown and Co., 2005.

Taylor, John Martin. *Hoppin' John's Lowcountry Cooking: Recipes and Ruminations from Charleston and the Carolina Coastal Plain.* Bantam Books, 1992.

Tipton-Martin, Toni. *The Jemima Code: Two Centuries of African American Cookbooks.* University of Texas Press, 2015.

Twitty, Michael W. *The Cooking Gene: A Journey Through African American Food in the Old South.* HarperCollins, 2017.

Twitty, Michael W. *Koshersoul: The Faith and Food Journey of an African American Jew.* HarperCollins, 2022.

Twitty, Michael W. *Rice: A Savor the South Cookbook.* University of North Carolina Press, 2021.

Wallace, Ira. *The Timber Press Guide to Vegetable Gardening in the Southeast.* Timber Press, 2013.

Walter, Eugene. *American Cooking: Southern Style.* Time-Life Books, 1971.

INDEX

Page numbers in *italic* refer to the illustrations

ABOUT THE AUTHOR

Michael W. Twitty is an award-winning culinary historian and food writer living in Fredericksburg, Virginia. His 2017 book *The Cooking Gene* received two James Beard Awards, for best writing and for book of the year. He is also the author of *Rice*, noted as one of the best cookbooks of 2021 by the *New York Times*, and *KosherSoul*, named the 2023 Book of the Year by the National Jewish Book Awards. Twitty is a National Geographic Explorer, TED Fellow, and member of the 2022 TIME 100 Next class. He is the first Revolutionary in Residence at the Colonial Williamsburg Foundation.

ACKNOWLEDGMENTS

Acknowledgments are never easy because they promise the ever-present sin of forgetting someone we should acknowledge. I hope this acknowledgment has all the appreciation and credit the community that produced this book deserves.

First, I think of my Ancestors. I come from anywhere from eight to over thirty generations of Southerners. Many were West and Central African from many lands; many British, Celtic, and German; and a few Native Americans from the Virginia Piedmont (Tutelo-Saponi) and the river bottoms of Alabama and Georgia (Muscogee). Thanks to the miracles of genetic genealogy and family oral history, I honor my Mende, Igbo, Serer, Fulani, Mandinka, Asante, Fante, Yoruba, Kongo, Mbundu, Wolof, and Malagasy Ancestors brought to the American South so long ago who among many others who survived the Middle Passage, used every part of their being and spirit to give me a heritage that changed the planet despite all of the pain and sacrifice they endured. Their blood moves in me, and their spirit and civilization push me any chance I receive the opportunity to tell their story. My late mother, Patricia Townsend, and maternal grandmother, Hazel Todd, were, along with my late father, William Twitty, my primary cooking instructors. I must acknowledge them and all the people in my family and beyond who taught me so much about Southern food and its culture. I am lucky. In some ways, I learned from the past two generations and the two going forward.

Emily Takoudes, thank you for giving me such a fantastic opportunity. This project came with extraordinary responsibility because this series is essential for many reasons. I wanted to learn new skills and ways of writing about food, and in faith and wisdom, you paired me with a fantastic project editor, Dr. Jessica Carbone. I am grateful to have the privilege of working with someone who knows my work and is familiar with my voice and perspective. How outrageously helpful not to have to translate! I am grateful for Jessica's patience, next-level assistance, and many phone and computer calls. Thank you also to the copyeditor Kate Slate, the proofreader Maria C. Hunt, the indexer Hilary Bird, the designers Ken Deegan, Brankica Harvey and Pedro Mendes, and to Nico Schinco and Kaitlin Wayne, the photography and food styling team!

Jordan Wimby, a remarkable young chef, helped me assemble the bulk of the recipes in this volume and mitigated my stress in meeting our early deadlines. Jordan, it is a joy to work with you, and I'm grateful for your contribution and high energy. Nancie McDermott—thank you for being a friend and mentor for much of my food journey and for being my go-to for baking and preserves. Our conversations and knowledge of sources, including your work, were pivotal. Your precision with testing and helping me navigate curation made this book happen. Phil Lueck—your craft with grammar and flow is irreplaceable, and you got me through my first big edit and my essays! I must thank expert baker Cheryl Day, her husband, Griff, Sandra A. Gutierrez, Ben Mims, Dr. Marcie Cohen Ferris, and Chef Bill Smith for helping me with recipes for this volume. There are too many friends and teachers to mention as well: Dr. Leni Sorenson, Mrs. Janice Canaday, Barbara Scherer, Harold Caldwell, Andre Taylor, Cheyney McKnight, Chef Wanda Blake, Ada Anago Brown, Toni Tipton-Martin, Tonya Hopkins, Eve Otmar, Emanuel Dabney, Jennifer Wender, Josmine Evans, Chef Angie Brown, and David and Tonya Thomas.

Most significantly, I want to thank my patient and caring husband, Taylor, and our brood of fur bugs, our late Felix, Dodger, Drifter, and Lorelai, for being by my side in the middle of the night. Thanks for eating so many test meals!

RECIPE NOTES

SUGAR is white US granulated (UK caster sugar), unless otherwise specified.

EGGS are US size large (UK size medium), unless otherwise specified.

FLOUR is always unbleached all-purpose US flour, unless otherwise specified.

MILK is whole milk, unless otherwise specified.

SALT is fine table salt, unless otherwise specified.

PEPPER is freshly ground black pepper, unless otherwise specified.

BUTTER is unsalted US butter, which is 80% butterfat, unless otherwise specified.

VANILLA is always pure vanilla extract, unless otherwise specified.

INDIVIDUAL FRUITS AND VEGETABLES are assumed to be medium unless otherwise specified, and should be washed unless otherwise specified.

Where **NEUTRAL OIL** is mentioned, use vegetable, canola (rapeseed), grapeseed, sunflower, or corn oil.

POTS OR SKILLETS are used throughout. Skillets are generally considered to be medium-size and cast-iron, unless otherwise specified.

METRIC, IMPERIAL, AND CUP MEASUREMENTS are used in this book. Follow one set of measurements throughout, not a mixture, as they are not interchangeable.

ALL TABLESPOON AND TEASPOON MEASUREMENTS given are level, not heaping, unless otherwise specified.
1 teaspoon = 5 ml; 1 tablespoon = 15 ml. Australian standard tablespoons are 20 ml, so Australian readers are advised to use 3 teaspoons in place of 1 tablespoon when measuring small quantities.

WHEN NO QUANTITY IS SPECIFIED for oils for deep-frying, use the depth of oil specified in the recipe to determine how much you will need. As a general guideline, to get a depth of 1 inch (2.5 cm) of oil in a 10-inch (25 cm) pot you will need 4 cups (32 fl oz/950 ml).

WHEN DEEP-FRYING, heat the oil to the temperatures specified, or until a cube of bread browns in 30 seconds. Exercise a high level of caution when following recipes involving any potentially hazardous activity, including the use of high temperatures and open flames and when deep-frying. In particular, when deep-frying, add food carefully to avoid splashing, wear long sleeves, and never leave the pan unattended.

COOKING AND PREPARATION TIMES are for guidance only.

Unless otherwise specified, **THE POSITION OF THE OVEN RACK** is in the center of the oven.

WHEN MAKING PICKLES OR PRESERVES, see Storing Preserves (page 307) for information on the recipes in this book. For more detailed information, consult the USDA Complete Guide to Home Canning.

DO EXERCISE CAUTION when foraging for ingredients, which should only be eaten if an expert has deemed them safe to eat. In particular, do not gather wild mushrooms yourself before seeking the advice of an expert who has confirmed their suitability for human consumption. As some species of mushrooms have been known to cause allergic reaction and illness, do take extra care when cooking and eating mushrooms and do seek immediate medical help if you experience a reaction after preparing or eating them.

Phaidon Press Limited
2 Cooperage Yard
London E15 2QR

Phaidon Press Inc.
111 Broadway
New York, NY 10006

Phaidon SARL
55, rue Traversière
75012 Paris

phaidon.com

First published 2025

ISBN 978 1 83729 087 1
ISBN 978 1 83729 155 7 (signed edition)

A CIP catalogue record for this book is available from the British Library and the Library of Congress.

Commissioning Editor: Emily Takoudes
Project Editor: Jessica Carbone
Production Controller: Andie Trainer
Photography: Nico Schinco
Food Styling: Kaitlin Wayne
Design and Illustration: Associate Studio

Printed in China

The publisher would like to thank Hilary Bird, Maria C. Hunt, Kate Slate, Ellie Smith, and Tracey Smith.